RE-IMAGINING DEFA

RE-IMAGINING DEFA

EAST GERMAN CINEMA IN ITS NATIONAL AND TRANSNATIONAL CONTEXTS

Edited by
Seán Allan and Sebastian Heiduschke

berghahn
NEW YORK · OXFORD
www.berghahnbooks.com

Published in 2016 by
Berghahn Books
www.berghahnbooks.com
© 2016 Seán Allan and Sebastian Heiduschke

All rights reserved. Except for the quotation of short passages for the purposes of criticism and review, no part of this book may be reproduced in any form or by any means, electronic or mechanical, including photocopying, recording, or any information storage and retrieval system now known or to be invented, without written permission of the publisher.

Library of Congress Cataloging-in-Publication Data
Names: Allan, Sean, editor. | Heiduschke, Sebastian, 1974- editor.
Title: Re-imagining DEFA : East German cinema in its national and transnational contexts / edited by Sean Allan and Sebastian Heiduschke.
Description: First edition. | New York : Berghahn Books, 2016. | Includes bibliographical references and index.
Identifiers: LCCN 2016021754| ISBN 9781785331077 (hardback) | ISBN 9781785331053 (pbk.) | ISBN 9781785331060 (ebook)
Subjects: LCSH: DEFA--History. | Motion picture industry--Germany (East)--History. | Motion pictures--Germany (East)--History.
Classification: LCC PN1999.D4 R45 2016 | DDC 384/.8/09431--dc23 LC record available at https://lccn.loc.gov/2016021754

British Library Cataloguing in Publication Data
A catalogue record for this book is available from the British Library

ISBN 978-1-78533-107-7 hardback
ISBN 978-1-78533-105-3 paperback
ISBN 978-1-78533-106-0 ebook

Contents

List of Illustrations	viii
Acknowledgements	xi
Introduction. Re-imagining East German Cinema (Seán Allan and Sebastian Heiduschke)	1

PART I: INSTITUTIONS AND IDEOLOGY

1. The State-Owned Cinema Industry and Its Audience (Rosemary Stott)	19
2. History and Subjectivity: The Evolution of DEFA Film Music (Larson Powell)	41
3. 'Fatal Attractions': Modernist Set Design and the East–West Divide in DEFA Films of the 1950s and early 1960s (Annette Dorgerloh)	61

PART II: NATIONAL AND TRANSNATIONAL CONTEXTS

4. DEFA and the Legacy of 'Film Europe': Prestige, Institutional Exchange and Film Co-Productions (Mariana Ivanova)	85
5. Betting on Entertainment: The Cold War Scandal of *Spielbank-Affäre* [*Casino Affair*, 1957] (Stefan Soldovieri)	106

6. 'Operación Silencio': Studio H&S's Chile Cycle as Latin American Third Cinema
(Dennis Hanlon) 127

7. Deconstructing Orientalism: DEFA's Fictions of East Asia
(Qinna Shen) 146

8. Transnational Stardom: DEFA's Management of Dean Reed
(Seán Allan) 168

PART III: GENRE AND POPULAR CINEMA

9. Walter Felsenstein and the DEFA Opera Film
(Sabine Hake) 191

10. Dreams of 'Cosmic Culture' in *Der schweigende Stern*
[*The Silent Star*, 1960]
(Sonja Fritzsche) 210

11. The DEFA *Indianerfilm*: Narrating the Postcolonial through Gojko Mitic
(Evan Torner) 227

12. Defining Socialist Children's Films, Defining Socialist Childhoods
(Benita Blessing) 248

PART IV: DEFA'S LEGACY

13. DEFA's Last Gasp: Ruins, Melancholy and the End of East German Filmmaking
(Nick Hodgin) 271

14. DEFA's Antifascist Myth Revisited. *KLK an PTX – Die Rote Kapelle*
[*KLK calling PTX – The Red Orchestra*, 1971]
(Sebastian Heiduschke) 292

15. DEFA's Afterimages: Looking Back at the East from the West in *Das Leben der Anderen* [*The Lives of Others*, 2006] and *Barbara* (2012) (Daniela Berghahn)   312

Select Bibliography   335

Index   357

List of Illustrations

1.1 Workers in a print laboratory on the DEFA Studio site, Babelsberg, 1950s. — 23
1.2 (From left to right) Heiner Carow, Heidemarie Wenzel, Regina Teichmann and Winfried Glatzeder on the set of *Die Legende von Paul und Paula* (1973). — 30
3.1 *Frauenschicksale* (1952). West Berlin nightclub. — 66
3.2 Erika's experience of Western modernist décor in *Das Leben beginnt* (1960). — 72
3.3 *Das Leben beginnt* (1960). The Schenks' rented accommodation in West Berlin. — 74
3.4 Willy Schiller's design for a room in the Senator's house. — 75
3.5 Solter's office in *Der Frühling braucht Zeit* (1965). — 79
5.1 *Spielbank-Affäre* (1957). Sybille and Gerhard in their apartment. Too many comforts for East German eyes? — 118
5.2 Mafioso Martinez in his Mediterranean penthouse. — 119
5.3 Casino Boss Gallinger in his ultra-modern office. — 120
6.1 Studio H&S's footage of the bombing of the Palacio Moneda as seen in the opening titles of *La batalla de Chile*. — 128
6.2 Capturing as many faces as possible for later identification in *Ich war, ich bin, ich werde sein* (1974). — 134
6.3 The redacted face of the sound engineer in *Eine Minute Dunkel macht uns nicht blind* (1975). — 136
7.1 The collision of Old and New in *China – Land zwischen gestern und morgen* (1957). — 148
7.2 The ensemble sings songs that echoed the Chinese government's rhetoric about overtaking England and America in *Wir sangen und tanzten in China* (1959). — 158
7.3 Dawadorshi passes the Water-Khan's test and receives three magic gifts in *Die goldene Jurte* (1961). — 162
8.1 Dean Reed on the set of *Aus dem Leben eines Taugenichts* (1973). — 172

8.2	At home with the Reeds.	178
8.3	Dean Reed in *Aus dem Leben eines Taugenichts* (1973).	179
10.1	*Der schweigende Stern* (1960) with Professor Saltyk, Professor Harringway Hawling and Raimund Brinkmann (top row) and Professor Sikarna (below).	211
10.2	*Die gefrorenen Blitze* (1967) with Wernher von Braun and the V-2 rocket in the background.	222
11.1	Dancers perform fabricated choreography in *Chingachgook* (1967).	230
11.2	*Chingachgook* (1967): Mitic pretends to knife-fight with the audience.	231
11.3	Farseeing Falcon (Mitic) lies dead at the conclusion of *Weiße Wölfe* (1969).	241
12.1	Anne and Jörg plot how to free the villagers from the enforced use of the town mill in *Der Teufel vom Mühlenberg* (1955).	254
12.2	Matthias 'flies' around his neighbourhood in *Ikarus* (1977).	258
12.3	The band of children set off in disguise to save the *Tscheljuskin* crew at the North Pole in *Das Eismeer ruft* (1984).	261
13.1	Symbolic excavation: the older generation preparing a grave for the younger generation in *Ein brauchbarer Mann* (1989).	279
13.2	Henning (Holger Kubisch) helpless against the region's redevelopment in *Abschiedsdisco* (1990).	280
13.3	The GDR province as ethereal environment in *Der Magdalenenbaum* (1989).	283
14.1	Changing of the guard at the Neue Wache, Berlin, in *KLK an PTX* (1971).	297
14.2	'Authentic' *mise en scène* in *KLK an PTX* (1971).	305
14.3	Broken illusion: restaging the arrest by the Gestapo in modern-day Berlin in Stefan Roloff's *Die rote Kapelle* (2003).	306
14.4	Morphing faces using Gestapo mug shots of members of the Red Orchestra in Stefan Roloff's *Die rote Kapelle* (2003).	307
15.1	Wiesler discovers Dreymann's novel at the Karl Marx bookshop.	320

15.2	Wiesler's hands holding Dreymann's novel *Sonata for a Good Man* in *Das Leben der Anderen* (2007)	320
15.3	Dreymann's hands picking up the piano score 'Sonata for a Good Man' in *Das Leben der Anderen* (2007)	321
15.4	Wiesler is listening to the 'Sonata for a Good Man' with tears in his eyes in *Das Leben der Anderen* (2007)	321
15.5	The workplace is the site where Barbara and André's love blossoms. *Barbara* (2012).	326
15.6	Wherever Barbara goes, she feels that somebody might be watching her. *Barbara* (2012).	330

Acknowledgements

Many people contributed in all sorts of ways to the making of this volume. The editors would particularly like to thank the following:

The DEFA-Stiftung, the DEFA Film-Library, University of Massachusetts Amherst, the Humanities Research Centre (University of Warwick), Center for the Humanities (Oregon State University), Oregon State University Valley Library.

Frau Ute Klawitter (Bundesfilmarchiv, Berlin), Frau Birgit Scholz (Filmmuseum, Potsdam), Tim Storch (Bundesarchiv, Berlin), Hans Jürgen Furcht (www.film-stadt-quedlinburg.de), Richard Parker and Richard Perkins (University of Warwick Library), Renate Göthe (Filmuniversität Konrad Wolf, Babelsberg).

Frank-Burkhard Habel, Sabine Hake, Ralf Schenk, Sabine Söhner, Jo Gerbeth, Hiltrud Schulz, Barton Byg, Sky Arndt-Briggs, Birgit Röder, Victoria Naipavel-Heiduschke, Melissa Weintraub, Bradley Boovy, Rebecca Olson, Kara Ritzheimer, Stefan Roloff.

Chris Chappell, Charlotte Mosedale, Caroline Kuhtz, Kate Pedlar, Ben Parker and Carlos Esparza at Berghahn Books.

INTRODUCTION
Re-imagining East German Cinema

Seán Allan and Sebastian Heiduschke

For many scholars, the term DEFA has become a byword for the national cinema of the German Democratic Republic (GDR); yet conceptualizing film historiography in such terms raises almost as many issues as it resolves, and is particularly complex in the case of the GDR because of its changing status as a geopolitical and cultural-political entity during the period 1949–1990. The founding of the DEFA studio (on 17 May 1946 it was granted a licence for film production) pre-dates the founding of the GDR itself by almost two-and-a-half years; and the liquidation of the company (on 9 August 1994 the name DEFA was expunged from the official register of German companies) occurred almost four years after the state's collapse. The studio's name is also deceptive; at one level the acronym DEFA (Deutsche Film-Aktiengesellschaft) invokes memories of its illustrious precursor, UFA (Universum Film Aktiengesellschaft), the prewar production company that had occupied the same site in Potsdam-Babelsberg; yet, in theory at least, the aims of the two organizations could hardly have been more different. Finally, even the designation of the DEFA studio as a so-called 'Aktiengesellschaft' (usually glossed as 'joint stock company') is misleading; for the term is to be understood not in terms of free-market capitalism, but rather in the sense of a 'Soviet joint stock company' – an economic model developed by the Soviets in order to facilitate the transfer of reparations from Germany to the USSR at the end of World War II.

It is perhaps understandable that some of the first publications on DEFA to appear after the *Wende* tended to see East German cinema predominantly in isolation from other Eastern European cinemas and to approach it as a national cinema (albeit one of a small nation) in its own right.[1] Although DEFA produced over 600 feature films in addition to a large number of animation films, films for children, and documentaries, relatively few of these films were known outside the GDR and the Eastern Bloc. On the one hand, regarded as largely free from the constraints of a capitalist market economy, film production and consumption in the GDR was seen by many (incorrectly as it turned out) as having no real relationship to the traditions of popular cinema in the West and in Hollywood. On the other hand, DEFA's collectivist approach to filmmaking – a practice embodied, above all in its system of artistic ensembles (or *Künstlerische Arbeitsgruppen*) – seemed fundamentally at odds with the more individualistic auteurist approach underpinning the study of arthouse movements such as the New German Cinema in the Federal Republic. Finally, even before the Wende, the cinema of the GDR had, for the most part, been consigned to a scholarly no-man's land and treated in isolation from other cinemas.[2] Almost always excluded from surveys of 'German' national cinema and the cinema of Western Europe,[3] it rarely features in studies devoted to the study of Eastern European film largely because of an assumption that the GDR's pivotal position in a divided Europe meant that its filmmakers were subject to a more radical censorship than their counterparts in Poland and Czechoslovakia.[4]

With the collapse of the GDR, and the end of the Cold War, many of these assumptions have been challenged as DEFA's output has reached new audiences. First, the Wende provided an historic opportunity for the screening of a number of films that had been banned in the wake of the Eleventh Plenum in 1965/66; and the subsequent wave of so-called *Ostalgie* (nostalgia for the GDR) in the early 1990s prompted regular screenings of DEFA films by the two regional television networks RBB (Rundfunk Berlin-Brandenburg) and MDR (Mitteldeutscher Rundfunk) most closely associated with the GDR. The availability of the films themselves in DVD format, together with the accessibility of archive material on almost every aspect of East German film production, has proved that DEFA was not the propaganda machine many assumed it must have been, and, as a result, a more differentiated picture of film culture in the GDR has emerged over the last decade. Now that the study of East German cinema is no longer quite the marginal activity it once was, the past decade or so has seen a proliferation of diverse historiographical approaches to the film culture of the GDR.[5] These different approaches have, in turn, given rise to the following research questions that underpin the overall agenda of the present volume. First, to what extent can DEFA be regarded as a national cinema in its own right? Second, given the involvement of DEFA's employees in both prewar and post-Wende cinema, how far can East German cinema be regarded as a homogeneous entity that is coterminous with the existence of the GDR itself? Third, to what extent is film culture in the GDR (considered both in terms of production and consumption) a transnational phenomenon that is bound up not only with the cinema of the Federal Republic, but also with other (non-German) cinemas? Fourth, what is the role of popular/genre cinema in East German film culture and how does it assimilate the traditions (both socialist and nonsocialist) on which it draws? Fifth, given the existence of independent studios (such as Studio H&S) and underground filmmakers working alongside mainstream television in the GDR, is it misleading to see East German cinema simply as synonymous with DEFA? (What forms does media convergence take in the GDR?) Finally, is it possible to speak of a 'DEFA style', and does DEFA have what might be termed 'an afterlife'?

At first sight, Andrew Higson's seminal essay of 1989, 'The Concept of a National Cinema' would appear to offer a promising framework for conceptualizing DEFA as a national cinema, even though for the first two-and-a-half years of the studio's existence it was, paradoxically, a cinema in search of a nation.[6] The difficulties of re-establishing a national cinema in Germany immediately after World War II are reflected in the very different cultural politics operating in the Soviet and American Zones of Occupation. While the understanding shown by Soviet Cultural Officers such as Alexander Dymschitz and Sergei Tulpanov pointed to a greater willingness to allow the involvement of German returnees in the development of the film industry in the East, the Americans' desire to reap the financial rewards of screening Hollywood films banned during the Third Reich was a considerable obstacle to the development of a new film industry in the West. The East's determination to stake its claim as the true guardian of Germany's cultural heritage is evident as early as the First German Film Congress of 6–9 June 1947 (an event organized under the auspices of the left-wing Cultural League for the Democratic Renewal of Germany that was designed to persuade German filmmakers to support the newly established DEFA studio). Alfred Lindemann's opening address, 'The Situation of German Cinema', highlighted the ways in which the entertainment cinema of the 1930s and 1940s had been transformed into a propaganda tool by the Nazis, and underlined the key role of cinema in the process of postwar political re-education.[7] Five years later, the message disseminated to delegates at the second film conference, of 17–18 September 1952, was even more clear-cut; in stark contrast to the GDR, which could boast its own independent film industry, the neighbouring Federal Republic was, it was claimed, merely a 'film colony' and a victim of American cultural imperialism.[8]

Seen from this perspective, one way of reading the constant attacks on so-called 'cosmopolitan tendencies' in art, literature and film during the early 1950s is to interpret them as a rearguard action designed to preserve the integrity of the GDR's concept of a national (German) culture. Yet the difficulties DEFA experienced in persuading ordinary East German citizens to embrace its own version of a national film culture based on socialist realism, underlines just how problematic that concept itself was. Conceived (at least in theory) in opposition to both Hollywood's model of commercial film production and the entertainment features served up by UFA's prewar *Traumfabrik*, DEFA's productions of the early 1950s rejected cinematic modernism and, by and large, eschewed popular entertainment in favour of an approach that was often overly didactic. The inevitable result was a steady decline in ticket sales during the 1950s. Ultimately, the only way DEFA could counter the lure of those cinemas showing popular Hollywood films just across the border in the West, was to develop its own forms of popular/genre cinema, produce more films about young people in the contemporary GDR, and to cultivate its own system of stars, or *Publikumslieblinge* (audience darlings) as they were known. Finally, during the 1970s and 1980s – a period when increasing numbers of East Germans were able to access West German television relatively easily – these strategies were supplemented by the regular import of carefully selected popular films from the West.[9] At various points in the history of the studio all of these practices were singled out for criticism by dogmatic cultural theorists; nonetheless, the fact remains that, even in the earliest years of its existence, DEFA could not seal itself off altogether from external influences and had no choice but to engage with viewer expectations generated by an increasingly global film industry.

The arguments for regarding DEFA as a national cinema in its own right are grounded, above all, in the studio's role in promoting an alternative German national identity based on a concept of antifascism, and its contribution to the self-legitimization of the GDR. Not surprisingly, a number of the studio's most prestigious productions focused on antifascist resistance during World War II and the Spanish Civil War. Even if they were not received as enthusiastically by the broader viewing public as the leaders of the ruling Socialist Unity Party (SED) might have hoped, films like Kurt Maetzig's monumental epics of the 1950s *Ernst Thälmann – Sohn seiner Klasse* [*Ernst Thälmann – Son of his Class*, 1954] and *Ernst Thälmann – Führer seiner Klasse* [*Ernst Thälmann – Leader of his Class*, 1955] were instrumental in forging a link between the fledgling state and the prewar traditions of progressive politics. In the early 1960s too, films such as Frank Vogel's *Und deine Liebe auch* [*And Your Love Too*, 1962], Heinz Thiel's *Der Kinnhaken* [*The Punch to the Jaw*, 1962] and Konrad Wolf's *Der geteilte Himmel* [*Divided Heaven*, 1964] looked to a combination of rising East German stars (Armin Mueller-Stahl, Manfred Krug and Renate Blume) and *nouvelle vague* aesthetics in order to make the case for the GDR as the 'better' Germany during a period of crisis triggered by the building of the Berlin Wall.

Writing from the perspective of 2002, Barton Byg notes, quite rightly, that 'a fundamental inadequacy of film criticism since 1989 has been the fact that the films of the DEFA ... are primarily valued as evidence for the history of the German Democratic Republic'.[10] Yet as the title of Harry Blunk's 1987 monograph *Die DDR in ihren Filmen* [*The GDR in its Feature Films*] on the representation of East German society in contemporary DEFA films suggests, this type of approach was established well before the Wende.[11] Despite being one of the more even-handed attempts to gain an understanding of East German society through the study of its cinema, Blunk's study suffers from a tendency to see film simply as a window onto social reality rather than as an aesthetic product in its own right. Nonetheless, it offers a more nuanced set of interpretations than those studies which, by contrast, portray East German film primarily as a propaganda tool in the service of the SED. Perhaps the most striking example of such an approach is Heinz Kersten's 1963 study *Das Filmwesen in der sowjetischen Besatzungszone Deutschlands* [*Film Culture in the Soviet Zone of Occupation*].[12] Kersten's survey, however, remains entrenched in the vicissitudes of Cold War rhetoric; not only is the GDR portrayed simply as a satellite state of the Soviet Union, but DEFA's output is analysed almost exclusively in terms of its role as anti-Western propaganda. Nonetheless, although written almost forty years later, Klaus Finke's keynote essay in a volume provocatively entitled *DEFA-Film als nationales Kulturerbe?* [*DEFA – The Cultural Legacy of a Nation?*] serves as a reminder of the enduring character of such ideologically reductive approaches to East German cinema.[13] For Finke, East German cinema remains first and foremost a visual embodiment of the premises underpinning the dominant ideology of the SED, and as such, charts the decline of the party and the decline of the GDR generally. In the light of this, Finke argues that future generations of scholars – and the DEFA-Stiftung (DEFA-Foundation) itself – must resist the temptation to judge the works primarily in terms of their aesthetic qualities and, instead, focus primarily on the ideological context in which they were created.[14] The polemical tone of Finke's approach cannot, however, conceal its limitations. It may be hard to conceptualize DEFA without reference to the ideological underpinnings of cultural politics in the GDR; yet, as documents from the DEFA studio's production files confirm, SED policy directives were not always systematically followed, and some directors (Konrad Wolf is an obvious example) were subject to far less rigid constraints than others. Likewise, DEFA's co-productions often involved foreign partners whose own agendas were clearly at odds with those of the GDR's Ministry of Culture.[15]

Given the complexity of the conditions under which films were made in the GDR, it comes as no surprise that, increasingly, scholars have moved on from the study of DEFA as an isolated phenomenon and sought instead to situate East German cinema within a broader context of German–German relations. In this respect Hans Joachim Meurer's 2002 study *Cinema and National Identity in Divided Germany 1979-1989 – The Split Screen* represents something of a landmark in DEFA scholarship.[16] Meurer's study probes one of the key questions for film scholars, namely what exactly is to be understood by the term 'German' in the context of postwar cinema. Following the catastrophe of World War II, the GDR defined itself as a *Staatsnation* (or 'political nation') in which the members of that nation inhabit a given territory and share a common ideology. By contrast, the Federal Republic embraced the essentially nineteenth-century notion of the *Kulturnation* (a concept which Marc Silberman has explained as 'meaning variously a cultured nation and a nation unified through its cultural achievements').[17] The use of the term *Kulturnation* was designed to define German national identity in terms that transcended the political reality of the recently founded Federal Republic and the GDR, while at the same time maintaining the possibility of a unified Germany at some point in the future. However, in the revised version of its constitution of 1974 the GDR redefined itself as 'a socialist state' that was complete in itself and not part of any larger entity; and all references to reunification were removed. As a result, Meurer argues 'it is not only possible to deny the existence of one "German national cinema", but also to deny that the production of films took place within a national framework *per se*, since the two industries were shaped by strong international forces'.[18] Yet the aim of Meurer's study is not to argue for a compartmentalized approach to the study of postwar German cinema, but rather to suggest that the quest to maintain the internal coherence of these two 'national cinemas' has obscured the fact that 'national cinemas are not confined, but hybrid and in interaction with multiple external influences'.[19]

Meurer's concept of the 'split screen' has proved extremely influential in promoting a more all-encompassing approach to the study of postwar German cinema, not least because it moves beyond textual readings of key works and engages with a much wider range of issues including not only production, but also distribution and exhibition. However, just as film studies has moved towards a more integrated model of film culture in East and West, so too there has also been a corresponding reassessment of the relationship between the pre- and postwar traditions of German filmmaking and, in particular, DEFA's relationship to UFA. As David Bathrick has pointed out, DEFA's much heralded desire to make films that had nothing in common with the entertainment films produced by UFA in the prewar era was a task that was much easier said than done.[20] One of the problems with which the new studio was immediately confronted was that, in the early years, a large proportion of its directors, producers and camera operators had previously worked for either UFA or Terra.[21] Artur Pohl, Arthur Maria Rabenalt and Wolfgang Schleif were just some of the better known employees who had been active in the film industry during the Third Reich. As a result, it is hardly surprising that many of DEFA's early feature films (Kurt Maetzig's *Ehe im Schatten* [*Marriage in the Shadows*, 1947] is an obvious example) have the look and feel of UFA productions of the 1940s. This cannot, however, be adequately explained purely in terms of an overlap of personnel. Detlef Kannapin identifies a number of additional factors that contributed to the extended legacy of the 'UFA-style' in East German film production.[22] These include a reluctance on the part of East German film theorists to engage with the visual language of Nazi cinema,[23] and a desire on the part of the SED to deflect attention away from the aesthetics of totalitarian film and onto the traditions of proletarian filmmaking in the Weimar Republic instead. In addition, some sixteen unfinished UFA productions from the years 1943–1945 were completed and premiered in the Soviet Zone of Occupation primarily to raise capital for the struggling film industry.[24] At the same time, a surprisingly high number of films made during the 1930s and 1940s – including films such as Luis Trenker's *Der Berg ruft* [*The Mountain Calls*, 1937] and Werner Singler and Herbert Selpin's (anti-British) *Titanic* (1943) – were screened in cinemas in the GDR, often attracting large audiences.[25] All of this goes some way to explaining why the visual habits not only of filmmakers but, more importantly, of cinema-goers in the East were so resistant to change, and why the realization of a cinematic 'zero hour' in the East proved to be far more difficult than originally envisaged.

The studies by Meurer, Kannapin and Bathrick all underline the difficulties of approaching the study of East German cinema in terms of a narrow conception of national cinemas. The enduring legacy of UFA in the postwar period, too, highlights the problem of seeing DEFA in isolation from the cinematic traditions that preceded it. By the same token, recent scholarship has focused increasingly on the transnational dimension of East German cinema. As a result, a number of studies have taken their cue from Katie Trumpener's exhortation to explore the ways in which DEFA engages with the cinemas of Eastern Europe.[26] Throughout its history, DEFA engaged in a number of co-productions with Eastern partners, and the international film festival at Karlovy Vary in Czechoslovakia was a key date for the studio's production schedule. But it would be wrong to think of DEFA purely in terms of its relations with other film producing nations in the Eastern Bloc. The DEFA Studio for Newsreels and Documentary Features together with Studio H&S (a quasi-independent organization set up by the documentarists Walter Heynowski and Gerhard Scheumann) made a crucial contribution to the internationalization of DEFA's output. On the one hand, documentaries about Chile and Vietnam played a key role in strengthening the political links with those countries which, in defiance of the Federal Republic's 'Hallstein doctrine', were prepared to enter into diplomatic relations with the GDR; and on the other, the screening of these documentaries in the GDR itself gave East German viewers a sense that their nation was an active player on the wider global stage.

While it was almost inevitable that the relations between DEFA and other socialist nations in both the developed and developing world would become increasingly important for scholars of East German film, the increased emphasis now placed on popular and genre cinema (and the impact of Hollywood) is perhaps more unexpected. DEFA's children's films, and its contribution to the fairy-tale genre in particular, are perhaps its most enduring legacy in the post-Wende era.[27] In the case of science fiction, the studio's experiments can be seen as an attempt to embrace a popular genre that was already well established in the Soviet Union and other Eastern Bloc nations. But the impact of classic science fiction productions from the West, such as Stanley Kubrick's 1968 production *2001. A Space Odyssey* and the US television series *Star Trek*, cannot be ignored either.[28] More remarkable still is the East German appropriation of the American genre of the Western in the highly popular series of so-called *Indianerfilme* that were released between 1965 and 1983. Yet in so doing, DEFA tapped into an existing tradition of popular German literature (the novels of Karl May) and combined this with its own distinctive take on Hollywood's cowboys.[29] Last but not least, the 'popular/genre turn' in DEFA scholarship has also been accompanied by a range of studies exploring the ways in which East German film culture has developed its own take on the discourse of stardom – both in film production and in popular magazines such as *Filmspiegel, Film für alle,* and *Film und Fernsehen dabei* that were designed to stimulate audience interest.[30]

The fact that DEFA is no longer seen simply as an isolated national cinema is, to a large extent, a reflection of the globalization of DEFA scholarship itself. Since the Wende, scholarly interest in East German cinema has expanded rapidly. This is due, at least in part, to the opening up of archives that allowed insight into the workings of the GDR film industry, and to the emergence of a wide range of research agendas both in and beyond Germany. These contrasting agendas highlight an interesting dichotomy as far as approaches to DEFA are concerned, something that Brigitta Wagner sees as reflecting an 'unbiased appreciation of the work of filmmakers from the former GDR in the United States and elsewhere abroad in comparison to the reception of DEFA films in the unified Federal Republic of Germany'.[31] Although Wagner's assessment of contemporary DEFA scholarship is perhaps too polarizing, her commentary serves nonetheless as a reminder of the importance of global scholarship in stimulating what is now a multifold interest in East German cinema. By providing a more nuanced complement to the (often lukewarm) appreciation of DEFA in Germany, scholars in Austria, Australia, Japan, the UK, the United States and other locations have opened up innovative avenues of research that, in turn, have led to new discoveries and, generally speaking, promoted a more balanced view.

Since 1993, a research centre and film archive dedicated to the study of GDR film has existed in the United States. Housed at the University of Massachusetts, Amherst, the DEFA Film Library was founded with the twofold mission of preserving the collection of 16mm and 35mm film prints obtained from the defunct GDR embassy in New York, and establishing a physical location for the continuous research into DEFA at a time when East German studies seemed in danger of becoming obsolete.[32] Over the years to follow, the DEFA Film Library expanded its collection with film prints from the US–GDR Friendship Committee and a substantial collection of film journals and research material on film culture in the GDR. Since 2002, the film prints have been stored in the climate-controlled library depository, which (somewhat ironically) is housed in a Cold War bunker located underground in the Holyoke Range in Massachusetts. The DEFA Film Library also took on the distribution of English-subtitled DEFA films on DVD from Icestorm International in 2001 and the subtitling of films, in 2003, to serve the predominantly academic North American market. In addition to curating travelling film programs, hosting annual visitors and staging the biannual film institutes, it has made a major contribution to the development of DEFA studies in a transnational context. Its collaboration with the Museum of Modern Art in New York for the film retrospective *Rebels with a Cause: The Cinema of East Germany* in 2005 attracted international attention, and the release of the *Wendeflicks* series in Los Angeles in 2009 triggered the rediscovery and release of some of the last DEFA films in Germany.

While DEFA films have a predominantly academic following outside Germany, the situation in Germany itself is very different. There, in addition to scholarly engagement, a commodification of East German cinema has taken place that has resulted in an ever-growing interest in the films produced in Potsdam-Babelsberg.[33] Founded in 1999, the DEFA-Stiftung became the legal successor to DEFA itself,[34] and took administrative control of the rights to the films.[35] The heated legal battle between the DEFA-Stiftung, film distributors, and other stakeholders regarding the licensing and distribution contracts for DEFA films in 2011 underlines just how hot a commodity East German cinema had become within the German film market.[36] The revenue stream from the sale of DEFA video cassettes, DVDs, and Blu-rays was so substantial that the home video distributor Icestorm, a start-up founded in 1998 to sell DEFA films on VHS (and later DVD), was able to purchase the distribution company Progress that held the distribution rights for TV and cinemas, and to launch a video-on-demand portal, Icestorm TV, that allows the streaming of DEFA films via the world wide web. As far as German audiences are concerned, there is little to suggest that this enthusiasm for, and interest in, GDR films is on the wane.

Perhaps the most striking manifestation of a renewed and seemingly ever-expanding audience interest in DEFA is the development of a vibrant fan culture. During the existence of the GDR, cinema-goers often favoured films imported from abroad over DEFA's own productions (despite the efforts of the GDR media to cultivate its own version of stardom and fandom). Paradoxically, the collapse of the state prompted something of a rediscovery of DEFA. The East Germans' struggle for identity in the wake of reunification triggered the phenomenon of *Ostalgie*,[37] and with it a strong interest in DEFA films as a way of visually reliving and commemorating the GDR. These audiences were instrumental in boosting the market for DEFA films as they wrote letters to Icestorm requesting film titles for release on DVD. The launch of fan websites for DEFA cinema in general (and also for specific film genres, actors, and even individual films) soon followed. Some fans tailor film costumes for fan conventions, create jewellery, and even re-record film music,³⁸ while others self-publish DEFA books about their favourite GDR cinema moments.³⁹

The continued production of DVDs with English subtitles, the existence of a vibrant community of fans, plus an ever-increasing volume of academic scholarship that shows little sign of abating all suggest that DEFA is enjoying an 'afterlife' that, in 1989, seemed scarcely imaginable. Yet just as the division between the UFA and DEFA eras – both in terms of personnel and aesthetics – has been shown to be much more blurred than appeared to be the case at first sight, so too the legacy of DEFA and its impact on post-Wende film production in the Berlin Republic throws up a range of methodological challenges for scholars. Where, for example, are we to place, aesthetically speaking, the films produced during the final phase of the studio's existence?⁴⁰ Is it legitimate to refer to international stars such as Corinna Harfouch and Katrin Sass as 'East German' actresses? Does it make sense to talk about Andreas Dresen as an 'East German' director? And in what way could a film such as Christian Petzold's *Barbara* (2012) be described as an 'East German' film? How, as Barton Byg has put it, can GDR cinema be said to 'haunt the films of the present'?⁴¹ Following the demise of the GDR, all of these questions might be seen as variants on a single theme, namely the question of whether it is possible to identify a specific DEFA aesthetic. In an essay of 2000, Detlef Kannapin posed this very question; yet as he himself acknowledges, any attempt to reduce over forty years of film history to a single set of aesthetic principles is almost bound to fail.⁴²

Rather than treat East German cinema as essentially an isolated national phenomenon, our volume seeks to invite readers and researchers to re-imagine DEFA within a much broader notion of both German filmmaking and an increasingly global film industry. As such our volume seeks to consolidate – and go beyond – existing scholarship of the kind reflected in such important collections of essays as *DEFA International* (edited by Michael Wedel, Barton Byg et al.) and *DEFA at the Crossroads of East German and International Film Culture* (edited by Marc Silberman and Henning Wrage). Over twenty-five years have elapsed since the fall of the Berlin Wall, and during this period scholarship on DEFA has evolved very considerably. One consequence of that, however, is that we have now reached a point where that scholarship itself is ready to be subjected to a process of meta-reflection.

It is, of course, perfectly legitimate to explore the impact of East German cultural politics on the films produced by the DEFA studio – and there is still much important work to be done on this front. Nonetheless, underpinning almost all the essays in the volume is the assumption that attempts to consider DEFA solely within the geopolitical context of the GDR itself raise almost as many issues as they resolve. Rosemary Stott's analysis of the economics of filmmaking in the GDR reminds us that, contrary to what many have assumed, financial considerations (and the need to keep abreast of international trends in the European import/export market) did play an important role in East German film programming, and had a profound impact on the landscape of cinema exhibition. Stefan Soldovieri's discussion of Artur Pohl's *Spielbank-Affäre* [*Casino Affair*, 1957] demonstrates how DEFA's attempts to access international markets via the production of popular entertainment features were heavily conditioned by developments in German–German politics. In a similar vein, Annette Dorgerloh's focus on set design in the films of the 1950s and early 1960s highlights the extent to which, even after the construction of the Berlin Wall, modernist design was a phenomenon that transcended the border between East and West.

As many of the contributors to the volume argue, films produced at the Potsdam-Babelsberg studio were not simply vehicles for SED ideology, but were deeply embedded within a wider process of transnational cultural exchange that involved filmmakers not just from the Federal Republic and the Eastern Bloc, but also from other continents. As Dennis Hanlon and Qinna Shen point out in their essays, political developments in Asia and Latin America were to shape film production in the GDR in often quite unexpected ways that we are only now just beginning to recognize and understand. Likewise, the contributions by Evan Torner and Sonja Fritzsche suggest that rethinking DEFA from the related perspectives of race, postcolonial theory and utopian thought not only opens up new readings of individual films, but also confirms the status of the GDR's science fiction films and *Indianerfilme* as important contributions to a transnational concept of genre cinema. And while few would now deny the existence of a star system in the GDR, as Seán Allan's chapter on Dean Reed underlines, there were moments when this system of stardom was inflected with a transnational aspect that simply could not be subsumed within the prevailing model of the *Publikumsliebling*.

While at one level our volume seeks to re-imagine DEFA by considering its relation to global concepts of popular cinema (and in the case of Benita Blessing's contribution, internationalist traditions of the *Kinderfilm*) it also explores the way in which filmmakers sought to democratize highbrow culture. As Larson Powell's essay on film music (surely one of the most underexplored areas in DEFA scholarship) demonstrates, for many East German composers, cinema constituted a crucial opportunity for self-expression; and many of DEFA's soundtracks, precisely because of their complex allusions to classical and modernist traditions in European music, suggest that musicology in the GDR was a much more complex and transnational phenomenon than many have assumed. For her part, Sabine Hake, in her pioneering essay on the politics of the DEFA 'opera film', examines the ways in which media convergence in the work of Walter Felsenstein is deployed as a tool to negotiate a pathway through the intricate complex of high culture, socialist culture and mass culture.

Finally, a number of the contributions to the volume reflect on questions of temporality, and the difficulties in confining the study of DEFA to the period 1946-1992. Mariana Ivanova's essay on the legacy of the prestige agenda of 'Film Europe' and its impact on postwar film production in the East, serves as a reminder that, for all the insistence on a new start in German filmmaking in 1945, the history of pre and postwar cinema is more one of continuity than rupture. As the chapters by Nick Hodgin, Sebastian Heiduschke and Daniela Berghahn suggest, the same is true of the (increasingly problematic) term 'German cinema' in the pre- and post-Wende periods. Hodgin's discussion of melancholy in the field of documentary – another form of filmmaking that is all too often overlooked – is followed by two contributions that, albeit in different ways, consider the ways in which contemporary German-language cinema and documentary engage in a process of creative dialogue with DEFA's cinematic and ideological legacy. In this way, all three contributions point to an 'afterlife' of East German cinema that has yet to be fully explored. Accordingly, our volume is an invitation to re-imagine not just DEFA, but also 'post-DEFA' cinema from a transnational – and indeed transtemporal – perspective. No edited collection can claim to offer comprehensive coverage of what is an increasingly diverse and complex phenomenon; and our volume is no different in that respect. But we hope that the gaps that were always there from the outset – and those that have emerged in the course of the editing process – will serve as an inspiration for DEFA scholars in the future.

Seán Allan is Professor of German at the University of St Andrews. He is co-editor (with John Sandford) of *DEFA: East German Cinema, 1946-1992* (1999), and has published widely on the films of Konrad Wolf, Kurt Maetzig and Jürgen Böttcher, and on East German identity in post-unification cinema.

Sebastian Heiduschke is Associate Professor in the School of Language, Culture, and Society, and Affiliate Faculty in the School of Writing, Literature, and Film at Oregon State University. He has published the monograph *DEFA: East German Cinema and Film History* (2013) and essays on the marketing, distribution, and fan cultures of DEFA film.

Notes

1. See, for example, Harry Blunk and Dirk Jungnickel (eds), *Filmland DDR. Ein Reader zu Geschichte, Funktion und Wirkung der DEFA*, Cologne: Verlag für Wissenschaft und Politik, 1990; Ralf Schenk (ed), *Das zweite Leben der Filmstadt Babelsberg. DEFA-Spielfilme 1946–1992*, Berlin: Henschel, 1994; Seán Allan and John Sandford (eds), *DEFA. East German Cinema, 1946–1992*, New York, Oxford: Berghahn, 1996. All translations are our own, unless specified otherwise.
2. See, for example, Peter W. Jansen and Wolfram Schütte (eds), *Film in der DDR*, Munich: Hanser, 1977.
3. For three of the earliest attempts to integrate DEFA into a more general history of German national cinema see Marc Silberman, *German Cinema. Texts in Context*, Detroit: Wayne State University Press, 1995; Sabine Hake, *German National Cinema*, London, New York: Routledge, 2002; and John E. Davidson and Sabine Hake (eds), *Framing the Fifties. Cinema in a Divided Germany*, New York, Oxford: Berghahn, 2007. For a more recent study see Stephen Brockmann, *A Critical History of German Film*, Rochester, NY: Camden House, 2010.
4. Notable exceptions in this respect include: Mira Liehm and Antonín J. Liehm, *The Most Important Art. Eastern European Film after 1945*, Berkeley, Los Angeles, London: University of Berkeley Press, 1977; Daniel J. Goulding (ed), *Post New Wave Cinema in the Soviet Union and Eastern Europe*, Bloomington and Indianapolis: Indiana University Press, 1989; and Dina Iordanova, *The Cinema of the Other Europe*, London: Wallflower, 2003.
5. For example, Joshua Feinstein, *The Triumph of the Ordinary. Depictions of Daily Life in the East German Cinema, 1949–1989*, Chapel Hill & London: University of North Carolina Press, 2002; Daniela Berghahn, *Hollywood Behind the Wall. The Cinema of East Germany*, Manchester: Manchester University Press, 2005; Anke Pinkert, *Film and Memory in East Germany*, Bloomington and Indianapolis: Indiana University Press, 2008; and Sebastian Heiduschke, *East German Cinema. DEFA and Film History*, New York, London: Palgrave Macmillan, 2013.
6. Andrew Higson, 'The Concept of National Cinema', *Screen* 30.4 (1989), 2–26.
7. Alfred Lindemann, 'Die Lage des deutschen Films', in *Der deutsche Film. Fragen – Forderungen – Aussichten. Bericht vom Ersten Deutschen Film-Autoren-Kongreß. 6–9. Juni 1947 in Berlin*, Berlin: Henschel, 1947, pp. 9–19.
8. Hermann Axen, 'Über die Fragen der fortschrittlichen Filmkunst', in *Für den Aufschwung der fortschrittlichen deutschen Filmkunst*, Berlin: Dietz, 1953, pp. 15–46 (esp. pp. 17–21).
9. See Rosemary Stott, *Crossing the Wall. The Western Feature Film Import in East Germany*, Oxford: Lang, 2012.
10. Barton Byg, 'Introduction. Reassessing DEFA Today', in Barton Byg and Betheny Moore (eds), *Moving Images of East Germany. Past and Future of DEFA Film*, Washington DC: AICGS, 2002, pp. 1–23 (p. 1).

11. Harry Blunk, *Die DDR in ihren Spielfilmen. Reproduktion und Konzeption der DDR-Gesellschaft im neueren DEFA-Gegenwartsspielfilm*, Munich: Profil, 1984.
12. Heinz Kersten, *Das Filmwesen in der sowjetischen Besatzungszone Deutschlands*, Bonn, Berlin: Bundesministerium für Gesamtdeutsche Fragen, 1963.
13. Klaus Finke, 'DEFA-Film als "nationales Kulturerbe"? Thesen zum DEFA-Film und seiner wissenschaftlichen Aufarbeitung', in Klaus Finke (ed), *DEFA-Film als nationales Kulturerbe?* [= Beiträge zur Film- und Fernsehwissenschaft, vol. 58], (2001), pp. 93–108.
14. Finke, p. 107.
15. See, for example, the analysis of DEFA's co-productions with France in Marc Silberman, 'Learning from the Enemy. DEFA-French Co-productions of the 1950s', *Film History* 18.1 (2006), 21–45.
16. Hans Joachim Meurer, *Cinema and National Identity in Divided Germany, 1979–1989. The Split Screen*, Lewiston, Queenston and Lampeter: Edwin Mellen, 2002.
17. Marc Silberman, 'What is German in German Cinema?', *Film History* 8 (1996), 297–315 (297).
18. Meurer, pp. 17–18.
19. Ibid., p. 43.
20. David Bathrick, 'From UFA to DEFA. Past as Present in Early GDR Films', in Jost Hermand and Marc Silberman (eds), *Contentious Memories. Looking Back at the GDR*, New York, Washington: Lang 2000, pp. 169–88.
21. Thomas Heimann, *DEFA, Künstler und SED-Kulturpolitik* [= Beiträge zur Film- und Fernsehwissenschaft, vol. 46], (1994), p. 57.
22. Detlef Kannapin, 'Was hat Zarah Leander mit der DEFA zu tun? Die Nachwirkungen des NS-Films im DEFA-Schaffen – Notwendige Anmerkungen für eine neue Forschungsperspektive', in Ralf Schenk, Erika Richter and Claus Löser (eds), *apropos: Film 2005* [= Jahrbuch der DEFA-Stiftung, 2005], Berlin: Bertz + Fischer, 2005, pp. 188–209.
23. For a useful overview of approaches to film historiography in the GDR, see Dorothea Becker, *Zwischen Ideologie und Autonomie. Die DDR-Forschung über die deutsche Filmgeschichte*, Münster, Hamburg, London: Lit, 1999.
24. Kannapin, 'Zarah Leander', p. 197.
25. Ibid., p. 201.
26. Katie Trumpener, 'DEFA. Moving Germany into Eastern Europe', in Barton Byg and Betheny Moore (eds), *Moving Images of East Germany. Past and Future of DEFA Film*, Washington DC: AICGS, 2002, pp. 85-104. See also: Mariana Ivanova, 'DEFA and Eastern European Cinemas: Co-Productions, Transnational Exchange, and Artistic Collaborations', unpublished PhD Diss., University of Texas at Austin, 2011; Oksana Bulgakowa, 'DEFA-Filme im Kontext der "neuen Wellen"', in Michael Wedel, Barton Byg, Andy Räder, Skyler Arndt-Briggs, and Evan Torner (eds), *DEFA International. Grenzen und Grenzüberschreitungen. Transnationale Filmbeziehungen der DEFA vor und nach dem Mauerbau*, Wiesbaden: VS Verlag, 2013, pp. 45–60; and Larson Powell, '"Wind from the East". DEFA and Eastern European Cinema', in Marc Silberman and Henning Wrage (eds), *DEFA at the Crossroads of East German and International Film Culture. A Companion*, Berlin, Boston: de Gruyter, 2014, pp. 223–42.
27. See Qinna Shen, *The Politics of Magic. DEFA Fairy-Tale Films*, Detroit, MI: Wayne State University Press, 2015.
28. See Sonja Fritzsche, 'The Natural and the Artificial. East German Science Fiction Film Responds to Kubrick and Tarkovsky', *Film & History* 40.2 (2010), 80–101 [Special issue: *Visions of Science and Technology in Film*]; and Rosemary Stott, 'Continuity and Change in GDR Cinema Programming

Policy 1979–1989. The Case of the American Science Fiction Import', *German Life and Letters* 55.1 (2002), 91–9.
29. Gerd Gemünden, 'Between Karl May and Karl Marx. The DEFA *Indianerfilme* (1965–1983)', *Film History* 10.3 (1998), 399–407.
30. See, for example, Claudia Fellmer, 'Stars in East German Cinema', unpublished PhD Diss., University of Southampton, 2002; Stefan Soldovieri, 'The Politics of the Popular. *Trace of Stones* (1966/89) and the Discourse of Stardom in the GDR Cinema', in Randall Halle and Margaret McCarthy (eds), *Light Motives. German Popular Film in Perspective*, Detroit: Wayne State University Press, 2003, pp. 220–236; and Sabine Hake, 'Public Figures, Political Symbols, Famous Stars. Actors in DEFA Cinema and Beyond', in Marc Silberman and Henning Wrage (eds), *DEFA at the Crossroads of East German and International Film Culture*, Berlin, Boston: de Gruyter, 2014, pp. 197–220.
31. Brigitta B. Wagner, 'Introduction. Making History ReVisible', in Brigitta B. Wagner (ed), *DEFA after East Germany*, Rochester, NY: Camden House, 2014, pp. 1–7 (p. 1).
32. See https://ecommerce.umass.edu/defa/about/history, accessed 23 April 2015.
33. Sebastian Heiduschke, 'GDR Cinema as Commodity: Marketing DEFA Films Since Unification', *German Studies Review* 36.1 (2013), 61–78; and Sebastian Heiduschke, 'Emerging from the Niche. DEFA's Afterlife in United Germany', *Monatshefte* 105.4 (2013), 625–40.
34. See also Stefanie Eckert, *Das Erbe der DEFA. Die fast unendliche Geschichte einer Stiftungsgründung*, Berlin: DEFA-Stiftung, 2008.
35. Stefan Haupt, *Urheberrecht und DEFA Film*, Berlin: DEFA-Stiftung, 2005.
36. See for example http://www.welt.de/regionales/berlin/article13639472/Verleih-will-DDR-Filmerbe-vermarkten.html, 3 October 2011, accessed 23 April 2015.
37. Daphne Berdahl, *Where the World Ended. Re-Unification and Identity in the German Borderland*, Berkeley: University of California Press, 1999.
38. One of the most active fan movements is that centered on Václav's Vorlícek's film *Drei Haselnüsse für Aschenbrödel* [*Three Wishes for Cinderella*, 1973]. Their website http://3hfa.jimdo.com shows the extent of fandom for a DEFA film.
39. See, for example, http://defa-filmfreund.de/schreiben-ist-auch-arbeit/ for a list of Jens Rübner's self-published fan books.
40. See, for example, Reinhild Steingröver, *Last Features. East German Cinema's Lost Generation*, Rochester, NY: Camden House, 2014.
41. Barton Byg, 'Spectral Images in the Afterlife of GDR Cinema', in Wagner, *DEFA after East Germany*, pp. 24–50 (p. 24).
42. Detlef Kannapin, 'Gibt es eine spezifische DEFA-Ästhetik? Anmerkungen zum Wandel der künstlerischen Formen im DEFA-Spielfilm', in Ralf Schenk and Erika Richter (eds), *apropos: Film 2000* [= Das Jahrbuch der DEFA-Stiftung, 2000], Berlin: Das Neue Berlin, 2000, pp. 142–64.

PART I
INSTITUTIONS AND IDEOLOGY

CHAPTER 1

The State-Owned Cinema Industry and Its Audience

Rosemary Stott

In recent scholarship the term DEFA has become synonymous with East German cinema generally; however, it is important to remember that the remit of this organization extended far beyond the production of feature films for the national cinema of the GDR. Subsidiary companies of DEFA managed not only the production of documentary and animation films, but also the sales of licenses for home-produced films, the purchase and dubbing of imported films, and the distribution and exhibition of all films across the national cinema network. Most of these companies were based in Berlin and Potsdam; but a number were located in outlying regions of the GDR, such as the animation studios which were based in Dresden.[1]

The cinema industry was one of the most significant cultural sectors in East Germany. Even in 1988, just one year before the collapse of the GDR, there were still some 808 cinemas[2] serving a population of just under seventeen million.[3] This was the equivalent of fourteen cinema seats to every individual, a more favourable ratio than in the Federal Republic, which had the equivalent of just 9.9 seats per member of the population.[4] Although the cinema network had declined slightly during the 1980s (with eighteen closures), in that same period the number of venues for live theatre had increased from 152 to 213, confirming that there was still a great appetite amongst the East German population to experience culture en masse. Nonetheless, cinema remained the most popular form of entertainment. In 1988 there were 50.2 million visits to the cinema as opposed to 9.6 million visits to the theatre; and 7,045 people were employed by cinemas, representing a total of 7.76% of employees in the cultural industries. The importance of cinema in the state's eyes is also confirmed by the fact that spending on the film industry increased steadily despite a slight fall in the number of cinemas; in 1980, government spending was 209.5 million (East German) marks and by 1988, it was 281.5 million marks.⁵

Originally set up under the auspices of the Soviet Military Administration in 1946, DEFA came under the control of the newly established GDR in 1949. It comprised a number of studios (feature, animation and documentary film) which produced some 950 feature films (including shorts), 820 animation films, and 5,200 documentary films and newsreels between them. Taking the year 1988 as an example, some 14 feature films were produced, of which 2 were children's films, together with a further 44 documentary films and 28 animation films. As far as distribution was concerned, some 143 films were released that year, comprising 19 DEFA films, 75 from other socialist countries, 36 from capitalist countries and 13 children's films. The DEFA dubbing studios worked on German versions of a significant proportion of the foreign imports (approximately 4,000 were dubbed in total over the course of the studio's existence), which were scripted by a team of East German writers and translators and subsequently dubbed by actors. The remaining proportion of imported films was purchased as dubbed versions from West German dubbing studios.

Film production and distribution in the GDR reflected the socialist politics, ideology and culture of the state. In stark contrast to the model of Hollywood, East German film production was not run as a business driven primarily by competitive, commercial interests. Nonetheless, while the studio complex at Potsdam-Babelsberg was a state-owned company (a so-called *Volkseigener Betrieb*) it still had to balance its books and ensure that film production was carried out in accordance with certain predetermined plans, budgets, shooting schedules and contracts. DEFA's main role was to inform and educate the cinema-going public, ideally through popular and entertainment forms of the medium. Most spheres of life in the GDR were subject to state control and surveillance and the cinema industry was no exception in this respect; through the control of film industry personnel, the ruling Socialist Unity Party (SED) tried to ensure that the films exhibited in East German cinemas promoted party interests and did not fuel audience discontent or disillusionment with the government. Even so, despite – or possibly even because of – the repressive aspects of such a top-down system of control and indoctrination – many individuals found ways of adapting and even subverting the system to serve their own interests; and some of these more personalized accounts – of the kind to be found in the volume *Spur der Filme* for example – offer a very different kind of 'history from below' regarding the way the studio operated than that which is to be found in more conventional histories of DEFA.⁶

Socialist Film Production at DEFA

DEFA mirrored a number of aspects of its predecessor UFA: not just in its name, which had connotations of a commercial production company, but also because it was a horizontally and vertically integrated film company.[7] Established during the Weimar Republic, the Babelsberg studio was a 'factory of dreams' capable of realizing projects on a grand scale. Although the infrastructure was in ruins in 1945, just one year before the Soviets granted the license for films to be made in the zone of occupation, the basis for film production was still there. Once the facility had been rebuilt, it comprised nine studio buildings, a large backlot, production office space and support buildings, uniting all the divisions that were necessary to produce films on one site of approximately 500,000 square metres. DEFA also inherited a longstanding legacy of technical innovation and knowledge and was proud to promote this tradition. In the 1960s and 1970s, for instance, it was the only country other than the United States and the USSR that could make 70mm productions.

From 1961 onwards, both feature and documentary films were produced at DEFA using the principle of so-called *Künstlerische Arbeitsgruppen* (film units). This approach also had a precedent in German studios of the Weimar era, but in socialist countries it had first been introduced by Soviet studios and subsequently by the majority of film studios in Eastern Europe.[8] These film units were semi-independent and underpinned a structural framework for socialist cinema, in which film was conceived both as a collective endeavour, and as an artistic medium with an educational role to play. The units founded in 1961 and focusing on feature film production were called Berlin (led by Slatan Dudow), Roter Kreis (Kurt Maetzig), Heinrich Greif (Konrad Wolf), Gruppe 60 (Alexander Löscher), Solidarität (Adolf Fischer), Konkret (Anni von Ziethen) and Stacheltier (Rudi Hannemann).

Günter Giesenfeld has drawn a parallel between the establishment of the artistic units in the GDR and the rise of auteurist cinema in the FRG, insofar as the latter was consciously set up to challenge the strictly industrial model of Hollywood and was committed to producing arthouse films with an often left-wing agenda.[9] The emergence of the film units at DEFA in the early 1960s also coincided with a period when arthouse cinema was beginning to flourish in a number of Eastern as well as Western European countries. However, it is important to remember that in the GDR all film was conceived of as 'art' (*Filmkunst*), and regarded as having the same status as – and similar purpose to – theatre, music and opera, whereas in the Federal Republic, the New German Cinema represented an alternative to the predominantly commercial film industry. In the GDR, the purpose of cinema was not first and foremost film as a commodity, but rather film as a contribution to a notion of culture (broadly understood).

The film units developed a range of ideas for films and pitched them to the studio administration. If an idea was accepted, it became part of the yearly production plan and its budget was provided by the studios. Unlike in the West, production teams in the East were not responsible for securing finance. Although they were semi-autonomous, politically, the film units were still an integral part of the bureaucratic machine of the film industry and were beholden to the overall administrators at the studios, who themselves had to toe the party line imposed from above. As we shall see, there were a number of levels of approval that a film script had to go through before the green light was granted. Accordingly the same processes that had a positive impact on GDR film production – consultation and collective decision making – also ensured that the end product remained subject to state control. Although this may give the impression that, while the film units were democratic spaces for creative free thinkers, the studio administrators were, by contrast, narrow-minded censors, such a view is too simplistic. As Ralf Schenk notes: 'it would be wrong to conclude that standing on one side of the barricades were the dogmatic SED functionaries, and on the other side, the more-or-less brave, resistant, and subversive filmmakers. The truth was much more complicated: those who conformed and those who resisted actually stood on both sides; even within any given individual, two souls raged'.[10]

The Film Collective

The variety of roles and professions in the East German film industry was similar in scope to that of most European national cinemas. As with all other areas of work in the GDR, the government controlled the number of young people trained for these roles according to society's need. There was a strong emphasis placed on professional training and qualifications and little prospect of entering a profession without passing the approved stages of training. For the majority of young people in the GDR, the aspiration to become a film director would have been quashed by lack of opportunity. For example, the Film and Television

Figure: 1.1 Workers in a print laboratory on the DEFA Studio site, Babelsberg, 1950s © DEFA-Stiftung.

School – also located close to the DEFA studio in Potsdam Babelsberg – offered only six to eight places every two years for trainee directors.[11] In the more technical areas of the profession, opportunities were greater.

The feature film studio was one of the largest employers in the region of Potsdam, employing 2,500 people alone.[12] Nearly all employees were employees of the state, with a regular source of work and income guaranteed. The state provided the workers with the means of production, but also expected something back, which could be broadly defined as a sense of responsibility to the collective, something which all citizens were educated to respect through their socialization at school and at work. For the creative employees at the studio, as Helmut Morsbach noted in 2006, DEFA meant home, family, variety, hope, disappointment, failure and guilt ('Heimat, Familie, Vielfalt, Hoffnung, Enttäuschung, Versagen und Schuld').[13]

Directors

The role of the director was not given as much emphasis as it was in the Federal Republic and other states in Western Europe, since in the GDR the director's individual contribution was subsumed into that of the collective. Production was not organized around the notion of 'auteurs' and only a few directors – Heiner Carow, Siegfried Kühn, Rainer Simon, Lothar Warneke and Konrad Wolf would be the obvious examples – could be said to have developed a 'signature style' comparable with that of some of the New German Cinema directors in the West. The socialization and training of directors within the established state-run structures led to an inherent understanding of what was possible, and to a type of 'responsible' self-censorship. Rather than a drive to express themselves in an artistically individual way and thus to differentiate themselves – in an auteurist sense – from other directors, East German directors were united by a sense of collective responsibility. At times, as Giesenfeld has argued, this contributed to a nationalist and ideological agenda in which cinema (like sport) could be presented as an area in which the GDR was superior to its capitalist German neighbour, the Federal Republic.[14]

Film directors and the other creative professionals contributing to the artistic development of a film were familiar with trends in international filmmaking. When it was set up, DEFA inherited both a historical site and a history of German filmmaking, which for decades had engaged in dialogue with international trends in genre, style, narrative, character development and aesthetics. In postwar East Germany such dialogue inevitably involved the cinema industries of other Eastern Bloc states. However, precisely because of their proximity, accessibility and shared history, the filmmakers of the New German Cinema in the Federal Republic were also important partners in a transnational dialogue between two filmmaking states which were of mutual fascination to one another and which shared more than just their language. While it was often claimed in public that the cinema of the GDR was shaped in contra-distinction to that of the Federal Republic, the reality was that both officials at the Ministry of Culture and film industry professionals kept a close eye on developments across the border. The administrators at the Central Film Administration, who worked with Progress Film-Verleih, DEFA's distribution arm with responsibility for importing foreign films, researched the West German print media film reviews to assess the suitability of films already released in the Federal Republic. Those who were allowed to travel (*Reisekader*) regularly went over the border to West Berlin to view films they were interested in purchasing for

East German exhibition. Most film directors – even those without permission to travel to the West – could access almost any film they wished; and like many East German citizens, became familiar with developments in international cinema via West German television (which could be received relatively easily in the GDR in the 1970s and 1980s).

Dramaturge

The role of the dramaturge originated from the Western theatre tradition and was already incorporated into German filmmaking during the early Weimar period. It was a particularly important creative role in the DEFA studios as well as in the cinema industries in other socialist countries as it reflected the conception of film as art rather than commerce. The dramaturge (sometimes glossed as 'literary advisor'), was usually a film professional with a strong literary background: a writer or critic, who had a variety of responsibilities at every stage of film production. S/he had the responsibility of sourcing new material for films, finding suitable authors, networking between writers and directors and mediating conflicts between filmmakers and bureaucrats, studios and co-production partners, and the production community and the general public. The dramaturge worked on the development of the screenplay of individual films, editing, reviewing and approving the final version. S/he also devised the thematic plans of the whole film unit, paying attention to the prevailing political and cultural agendas and the annual studio production plans. Every year, the dramaturge sorted through approximately 200 proposals and treatments to determine which would be suitable for development.[15]

The dramaturge was one of the most important creatives in the film unit and some of the long-standing dramaturges at the studio were held in very high esteem by directors and scriptwriters at DEFA. As Dieter Wolf, head of dramaturgy for the Babelsberg film unit for twenty-six years has noted, both the author's,[16] and the director's success was dependent on a successful working relationship with the dramaturge.[17] Lothar Warneke's remarkable run of creative successes in the 1980s, for instance, was due in part to his dramaturge Erika Richter securing three literary debuts for film scripts. Firstly, Richter engaged the psychologist and writer Helga Schubert for the screenplay of *Die Beunruhigung* [*Apprehension*, 1982]. Richter herself worked on the script for *Eine sonderbare Liebe* [*A Strange Love*, 1984] in collaboration with Wolfram Witt, a graduate of dramaturgy from the national Film and

Television School. Finally, it was Richter who brought Warneke's attention to the novel *Blonder Tango* [Blond Tango, 1982], written by the exiled Chilean author, Omar Saavedra Santis and who commissioned Santis to write a screenplay based on the novel. The film of *Blonder Tango* was released in 1986.[18] Nearly every film had a dramaturge, but there was also a higher level of dramaturge: the studio head of dramaturgy (DEFA-*Chefdramaturg*), who had overall artistic responsibility for the films produced by DEFA. This role was more associated with central planning and ideological control of the industry. An indication of the importance and responsibility attached to this role can be drawn from the fate of Klaus Wischnewski, who was the head of dramaturgy at the time of the notorious Eleventh Plenum in 1965 and who, as a consequence, was dismissed from the studio.[19]

Film Finance

The acronym DEFA stood for 'Deutsche Film-Aktiengesellschaft' (in which the final term 'Aktiengesellschaft' is the usual German term for 'limited company'). Although officially referred to as a corporation when established, DEFA became – like most businesses in the GDR – a state-run industry with no competition between companies, no market forces and no shareholders to answer to. In German film history, DEFA has acquired something of a special status as one of the few major film companies in Germany to have operated under non-capitalist conditions. Yet as Giesenfeld has argued, this difference does not appear to have been the decisive factor in shaping a distinctively East German film aesthetic and/or approach to filmmaking. For many of the obstacles faced by filmmakers in both East and West were very similar, namely the battle against the declining cinema-going audience as a result of competition from television, and the necessity to repackage serious issues in entertaining forms. Nonetheless, these issues had a different ideological inflection in the GDR.[20]

Taking the model of Hollywood as the norm, it is, of course, difficult to conceive of film production outside the context of capitalism on an industrial scale. However, from the 1970s onwards it was (and still is) common in Western Europe to have public service broadcasting companies, which use economic models that were not so very different from those of the East German film industry. Indeed this is a useful starting point for understanding how film finances worked in the GDR. It was certainly not the case that the budgets were limitless but, as with the public service model in the West, East German employees of the state were responsible for managing and administrating the film industry and ensuring value for money. The employees on the production side worked collaboratively with the administrators of the industry, but were held to account by them if they did not produce to time or budget. Thus the film administrators at DEFA were like executive producers, responsible to the government for the financial setting and controlling of film budgets.

The decisive factor in production was the theme of any given film and its so-called 'progressive message' (*fortschrittliches Gedankengut*).[21] Films were made to express the values and politics of socialism and cinema was conceived as a sphere where political and cultural debate could take place. The motivation for film producers was therefore not primarily commercial; but it was still important – albeit for ideological rather than financial reasons – that audiences would want to view the films. Criteria of efficiency and financial prudence were still imposed, but these were secondary to the educational value of the end product. This was especially the case with films set in the contemporary GDR and targeted at a national audience. It was also true for genre films even though, superficially at least, DEFA's genre films mimicked the more traditional consumer-driven patterns of the industrial film production model in matters of iconography, star and settings.

Key themes were set out in yearly production plans produced by the studio and were aimed at addressing and promoting both the values and attributes of the 'socialist personality', and an understanding of communist history. Following the collapse of the GDR in 1989, it became clear that not all cinema industry workers had felt included in this process because, for the first time in forty years, there was a revolt amongst the technical and economic personnel. They demanded an independent commission, whose members would be democratically elected from members of staff, to decide upon which films should be planned.[22] These and other idealistic initiatives during the short-lived honeymoon period of the Wende underline just how deep-rooted the desire for a genuinely socialist model of filmmaking was at the studio, before the commercial imperatives of Western models of filmmaking swept in and led to the demise of DEFA itself.

When we look more closely at one of the yearly production plans, the extent to which the theme and/or ideological content of the films was the dominant consideration becomes very clear. The ideas put forward by the various production groups were assessed in terms of their potential to engage audiences and their appropriateness to the prevailing political imperatives. Much like the principles of public service broadcasting, planning was based on a notion of creating a balanced and representative output, which mirrored the interests and tastes of all groups in society. Accordingly, in 1969 filmmakers were told:

> With reference to the twentieth anniversary of the GDR in all respects, the thematic plan for 1969 is intended to contribute towards providing a multifaceted and interesting picture of the people in this Republic, to the development of the socialist community, and to satisfy the differentiated cultural needs of the cinema-going public. The emphasis is on the challenges that face people in a developed social system of socialism. In contemporary films, a variety of themes in a variety of genres will be presented.[23]

In 1969, nineteen new films were taken into production and six films were still in production from the previous year's plan. The administrators who authored the report stated that in the future more films which addressed the interests of the rural population and the armed forces would be required and it was considered regrettable that there was a shortage of films featuring working-class protagonists.[24]

Once a film was approved, it was assigned a budget as part of the yearly financial plan and an income target for both national and international exhibition. Each film cost on average two million East German Marks to produce[25] and some large-scale productions substantially more. The income targets were typically a half to two-thirds of the production costs; therefore film was a government-subsidized industry. *Spur der Steine* [*Traces of Stones*, 1966] was made at a cost of 2.5 million marks,[26] only to be locked away in the cellar for twenty-five years by the same group of film administrators who had commissioned it and sanctioned its budget. Thus the state made no return on its original cost: a stark illustration of the precedence of ideology over commerce. Genre films were more ambitious both technically and aesthetically than the majority of contemporary realist films and were more expensive as a consequence. Gottfried Kolditz's science fiction film, *Signale – Ein Weltraumabenteuer* [*Signals – A Space Adventure*, 1970] had a budget of 2.7 million.[27] DEFA made a total of eight 70mm productions and these could cost up to five million marks each.[28] *Goya* [1971], a 70mm co-production with the Soviet Union, had a budget of four million marks.[29] At the opposite extreme, some filmmakers experimented with a more modest style of production. The documentary realist style, which became predominant in the 1970s and 1980s was far less costly.

Lothar Warneke's *Die Beunruhigung*, for instance, experimented with a partly improvised script, handheld camera techniques and black-and-white film stock, and was made with a budget of some 800,000 marks.[30] The cost of making a film did not rise substantially, since there was little or no inflation in the economic system.[31]

Theory and Praxis. The Case of *Die Legende von Paul und Paula*

In order to show how DEFA's infrastructure shaped film production in the GDR and, in particular, how the issues of finance and censorship operated within the studio itself, I propose to take one of DEFA's most popular films, *Die Legende von Paul und Paula* [*The Legend of Paul and Paula*, 1973] as a case study. Few films could be considered 'typical' in terms of cost and production time, but Heiner Carow's *Die Legende von Paul und Paula* exemplifies many of the aspects of film production I have referred to above. When considering the way in which film production in the GDR was financed, it is important not to lose sight of the time it took to produce a film over the different phases of its production. At DEFA, the development phase was usually relatively long as the sourcing and development of an idea and scenario was considered crucial. *Die Legende von Paul und Paula* had a particularly long development phase because it had first been assigned to the director Ingrid Reschke, who worked on the original scenario with the author Ulrich Plenzdorf. When Reschke died in a car accident in May 1971, the project was taken over by the director Heiner Carow, who reworked the scenario with Plenzdorf soon after. In the assessment written by the film unit KAG Berlin, which made the film, it was recognized that the authors had the basis for an 'exceptional film'.[32] The scenario was also praised for its presentation of a relationship based on an equal partnership: 'Our society is the first which has enabled the full potential of love to contribute to the development of the personality, without coming into conflict or even failing because of social traditions, conventions or economic pressures'.[33] Despite this, however, the head of dramaturgy was not content with the scenario and a rewrite was requested.[34] In a protocol produced by the artistic director and signed by three people, the originality of the scenario was acknowledged, but the criticisms were harsh and bore the hallmarks of state censorship. The experimental aesthetic approach was criticized, and they believed that the film focused on individuals as opposed to their social environment. They found the treatment of some of the characters, for example the character of Reifen-Saft, one-dimensional, even satirical.[35]

The final version of the script was submitted on 31 January 1972,[36] but before that, the pre-production stage had already begun. The formal request to embark on pre-production and for funds to be released was made by the production manager to the studio's director for production on 7 January 1972 and was accompanied by a detailed pre-production budget plan of 158,600 marks.[37] Prior to that, on 20 December 1971, discussions were held between the production manager Erich Albrecht and the director Heiner Carow and reported to the director for production, Gert Golde. The letter from Albrecht to Golde focused on the budget required for the film.[38] Albrecht had informed Carow that the original budget figure of 1.3 million marks had to be met. In his letter to Golde, however, he argued that the real figure would be 1.75 million marks owing to the required meterage being longer than average, as well as the large number of location shoots, props and outside sets required.[39] The requested pre-production budget was approved, with a

Figure 1.2 (From left to right) Heiner Carow, Heidemarie Wenzel, Regina Teichmann and Winfried Glatzeder on the set of *Die Legende von Paul und Paula* (1973) © DEFA-Stiftung/Manfred Damm, Herbert Kroiss.

requirement that a draft production plan and a draft production budget be submitted within two weeks of receipt.[40]

The pre-production stage consisted of a search for actors and locations, the creation of shooting plans, rehearsals, scene planning, securing permission to shoot, negotiations with state institutions and businesses, test shooting, arrangements for set design, costume and make-up, planning for shoots, confirmation of arrangements with the studio directorate and preparation of all necessary production records.[41] On average, pre-production would take about three months prior to commencement of shooting, but in the case of *Die Legende von Paul und Paula* it took somewhat longer. Production had been due to start in March, with the first of two shoots planned for 10–24 March 1972,[42] but was delayed because the actor playing Paul (Winfried Glatzeder) was in rehearsals for a play at the Volksbühne theatre in Berlin. Screen tests and auditions with other actors had come to nothing and Heiner Carow and the production team were convinced that the success of the film rested on the participation of Glatzeder.

Negotiations with the theatre director had broken down to such an extent that the head of the studio, Albert Wilkening, wrote to the Deputy Minister for Culture, Günter Klein, drawing his attention to the general problem of the availability of actors and asking him to intervene in this particular case by sending a directive to the artistic director of the Volksbühne. The request was strongly justified with recourse to both artistic and economic arguments: 'It is clear to me that this is a complex problem, but we are obliged to strictly respect not just the artistic, but above all the financial requirements and in this case we are not able to move forward on our own'.[43] Subsequently, a compromise was reached during negotiations between the deputy director and head dramaturge of the Volksbühne, Heiner Müller, Heiner Carow, and Erich Albrecht (the production manager of the film). Both Glatzeder and his co-star, Angelica Domröse, travelled with the theatre for guest performances in Italy in April, but returned on 29 April 1972 to begin the shoot for the film on 2 May 1972.[44] Despite the compromise, the arrangements for getting the two of them on set were complex because they both had other television and film commitments too. A similar conflict to the one with the Volksbühne arose with the producer Erich Kühne and the director Frank Beyer of the TV mini-series *Die sieben Affären der Doña Juanita* [*The Seven Affairs of Doña Juanita*, 1973], who planned to shoot night scenes with Glatzeder in Cottbus on the same days that he was involved in shooting for

Carow's film. Because of Domröse's other commitments, the shooting plan for *Die Legende von Paul und Paula* had to take place in two separate periods, finishing on 10 August 1972.[45]

The DEFA studio director, Albert Wilkening formally signed off the commencement of the production phase of the film on 25 April 1972. The budget was calculated as 1,819,200 marks. The national box office target was set at 900,000 marks and international receipts at 150,000 marks. A special clause requested that the 'Datsche' (holiday home) scene be moved from the Baltic Sea to the Potsdam region to make cost savings.[46] The production team were briefed on the same day that production was formally approved. The briefing covered the length of the shoot (55 days) and details about the locations, the main one being at 62 Singerstrasse in Friedrichshain, Berlin, where old tenement blocks were being cleared for new apartment buildings.[47] During the briefing, the production collective were asked to sign the 'Wettbewerbsverpflichtung' (the commitment to strive for continuous improvement). This was an East German approach to work in the collective: motivation and efficiency in completing the project were created through such declared commitment to the work and fulfilment of the targets and through the award of a bonus ('Prämie') to individuals on successful completion of the project. The document outlined the work that needed to be completed and the budget costs and appealed to the collective to commit itself to the work required:

> *Each worker is requested to give due consideration to and make suggestions towards how the workload required for the production can be made more efficient, how the workflow, continuity and planning can be improved despite the known obstacles, in order to keep to the confirmed budget and even reduce costs where possible. Every constructive idea should be used for the good of our collective work.*[48]

During the film production, protocols were kept to record the daily activities and costs. Any changes to the original production plans and budget had to be justified and communicated to the production director of DEFA. All costs were accounted for and any extra expenses justified. For instance, during the shoot of the 'dream sequence' on the barge at Alt-Stralau, one of the thirty-eight extras fell and laddered her tights. A claim for damages and replacement of the tights was made to the production department of the studios by the unit manager: a touching insight into the way in which, in the GDR, often mundane articles were a luxury that for many were either unavailable or unaffordable.

Post-production began in late August and the rough cut was viewed by the artistic director of the studios and other DEFA directors on 27 September 1972. The assessment was extremely positive, for example the director Günter Reisch said that it was 'the most beautiful love story that he had ever seen in a DEFA film'.[49] The 'Wettbewerbsverflichtung' for the production stage was exceeded since cost savings of four per cent of the budget (75,000 marks) were returned to the studio. Post-production also ran to time, with the final negative of the film delivered before the planned date of 7 December 1972.[50] The film was awarded the rating 'good' by the director of the studio on 6 December 1972 and this rating determined the amount of the bonuses awarded.[51] The director was awarded a bonus of 15,000 marks, the cameraman Jürgen Brauer 9,000 marks and the set designer Harry Leupold 6,250 marks. Production records for the same film show that the production manager also rewarded the cast and crew by organizing a visit for them and their families to a production of *Die schöne Helena* [*The Beautiful Helena*], a play by Peter Hacks, in which Angelica Domröse was acting at the *Volksbühne* theatre in East Berlin on 16 December 1972. The production manager made an official claim to reimbursement of the tickets with the justification that the visit should be seen as a reward for the fulfilment of the commitment to continuous improvement, as the final costs of the film were under budget.[52] The case study of *Die Legende von Paul und Paula* underlines how systems of financial planning, prudent budgeting, account keeping and financial incentives were still vital aspects of the filmmaking process even in a fully state-subsidized model of film production.

Censorship at DEFA

The case of *Die Legende von Paul und Paula* also offers some insights into the ways in which the process of censorship operated in East German film production. Ever since the formation in 1947 of the Film Commission (*DEFA-Kommission*), a committee of the SED Central Secretariat, which could intervene in both the production planning and the management of personnel, DEFA films had been subject to scrutiny. This commission had a devastating effect on production during the early 1950s, but had been replaced by the Central Film Administration (*Hauptverwaltung*

Film) in 1954, during a mild thaw in cultural politics following the death of Joseph Stalin in March 1953. During the remainder of the 1950s, the party functionaries only got involved at the final stage of approving the finished film. During this period, as Ralf Schenk has noted, the relative 'health' of the studio could be gauged from the annual number of productions released. In 1951, only eight DEFA feature films were produced and in 1952, as few as six, but later in the decade, production rose to between twenty or even thirty films a year.[53] From the mid 1960s onwards, the number of feature films produced was lower, but more stable, averaging twenty DEFA productions annually.

There was scrutiny at every stage of production to make sure that the content and themes reflected the required representation of the state. Overt criticism of the state or its institutions was strictly taboo. At the fifth conference of the Film and Television Workers' Congress, in 1988, Jörg Foth, one of the so-called 'lost generation' of younger directors, gave a speech in which he estimated that an average DEFA film went through sixteen instances of examination, rejection or alteration before it was approved, leaving no room for free expression, spontaneity or experimentation.[54] Only a small number of films got away with defying the official image, or with using new or individual film styles. Those films which did succeed were unlikely to be in mainstream feature filmmaking, but in the more peripheral forms, such as the documentary film.[55]

As the case of *Die Legende von Paul und Paula* underlines, aesthetic experimentation was viewed with particular suspicion and gave rise to cuts and changes for the nationally produced film. When the original scenario for the film was at the approval stage, the artistic director considered the attempt to use heightened artistic techniques and characteristics of the fairy tale to be a 'particular problem'.[56] One year later, when the rough cut was viewed by the studio's artistic panel, Carow succeeded in gaining approval, despite having adhered to his and Plenzdorf's original scenario. He said that it would have been terrible to watch the film if they had used documentary realist techniques to make it and that he did not want the use of the legend to be understood as an intellectual way of telling the story.[57] There was still a considerable amount of nervousness about the film once it had been finished. In January 1973, it was discussed in the directorate of the Union of Film and Television Workers. There was concern about the characterization of the figure of Paul, a high-ranking member of the diplomatic service, who ends up rejecting his career and marriage in favour of life with Paula and their respective children: a life which the film endorses as more authentic than his former life. The film was also criticized for its 'dismaying intellectual emptiness' and just escaped being banned.[58]

Even at the exhibition stage, films could be subject to censorship. *Die Legende von Paul und Paula* caused a sensation with the audience when it was released, to the extent that the authorities grew nervous and restricted the amount of screenings the film was given. Looking back at the time at which the film was released, the former head of dramaturgy at the studio, Klaus Wischnewski, notes how it was precisely the film's mass appeal that the GDR's Ministry of Culture found so disconcerting:

> *The thoroughly amusing and tragic, sad and defiant story touched the nerve of the times and expressed what many associated positively with the term socialism. Much social potential and moral energy was revealed by these reactions, and was also present in the poetry, the songs, films, plays and books of the era, and in youth and singing clubs. Instead of being encouraged and used, it was controlled and administratively channelled. And yet the situation could have been dealt with so easily: the three most popular DEFA films in 1973 were: 1. Apachen [Apaches] 2. Die Legende von Paul und Paula 3. Nicht schummeln, Liebling [Don't Cheat, Darling!]. Any mediocre media manipulator can cope with this typical constellation. However after the disturbingly spontaneous and mass audience interest in Carow's Legende, the hardliners gained more power, the brakes were applied and the studios brought back into line.*[59]

Spectatorship and the Audience

Going to the cinema in the GDR was a cheap form of entertainment. Ticket prices were very low indeed, relative to income: for children, 0.25 to 0.5 marks; for adults, two marks on average; and pensioners paid half price. There was not a direct financial relationship between the number of tickets sold and the budgets available to make new films. If audiences stayed away from the cinema, it was obviously a concern for the film industry employees and administrators. However, it was not first and foremost financial factors which caused the concern, but rather the failure of individual films to communicate with the audience. Most DEFA filmmakers felt a strong affinity with their audience and a responsibility towards them. Because of the lack of a democratic press, the arts could serve the function of raising contemporary issues related to everyday life which were taboo in the print media. 'Some filmmakers', René Beyer notes, 'tried to communicate free moral concepts and lifestyles in their works. An indirect, encoded kind of communication, which occurred between the images, in gestures and in the way situations were presented'.[60]

Whilst it may be the case that studies since the Wende have neglected to investigate the viewing public in the GDR, during the time of the country's existence, the state was interested to find out about audience reaction to films, even if their motive was to preserve the political status quo. Preview screenings of DEFA films to test the audience reaction were normally conducted. In the case of films that the *Hauptverwaltung Film* considered a potential threat, additional screenings and focus group discussions were undertaken, much as they are by Western film companies today. As with everything else in the East German film industry though, the principal motivation was to find out whether the professed educational aims of the film were fulfilled (and not how to maximize the box office returns). In some respects, the preview screenings were to test whether the film did in fact elicit the reactions that had been anticipated in the original production plans.

Taking *Die Legende von Paul und Paula* as an example once again, there were fourteen test groups, ranging from a group of six hundred employees of a steel works in Brandenburg to fifteen officers and soldiers in the army in Bernau. Carow, the director, Plenzdorf, the author, both Glatzeder and Domröse, the principal actors, Werner Beck, the head of the film unit Berlin, as well as Peter Gotthardt, the composer, were present at the screenings. The conclusion of the eight-page report on the previews of the film, which took place in March and April 1973, was that the reactions of the public corresponded with the original conception for the film. Only in Dresden and to some extent in Potsdam was the character of Paul interpreted as a criticism of society. Some members of the audience spoke openly about how they disagreed with the negative reviews in the newspapers *Neues Deutschland* and *Junge Welt*. In all the discussions, the spectators expressed how important it was for them to be able to admire and respect DEFA films and for there not to be artistic or political compromises made during production. The film was seen by a number of the spectators as an example of how this could be achieved.[61] In the case of this film, the authorities appear to have been satisfied with the audience reactions at this stage. Only later, when the film was on general release (from 29 April 1973) and became a sensation, did the authorities grow nervous about the reaction.

The real viewing public ensured that the purely propagandistic aims of the cinema administrators were undermined. As the case study of *Die Legende von Paul und Paula* has demonstrated, it was possible for individual, nationally produced films to overcome the hurdles of censorship and to communicate authentically with the audience. There was great interest in films which tested the limits of political expression. The audience passed on recommendations of controversial films and these were hotly debated in the private sphere. When DEFA failed to produce films which were of interest to the audience, they did resort to the film imports. What was to stop individuals from reading films in whatever way they cared to? What was to stop them enjoying a film 'against the grain'? For example, a Hollywood political thriller, such as *All the President's Men* (1976), exhibited in the GDR in 1978, could be enjoyed for its compelling storytelling or characterization, without relating it to the failings of Western democracies. Or *One Flew over the Cuckoo's Nest* (1975), also released in the GDR 1978, could be read as a parable of rebellion in Eastern Europe or in the GDR itself and not just as a mirror of American society. Or, to quote the title of a publication on media in the GDR by Stefan Zahlmann, spectatorship and cinema was: 'Just like in the West, only different' ('Wie im Westen, nur anders').[62]

Rosemary Stott is Associate Dean in the School of Media at Ravensbourne (UK). She is the author of *Crossing the Wall. The Western Film Import in the GDR 1971–1989* (2012). She has published widely on film censorship and programming policy in the GDR and on the representation of the GDR in post-unification German films.

Notes

1. As Ralf Forster and Volker Petzold have shown, DEFA was not an absolute monopoly. Their study examines the approximately forty private film producers who engaged primarily in film-making for education and advertising purposes. Together with artist and amateur films, such productions form an integral part of the historiography of filmmaking in the GDR. See Ralf Forster and Volker Petzold, *Im Schatten der DEFA*, Constance: UVK Medien, 2010, and Karin Fritzsche and Claus Löser (eds), *Gegenbilder. Filmische Subversion in der DDR 1976–1989*, Berlin: Janus, 1996.
2. The figure provided is for 1988. Institut für Kulturforschung beim Ministerium für Kultur (eds), *Kultur in der DDR. Daten 1975–1988*, Berlin: Institut für Kulturforschung, 1989.

3. The GDR's population in 1978 was 16,757,857. Peter Christian Ludz and Johannes Kuppe (eds), *DDR Handbuch*, Cologne: Wissenschaft und Politik, 1979, p. 195.
4. Hans-Eckart Wenzel, 'Nur was sich zählen lässt, das ist auch wahr ...' [= www.ddr-klubkinos.de/lsw_statistik.htm], accessed 16 June 2016.
5. Institut für Kulturforschung beim Ministerium für Kultur, pp. 7–13.
6. Ingrid Poss and Peter Warnecke (eds), *Spur der Filme. Zeitzeugen der DEFA*, Berlin: Christoph Links, 2006.
7. René Beyer, 'Die Etablierung der Merseburger DEFA-Filmtage', in René Beyer and Alfred Georg Frei (eds), *Die Traumfabrik von gestern. Die Merseburger DEFA-Filmtage*, Halle: Cornelius, 2008, pp. 23–52 (p. 24).
8. See, for example, Dorota Ostrowska, 'An Alternative Model of Film Production. Film Units in Poland after World War Two', in Anikó Imre (ed), *A Companion to East European Cinemas*, Oxford: Wiley, 2012, pp. 453–65.
9. Günter Giesenfeld (ed), *Der DEFA-Film. Erbe oder Episode?*, Marburg: Schüren, 1993, p. 6.
10. Ralf Schenk, 'DEFA (1946–1992)', in Michael Wedel, Chris Wahl and Ralf Schenk (eds), *100 Years Studio Babelsberg. The Art of Filmmaking*, Kempen: teNeues, 2012, pp. 114–168, (p. 135).
11. Interview with Andreas Dresen, Deutsche Welle, *typisch deutsch*, 6 November 2011 [= www.youtube.com/watch?v=jyg-zu8U5cU], accessed 1 June 2016
12. Schenk, 'DEFA (1946–1992)', p. 142.
13. Helmut Morsbach, 'Vorwort zur Festschrift', in Ralf Schenk, *Eine kleine Geschichte der DEFA*, Berlin: DEFA-Stiftung, 2006, pp. 8–9 (p. 8).
14. Giesenfeld, p. 6.
15. Leonie Naughton, *That Was the Wild East. Film Culture, Unification, and the 'New Germany'*, Michigan: University of Michigan Press, 2002, p. 37.
16. Dieter Wolf, *Gruppe Babelsberg. Unsere nichtgedrehten Filme*, Berlin: Das Neue Berlin, 2000, p. 7.
17. Klaus-Detlef Haas and Dieter Wolf (eds), *Sozialistische Filmkunst,* Berlin: Karl Dietz Verlag, 2011, p. 176.
18. Ibid.
19. Ibid., p. 296.
20. Giesenfeld, p. 6.
21. Karl Knietzsch, 'Kino in den Nachkriegsjahren', in *Kinos, Kameras und Filmemacher. Kinokultur in Dresden* [= Dresdener Hefte, 23/2 (2005)], 34–39 (38).
22. Schenk, *DEFA (1946–1992)*, p. 143.
23. *Thematischer Produktions-Plan*, Potsdam Babelsberg: DEFA, 1969, p. 4. All translations from original German sources are by the author unless otherwise indicated.
24. Ibid.
25. Haas and Wolf, p. 241.
26. 'Antrag auf Mittelfreigabe. *Spur der Steine*' dated 29 April 1965 [BArch DR 117 / 33063].
27. *Thematischer Produktions-Plan*.
28. Schenk, 'DEFA (1946–1992)', p. 142.
29. *Thematischer Produktions-Plan*.
30. Haas and Wolf, p. 241.
31. To put these costs into context, an average salary in the GDR was 600 to 800 (East German) marks for a retail worker, 900 to 1,800 marks for a builder; a Trabant cost 10,000 marks and flat rental cost between 30 and 120 marks a month without utilities.

See: www.ddr-museum-muehltroff.de/ddr-geschichte-einkommen-und-konsum.html, accessed 16 June 2016.
32. 'Betr.: *Paul und Paula*' no signature or date [= BArch DR 117 / 29493].
33. Ibid.
34. 'Vertragsaufgabe *Paul und Paula*' signed Werner Beck and dated 1 October 1971 [= BArch DR 117 / 29493].
35. 'Betr.: Szenarium *Paul und Paula*' signed Schröder and two other names (illegible) dated 27 September 1971 [= BArch DR 117 / 29493].
36. 'Drehbuchbestätigung' signed Hauptdramaturg and dated 17 April 1972 [= BArch DR 117 / 29493].
37. 'Freigabe der Produktionsvorbereitung für den Spielfilm 557 *Die Legende von Paul und Paula*' signed Albrecht and dated 7 January 1972 [= BArch DR 117 / 29493].
38. 'Vorbereitung des Spielfilms *Die Legende von Paul und Paula*' signed Albrecht and dated 29 December 1971 [= BArch DR 117 / 27936].
39. Ibid., p. 2.
40. 'Kostenfreigabe für das Filmvorhaben *Die Legende von Paul und Paula*' signed Golde and dated 12 January 1972. [= BArch DR 117 / 27936].
41. 'Plan der Vorbereitungsperiode' not signed or dated [= BArch DR 117 / 25777].
42. 'Arbeitszeitregelung für die Mitarbeiter des Spielfilms *Die Legende von Paul und Paula*' signed Albrecht and dated 22 February 1972 [= BArch DR 117 / 26437].
43. 'An den Stellvertreter des Ministers für Kultur' signed A. Wilkening and dated 3 April 1972 [= BArch DR 117 / 26437].
44. 'Durchführung der Produktion *Die Legende von Paul und Paula*' signed Albrecht and dated 7 April 1972 [= BArch DR 117 / 27936].
45. 'Drehplanbestätigung' signed Albrecht and Wilkening and dated 25 April 1972 [= BArch DR 117 / 26437].
46. 'Antrag auf Mittelfreigabe' signed Wilkening and dated 25 April 1972 [= BArch DR 117 / 26437].
47. 'Produktionsberatung Spielfilm *Die Legende von Paul und Paula*' signed Albrecht and dated 25 April 1972 [= BArch DR 117 / 26437].
48. 'Spielfilm *Die Legende von Paul und Paula*. Wettbewerbsverpflichtung' signed Dressel, Leupold and Albrecht and dated 25 April 1972 [= BArch DR 117 / 27936].
49. 'Protokoll über die Rohschnittabnahme *Paul und Paula* am 27.9.1972' signed Wilkening and dated 4 October 1972 [= BArch DR 117 / 29493].
50. 'Spielfilm *Die Legende von Paul und Paula*. Wettbewerbsverpflichtung' signed Dressel, Leupold and Albrecht and dated 25 April 1972 [= BArch DR 117 / 27936].
51. 'Aktenvermerk' signed Wilkening and dated 6 December 1972 [= BArch DR 117 / 29493].
52. 'Wettbewerbsverpflichtung Spielfilm *Die Legende von Paul und Paula*' signed Albrecht and dated 18 December 1972 [= BArch DR117 / 29493].
53. Schenk, 'DEFA. 1946–1992', p. 128.
54. Reinhild Steingröver, *Last Features. East German Cinema's Lost Generation*, Rochester, NY: Camden House, 2014, p. 5.
55. Nick Hodgin, 'Alternative Realities and Authenticity in DEFA's Documentary Films', in Marc Silberman and Henning Wrage (eds), *DEFA at the Crossroads of East German and International Film Culture*, Berlin, Boston: de Gruyter, 2014, pp. 281–304 (p. 282).
56. 'Betr.: Szenarium *Paul und Paula*' signed Schröder and dated 27 September 1971 [= BArch DR 117 / 29493].

57. 'Protokoll über die Rohschnittabnahme *Paul und Paula* am 27.9.1972' signed Hübsch and dated 4 October 1972 [= BArch DR 117 / 29493].
58. Poss and Warnecke, p. 253.
59. Klaus Wischnewski, 'Träumer und gewöhnliche Leute. 1966 bis 1979', in Ralf Schenk (ed), *Das zweite Leben der Filmstadt Babelsberg. DEFA-Spielfilme 1946-92*, Berlin: Henschel, 1994, pp. 212–63 (p. 248).
60. Beyer, p. 26.
61 'Die Legende von Paul und Paula' no signature or date [= BArch DR 117 / 29493], pp. 1– 6.
62. Stefan Zahlmann (ed), *Wie im Westen, nur anders. Medien in der DDR*, Berlin: Panama, 2010.

CHAPTER 2
History and Subjectivity
The Evolution of DEFA Film Music

Larson Powell

In recent scholarship the long-assumed subservient and secondary function of film music relative to the image has increasingly been called into question. For example, the introduction to *Beyond the Soundtrack* programmatically declares: 'We want to consider film as representing music, not simply as adding music as a supplement to a cinematic representation formed by image or narrative'.[1] Such a perspective reverses the usual view of music as a mere heightening or 'accent' added to an existing representation, and suggests that music itself – traditionally thought to be a non-representative art – can be represented by the image. In this perspective, the images on screen may be grasped as themselves 'representing' the actions or emotions suggested by film music. Rather than being subordinate to the image simply as 'unheard melody' (in Claudia Gorbman's formulation), or an aspect of 'style' as 'excess' (as in Caryl Flinn's work on New German Cinema), music works together with image in an audio-visual or intermedial relationship.[2] As we shall see, such a view can offer a fresh understanding of the evolving role of music in DEFA film.

The relevance of newer film music theory to DEFA becomes even clearer with another quote from *Beyond the Soundtrack*, suggesting that one should 'ask not how to conceptualize the use of music in film, but rather how to understand the ways in which film conceptualizes music'.[3] This formulation is again counterintuitive, given that music, especially absolute music (a tradition in which the GDR took great pride) has been seen as a nonconceptual art. Yet music in the GDR was not, for all the reference to the 'humanist legacy' of Bach and Beethoven, primarily seen as autonomous, but rather as functional, in accordance with the doctrine of socialist realism. Despite the ironies of GDR composers like Hanns Eisler (who famously quipped that he did not know what a socialist realist string quartet should sound like), this aesthetic remained more or less valid for most of the GDR's existence. Film music was not only no exception to this rule, but may even have had an easier time fulfilling its social function than symphonic or chamber music. For film music must indeed 'conceptualize' music, making it serve not only specific political interests, but also social and historical content needing to be conveyed, and exemplified in particular character types, viewed through the overall lens of *Parteilichkeit* (or 'adherence to the Party line').[4] The specific musical means by which this was to be done were, however, difficult to specify. Thus, as we will see, the concepts film music was meant to serve, and how it served them, changed significantly over the history of DEFA and the GDR.

A full analysis of DEFA film music would require book-length treatment. Among the many composers for film in the GDR, one would want to mention Andre Asriel, Reiner Bredemeyer, Rainer Böhm, Gerhard Rosenfeld, Karl-Ernst Sasse, Kurt Schwaen and Georg Katzer; special attention should also be given to the prominent returning exiles Hanns Eisler and Paul Dessau, who in turn influenced and mentored many younger composers. Given the impossibility of an inclusive overview of the wide range of film compositions produced for DEFA, what follows will roughly group film music production according to three larger periods within the GDR's history. The first corresponds to the era of Stalinism that ended in 1956 with Khrushchev's secret speech to the Twentieth Congress of the Communist Party of the Soviet Union. This period was still dominated by a socialist realist aesthetic interpreted in the narrow sense of the term, and exemplified in Kurt Maetzig's two monumental Thälmann biopics of 1954–1955. The second period is that of the subsequent 'thaw' or liberalization that lasted into the mid 1960s, and ended with the Eleventh Plenum of 1965; this is also the heyday of Ulbricht's so-called New Economic System (*Neues Ökonomisches System*, NÖS) and it finds its emblematic expression in Konrad Wolf's *Der geteilte Himmel* [*Divided Heaven*] of 1964. The third period begins in the 1970s, including another brief window of liberalization after Honecker's coming to power in 1971, that ended somewhere between Wolf Biermann's expatriation in 1976 and the Soviet invasion of Afghanistan in December 1979. During this window, filmmakers, like writers and musicians, took to heart Honecker's adage that there were 'no taboos in the field of art and literature' as long as one 'sets out from the firm position of socialism'.[5] The brief moment of tolerance allowed for a range of experimentation that came close to the avant-gardism of Western postwar art, as can be seen in the films of Rainer Simon, DEFA's last auteur director, and especially in his collaboration with composer Friedrich Goldmann in *Das Luftschiff* [*The Airship*, 1982]. Although the film was made after the end of Honecker's liberal period, Simon still tried to continue the auteurist experiments of his earlier works such as *Jadup und Boel* [*Jadup and Boel*, 1981/1988], but transposed now to a safer setting in the historical past. These three film projects are thus seen as typifying the three periods of DEFA and GDR history in which they were produced. In each of them, music contributes centrally to the overall aesthetic and effect of the work.[6]

The overall evolution of DEFA film music followed broadly the same pattern as that in the West, moving away from the grand symphonic scores typical of classical sound film to more eclectic mixes that could include jazz or popular music, and eventually even aspects of musical modernism. This happened in DEFA slightly later than in Hollywood, where such postclassical scores were already being produced in the early 1950s (as in the scores to Elia Kazan's *A Streetcar Named Desire* (1951), and *On The Waterfront* (1954), or Nicholas Ray's *Rebel Without a Cause* (1955)); yet already Joachim Werzlau's music for Konrad Wolf's *Lissy* (1957) was sparer and more understated than Wilhelm Neef's Thälmann scores only a year previously. Orchestral film music did not of course entirely vanish from DEFA films after this point, as Neef's scores for several of the *Indianerfilme* of the 1960s attest (Richard Groschopp's *Chingachgook, die große Schlange* [*Chingachgook, The Great Snake*, 1967]; and Josef Mach's *Die Söhne der großen Bärin* [*Sons of Great Bear*, 1966]). These colourful epic and symphonic scores have benefited from the continued cult popularity of the *Indianerfilme*; the first post-Wende re-release of DEFA film music played by the DEFA Symphony Orchestra, entitled *Ein Wigwam steht in Babelsberg* [*A Wigwam in Babelsberg*, Allscore/Indigo, 1999], featured much of Neef's music, and two subsequent albums on the same label have also centred on *Indianerfilme*.[7] These symphonic scores are thus among the best-known DEFA film soundtracks.

As in the West, popular music came to be used in DEFA films as well from the 1960s onwards, most famously in Joachim Hasler's *Heißer Sommer* [*Hot Summer*, 1968], Heiner Carow's *Die Legende von Paul und Paula* [*The Legend of Paul and Paula*, 1973] and Konrad Wolf's *Solo Sunny* (1980), with music by Gerd Natschinski, The Puhdys and Günther Fischer respectively. Yet 'the major debate on music and narrative has taken place, for better or for worse, on the terrain of the background score',[8] meaning the orchestral nondiegetic score. In order to link DEFA film music to these methodological questions, what follows will also concentrate on background scores, while noting the inclusion of popular music in the composite score of *Der geteilte Himmel*.

From Melodrama to Oratorio: The Thälmann Films

Socialist realist film music, as evinced in Wilhelm Neef's grandiose scores for the two Thälmann films, has much in common with classical Hollywood's scoring practice; like the latter, it relies on 'selective use of nondiegetic music; correspondence between that music and the implied content of the narrative; a high degree of direct synchronization between music and narrative action; and the use of the leitmotiv as structural framework'.[9] This similarity is less ironic than it seems. After a brief period of artistic experiment that, in Germany, found expression in Dudow and Eisler's *Kuhle Wampe [Kuhle Wampe or Who Owns the World?]* of 1932, with its use of ironic audio-visual counterpoint (as in the combination of natural scenery with Eisler's dissonant setting of Brecht's poem 'Das Frühjahr' ['Spring']), the aesthetics of socialist realism had settled into a more normative pattern of identificatory rhetoric. The deployment of music in Gyorgi and Sergei Vasilyev's *Chapayev* (1934) was not far from classical Hollywood's. After 1945, a brief window of relative freedom in the GDR ended with the formalist debates of the early 1950s which 'put an end to aesthetic experimentation' and favoured an aesthetic 'modelled after the Stalinist epics of the 1930s'.[10] Interestingly, the composer Neef himself was no hardliner, and protested publicly against the strict application of these rules at the Second Composers' Union Congress of 1954 in Leipzig.[11] Yet the Thälmann myth and cult were central aspects of the GDR's self-legitimation in the 1950s as heir to the antifascist struggles of Weimar, and Maetzig's two films ended up being monumental, hieratic historical panoramas, seeking to centre the entire history of the working class around one heroic life.[12]

Two related interpretative problems arise in understanding this music. One is the temptation to see this intermedial collaboration of music and film as a socialist *Gesamtkunstwerk*, following Boris Groys's suggestion that Stalinist aesthetics were the continuation of this Wagnerian idea.[13] The second is to assert the similarity of Neef's Wagnerian practice to that of Nazi film, especially in the work of composer Herbert Windt for Leni Riefenstahl in *Triumph des Willens* [*Triumph of the Will*, 1935] and *Olympia* (1938). Such a reading would underline connections between different types of 'totalitarian art' through their common descent from Wagner.

A closer look at the films, however, does not bear this out. First, sound film practice had paradoxically less in common with Wagner than had that of silent film. If one were to look for a stepchild of Wagner in film, Fritz Lang's *Die Nibelungen* [*Siegfried/Kriemhild's Revenge*, 1924], with music by Gottfried Huppertz, would be a better candidate.[14] Silent film required a musical continuity that resonated with Wagner's own idea of 'unendliche Melodie' (unending melody). Sound film, by contrast, was more sparing with music due to the imperative of allowing spoken dialogue to be heard. As Kalinak puts it, 'the sound film score was freed from the necessity of seamlessness, but inherited from the silent film its function as arbiter of narrative continuity'.[15]

Secondly, Neef's score, although indebted to Wagner, is much sparer and less continuous than Windt's. In both *Triumph of the Will* and *Olympia*, the opening 'overture' lasts for around twenty minutes before any words at all are spoken. Music thus plays a disproportionately greater role in Nazi film aesthetics than in DEFA, even at the height of Stalinism. The two 'overtures' to the Thälmann films are only about three minutes each, and there are long passages with no music at all. This goes hand in hand with a larger Marxist preference for logos and ethos over pathos: the Thälmann films are meant to explicate a relation to the master narrative of history, and an ethos of discipline and restraint, not the ecstasy of self-loss in the mystic racial collective of the *Volk*. In fact, the Thälmann films are more sparing in their use of music than Kurt Maetzig's earlier DEFA melodrama *Ehe im Schatten* [*Marriage in the Shadows*, 1947] – the composer of which, Wolfgang Zeller, had worked for the Nazis, specifically on the score for Veit Harlan's *Jud Süß* [*Jew Süss*, 1940].[16] A scene like Thälmann's nocturnal visit to his soldiers on the barricades in Hamburg, so reminiscent of *Henry V* Act IV ('a little touch of Harry in the night'), virtually cries out for musical underscoring; yet there is none in the film.[17] Even High Stalinism thus emerges as more musically restrained than either Nazi film or melodrama.[18]

Nonetheless, the Thälmann films have their specifically 'melodramatic' moments as well, along with many oratorical ones. The opening music for the first of the two films contrasts, in the symphonic manner of a sonata form, two types of music that will recur throughout the film. The first is a dissonant, minor key fanfare akin to the beginning of Wagner's *Götterdämmerung* (or that of the finale of Mahler's Sixth Symphony), emphasizing the dissonant intervals of seventh and tritone, and scored for brass. This music may be said to represent the tragic dimension of the Thälmann narrative, which ended in the hero's death, and was punctuated by repeated defeats at the hands of reactionary forces. The second theme is, however, an energetic march with dotted rhythms, which might be said to hearken back to the spirit of Weimar workers' songs and agitprop. The film's score in fact quotes repeatedly from Eisler and Brecht's 'Solidaritätslied' – as if in homage to *Kuhle Wampe* – along with the 'Internationale', and closes with a setting of the 'Thälmannlied' (1951), composed by Eberhard Schmidt to words by Kurt Barthel (KuBa). These songs are alternately sung diegetically by workers in the film or given orchestral settings as nondiegetic background to action-packed, dramatic moments of crisis or struggle. The score to the first Thälmann film may thus be said to imply almost an underlying dialectic between the symphonic legacy of Wagner and popular march music. (As film music scholars have remarked, classical film narrative has inherent kinship with the narrative patterns of nineteenth-century symphonic music.)[19] In the second Thälmann film, the march music comes to be increasingly associated with the liberating advance of the Red Army, and it is hard for the listener not to be reminded of similar marches in Tchaikovsky, another favourite model for the eclectic aesthetics of musical socialist realism; the musical 'dialectic' of the film thus subtly shifts toward one between Wagner and Tchaikovsky.

In two cases, Neef's score approaches specific musical forms. The first is his use of underscoring beneath Thälmann's speeches, a central part of the films. At the end of the first film, Thälmann gives a speech on the occasion of the commuting of the fictitious character Fiete Jansen's death sentence. Below his words, we hear the faint sounds of the energetic march music, mimicking Thälmann's own sturdy resolve to be a model for the workers. In this context it is important to remember that the use of music to accompany a spoken (not sung) text was a nineteenth-century practice known as 'melodrama', and was a specifically bourgeois form, originating in the eighteenth century; it should not be mistaken for the better-known dramatic and filmic genre with which it is sometimes confused.[20] Early film arose in part from the literally melodramatic practices of nineteenth-century incidental music, and these practices continued to influence sound film.[21] The same 'melodramatic' form of spoken text over underlying music was also used by Aaron Copland in his *A Lincoln Portrait* (1942), another depiction of a great leader as a common man. The melodrama in this sense is thus a formal legacy from another revolutionary period (that of the bourgeois eighteenth century), and it is a mixed genre, that is, an intermedial one. It is close to opera without being identical to it. We can thus designate Thälmann's rhetorical pathos as 'melodramatic' in a genuinely historical – and not simply quasi-metaphorical – sense: it is not only his individual drama, but that of history itself.

The other musical form in the background here is that of the oratorio, which comes into its own in the grand finale to the second Thälmann film: the central figure marches straight into the camera and towards his death, while the background of his prison is replaced by a fluttering red flag and the soundtrack yields to a choral rendition of the 'Thälmannlied'. The oratorio was one of the preferred musical forms of socialist realism, especially in the early GDR, when Ernst Hermann Meyer's *Mansfelder Oratorium* of 1950, to a text by Stefan Hermlin, became the exemplary model to be followed by other GDR composers. Meyer's music – stern, austere and heroic – treats a subject also depicted in the Thälmann film, namely the life of the miners of Mansfeld, who are shown as heroic subjects of class struggle. Like the melodrama, the oratorio was also originally an eighteenth-century bourgeois form, but it would be revived for Marxist purposes in the GDR, as in Brecht and Dessau's ill-fated oratorio *Die Verurteilung des Lukullus* [*The Condemnation of Lucullus*, 1951], which was at the centre of the formalism debates of the early 1950s.[22] Both melodrama and oratorio are intermedial, mixed forms, and both are highly rhetorical: their discursive nature is put to the service of a conceptualization of history, the master signifier of these films. Moreover, the subordination of music to text – a feature of all GDR music in the 1950s – fits well with the Thälmann films' central motif of self-restraint and Party discipline. Again and again, Thälmann reminds his co-workers that individual activism without organization is useless. Here, 'music imitates carefulness (*Vorsicht*)', as Adorno and Eisler remark on the function of film music.[23] That Neef's score to the Thälmann films should pay homage to these forms shows how deeply linked to the GDR's larger musical culture, film music practice was.

Between Mourning and Presence: *Der geteilte Himmel*

The early 1960s are separated from the Thälmann films not only by different state cultural policies, but also by the rise of New Wave cinema, which made its mark in Eastern European and Soviet film as well. Along with the better-known examples of this latter group, such as Andrzej Wajda's *Popiół i diament* [*Ashes and Diamonds*, 1958] or Mikhail Kalatozov's *Letyat zhuravli* [*The Cranes are Flying*, 1957], which rewrote national war narratives with new cinematic techniques, there were also films of everyday life, such as Wajda's *Niewinni czarodzieje* [*Innocent Sorcerers*, 1960] and Marlen Khutsiyev's *Vesna na Zarechnoy ulitse* [*Spring on Zarechnaya Street*, 1956] or *Zastava Iliycha/Mne dvadtsat let* [*Lenin's Guard/I am Twenty*, 1961/1965], which often made use of popular music, including jazz. In France, many New Wave films had jazz soundtracks, and Malle's *Ascenseur pour L'échafaud* [*Elevator to the Gallows*, 1958, with music by Miles Davis], or Godard's *À bout de souffle* [*Breathless*, 1960, with music by Martial Solal] are but two examples of this trend. Godard applied the same ironic montage techniques to music as to the image, deliberately chopping up bits of sound or quoting them in homage to classical Hollywood practice.[24]

Although Konrad Wolf's *Der geteilte Himmel* of 1964 may seem superficially less radical than a film such as Godard's *Une femme est une femme* [*A Woman is a Woman*, 1961] in its audio-visual montage, the soundtrack to Wolf's film is, nonetheless, extremely subtle and complex in its levels of meaning, and merits further analysis. Wolf's composer for this film was Hans-Dieter Hosalla, who was for years the music director of the Berliner Ensemble and composed songs to texts by Brecht along with incidental music for his plays.[25] The score to *Der geteilte Himmel* is extremely understated, eschewing symphonic grandeur in favour of solo instruments and smaller ensembles, including jazz bands; even in underscored passages, winds are also preferred to the string choir, in order to avoid the kind of pathos to be found in the Thälmann films' love scenes. The most extended musical passages occur during the opening credits and at several crucial narrative junctures in the film. As in the Thälmann films, the musical material is divided into two main thematic areas. The first is the deliberately brash and upbeat opening, for trombone, with jazzy syncopations. The second is the guitar theme occurring under the credits, usually in the minor key, and slightly recalling the main theme from the first movement of Dvořák's Piano Concerto in G minor. This second theme is based on the German folksong 'Ich hab' die Nacht geträumet'. These two themes are opposed in character, the first major and descending, while the second is minor and ascending. If the first theme is a musical embodiment of presence and immediacy, the second is linked to Rita's memory and mourning. The first theme is heard much less often than the second, only at the opening and close of the film, and alluded to during the (very Godard-esque) driving scene (ca. 28' 40"; compare the famous driving scenes in *À bout de souffle*). The second, however, recurs at every flashback, and is usually associated with the image of the aqueduct near Rita's mother's house, where she goes to recover from her trauma.[26] It thus suggests to the viewer the process of Rita's 'working through' her trauma.

Along with these nondiegetic uses of music, there are also important instances of diegetic music, such as: the popular dance music for Rita's recollection of meeting Manfred, or the waltzes at the factory party, and frequent snippets of radio, whether East German pop tunes of the period (like Robert Stefan's 'Schwarze Maria') or bits of Western radio broadcasts suggesting the atmosphere of crisis at the time of the building of the Berlin Wall. These passages serve to underline the documentary aspect of the film: its claim to represent a moment of specific historical crisis between East and West, in accordance with Marshall McLuhan's idea that radio is a 'hot' medium.[27] In one scene, where Manfred and Rita are guests at a party of scientists (ca. 73' 40"), the hard cuts between diegetic radio music (linked to the external setting) and nondiegetic soundtrack (linked to Rita's thoughts) are often abrupt, lopping off the music mid phrase, in the manner of Godard. The ironic use of radio as simultaneous commentary on the characters' speech, juxtaposing the collective and historical dimension of the mass media to the intimate and individual domain of love, points ahead toward the later practice of Fassbinder in such films as *Die Ehe der Maria Braun* [*The Marriage of Maria Braun*, 1979].

In general, the dominance of solo instruments, especially guitar and saxophone, may be correlated to the centrality of Rita's individual mourning to the narrative. If it is the task of the film to lead Rita out of her traumatic past into a positive (socialist) present and future, the music must also participate in this process. It does so by expanding the solo guitar into ensemble writing, which is by its nature collective. 'Polyphonic music says "us"', as Adorno observes,[28] and this is true for film music as well as autonomous concert music. Thus Hosalla's score again and again extends the guitar's memory-leitmotif into dialogue with other instruments, as Rita remembers her past, and her own 'banal story' is interwoven with that of other characters. The flexibility of this theme, like that of the classical instrumental tradition as a whole, allows for great semantic variability. Thus at the end, Hosalla shifts the theme's key to major, to suggest Rita's hard-won optimism, and harmonizes it with a Neapolitan lowered second,[29] to hint at her painful loss of Manfred. Most interesting is that we rarely hear more than the opening of the memory theme (what one might call its 'head motif' or *Kopfmotif*). Only during the credits is it extended into a full melodic statement, as if to underline the film's idea that the entire meaning of Rita's narrative only becomes clear in retrospect. The theme is so varied in its renditions as to move between popular and classical connotations. During the credits, it is extended into a deliberately archaic, modal close, suggesting the epic or legendary narrative tone of 'once upon a time'. In Rita's first flashback, the theme briefly suggests the texture of a Bach invention; elsewhere it ends in jazzy chords with added sevenths. Only once is the music directly synchronized with visual action, in a technique known to film music scholars as 'Mickey-Mousing'.[30] This is when Manfred suddenly reasserts his love for Rita, at a moment when their relationship is already disintegrating (80' 05"), so that the dramatic synchronizing of the sound has an ironic effect, as if it were overdoing itself, like Manfred in his desperation. Certain passages are partly athematic, as when Manfred admits to Rita (83' 36") that he lacks a 'festen Punkt' (secure point) or when Rita weeps after receiving Manfred's letter from West Berlin (86' 30", with a rare use of piano); the dissonance of these sections, and their disconnection from the rest of the music, may be linked to the narrative's moments of doubt or pain. The sound engineers also make subtle use of added reverb or echoing resonance to suggest the dimension of remembrance at certain points in the narrative.

The most complex moment in a film full of modernist techniques is the Yuri Gagarin sequence near the end. Here the film's multiple narratives – of Rita and Manfred, of Rita and the railway carriage factory, with Meternagel and Wendland – are metonymically juxtaposed with the simultaneous occurrence of the first manned space flight on 12 April 1961. The technological accomplishment of the Soviet cosmonaut, who was the object of an immense public propaganda campaign[31] (thereby vindicating Manfred's sarcastic comment: 'I know what's coming – a big propaganda campaign'), is set in parallel to the railway carriage factory's work on brake testing. As Christa Wolf's text and script soar off into the sublime heights of metaphor, the film cuts rapidly between its diegesis and documentary still shots of ground control personnel monitoring Gagarin's flight. We do not see Gagarin himself, although the camera zooms up heavenward at one point, and a voiceover reads a quote from Gagarin in German translation, before Rita's voiceover goes on to comment on it. Christa Wolf's novel, to which the film has remained fairly faithful, is at its most problematic in such metaphoric passages, where the 'scientific-technical revolution' (as it was called in the GDR in the 1960s) is blended with evocations of maternal Nature: Gagarin, the 'peasant's son', 'ploughs the heavens', and the stars are like 'seed corn'.

Music plays a crucial role in this sequence. Just as the images are an intrusion of the extradiegetic world into the fictional narrative, so Hosalla's score here breaks with its normal reserve. Massive, slow string chords enter at precisely the moment when Wolf's film includes an image of the Vostok rocket's take-off (81' 57"), underlining the sublimity of this historical moment. The musical material itself is also unrelated to the rest of the film, in accordance with the event's exceeding the limits of Rita's story. After the string passage, a solo flute continues with a deliberately archaic passage, suggesting again the tone of a legend or fairy tale. In the tension between modernist image and archaizing text that defines this film,[32] has the music simply taken the side of the text and its metaphorical claims to ideological legitimacy? The archaic, modal sound of the music here is clearly meant to suggest the overarching authority of history, which was the main concept underpinning the Thälmann films.

To answer this criticism requires looking at Hosalla's score as a whole. Wolf's film may be said to participate in a tendency toward abstract 'parametric' narration theorized by Noel Burch in 1967.[33] This tendency treated individual aspects of film as constructive 'parameters', following the model of 1950s musical serialism (especially that of Boulez, one of the chief theoreticians of serialism). As David Bordwell describes it, the parametric model provided 'a conception of spatial form which treats any discrete configuration as one paradigmatic possibility, and thus only a variant of a hidden order'.[34] Thus in *Der geteilte Himmel*, the story appears spatialized, simultaneous in Rita's memory, unified by recurring iconic images and sounds. Each occurrence of an image or sound is felt to be a 'musical' or parametric variation on a hidden order of memory. Within the story, the Gagarin episode feels like a foreign body, a utopian attempt to 'break out' of the confines of the personal into the domain of history. For it to be convincing, and not merely a heavy-handed imposition from above, this segment has to have some relation to what surrounds it. We may see this problem as akin to the modernist moment Adorno found in Mahler's music, namely the breakthrough (*Durchbruch*) out of classical sonata forms. For Adorno, Mahler's compositional reflection meant recognizing that even radically new musical materials, which broke through the logical unity of the sonata form, had somehow to be 'mediated' with that form.[35] Is Hosalla's music also integrated with the larger that narrative surrounds it? If one listens repeatedly to the score, one recognizes that the archaic, legendary ('medieval') tone of the Gagarin sequence was already hinted at during the credits sequence. As with the Thälmann films, closer attention to the film's music can change the way we evaluate it as a whole.

Fantasy and Satire: *Das Luftschiff*

Like *Der geteilte Himmel*, Rainer Simon's *Das Luftschiff* [*The Airship*, 1982] was based on a novel, in this case by the East German modernist writer Fritz Rudolf Fries. The book retells the story of a fictitious aeroplane inventor, Franz Xaver Stannebein, who was loosely based both on a real historical figure and on one from Fries's family; its setting shifts from Leipzig to Berlin and Spain during the period between the world wars. Fries's book thematizes the political errors of the grandfather, a naively apolitical inventor who refuses to see how his work will be misused for politically sinister aims. In accordance with Simon's art-film auteurist aspirations, Stannebein is linked with a recurring windmill imagery clearly meant to remind the viewer of Don Quixote. The most drastic revision of the novel occurs at the film's end. Where Fries's novel ends with Stannebein's belated and half-unwitting political intervention in the Spanish Civil War (by freeing a group of Republican prisoners from the Falangists with a homemade grenade thrower), the film ends with a harsh awakening of the grandson to the reality of his grandfather's powerlessness and defeat, almost as Don Quixote comes to his senses at the end of Cervantes' novel.

Fries's novel may be said to be 'reform socialist' or 'moderate modern', in that it balances its narrative experiments with frequent addresses to the reader, a tactic common among East German writers, who treated their public as their intimate friend or relative, as part of a closer community. By the 1970s, this community was beginning to break down, as writers in the GDR experimented with modernist techniques that could no longer be contained within it;[36] Simon's film arguably intensifies the modernism of the novel, both through the rewriting of the filmscript and also through the use of Friedrich Goldmann's atonal film score. Goldmann had previously written similarly unusual music for Simon's *Till Eulenspiegel* (1974). In addition, several abstract animated sequences were interpolated, made by the artist Lutz Dammbeck (later famous for his film on the prehistory of the Internet, *Das Netz* [*The Net*, 2004]). One of the difficulties faced by DEFA filmmakers who filmed subjectively narrated novels was how to transpose the narration into film. Frank Beyer's *Jakob der Lügner* [*Jacob the Liar*, 1974] used colour stylization for this, reducing the soundtrack to a minimum. *Das Luftschiff*, by contrast, relies partly on its soundtrack to suggest the dreams and flashback structure of its story.

For just as in the Thälmann project and in *Der geteilte Himmel*, in *Das Luftschiff* history is once again the main subject of the film. Yet whereas in the Thälmann films, a heroic individual succeeds – even despite experiencing defeat in his lifetime – in becoming the subject of history, and *Der geteilte Himmel* suggests a healing of the private wounds caused in Rita's life by the division of Germany, by contrast Simon's Stannebein stands in contradiction to the larger course of history right until the end. The resulting dissonance between individual and collective is thus manifest in that of the atonal music. The semantics of Goldmann's predominantly atonal score oscillate between suggesting the unreality of Stannebein's utopian visions of flight and technological progress on the one hand, and satirical irony about his political blindness on the other. In musical-historical terms, we might say that Goldmann's atonality thus alternates between the poles of Arnold Schönberg's Expressionism and the satirical use of dissonance typical of Hanns Eisler and Paul Dessau. Goldmann had in fact been closely associated with Dessau, who had been a strong patron of atonal music in the GDR. By the 1970s, the earlier strictures on atonality in the GDR had been loosened,[37] and Goldmann, who had (unusually for an East German composer) studied briefly with Karlheinz Stockhausen in 1959, had more freedom as a composer than had been possible earlier. The central ambivalence in the film score's semantics corresponds to one in Fries's novel, which constantly alternates between wanting to tell a satisfyingly rounded moral parable and criticizing this impulse.[38] Stannebein's often eccentric character has early-modern characteristics about it: since Rousseau, 'naïvety' (*Blödigkeit*) must be added to the qualities of poet and artist as genius, as the flipside so to speak of their Promethean attributes'.[39] Thus Stannebein, for all his scientific genius, often appears odd, awkward or clumsy in the film, whether as lover or self-promoter.

Goldmann's music is itself a central component in this characterization. The score uses neither the large Romantic orchestra used by Neef for the Thälmann films, nor the jazz band of *Der geteilte Himmel*, but rather a small and flexible chamber orchestra of woodwind, strings and tuned percussion (vibraphone and marimba). Unlike the careful blending of Wagner's orchestration, Goldmann prefers to set extreme registers of piccolo and double bass in opposition, often for satirical or caricaturist purposes. This technique can already be found in Mahler, and was also used by Hindemith in the 1920s, and is called *Spaltklang* (or 'split sound'); it is the timbral equivalent to dissonance in harmony. There are recurring sonorities and motifs in the music, especially during the music for the credits sequence, which is a miniature symmetrical form (with the opening chord recurring at bar 40 and again at the end).[40] Yet most listeners will not perceive any recurring motifs in the nontonal context, nor will they know that the score contains aleatoric (improvisatory) episodes (cf. p. 16 in the score, flute and oboe, bars 10-14), or passages of deliberate noise (as in the Spanish march music sequence, where the woodwind instruments make a pitchless *Klappergeräusch* by clicking their keys without actually sounding a note). Goldmann's own music, which is non-diegetic, alternates with other quoted compositions (including, somewhat incongruously, a segment of Beethoven's Ninth Symphony played while the grandson is flying along the railway tracks alone; the quotation is heavily ironic, perhaps too much so, given the music's burden of semantic baggage).[41] Like the novel, which is also stylistically heterogeneous, the score includes segments that are less abstract and modernist than others, and which stick out from the rest of the film – as Hosalla's neo-medieval chorale for the Gagarin sequence of *Der geteilte Himmel*.

One sequence stands out in particular. About seventy minutes into the film, Stannebein's grandson encounters a travelling group of circus animals outside Leipzig's Monument to the Battle of the Nations (the *Völkerschlachtdenkmal*) – a monument that is repeatedly shown in the film, and thus has allegorical character. A Wilhelmine monstrosity completed in 1913 to commemorate Napoleon's defeat a century earlier, the monument is a shorthand for imperial German militarism. A dwarf leading a donkey informs the grandson that 'we are making our exit from the world stage', referring to the end of World War II. In the soundtrack, we hear a deliberately awkward, grotesque dance in 6/8 time, very much in the style of Gustav Mahler (p. 31 of the score). Not only does this music stick out from the rest of the score, but the entire sequence (not in the original novel, but added to the script) has a deliberately Brechtian, theatrical quality about it; the dwarf's words are clearly addressed not only to the grandson but also to the viewer.[42]

One could see the Mahlerian style of this sequence as tied to the Wilhelmine connotations of the *Völkerschlachtdenkmal*; alternately, Mahler was himself a pioneer of modernist ironic musical quotation, which had been taken up again by composers since the 1960s, including those in the GDR. Mahler's music frequently had connotations of a *theatrum mundi* as well, and his music is sometimes seen as the end of classical tonality, which corresponded historically to that of German imperial illusions shown in the film. Mahler's use of quotation and dissonance was still sufficiently modern to have been a provocation to official GDR aesthetics, and thus Goldmann's pastiche of his style has a particular GDR index to it.[43] This sequence, along with several others – a dialogue between Stannebein on a swing and an unnamed anarchist who chops up a table and chairs while they argue about politics (54'), or a racquetball game between Stannebein and his Spanish assistant

Sorigueta, also accompanying a political argument (85') – breaks the frame of the narrative to comment on the story's larger political questions in Brechtian estranged fashion.[44] In these segments, the characters' speeches quote larger political positions, didactically opposing Sorigueta's commitment to Stannebein's bourgeois belief in science's self-legitimation. The ironic, quoted character of the music is thus in accordance with that of the images; as Victoria Piel has pointed out (with specific reference to DEFA films of the 1970s), film music may 'counterpoint' the images not only through difference of mood, but also 'through a conscious break with filmic genre conventions or in the function of a stylistic counterpoint'.[45] Other modernist film scores have resorted to such stylistic pluralism (such as Lars Johan Werle's score for Ingmar Bergman's 1966 film *Persona*, which, though often atonal, also quotes tonal snippets for ironic contrast).[46] Common to the political debates, the Mahler pastiche and the Beethoven Ninth quote earlier mentioned is a deliberately ironic counterpointing of music to image, a practice Godard had pioneered in the 1960s.[47]

The other sequence to which music contributes centrally is the film's conclusion. In 1945, almost all the characters assemble, as if in an operatic finale, outside the insane asylum where the Nazis incarcerated Stannebein. The ground is strewn with papers, which we may infer are the inventor's plans, all come to naught. In the last shot of the film, the grandson, seen from below, rises from the ground to look into a harshly empty sky, and the film bleaches out to white. The implication is that he has lost all faith in his grandfather; history is meaningless, and the individual is thrown back upon himself. The music, in 6/4 time, first suggests an atonal chorale in the winds and then rises to a piercing dissonance in high violins as the screen goes white. With this, the semantics of atonality have shifted from dream and parody to the negativity of modernist shock associated with Schoenberg's music.[48] Narrative closure is as little possible for the film as it is for atonal musical composition.

In all three of these films, history, the Marxist master signifier of the GDR, plays a central role, and film music must thus serve to articulate this. Yet whereas the Thälmann films propose a triumphant merging of their hero's struggle with historical necessity, *Der geteilte Himmel* must work harder to reconcile Rita's pain with the implicit need for the Berlin Wall. Hosalla's score for the film is thus more oblique and more internally differentiated than Neef's grand symphonic drama. Hosalla nonetheless contains his contrasting musical styles of jazz, quoted folk-song, and neo-Baroque figuration within a larger tonal and motivic context, one that can therefore encompass Rita's mourning process and give it a conciliatory end. With *Das Luftschiff*, however, any such reconciliation of individual and history is rejected. If 'the preference for closed classical dramatic form in Hollywood's studio era no doubt underwrote a corresponding preference for tonal composition',[49] this held true for DEFA film in the 1950s as well, even though that preference was described with the moniker of socialist realism. The evolution of music in DEFA films ran roughly parallel to a growing complexity in DEFA's narratives and stylistic means, as well as to an increased autonomy for GDR composers. It is interesting that the overt modernism of *Das Luftschiff* did not pose a problem for the censors in the way that Simon's earlier film *Jadup und Boel* (1981/1988) had; what the authorities objected to in *Jadup und Boel* was not its modernity (which was in some ways less drastic than the later film's), but rather its depiction of everyday life in the GDR. Yet *Das Luftschiff* has not become part of the filmic modernist canon as *Persona*, or modernist films like Krzysztof Zanussi's *Illumination* (1973), with its frequently atonal score by Wojtech Kilar; within Simon's oeuvre, it is other films like *Jadup und Boel* or *Die Frau und der Fremde* [*The Woman and the Stranger*, 1985] – both with much sparer scores by Reiner Bredemeyer – that have received most attention. In the prominent role it gave to modernist music, *Das Luftschiff* remains, with a small number of other films, like Egon Günther's *Die Leiden des jungen Werthers* [*The Sorrows of Young Werther*, 1976],[50] an unusual experiment.

Larson Powell is Professor of German at the University of Missouri, Kansas City. His most recent book, *The Differentiation of Modernism. Postwar German Media Arts,* appeared in 2013. He has published on German film and literature, media theory, and musicology and aesthetics.

Notes

1. 'Introduction. Phonoplay: Recasting Film Music' to Daniel Goldmark, Lawrence Kramer and Richard Leppert (eds), *Beyond the Soundtrack. Representing Music in Cinema*, Berkeley: University of California Press, 2007, pp. 1–12 (pp. 4–5).
2. Claudia Gorbman, *Unheard Melodies. Narrative Film Music*, London: BFI, Bloomington: University of Indiana Press, 1989; Caryl Flinn, *The New German Cinema. Music, History and the Matter of Style*, Berkeley: University of California Press, 2004.
3. Goldmark et al., p. 3.

4. I have taken these chief characteristics of socialist realism in music from Carl Dahlhaus's discussion in Carl Dahlhaus, *Musikalischer Realismus*, Munich: Piper, 1982, pp. 8–13.
5. Gisela Rüss (ed), *Dokumente der Kunst-, Literatur- und Kulturpolitik der SED 1971-1974*, 3 vols., Stuttgart: H. Seewald, 1976, vol. 1, p. 287. All translations here and elsewhere are my own unless otherwise indicated.
6. It should be added that this essay will be concentrating on original music for the film, rather than compilations of borrowed music, like those used for documentary films. The soundtrack for Karl Gass's *Schaut auf diese Stadt* [*Look at this City*, 1962], put together by Jean Kurt Forest, or Dessau's music for the Thorndikes' *Du und mancher Kamerad* [*You and Many a Comrade*, 1956], both extremely tendentious Cold War products, might show some continuities with Weimar collage and montage practices (such as those by John Heartfield).
7. See, for example the albums *Wigwam, Weste(r)n und Weisse Wölfe* (2001); *Wigwam, Cowboys, Roter Kreis* (2002).
8. James Buhler, 'Analytical and Interpretive Approaches to Film Music, II: Interpreting Interactions of Music and Film', in Kevin J. Donnelly (ed), *Film Music. Critical Approaches*, New York: Continuum, 2001, pp. 39–61 (pp. 44–45).
9. Kathryn Kalinak, *Settling the Score*, Madison: University of Wisconsin Press, 1992, p. 113; compare also Claudia Gorbman's list of similar characteristics in her *Unheard Melodies*, p. 73. We will subsequently need to nuance this characterization, since as subsequent critics have pointed out, film music is less 'unheard' than once thought.
10. Sabine Hake, *German National Cinema*, London: Routledge, 2002, p. 100.
11. David Tompkins, *Composing the Party Line*, Lafayette: Purdue University Press, 2013, p. 63; Daniel Zur Weihen, *Komponieren in der DDR. Institutionen, Organisationen und die erste Komponistengeneration bis 1961*, Cologne: Böhlau, 1999, pp. 331–32.
12. Hunter Bivens has noted the films' hierarchical compositions, centred around the person of Thälmann, and their tendency to freeze into static *tableaux vivants* in the manner of academic history painting, with a 'use of color which is more symbolic than realistic', contrasting revolutionary red with the drab brown of factories and the green of reaction. See Hunter Bivens, '9 March 1954: *Ernst Thälmann – Sohn seiner Klasse* Marks High Point of Socialist Realism', in Jennifer Kapczynski and Michael Richardson (eds), *A New History of German Cinema*, Rochester, NY: Camden House, 2012, pp. 347–53 (p. 350).
13. Boris Groys, *Gesamtkunstwerk Stalin. Die gespaltene Kultur in der Sowjetunion*, Munich: Hanser, 2008.
14. See the recent French study of the score by Antoine Roulé and Violette Anger, *Les Nibelungen de Fritz Lang. Musique de Gottfried Huppertz*, Paris: L'Harmattan, 2012. The symphonic scores of the silent period were also politically ambiguous: Edmund Meisel, composer for Eisenstein's *Bronenosets Potemkin* [*Battleship Potemkin*, 1925], also worked with Arnold Fanck on *Der heilige Berg* [*The Holy Mountain*, 1926] and Ruttmann on *Berlin – Die Sinfonie der Grosstadt* [*Berlin – Symphony of a Great City*, 1927]. Lutz Koepnick has explored the complex relations between Hollywood and Nazi film music practices in *The Dark Mirror. German Cinema between Hitler and Hollywood*, Berkeley: University of California Press, 2002.
15. Kalinak, p. 80.
16. Questions of continuity in DEFA personnel with the Nazi period are worth noting: thus Erwin Roter, composer of the score to *Die Mörder sind unter uns* [*The Murderers Are Among Us*, 1946] and *Die Familie Benthin* [*Family Benthin*, 1950], had also worked with Veit Harlan on *Die Kreutzersonate* [*The Kreutzer Sonata*, 1937]. Neef, however, began his career only after 1945.

17. By contrast, Lawrence Olivier's 1944 film of *Henry V*, a classic of the patriotic epic genre in Technicolor, relies heavily on the music of William Walton during this scene. See the comments of James Agee in *Agee on Film*, New York: Random House, 2000, pp. 347–53 (esp. pp. 348–49).
18. One would need to check the production archives to determine whether the sparseness of music was based on economic grounds or aesthetic choice.
19. Peter Franklin, 'The Boy on the Train, or Bad Symphonies and Good Movies. The Revealing Error of the "Symphonic Score"', in Goldmark, Kramer and Leppert, pp. 13–26.
20. Laurenz Lütteken, *Das Monologische als Denkform in der Musik zwischen 1760 und 1785*, Tübingen: Niemeyer, 1998.
21. Michael Pisani, 'Music for the Theatre. Style and Function in Incidental Music', in Kerry Powell (ed), *The Cambridge Companion to Victorian and Edwardian Theatre*, Cambridge: Cambridge University Press, 2004, pp. 70–92; David Neumeyer, 'Melodrama as a Compositional Resource in Early Hollywood Sound Cinema', *Current Musicology*, 57 (1995), 61–94. See also James Buhler's note on melodrama in his 'Wagnerian Motives. Narrative Integration and the Development of Silent Film Accompaniment, 1908–1913', in Jeongwon Joe and Sander Gilman (eds), *Wagner and Cinema*, Bloomington: Indiana University Press, 2010, pp. 27–45 (esp. pp. 40–41 n7). On 'melodrama' in this sense in film, see Marcia Citron, *Opera on Screen*, New Haven: Yale University Press. 2000, pp. 197–98. Citron stresses the gliding transitions between speech and music made possible by melodrama.
22. As Jost Hermand notes, 'The SED functionaries believed that the best mode of expressing ... programmatic content was vocal music, in the forms of songs, choral works, or even oratorios'. Jost Hermand, 'Attempts to Establish a Socialist Music Culture in the Soviet Occupation Zone and the Early GDR, 1945–1965', in Edward Larkey (ed), *A Sound Legacy? Music and Politics in East Germany*, Washington: AICGS, 2000, pp. 4–19 (p. 8). On the aesthetics of the GDR oratorio, see Golan Gur, 'Classicism as Anti-Fascist Heritage. Realism and Myth in Ernst Hermann Meyer's *Mansfelder Oratorium* (1950)', in Kyle Frackman and Larson Powell (eds), *Classical Music in the GDR*, Rochester, NY: Camden House, 2015, pp. 34–57.
23. 'Komposition für den Film' , now in Rolf Tiedemann (ed), *Adorno. Gesammelte Schriften in 20 Bänden*, Frankfurt am Main: Suhrkamp, 1997, vol. 15, pp. 369–401 (p. 141).
24. On Godard's sound practice, see among other works Laurent Juillier, 'To Cut or Let Live? The Soundtrack According to Godard', in Graeme Harper (ed), *Sound and Music in Visual Media*, New York: Continuum, 2009, pp. 352–62; and Jürg Stenzl, *Jean-Luc Godard – Musicien. Die Musik in den Filmen von Jean-Luc Godard*, Munich: edition text + kritik, 2010. There is a documentary film on Godard's use of music, *À l'écoute de Godard* [*On Listening to Godard*, dir. Vincent Perrot, 2007].
25. Hosalla had previously collaborated with Wolf on *Professor Mamlock* (1961), and also wrote music for films as varied as *Das hölzerne Kälbchen* [*The Wooden Calf*, dir. Bernhard Thieme, 1960], *Apachen* [*Apaches*, dir. Gottfried Kolditz, 1973] and *Denk' bloß nicht, ich heule* [*Just Don't Think I'm Crying*, dir. Frank Vogel, 1965].
26. This supports Barton Byg's view of the centrality of mourning in the film (see his 'Geschichte, Trauer und weibliche Identität im Film. *Hiroshima mon amour* und *Der geteilte Himmel*', in Ute Brandes Ute (ed), *Zwischen gestern und morgen. Schriftstellerinnen der DDR aus amerikanischer Sicht*, Berlin: Lang, 1992, pp. 95–112.
27. See Chapter 2, 'Media Hot and Cold' in Marshall McLuhan, *Understanding Media*, Berkeley: Gingko Press, 2003, which was originally published in 1964 (New York: McGraw-Hill), the year *Der geteilte Himmel* was released.

28. *Philosophie der neuen Musik* [= Adorno. *Gesammelte Schriften*, vol. 12], p. 26. See also 'Ideen zur Musiksoziologie', *Klangfiguren* [= Adorno. *Gesammelte Schriften*, vol. 16], p. 18: 'jeder Klang allein sagt Wir'.
29. Neapolitan chords are built on the flattened second degree of the scale, usually in preparation for the dominant, and although already used in the eighteenth century, became commonly used by 1800 in the music of Beethoven, Schubert and their contemporaries. The effect is of a sudden distant colouring, remote from the main key.
30. Mickey-Mousing is the close, one-to-one correspondence of soundtrack to visual gesture, once common in the 1930s and 1940s. See Chuck Jones, 'Music and the Animated Cartoon', *Hollywood Quarterly* 1.4 (1946), 364–70.
31. See Klaus Gestwa, 'Kolumbus des Kosmos. Der Kult um Jurij Gagarin', *Osteuropa* 59.10 (2009), 121–52.
32. I have analyzed this tension at greater length in 'Une socialiste est une socialiste. *Der geteilte Himmel* zwischen Bild und Stimme', in Oksana Bulgakowa (ed), *Resonanz-Räume. Die Stimme und die Medien*, Berlin: Bertz + Fischer, 2012, pp. 130–37.
33. Noel Burch, *Theory of Film Practice*, trans. Helen Lane, New York: Praeger, 1973.
34. David Bordwell, *Narration in the Fiction Film*, Madison: University of Wisconsin Press, 1985, p. 277.
35. *Mahler. Eine musikalische Physiognomik* [= Adorno. *Gesammelte Schriften*, Vol. 13], pp. 149–320, esp. 190–95 (Chapter 3).
36. For a history of this process, see Colin Grant, *Literary Communication from Consensus to Rupture. Practice and Theory in Honecker's GDR*, Amsterdam: Rodopi, 1995, esp. Chapter 2.
37. Matthias Tischer (ed), *Musik in der DDR. Beiträge zu den Musikverhältnissen eines verschwundenen Staates*, Berlin: Kuhn, 2005; Michael Berg, Albrecht von Massow and Nina Noeske (eds), *Zwischen Macht und Freiheit. Neue Musik in der DDR*, Cologne: Böhlau, 2004.
38. Reinhard Hillich, 'Die Brüste der Göttin. Fiktion und Kritik der Fiktion als Gestaltungselemente in Fritz Rudolf Fries' Roman *Das Luft-Schiff*, *Sinn und Form* 33.1 (1981), 141–62 (150–51).
39. Georg Stanitzek, *Blödigkeit. Beschreibungen des Individuums im 18. Jahrhundert*, Tübingen: Niemeyer, 1989, p. 186. Stanitzek describes a semantic change in the word 'Blödigkeit' (the title of a poem by Hölderlin!) to designate not merely dim-wittedness, but rather the unworldly innocence of genius.
40. The composer's manuscript score is at the Archiv der Akademie der Künste, Berlin [= Goldmann-Archiv, 251].
41. Beethoven's Ninth has been co-opted by so many different ideologies that an entire history of its 'politics' has been written (see Esteban Buch, *Beethoven's Ninth. A Political History*, trans. Richard Miller, Chicago: University of Chicago Press, 2003). In this passage, Simon seems to have been attempting the Godard-like irony of musical quotation mentioned earlier, but the grand emancipatory connotations of Beethoven only swamp the images of the young boy on the railway tracks.
42. This circus theatricality also suggests a reference to other auteurist filmmakers, namely Fellini (the circus figures at the end of *8 ½*, 1963) and Bergman (the procession at the end of *Det sjunde inseglet* [*The Seventh Seal*, 1957]). This reference fits well with Simon's larger strategy of self-legitimation as an auteur director, to which his ironic and eclectic use of film music also contributes.
43. On Mahler's belated and ambivalent reception in the GDR, see Juliane Schicker, 'Beyond the Gewandhaus. Mahler and the GDR', in Frackman and Powell, pp. 135–56.
44. On these different levels, see Gérard Genette, *Narrative Discourse. An Essay in Method*, trans. Jane E. Lewin, Ithaca: Cornell University Press, 1980.

45. Victoria Piel, 'Dissonante Repräsentationen. Tendenzen der DEFA-Spielfilmmusik der 70er Jahre', in Matthias Tischer (ed), *Musik in der DDR*, Berlin: Kuhn, 2005, pp. 166–84, (p. 181).
46. Goldmann commented on his use of 'borrowed' musical material in his essay 'Klischee und Wirklichkeit. Komponierte Klischees', in Otto Kolleritsch (ed), *Klischee und Wirklichkeit in der musikalischen Moderne,* Vienna: Universal Edition, 1994, pp. 23–34.
47. Research still needs to be done on documenting the reception of Western European filmic modernism by DEFA directors, whether official or unofficial. Bergman's *Smultronstället* [*Wild Strawberries*, 1957] premiered in the GDR on 8 July 1966; and Fellini's *Roma* [*Rome*, 1972] was discussed by Hermann Herlinghaus in *Film und Fernsehen* 3 (1973), pp. 43–7. Barton Byg has discussed GDR reception of Resnais and Bergman: see Byg 1992. Many critics and filmmakers visited international film festivals from Warsaw to the West, and their international contacts, including ones as close as West Berlin, would also have allowed them to borrow prints. Thus an auteurist director like Tarkovsky, although not officially approved of, could still be a cult figure in the GDR (Oksana Bulgakowa, personal communication).
48. *Locus classicus* for this association: Adorno's *Philosophie der neuen Musik* [= Adorno. *Gesammelte Schriften* vol. 12].
49. David Neumeyer and James Buhler, 'Analytical and Interpretive Approaches to Film Music, I: Analysing the Music', in Kevin J. Donnelly (ed), *Film Music. Critical Approaches*, New York: Continuum, 2001, pp. 16–38 (p. 23).
50. Günther's film also had a score by a prominent GDR composer of classical music, Siegfried Matthus; see the discussion in Piel, 'Dissonante Repräsentationen'.

CHAPTER 3

'Fatal Attractions'
Modernist Set Design and the East–West Divide in DEFA Films of the 1950s and early 1960s

Annette Dorgerloh

The sky at night is pitch black and there are no stars to be seen. That's why the colourful neon advertising signs burn even more brightly than usual. Beacons of temptation they broadcast their wares – 'Dancing', 'Jewellery', 'Casino'. People out for a walk – some oblivious to everything, others with desire etched on their faces – stroll past a film poster bearing the title 'Pact with the Devil' as they go in search of 'work' or a brief moment of 'happiness'.

The glittering façades give the impression of warmth and wealth. But behind them there is nothing – neither on West Berlin's fashionable boulevards nor on the set at the DEFA studio in Potsdam-Babelsberg where an almost exact replica of just such a street has been recreated. But whether in the city or in the studio – everything is just a façade. But each serves a very different purpose.

Published in the East German daily, the *Berliner Zeitung am Abend* on 7 December 1951, the report above on the filming of Slatan Dudow's *Frauenschicksale* [*Destinies of Women*, 1952] is written in a dramatic style that, both in its tone and emotive vocabulary, is characteristic of many discussions of films made in the 1950s and dealing with the East–West divide from a socialist perspective.[1] Set design played a key role here as it was crucial to create an illusion of the luxurious look and feel of the grand boulevards in the West. At the same time, however, many of these settings were presented as a locus of moral decay that, in some cases, included criminal activity. For that reason the sets designed at DEFA often included allusions to such decadence; a film poster with the highly suggestive title 'Pact with the Devil', for example, could only be read symbolically as a warning of impending doom.[2] Readers of newspaper reports such as the one reproduced above were left in no doubt that, in the West, everything was merely a façade that was no less hollow than those constructed by DEFA's set designers. Nonetheless, whether in the city or in the studio, these illusions could conjure up associations that, if not quite the work of the devil, certainly had the potential to overwhelm anyone who set eyes on them.

In this essay I will examine the considerations underpinning set design in a series of films from the 1950s that address, in particular, the ideological and aesthetic confrontation with the West and postwar Western 'modernity'. I will focus primarily on Slatan Dudow's *Frauenschicksale* (set designer Otto Erdmann), Artur Pohl's *Spielbank-Affäre* [*Casino Affair*, 1956; set designer Gerhard Helwig] and an early work by Heiner Carow, *Das Leben beginnt* [*Life Starts Now*, 1960; set designer Willy Schiller] in order to highlight the different aesthetic strategies that were invoked when discussing the respective merits and shortcomings of the two ideological systems. As we shall see, however, during the early 1960s, the East German government became increasingly conscious of the need to develop a modern consumer culture; and this, together with new developments in design and technology, led to a very different attitude towards modernist décor and furnishings, and one that is reflected in a number of films from the mid 1960s, including Konrad Wolf's *Der geteilte Himmel* [*Divided Heaven*, 1964; set designer Alfred Hirschmeier] and Günter Stahnke's *Der Frühling braucht Zeit* [*Spring Takes Time*, 1965; set designer Georg Kranz].

The postwar division of both Germany and Berlin, and the ideological gulf that existed between the two states, posed a continual challenge to those overseeing cultural policy in both East and West. The Cold War was a key factor in many aspects of film production on both sides of the German–German border, and the rivalry between the two states was often played out via an intense exchange of images and counter-images in the cinema and, from the mid 1950s onwards, on television. Feature films did not have to be based on real-life stories in order to be convincing. Nevertheless, these films needed to be more than just exciting, and had to relate to everyday reality in ways that viewers could accept. That applied as much to the sets and the artificially constructed interiors and exteriors on display as it did to the main protagonists and their conflicts. Even in the fictional world of the cinema, those fighting for progress (and their opponents) operated in spaces in which décor functioned as a marker of character. Protagonists were often presented as either potential (or actual) adversaries by being associated with spaces and milieus that, in stylistic terms, were markedly different. Audiences had little difficulty in recognizing the significance of such visual cues, and drawing on them in their interpretation of the action.

The Danish director Urban Gad (1879–1947) was one of the first to acknowledge the importance of set design in his book *Der Film, seine Mittel – seine Ziele* [*Cinema – Goals and Techniques*] that was first translated into German in 1920. Writing about the relationship between the viewer's evaluating gaze and the onscreen décor, he notes: 'No amount of explanatory dialogue can contribute as much to the viewer's understanding of what he has seen as the visual information conveyed by the film'.[3] As we shall see, what was important was not simply to exploit the way in which the viewer's visual perception was (at least in some respects) already preconditioned, but rather to actively intervene in shaping the way the viewer perceived the onscreen 'reality' with which he or she was confronted.

Watching the Detectives: Hallmarks of a Genre

In the late 1940s and the early 1950s, a lack of basic raw materials and an obligation to pay reparations to the Soviet Union were just some of the factors that made it almost impossible for the GDR to satisfy its own citizens' demands for consumer goods; and the gulf between the GDR and the Federal Republic (FRG) in this respect was exacerbated by Marshall aid and the resulting flow of capital to the West from 1947 onwards. Cut off from the material benefits of postwar capitalism, the GDR had little choice, initially, but to make a virtue out of a necessity and to portray Western consumerism and the desire for luxury goods as something that was not only decadent, but also potentially criminal. As a result, many East–West conflicts were played out in the form of crime thrillers. The genre of the crime thriller, like that of the spy film to which it is closely related, has always been extremely popular in German cinema and could draw on traditions that dated back to the prewar era of the 1930s. Crime thrillers could mediate 'reality' in a way that few other genres could match; the action was exciting, and the crimes depicted in them almost always stemmed from conflicts in the everyday lives of the protagonists. Because of their unique blend of subversive and affirmative plotlines, such films could promote normative messages insofar as good is almost always rewarded and evil punished. As Michael Wedel has observed, criminal actions reflect, metaphorically speaking, the state of society; accordingly, the crime thriller is the fictional genre through which any given society articulates most clearly not just the norms that underpin it, but also the fantasy of transgressing these norms (and the consequences of so doing).[4] Moreover, since it is a key characteristic of the genre that the case in question should always be resolved, crime thrillers play, and have always played, a vital role in restoring and maintaining the social status quo.

In line with classical Marxist theory, crime in the GDR (during the 1950s at least) was understood primarily in terms of political ideology and as the result of unresolved class conflicts. All of this goes some way to explaining why, during the 1950s in particular, youth crime in the GDR was often accounted for in terms of an inadequate ideological upbringing and the negative influence of Western media, above all television and publications described as trashy and decadent (*Schund- und Schmutzliteratur*).[5] The conventional means of combating such negative attitudes to society and preventing criminal activity was to promote a firm commitment to socialism via a deliberate and targeted use of 'positive' role models across a wide range of diverse media. However, since theory and praxis seldom went hand in hand in socialist society, spy films and crime thrillers enjoyed an enduring popularity with East German filmmakers and viewers (and indeed with DEFA scholars).[6] For as Michael Hanisch quite rightly asks in his study of the East German crime thriller, where on earth do all the 'bad guys' in these films actually come from?[7] Up until 1961 and the building of the Berlin Wall, the answer was, almost inevitably, from the capitalist West (just as in Western thrillers, spies always came from the communist East). More often than not, the villains in these films, who have themselves been led astray by the lure of Western capitalism, manage to persuade naïve and ideologically confused East Germans lusting after Western consumer goods, to act as accomplices in their shady dealings. That such schemes are thwarted, although often only at the eleventh hour, and the appropriate punishment handed down is, more often than not, the result of the timely intervention of vigilant (socialist) comrades. Films set in the East often centred around problems of technological development and the production of high-end goods such as cars, artificial fabrics and telescopes made by Carl Zeiss (thereby reminding East German viewers that the GDR too was capable of producing high-value technology that was coveted by the West). By contrast, films set in the West took a hardline view of wealth and luxury goods and identified greed, the need to assert oneself, and a dog-eat-dog approach to business as key aspects of the so-called 'economic miracle' (*Wirtschaftswunder*) in the FRG. The considerable disparity between living standards in East and West was an enduring problem for the fledgling GDR during the 1950s; and depicting luxury goods and Western consumerism in such a negative light was designed to counter their appeal for as long as possible.

The Challenge of Western Modernism in the Postwar Period

The temporal setting of a film's plot can always be visualized using a range and combination of different styles; and the impact of the resulting images is a reflection of their capacity to embody the simultaneity of the non-simultaneous. Different styles and tastes have to be invoked in order to construct diverse milieus. Even though art historians often tend towards a theoretical model in which different styles appear to unfold consecutively in an essentially linear fashion, the reality is that often quite diverse styles coexist side by side in a given historical epoch and, depending on their acceptance by different social classes, connote a particular set of social meanings. This is particularly the case with the kind of modernist art and design that became established at roughly the same time as the medium of film. In the prewar film industry, directors such as Fritz Lang and set designers Emil Hasler and Karl Vollbrecht constantly sought to exploit the semantic tensions that resulted from juxtaposing contrasting styles and, as a result, the relationship of the central protagonists in their films to modern architecture and design came to be an increasingly important part of their characterization.[8]

By way of example we might consider the impact of Lang's 'Dr Mabuse' films, with their juxtaposition of traditional/historical and modern settings, on a range of DEFA productions in the decades immediately after the war. In *Das Testament des Dr Mabuse* [*The Testament of Dr Mabuse*, 1933], the villains are hardly ever associated with contemporary modern design; for the most part they are confined to lavish retro-interiors, historical artefacts and a décor that, right from the start, suggests that these characters should not be viewed positively. By contrast, in postwar East German film production, it is not until the mid 1960s that we can discern a similarly positive attitude towards modernist design of the kind that is evident in such films as *Der geteilte Himmel* and the (forbidden) DEFA film *Der Frühling braucht Zeit*.[9]

In the years immediately after the end of World War II, however, the tensions generated by such representations of modernity were of lesser significance. Nevertheless, the development of modern architecture and design in the West during the 1950s and 1960s was not only reflected in films of the period but, as

Donald Albrecht and, most recently, Doris Agotai have demonstrated,[10] was taken to an altogether new level. The new fashions not only set the tone for life in the West, but presented the GDR with a huge challenge; for the well-stocked shops made possible in the West by the Marshall plan were easily accessible to anyone from the East who happened to cross the border. In addition, there was the attraction of music and entertainment (predominantly jazz) that, as Uta Poiger has argued, cultural functionaries in the GDR regarded as highly dangerous.[11] As we shall see, the attempts to mobilize cinema as a means of discrediting such attractions were both ambitious and grotesque by turns.

In Slatan Dudow's *Frauenschicksale*, a film in which the influence of Otto Dix and George Grosz on Otto Erdmann's set design is plain to see (Fig. 3.1), the sequence where the decadent Conny and his aristocratic girlfriend visit a nightclub in West Berlin offers the viewer a nightmarish vision of a society that, out of control, has descended into a state of quasi-psychotic folly. Likewise, in Heiner Carow's film *Das Leben beginnt* the main female protagonist, Erika, undergoes a

Figure 3.1: *Frauenschicksale* (1952). West Berlin nightclub © DEFA Stiftung/Neufeld.

similar experience in a nightclub that both disturbs and disgusts her, while the patrons of such a milieu are presented as ugly and revolting. Here, too, tried and trusted devices borrowed from (prewar) German Expressionist cinema are deployed to underscore Erika's growing isolation and disenchantment, with the result that, visually speaking, the sequence conveys the impossibility of her establishing herself in her new 'home', West Berlin.

In the divided Germany of the 1950s it was simply impossible to ignore the comparisons that were being constantly drawn between the two systems in their respective media; and the East–West divide became an increasingly important topos in feature films produced in the GDR. The population of East Berlin and neighbouring Brandenburg also benefited from the cut-price tickets which West Berlin cinemas situated at the border (the so-called *Grenzkinos*) could offer their 'brothers and sisters' from the East thanks to Western subsidies.[12] In addition, a large number of films from the West were screened in East German cinemas and so, long before the spread of television, East Germans had an opportunity to get a sense of developments in international cinema and, as a result, made similar demands of their own film production.[13] In the recently founded FRG, individuals quickly adapted to the American way of life in the early 1950s and soon lost interest in seeing gloomy representations of life in the East on their cinema screens. However, in Potsdam-Babelsberg, DEFA and its employees were often required to address the (often contradictory) demands of their political leaders, and to present their audiences with clear-cut ideological positions, while at the same time ensuring that onscreen representations of East Berlin, the capital of the GDR, did not pale beside images of West Berlin, the 'shop window of Western capitalism'. Finally, the high status that art and literature enjoyed generally in the GDR, coupled with an at times almost unshakeable faith in the power of cinema to influence the individual, meant that, very often, DEFA's productions were, by turns, either subjected to often hopelessly unrealistic expectations, or viewed with quite undeserved suspicion.

The Lure of Western Modernity: Appearance and Reality

Following the uprising of 17 June 1953 in the GDR and the ensuing introduction of the so-called *Neuer Kurs* (new approach), there was a brief respite from the insistence on a doctrinaire approach to socialist realism of the kind we find in films of the very early 1950s such as Dudow's *Frauenschicksale*. This more liberal attitude to cultural policy was, however, short-lived; and from around 1958 onwards, filmmakers in the GDR found themselves confronted once again with the need to engage with socialist realist aesthetics. Made in 1956/57, the film *Spielbank-Affäre* reflects both the rise and fall of the *Neuer Kurs*, while *Das Leben beginnt* (1960) can be seen as an early example of an attempt to embrace a paradigm of filmmaking that was less schematic and offered a more differentiated perspective of the protagonists and their conflicts. Both films deal with naïve young women and their experiences in the West – including their responses to Western consumerism, their hopes and desires and, perhaps almost inevitably in a DEFA film, their disappointment and subsequent political reorientation in accordance with the socialist principles underpinning the GDR.

In the early 1950s it took a powerful argument to counter the usually unquestioned acceptance of the desirability of Western consumer goods. In Dudow's 1952 film *Frauenschicksale*, the female protagonists' fateful experience of the West is mediated via the seductive playboy, Conny, a figure who embodies everything that had become possible following the Marshall Plan and the establishment of a new regime in the Western zones: elegance, charm, an attention to detail and rakish humour. All three of the women, each very different in character, undergo a process of self-development following their humiliating experiences at the hands of the unscrupulous Conny. Eventually all come to recognize that it is only in the GDR that women can expect a better life with a prospect of a professional career, the availability of childcare, a modern and more sincere type of love relationship, and even the possibility of engaging in consumerism through the purchase of the highly symbolic (and now affordable) blue dress.

While in Dudow's *Frauenschicksale*, the foppish Conny (played, perhaps not uncoincidentally, by a West German actor, Hanns Groth) symbolizes the excesses of Western consumerism, in Artur Pohl's *Spielbank-Affäre,* by contrast, the male protagonist, Gerhard Fischer, is an essentially 'positive' figure, a committed socialist from the GDR, who tries to help the naïve young actress Sibylle Schilling. Following a moment of existential crisis one night, Sibylle runs out into the street and is injured after being knocked down by a car; the parallel with both Barbara's situation in *Frauenschicksale* and that of Erika in Carow's *Das Leben beginnt* is striking. In contrast to these films, however, we never see the East in Artur Pohls's film as all of the action is set in the West, on the Côte d'Azur and above all in the 'West German' international spa town of 'Weltbad' (the town itself is in fact modelled on

Wiesbaden).[14] In this 'Swedish'–East German co-production[15] we discover how the young Sibylle unwittingly gets drawn into criminal activity at a casino that involves the fabrication of counterfeit chips. She gets to know the young investigative journalist Gerhard with whom she falls in love, and the two marry. While Gerhard researches the background to what are clearly criminal activities on the part of rival casino proprietors, Sibylle, seduced by the prospect of making a fast buck, allows herself to become involved in the dubious activities of the charismatic but unscrupulous Dr Busch (played by the West German actor Peter Pasetti). It turns out that there is a very high price to be paid for the elegant furniture she acquired for what, at the time, seemed to be easy money. After much trouble and effort she succeeds, with Gerhard's help, in extricating herself from the affair with her reputation more or less intact; but the villainous Dr Busch falls victim to tensions between the rival gangs and pays with his life. For his part, Gerhard's journalistic efforts fall on stony ground as he runs up against a cartel of the rich and powerful in the city, who rush to each other's defence.

Once again the lure of modernist design and elegant fashions – commodities that the young couple can only acquire through dishonest means – lie at the heart of this film; and, as elsewhere, the desire for a modern, elegant way of life is exposed as something essentially shallow and morally questionable. The casino owners are painted in an even more reprehensible light; their expensive ultra-chic offices adorned with modernist works of abstract (i.e. 'formalist') art reflect both the decadence of capitalism and their indomitable drive to assert themselves at any cost. The Marseilles office of the gangster Martinez is decorated using a blend of red and beige hues, while in the offices of the German casino owner Gallinger and his colleague Balduin shades of brown and blue-green dominate. Here too the colour of the furniture contributes to the overall palette of the film.

An early version of the script dating back to May 1955 reveals that the decision to use modernist sets must have been made relatively late in the production process. In this earlier version Gerhard can contribute only old handed-down items of furniture to the joint family home; and Sibylle has a further problem (she is dependent on tranquilizers) that takes its financial toll. In this version, the fact that she strays from the straight and narrow can be explained by her addiction – a condition that has forced her to acquire drugs illegally via casino employees. Yet, although the casino's boardroom is depicted as the locus of criminal activity, no reference is made to its furnishings and décor. The far-reaching changes made to the character of Sibylle, who is transformed from a negative figure with criminal tendencies into an attractive young woman whose naivety allows her to be exploited by others, and who elicits the sympathy of the viewer, are evident in both the final version of the film and Hans von Oettingen's 1956 novel of the same name that was published in tandem with its release. Like the modernist aspect of the sets, these adjustments to the character of the female lead made the film more attractive to audiences.

In 1957 *Spielbank-Affäre* was the cause of some controversy on account of its failure to meet with the approval of the GDR's licensing body the *Hauptverwaltung Film*. In the GDR the film was criticized as an example of revisionism and as an embodiment of bourgeois tendencies; by contrast, in the FRG it was viewed as anti-Western propaganda. Although a ban was proposed, the film was still distributed in the GDR (albeit with a revised ending and only in black-and-white copies in a standard format). This was particularly remarkable given the trouble and expense of shooting the film in colour and the fact that it was supposed to be the first DEFA film to be realized in Totalvision (DEFA's answer to Cinemascope). The wide-format colour version was shown in the West, albeit with the title *Parkplatz zur großen Sehnsucht* [*A Car Park Named Desire*]; however, in the West the film was referred to not as a GDR–Swedish co-production, but rather as a 'German classic'.[16] The film's plot was set exclusively in West Berlin and Hamburg (some sequences were even shot on location in the two cities) and was designed to show the impact of the so-called 'economic miracle' on those at the lower end of the social scale. In his essay 'Zur Parteilichkeit in der Filmkunst' ['Political Commitment and the Cinema'], Anton Ackermann criticized the film for its 'complete failure to take sides', and commented on the way it even 'depicted relations under capitalism in a way that was uncritical and made them appear even harmless'.[17] As Gerhard Helvig's elegant sets confirm, the party official's concerns were not altogether unfounded.

Filmed in colour and in Totalvision at a cost of more than 3.8 million marks, *Spielbank-Affäre* was shot at a number of locations in Potsdam.[18] The setting for the casino is provided by the Orangerie in Potsdam's Sanssouci park; likewise the Sicilian Gardens function as the backdrop to the café where Sybille and the mysterious Dr Busch meet up and go for a drive together in an open-topped car. Shooting also took place in Lugarno over a period of ten days. Alexander Abusch, at the time Head of the Ministry of Culture, recognized that the film had a 'dangerous appeal'.[19] He demanded that sequences showing the young couple's two-room apartment be replaced with scenes showing a one-bedroom apartment with a room divider instead so that young audiences in the GDR could still identify with the film: students with their own, modern-furnished apartment with two rooms and a kitchen could only come across as an example of excessive luxury. Reducing the images to black and white would make showing the film less ideologically risky in the East but would not jeopardize the projected box office takings in the West. Not surprisingly, Artur Pohl and his team, whose project had been conceived as a production in colour, felt personally attacked by the criticism of the East German authorities and their decision to release the film in black and white. All of this led to Pohl declaring on the NDR (Norddeutscher Rundfunk) radio station in the West that he no longer wished to continue working for DEFA.

Shifting Perspectives: *Besuch aus der Zone* (1958/59) und *Das Leben beginnt* (1960)

During the 1950s there were also attempts in the West German film industry to tackle the contentious issue of the East–West divide from a more ideologically balanced perspective. One such example is Rainer Wolffhardt's *Besuch aus der Zone* [*Visitors from the Soviet Zone*; set designer Karl Wägele] – a West German TV film produced in 1958 by SDR (Süddeutscher Rundfunk) about an innovative manufacturer of artificial fibres, Reichert, who has chosen to remain in the GDR, and his relationship with his close friend and former colleague, Kleinschmidt, now in the West. With a remarkable lack of sentimentality, Wolffhardt's film shows how the decent businessman from the East fails in the Federal Republic. Although he is offered a position in Kleinschmidt's firm, he fails to get his Western partners to honour their commitments – the real purpose of his trip. Despite Kleinschmidt's efforts to persuade him to stay in the West, he returns, bitterly disappointed, with his wife and adolescent daughter to the GDR. Although dazzled by the range of consumer goods on offer in the West, neither wife nor daughter ever questions the decision to return to the East.

Given the state of German–German relations during the Cold War it is not that surprising that the film provoked widespread discussions and was even debated in the West German parliament.[20] Although the film was well received in the FRG, the elegance of the West as reflected in Karl Wägele's set design was singled out for criticism. As one viewer put it 'the film should have shown that not everyone in the West is a successful champagne-drinking individual with a luxury car'.[21] This film, too, depicts a young East German woman's first experience of a modern room furnished in accordance with the latest Western fashions. The room actually belongs to the daughter of the family with whom she is staying (who is the same age but away on a skiing holiday). Her brother takes pride in showing off his sister's well-appointed room to the new arrival from the East – a young and attractive woman in her own right – who admires both its décor and the clothes in the wardrobe. In a number of other sequences, too, the film deploys backdrops designed to highlight, in passing as it were, the availability of chic luxury goods in Western stores.

The relationship of mutual attraction between the two young protagonists in *Besuch aus der Zone* resembles that between Erika Schenk and her amusing laid-back cousin (the freelance journalist Benno Brenner from West Berlin), in Heiner Carow's *Das Leben beginnt*. But while the young man in *Besuch aus der Zone* is more a source of emotional confusion, Benno by contrast is a downright disappointment for Erika in *Das Leben beginnt*. Although Benno takes Erika to the theatre to see a play by Brecht in East Berlin's Berliner Ensemble, he turns out to be

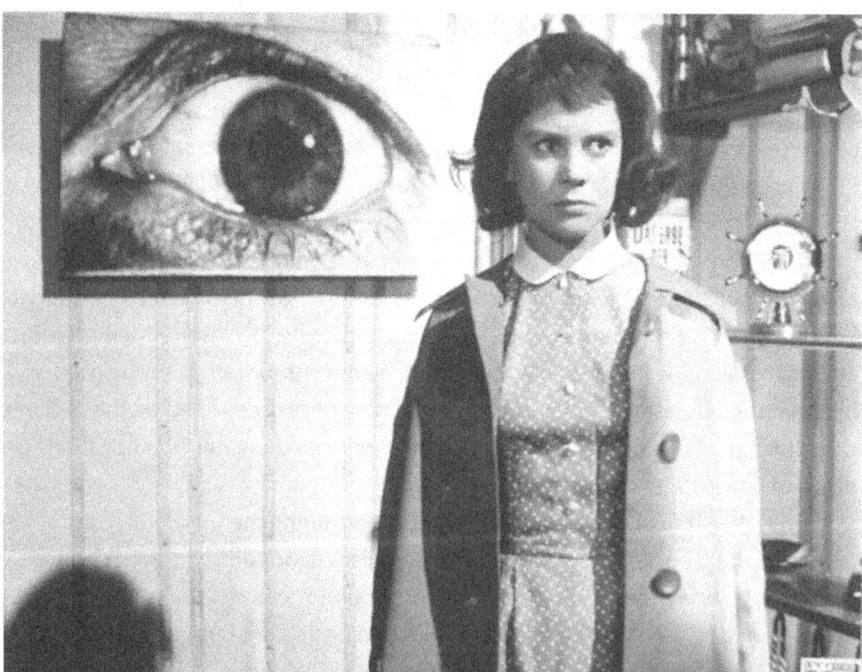

Figure 3.2: Erika's experience of Western modernist décor in *Das Leben beginnt* (1960) © DEFA Stiftung/Baxmann.

incapable of acting responsibly. When Erika believes herself to be pregnant, all he can do is turn to his father and ask for money to pay for an abortion. As a result, Erika no longer finds him as appealing as she did in the sequence when she first met him in his parents' house in the leafy suburb of Berlin-Dahlem in the West. There, everything seemed like an extravagant game: the modernist armchair, the amusing cigarette dispenser, the bed, and the portable radio she received as a present; but in this sequence, too, an extended pan exposes the superficial quality of such chic décor (Fig. 3.2).

Nevertheless, the high-school student Erika would never have made the journey to West Berlin from the provincial Brandenburg town of Krüselin had she found everything that was important to her there. In Krüselin she has her school, a communist youth group (*Jungpioniere*) that she looks after, and an (East German) boyfriend in Rolf Gruber, the headmaster's son. But Rolf's father, a former prisoner in a concentration camp, is an inflexible authoritarian figure who cannot bear the idea of his son going out with the daughter of an ideologically suspect doctor. It is certainly true that Dr Schenk, who used to be the senior clinician in a private institute, looks back nostalgically at his former prewar life and regards himself as restricted in his current professional role in the GDR. This impression is underscored by Willy Schiller's set design and, in particular, by the inherently conservative décor of his living room: bulky leather armchairs, oppressive wall coverings and antique furniture plus a television set that doubles as an unambiguous marker of his high income. When he decides to leave for the West, his daughter has no choice but to accompany him. Initially the family's wealthy relatives in Berlin-Dahlem welcome him and his daughter with open arms; but they begin to have second thoughts as, contrary to expectations, they struggle financially. The root cause of their difficulties is a surplus of doctors in West Berlin, caused by the mass exodus of doctors leaving the GDR. Erika, too, finds that gender relations are seen differently in the West and discovers that there is no expectation for a girl of her age to continue with her education at school. The social vacuum in which she finds herself is subsequently filled by two very different male characters: on the one hand her old boyfriend Rolf, who finds himself increasingly alienated from society; and on the other, the charming, attractive figure of Benno to whom she quickly succumbs. This marks the start of her decline. Father and daughter move out of the villa in Dahlem as their relatives' behaviour becomes increasingly intolerable. The elegant façade crumbles and behind it there is only frosty hostility (an attitude that is underscored by the treatment of the maid servant). The visits they pay to the member of the Berlin Senate (a friend of the father, who lives in an extravagantly futuristic dwelling) are all in vain as there simply are no jobs for doctors in West Berlin. The plot shifts into a new gear as father and daughter are forced to live together in low-quality rented accommodation, and their decline is reflected in aesthetic terms. While her father takes on the demeaning role as a rep for a pharmaceutical company, Erika has to stick it out in these old-fashioned lodgings that conjure up an image of petty bourgeois life in the days of empire (Fig. 3.3). The décor of this space stands in the sharpest possible contrast to all the others in the film, from the modernist elegance of the villa in Dahlem to the bourgeois furnishings of their former 1930s property in Krüselin.

To the disappointment of his daughter, the father eventually decides to enlist as a doctor in the (West) German military – a decision that means he is rarely physically present. Benno's behaviour in these circumstances, together with a disastrous encounter involving Erika and her landlady, lead to a catastrophe. In an almost Expressionist manner, the next sequence hints at a possible suicide attempt on a dimly lit street with heavy traffic, and the disturbed inner state of the

Figure 3.3: *Das Leben beginnt* (1960). The Schenks' rented accommodation in West Berlin © DEFA Stiftung/Baxmann.

protagonist completely transforms the way the urban exteriors are perceived. Filmed as it is in black and white, the final scene of *Das Leben beginnt* is highly reminiscent of the cinematographic style of UFA; the camera looks down onto a sparsely furnished room in a hospital in which Erika lies motionless in bed attended to by a sister sporting a huge old-fashioned nurse's cap. Only after Rolf hesitatingly enters the room do we get a sense of the notion encapsulated in the film's title, that life is only just beginning; and, or so we must imagine, it would appear to begin, or at least continue, in Krüselin. Thanks to the example of his independently minded son, the excessively dictatorial headmaster has finally recognized the error of his ways, and now Rolf is in a position to offer Erika in her old surroundings everything that her father had jeopardized by leaving for the West: warmth, emotional support, and a vision of the future. As the first part of the film has demonstrated, none of these are compatible with modernist postwar trappings of the West. The most strikingly modern room in the film belongs to the member of the West Berlin Senate (Fig. 3.4); but he is just another of those who let down the Schenks.

Figure 3.4: Willy Schiller's design for a room in the Senator's house. © Filmmuseum Potsdam. Every effort has been made to trace the original copyright holder.

Curiously, it is not the film itself, but rather the programme issued by the distributor, Progress, that offers us a series of images of the small-town idyll where it all began.[22] The provincial milieu itself is presented in the margins of the programme in the form of a colourful sketch in which the predominantly red tones are designed to convey a sense of optimism. The margins of the programme show thatched cottages, a church (both film and book refer to the cathedral in Stendal) and leafy trees together with, at the bottom of the page, a half-finished housing block complete with scaffolding. The urban modernity of West Berlin which promises so much, but which in reality delivers so much disappointment, is juxtaposed with an idyllic image of provincial town that, as the drawings suggest, has the potential for development; and the black-and-white sketches are superseded by a series of contrasting images in which red, the colour of the working class, predominates.

Heaven Divided: The Building of the Berlin Wall as a Caesura in History

We are also treated to 'a visit from the East' in Konrad Wolf's 1964 film *Der geteilte Himmel*, notably when Manfred goes to West Berlin to stay with his aunt who lives in a depressingly old-fashioned apartment that is devoid of any modernist influences. The viewer sees the room through the eyes of Rita, Manfred's girlfriend whom he has left behind in East Berlin and who has come to visit him for one last time. In stark contrast to the bizarre modern studio in the attic of his parents' home in Halle (Saale) where he used to live in the GDR, the room in his aunt's flat is an anonymous affair. Rita also finds it strange and unbecoming and, rather than stay indoors, they opt to go for a walk outside. As the camera pans along the facade of the famous Café Kranzler, we are offered some glimpses of West Berlin's modernity albeit only in the form of exteriors. In this way, in *Der geteilte Himmel* (on which Alfred Hirschmeier worked as the set designer) the discrepancy between the urban exteriors and the private interiors reflects a state of personal crisis; it also marks the point at which the relationship between Rita and Manfred breaks down, as he expresses his desire to remain in the West. However, as Wolf's film underlines, by the mid 1960s, it was no longer necessary to film on location inside such cafés (or to reconstruct their interiors in the studio): following the completion of East Berlin's Stalinallee, later renamed the Karl-Marx-Allee, and the construction of the Café Moskau in 1964/65 (using designs by Josef Kaiser and Horst Bauer) together with a number of other restaurants, East Berlin now had its own modernist buildings that, in visual terms, underlined the extent to which international developments in modern design had been integrated into the architecture of the GDR.[23]

A number of factors explain the greater acceptance of modernist design in *Der geteilte Himmel* and other films released during the early 1960s. In this context the production of the GDR's first science fiction film, Kurt Maetzig's *Der schweigende Stern* [*The Silent Star*] – filmed in colour and premiered on 26 February 1960 – was to play a key role.[24] Set in the not-too-distant future of 1970, and with sets designed by Anatol Radzinowicz and Alfred Hirschmeier, Maetzig's film was one of the very first DEFA productions to present contemporary modernist design in a wholly positive light. As the explicitly modernist character of the sets suggests, a paradigm shift in the concept of design (and abstract art) was underway in the GDR. These developments were not confined to DEFA but coincided with a radical change of policy in the GDR at the start of the 1960s regarding the production of high-end goods (including, in particular, fashion, modern household goods and appliances and furniture). As early as 1958, the Fifth Party Congress of the SED had announced its intention to raise standards of living in the GDR beyond those in the Federal Republic by 1961;[25] and at the same time, discussions were underway regarding the production of an East German brand of jeans.[26] The introduction of these policies meant that, from about 1960 onwards, East German manufacturers were, for the first time, able to supply modern consumer goods in larger quantities. In particular, the new programme of chemical engineering – captured in the slogan 'Chemie bringt Brot, Wohlstand und Schönheit' (Food, prosperity and good looks – it's all down to chemistry!) – made it possible to use Soviet oil to manufacture a wide range of plastic goods, and to do so in quantities that made the export of such goods to other socialist nations possible. New technologies coupled with a more systematic approach to production led to a new understanding of form, above all in the field of design. As a result, questions of design, in the modern sense of the term, came to be seen as a key area in many manufacturing processes. As early as 1958/59, Design (*Formgestaltung*) was an independent section alongside Applied Arts (*Gebrauchsgrafik*) and Arts and Crafts (*Kunsthandwerk*) at the Fourth Deutsche Kunstausstellung in Dresden; and it was not long before shops dealing in modern design products produced on an industrial scale started to emerge. The first of these opened in 1963 under the name 'Moderne Kunst' and offered both mass-produced goods that, in design terms, were functional and minimalist, as well as superior versions of the same. A year earlier, in 1962, the exhibition 'neues leben – neues wohnen' in Berlin had presented the East German government's new vision for the closely related concepts of architecture and interior design, a vision that, as we shall see, was to have a profound effect on set design at the DEFA studios.[27]

Günter Stahnke's *Der Frühling braucht Zeit* is a key work in the context of DEFA's attempt to both embrace modernist design while at the same time freeing it from the negative connotations that were so typical of earlier films of the 1950s. Following the film's premiere, on 25 November 1965, the East German press praised it as 'stylistically confident', while at the same time noting how the sparsely furnished interiors called to mind past intellectual debates about form and function.[28] In Stahnke's film we are confronted with a form of modernist aesthetic minimalism that is highly reminiscent of the works of the Italian directors Antonioni and Fellini. This minimalist style, which had gained wider acceptance in European art, architecture and design during the 1960s, was a reaction to the cluttered, 'busy' styles of earlier decades, and was characterized by a process of aesthetic reduction in favour of simplified forms that were essentially functional.

The sets were designed by Georg Kranz, one of the most prolific designers to work for DEFA; however, none of his subsequent designs would embody the same degree of aesthetic minimalism as that for *Der Frühling braucht Zeit*. The ways in which space is articulated in the film through the use of light and shade strike the viewer as reductive and austere, while at the same time evoking a concept of modernist design that, in its regular angularity, has its roots in the Bauhaus-style of the 1920s and 1930s. The principle of repeated geometrical sequences is used again and again, both in the composition of outdoor and indoor spaces, and further heightened through the use of black-and-white film stock. The focus on minimalist design is sustained throughout the film, and for the most part the characters are positioned in front of bare walls; yet by means of carefully selected items of furniture, the set design enables the viewer to differentiate clearly between the different protagonists and the values associated with them. In stark contrast to the earlier films of the 1950s, in Stahnke's film modernist design is associated primarily with those characters who embody a progressive socialist outlook – the engineer Solter (Fig. 3.5), his daughter, Inge, and the wife of the plant manager, Luise Faber.

By the same token, those figures who are characterized as essentially subservient to the state (for example, the plant manager, Faber, and the state attorney, Burger) are aligned with antiquated furnishings and décor; and the representative

Figure 3.5: Solter's office in *Der Frühling braucht Zeit* (1965) © DEFA Stiftung/ Schütt.

power of the state is itself visually critiqued through its association with a style that is clearly rooted in the past. While Solter's minimalist apartment is characterized by clean lines, Faber's attempt to maintain a position of patriarchal authority within the domestic sphere, and his reluctance to abandon traditional belief systems that are now outmoded, is symbolized by the ponderous old-fashioned writing desk that dominates the family home. His more open-minded wife, Luise, by contrast works in a modern, brightly lit office; and to enter this office the young student Inge Solter has to first pass through an elaborately carved wooden door not unlike that leading to the state attorney's office. Confronted with such a symbol of power, Inge is initially overawed and declares her intention to abandon her studies. Yet Luise Faber's intelligent and open-minded response is underscored by the film's scenography and the image of her as an elegant woman at work at the corner desk in her modern twentieth-century office. Finally, as we see in the figure of Inge's friend Jensen, the juxtaposition of design elements serves as a means of articulating ideological confusion. The apartment that Jensen lives in, and that Inge tries to jazz up with a daring pyramid constructed from empty bottles, is an ensemble of contradictory styles, both modern and antiquated; and this indecisiveness in aesthetic matters mirrors the inner ethical uncertainty of the apartment's male inhabitant.

By the 1960s, modern designs of the type featured in the Solters' family apartment were being produced on an industrial scale in the GDR by the Deutsche Werkstätten Dresden-Hellerau; and, as the extensive export of these designs underlined, the popularity of such modular furniture and stackable assembly units was by no means confined to the GDR. Indeed it is one of the paradoxes of East German history that those modernist developments which so quickly gained acceptance in the fields of industrial construction and furniture design, met with such resistance in the sphere of literature, cinema and the visual arts. *Der Frühling braucht Zeit* might have been a beacon of modernist filmmaking in the history of DEFA; however, it was just one of a number of modernist *nouvelle vague* films that were banned after the infamous Eleventh Plenum of 1965. Modernist tendencies had always been viewed with suspicion in the GDR; and for much of the 1950s it had been argued that such an overemphasis on aesthetic form at the expense of content reflected a state of alienation that itself was fundamentally incompatible with socialist goals. Following the Eleventh Plenum the formalist debates of the 1950s were once again revived in the form of a full-scale attack on modernism and abstraction across a wide range of media, and contributed to a period of aesthetic stagnation in the GDR that was to last until the early 1970s.

The ways in which modernist design and architecture of the 1950s and 1960s is reflected in both interior and exterior shots in the films released by DEFA tell us much about the GDR's rejection and assimilation of Western visual aesthetics at different phases in its history. This can be traced from the initial attempts to engage with the phenomenon of Western consumerism in the films of the 1950s, to the more differentiated position of a film such as Konrad Wolf's *Der geteilte Himmel* and the emphatic defence of modernity articulated in *Der Frühling braucht Zeit*. In the wake of the Eleventh Plenum, the vision of reshaping the GDR along modernist lines was shattered. After 1961, the East–West dichotomy had to be recast in new ways; but in some shape or form it was always present in the East German social imaginary.

Annette Dorgerloh is Privatdozentin for History of Art at the Humboldt Universität, Berlin. She has published widely on set design in DEFA film as part of an interdisciplinary research project between the Humboldt Universität and the Filmmuseum Potsdam.

Notes

This essay is based on a slightly shortened version of 'Nachkriegsmoderne als Herausforderung', in: kunsttexte.de, 1/2014 [= http://edoc.hu-berlin.de/kunsttexte/2014-1/dorgerloh-annette-2/PDF/dorgerloh.pdf], accessed 20 June 2016

1. All translations are by the author unless otherwise indicated.
2. This is an allusion to René Clair's French–Italian co-production *La Beauté du diable* [*Beauty and the Devil*, 1950] an adaptation of the Faust legend in which the quest for youth, power and wealth is exposed as an illusion. It was distributed in the Federal Republic under the title *Der Pakt mit dem Teufel*.
3. Urban Gad, *Der Film. Seine Mittel – Seine Ziele*, Berlin: Schuster und Loeffler, 1920, p. 116.
4. Michael Wedel, 'Schuld und Schaulust. Formen und Funktionen des deutschen Kriminalfilms bis 1960', in Rainer Rother and Julia Pattis (eds), *Die Lust am Genre. Verbrechergeschichten aus Deutschland*, Berlin: Bertz + Fischer, 2011, pp. 25–40 (p. 36).
5. Andrea Guder, *Genosse Hauptmann auf Verbrecherjagd. Der Krimi in Film und Fernsehen der DDR*, Bonn: ARCult Media, 2003, p.14.
6. Michael Hanisch, *Nachrichten aus einem Land ohne Schurken, oder In Diktaturen hat der Krimi nicht viel zu melden*, in Ralf Schenk and Erika Richter (eds), *apropos: Film 2001* [= Das Jahrbuch der DEFA-Stiftung, 2001], Berlin: Das Neue Berlin, 2001, pp. 194–222.
7. See Hanisch, and Guder (esp. Ch. 3 'Der Kriminalfilm der DEFA'), pp. 39–72.
8. See, for example, Helmut Weihsmann, *Gebaute Illusionen*, Wien: Promedia, 1988, and Dietrich Neumann, *Filmarchitektur. Von Metropolis bis Blade Runner*, Munich, New York: Prestel, 2002.
9. See Annette Dorgerloh, 'Die Räume des Ingenieurs. Zur Szenographie des verbotenen DEFA-Films *Der Frühling braucht Zeit*', in Christof Baier, André Bischoff and Marion Hilliges (eds), *Ordnung und Mannigfaltigkeit. Beiträge zur Architektur- und Stadtbaugeschichte für Ulrich Reinisch*, Weimar: Vdg, 2011, pp. 85–90.
10. Donald Albrecht and Ralph Eue, *Architektur im Film. Die Moderne als große Illusion*, Basel, Boston, Berlin: Birkhäuser, 1989; and Doris Agotai, *Architekturen in Zelluloid. Der filmische Blick auf den Raum*, Bielefeld: transcript, 2007.
11. Uta Poiger, *Jazz, Rock and Rebels. Cold War Politics and American Culture in a Divided Germany*, Berkley, Los Angeles, London: University of California Press, 2000.
12. Cf. Elizabeth Prommer and Andy Räder, 'Kinogrenzgänger im geteilten Deutschland (1949–61). Filmgeschmack, Nutzung und Motive des Kinobesuchs', in Michael Wedel, Barton Byg, Andy Räder, Skyler Arndt-Briggs and Evan Torner (eds), *DEFA International. Grenzen und Grenzüberschreitungen. Transnationale Filmbeziehungen der DEFA vor und nach dem Mauerbau*, Wiesbaden: VS Verlag, 2013, pp. 131–148.
13. Cf. Herbert Janssen and Reinhold Jacobi (eds), *Filme in der DDR 1945–86*, Bonn: Katholisches Institut für Medienforschung, 1987.
14. Cf. Artur Pohl 1955, *Spielbank-Affäre*, Drehbuch, Version vom 25.7.1955, p. 156, Filmmuseum Potsdam.
15. The film was only a GDR–Swedish co-production in a technical sense. The 'Swedish' production partner 'Pandora' was essentially a German partner with a Swedish address set up by the German, Erich Mehl, in order to circumvent the restrictions of the Hallstein Doctrine. See Mariana Ivanova, 'Die Prestige-Agenda der DEFA. Koproduktionen mit Erich Mehls Filmfirma Pandora (1954–1957)', in: Michael Wedel, Barton Byg, Andy Räder, Skyler Arndt-Briggs and Evan Torner

(eds), *DEFA International. Grenzen und Grenzüberschreitungen. Transnationale Filmbeziehungen der DEFA vor und nach dem Mauerbau*, Wiesbaden: Springer VS Verlag, 2013, pp. 217–32 (esp. p. 222).
16. See the advertising blurb on the back of the commercially distributed VHS version of the film.
17. Anton Ackermann, 'Zur Parteilichkeit in der Filmkunst', *Einheit. Zeitschrift für Theorie und Praxis des wissenschaftlichen Sozialismus* 13.4 (1958), 527–38 (536).
18. Cf. Heinz Kersten, *Das Filmwesen in der sowjetischen Besatzungszone Deutschlands*, Bonn, Berlin: Bundesministerium für gesamtdeutsche Fragen, 1963, p. 137.
19. Alexander Abusch, cited in 'Die gefährliche Farbe', *Der Spiegel*, 44/1957.
20. A report of the debate is available on the website of the Bundeszentrale für politische Bildung: [= http://www.bpb.de/gesellschaft/medien/deutsche-fernsehgeschichte-in-ost-und-west/147350/die-1950er-jahre-anfaenge], accessed 16 June 2015.
21. 'Leserzuschrift W.W. aus Köln-Ehrenfeld', *Hörzu* 11/1958, 49.
22. Cf. Progress Film-Programm 1960, *Das Leben beginnt*.
23. This section of Stalinallee/Karl-Marx-Allee with the Café Moskau is used as a backdrop in many DEFA films. See Bruno Flierl, *Gebaute DDR. Über Stadtplaner, Architekten und die Macht*, Berlin: Verlag für Bauwesen, 1998; and Stephanie Warnke, *Stein gegen Stein. Architektur und Medien im geteilten Berlin 1950–1970*, Frankfurt am Main, New York: Campus, 2009.
24. In the Federal Republic the film was released under the title *Raumschiff Venus antwortet nicht*.
25. See the article 'Umfangreiche Maßnahmen zur weiteren Verbesserung der Lebenslage', *Neues Deutschland*, 28 April 1958.
26. See Rebecca Menzel, *Jeans in der DDR*, Berlin, 2004, esp. pp. 27–28.
27. For a more detailed discussion of the politics of interior design, see Katherine Pence and Paul Betts (eds), *Socialist Modern: East German Everyday Culture and Politics*, Ann Arbor: University of Michigan Press, 2008 (esp. Paul Betts 'Building Socialism at Home. The Case of East German Interiors', pp. 96–132).
28. Hartmut Albrecht, 'Konflikte beim Vorwärtsschreiten', *Nationalzeitung*, 27 November 1965.

PART II
NATIONAL AND TRANSNATIONAL CONTEXTS

CHAPTER 4
DEFA and the Legacy of 'Film Europe'
Prestige, Institutional Exchange and Film Co-Productions

Mariana Ivanova

> *What was utopian just yesterday is today beginning to become reality: the most accessible avenue forward ... was that of European production partnerships.*
> Felix Henseleit, 'Film-Europa'[1]

Reconstructing the historical context of UFA's and DEFA's partnerships with European film industries reveals continuities in their approach and institutional practices that should not be ignored in the history of European cinema. Moreover, the ideas about European cinema that both these film studios shared, challenges the traditional view of a break between the cinematic cultures of pre- and postwar Germany. It is true that DEFA, in stark contrast to UFA in the early 1920s, never dreamt of establishing a European-wide consortium to rival Hollywood. Nevertheless, the Babelsberg studio's agenda during the 1950s to produce prestige films as a way of reclaiming its former prominence within Eastern and Western markets points to the lasting legacy of UFA's self-conception as a studio at the very heart of Europe. DEFA filmmakers' idea of cinema as a means of demonstrating both the high quality and the political importance of film art curiously resonated with the agenda of an earlier European movement called 'Film Europe'.

The term 'Film Europe' can be traced back to the 1920s, when producers and exhibitors on the continent developed a proposal for a form of cinematic cooperation that could challenge the control by US distributors. Although short-lived, this ideal laid the foundation for dialogue among national film industries and engendered numerous international co-productions that enhanced European domestic markets. In addition, the leading film studios of Germany, France, Britain, Italy, Czechoslovakia, Hungary and others, introduced a set of industrial policies in order to promote their products and enable the free movement of cinematic talent, technical equipment and expertise. Such practices included creating protocols for co-productions, the use of international casts for nationally based films, or the exploitation of international settings and storylines. On another level, 'Film Europe' meant reciprocal agreements between distributors in different nation-states, in response to their efforts to rationalize and secure a long-term market share.[2]

One of these companies was the film studio in Potsdam-Babelsberg, which first hosted UFA (Universum Film Aktiengesellschaft, 1917–1945) and, subsequently, the East German production company DEFA (Deutsche Film-Aktiengesellschaft, 1946–1992). UFA paved the way for French, Czech and Russian directors and actors to make prestige films on German soil and/or to work with such renowned filmmakers as Fritz Lang, Georg W. Pabst, and Max Ophüls.[3] At the same time, the studio actively pursued institutional and personal exchanges with European partners, for instance, by participating in a number of film congresses between 1926 and 1930 and by working towards establishing a lasting presence on markets in Western and Central Europe.[4] As UFA's successor, DEFA inherited not only a range of institutional contacts to the once wide-reaching network of the 1920s, but also an interest in sustaining its precursor's standing in the international market. Formal alliances were pursued for an essentially national agenda, namely the need to promote socialist art as a means of securing the diplomatic recognition of the East German state. While UFA's desire for cooperation with European partners in the 1920s came as a response to Germany's exclusion from the League of Nations after World War I, DEFA's co-productions with French partners, in particular in the late 1950s, served to win Western support for the GDR's sovereignty.

Little is known about the historical continuity between the interwar debates on Germany's place within the European film scene, and DEFA's interest in reclaiming this place coupled with reviving the agenda to co-produce prestige films. To date, UFA's legacy in the postwar period has been seen primarily in terms of a re-appropriation of film genres, re-employment of cinematic talent, or recycling of prewar film aesthetics.[5] Yet numerous affinities between, on the one hand, the cosmopolitan aspirations of Weimar producers and, on the other, the desire of East German filmmakers for prestige and presence on wider European markets suggest that the relationship between pre- and postwar German cinema needs to be rethought. This essay, therefore, compares institutional and transnational strategies for film (co-)production in Germany of the 1920s and the 1950s. Such strategies involve responses to the historical situation of exclusion, appeals for unity and international solidarity among filmmakers, the need for networking with other European industries, active participation in film congresses, production of multiple-language version films, and the provision of various technical services and expertise. Even though the DEFA studio management and cultural functionaries never explicitly mention Film Europe as a model, it is striking how often their rhetoric both invoked and re-rehearsed the premises of this anti-American utopian ideal.

The key to a productive analysis of the continuities between UFA and DEFA in this respect is a step-by-step engagement with three issues that both studios had in common: first, their initial anti-American sentiments and related critique of cultural imperialism; second, a national agenda driving international collaborations; and, third, the wish to co-produce with other European nations in order to gain prestige and to promote international solidarity. The example of postwar French and East German cooperation, outlined at the end of this essay, illuminates the intersection of these three issues and reveals the lasting legacy of Film Europe and its impact on DEFA's programme to co-produce with other nations. In both cases, the Germans ventured into reciprocal agreements with French partners ostensibly with the agenda to co-produce and circulate European films; yet, as we shall see, much larger political issues were at stake.

Anti-Americanism and Critique of Cultural Imperialism

By the mid 1920s, certain groups within the German film industry saw Hollywood's encroachment on European markets as a major challenge to their commercial and artistic success. While Weimar society welcomed the process of Americanization in popular culture and everyday life, several German producers and exhibitors assumed a leading role in the emerging European film association. Behind their promise to consolidate the European market, UFA and other companies envisioned breaking the American monopoly and promoting their own products. The proponents of Film Europe articulated several points of criticism that display a striking similarity to DEFA's cultural policy twenty-five years later: first, they condemned the so-called cultural imperialism of Hollywood while at the same time emphasizing the need to enhance competition by producing prestige films with other strong European film companies; second, they insisted on the need to reclaim existing film markets and, to that end, pointed to German audiences' apparent preference for domestic productions over American imports; and, third, they criticized Hollywood scripts for their compromised aesthetic and artistic qualities and articulated a conviction that the screenplay was the key to a good film. Generally speaking, anti-American sentiment was expressed in a critique of Hollywood cinema that portrayed the latter as a propaganda tool for American culture, values and way of life.

After most large European film companies had signed trading and co-production agreements in 1924, one of Germany's leading film trade papers, *Lichtbildbühne*, suggested that 'the new guiding principle for European film politics must be: band together' so as 'to establish a general principle of regulating mutual distribution according to existing levels of production'.[6] This seemed a lucrative deal for the prolific German industry. However, in late 1925, UFA was forced by political and economic interests to enter into a partnership with the US studios Universal, Paramount and Metro-Goldwyn-Mayer that came to be known as the 'Parufamet agreement'. UFA benefited financially to the tune of four million dollars, but in return the American companies demanded 50% of screening time in German cinemas. *Lichtbildbühne* grimly described Parufamet as 'UFA's Americanization' while deploying terms such as 'rivals', 'conquer' and 'domination' to criticize Hollywood's cultural and economic monopoly.[7] Under these circumstances, the prospect of a European-wide association seemed the only way out of UFA's subjugation to Hollywood. In support of this, the trade journal *Film-Kurier* called on the German film industry to develop a global policy and to embark on large-scale prestige European productions in order to shake off US dominance.[8] Pressed by similar demands, in 1927, UFA representative Salomon Marx publicly declared his intention to offset Hollywood's 'invasion' of European film markets by establishing a pan-European coalition. His speech was commended in *Lichtbildbühne* and in other journals as 'UFA's New Course'.[9]

In 1946, DEFA, also announced a new beginning, or 'Stunde Null', and, much like the proponents of Film Europe in the 1920s, the studio used anti-American discourse to entice German artists and filmmakers to Babelsberg. One of DEFA's founders, Alfred Lindemann, declared: 'We have to expect that we will be operating in a free market one day. ... Therefore, it is of great importance to produce as many German films as possible',[10] adding 'We welcome all those who want to help the new, true democracy with creativity, directing, and acting, no matter in which zone they live.'[11] This desire to make specifically German films while others (notably the cultural officers in the American sector) sought to saturate the devastated country's film market with US imports, reflects DEFA's early agenda of developing a strong national film industry. Much like Weimar producers, those running the East German studio sought to re-create a strong domestic market, which went hand in hand with the employment of qualified former UFA filmmakers.

In this sense, DEFA's anti-Americanism is articulated both in the opposition to American cinematic hegemony, and to proponents of US cultural policy in the immediate postwar years, which was characterized by a reluctance to allow Germans to make their own films. A case in point here is the first German film made after World War II, namely Wolfgang Staudte's *Die Mörder sind unter uns* [*The Murderers Are Among Us*, 1946]. The eagerness with which the East Germans and the Soviet cultural administration pursued a project that had been rejected in the other sectors attests to the fierce competition among film officers. In the West, those were predominantly returnees from the US, who had earned respect in the film business and made successful careers at Hollywood. The most prominent among them, Erich Pommer, UFA's prolific producer and one-time active proponent of Film Europe, returned to Berlin in 1946 to assume the post of cultural officer in the American sector. Likewise, Billy Wilder and Peter van Eyck arrived from California to help reorganize what was left of Germany's film industry. Nevertheless, their efforts at reconstruction, as Tim Bergfelder suggests, 'became trapped between conflicting objectives of German politicians and filmmakers who were eager to resume an autonomous and strong national film industry, and of Hollywood's major studios intent on keeping competition neutralized'.[12]

Despite their initial hesitancy, film officers in the American sector soon began competing with DEFA for directors and actors. Pommer played a key role in attracting former colleagues to the Western sectors in the late 1940s, such as Joseph von Sternberg, but also the British directors Alfred Hitchcock and Paul Rotha. In response, East German intellectuals launched a campaign to persuade former UFA filmmakers to join their cause. Friedrich Wolf, for instance, wrote on 30 May 1946 to Leonard Mins, a member of the US Communist Party: 'By the way, I am a member of the artistic advisory board of our new film company Film A.G. DEFA ... If only we could get someone like William Dieterle or even Fritz Lang to come here! Do you think that might be possible?!'[13] These endeavours to contract renowned UFA employees reflect the East German studio's prestige agenda, which at the time pointed to a desire to reconnect with the successes of the 1920s in an attempt to succeed in the present.

Like his East German colleagues, Pommer believed in 'a reputable German film' in contrast to 'mass films'. In his opinion, Germany needed films without 'pomp and spectacular wizardry' where 'the decisive factor is the script'.[14] This view harked back to similar sentiments in the mid 1920s of which Pommer must have been well aware. In 1924/25, film critics and cinema owners highlighted fundamental flaws in Hollywood productions that, in their view, made them ill-suited for German viewers.[15] They also claimed that audiences preferred domestic films, which attested to their alienation from American cinema. In a similar vein, the Soviet officials in 1945 Berlin appealed for the production of 'cultural films' and for the careful selection of scripts. While such restrictions were adopted early on in the Western sectors as well, the approval of the screenplay became the first and most important step for any DEFA film throughout the studio's existence. The emphasis on story and dialogue allowed DEFA to concentrate on the film's content and political message, and to avoid the Hollywood-style focus on genre or entertainment.

DEFA perceived Hollywood films as vehicles for capitalist propaganda. This conviction was reflected in its insistence on the need for a new form of socialist art that should reflect the reality of the working classes (and a corresponding rejection of 1940s UFA entertainment productions that, together with US cinema, were viewed as misleading and as obscuring socialist values and everyday experience). Similarly, the supporters of Film Europe in the 1920s had viewed Hollywood as a repository of national character and values that distinguished US film culture from its German counterpart. American pictures were described in blunt terms as entertainment and profit-oriented and contrasted with German films that possessed not only inherent artistic quality but also cultural and even educational value. These stereotypes were underpinned by a critique of the 'typical' Hollywood screenplay that was described unflatteringly as a compilation of improbability and false characterization, and as resorting to sentimentality in order to resolve social conflicts.[16]

Another critical stance that DEFA shared with Film Europe supporters in the 1920s was the insistence on (East) German audiences' need for films that reflected their own experiences rather than the glamorous fantasies on display in Hollywood productions. A common way to discredit US cinema in the 1920s was through the exaggeration of the audience's alleged aversion to American films. For instance, a lead article entitled 'America, can you hear our whistles of disapproval?' that appeared in *Film-Kurier* of 1926, sharply critiqued the methods for advertising

Hollywood premieres in Berlin and claimed that such sentimentality was intolerable to German viewers.[17] In that year, resistance to American strategies for film exhibition culminated in an appeal to boycott Hollywood films on the grounds of existing nationally conditioned taste differences. 'European audiences want European themes' was the reasoning behind such criticism, 'such a view is not the result of theoretical hair-splitting but an experienced fact: a German will always find a domestic picture – taken on average – more accessible than a roughly equivalent American film'.[18] This claim for national exclusivity and for German audiences' preference for homegrown genres returned in the early days of DEFA. 'Shallow entertainment' was no longer an option for East German audiences who, according to the Soviet officials, had for too long been duped and diverted by musicals and costume dramas during the Third Reich.[19] As suggested by Thomas Heimann, new genres were said to be more attractive to socialist audiences: the *Zeitfilm* and the *Gegenwartsfilm* (films about contemporary time and life).[20] These films promoted a new everyday-life aesthetic that masked the attempt at ideological education of the masses; but they also represented a policy of securing the East German market for domestic and Soviet productions. The effort to control Weimar and East German audiences and to develop their tastes in favour of a domestic film market points to a strong national agenda behind the proclaimed internationalism of both DEFA and Film Europe.

The National Agenda Behind the Claim for Internationalism

Both pre- and postwar international cooperation was driven by an essentially national agenda: while UFA's desire for co-productions with European partners was a response to Germany's exclusion from the League of Nations after World War I, DEFA's collaborations with other film studios were seen as means of promoting the GDR's international recognition in the wake of the 1955 Hallstein Doctrine.[21] In both cases, the German film industry suffered the consequences of political and economic isolation after a world war and responded with an effort to overcome the state's exclusion from vital alliances with European neighbours. Even before the end of World War I, the Allies convened to discuss an international League of Nations in order to secure nonviolent resolutions of future political disputes. The aggressor of World War I, Germany, was notably not invited to participate; as per the 1919 Treaty of Versailles it was excluded from European-scale decision making. But in its struggle to secure a role on the world stage, Germany subsequently applied to join the League of Nations, a political move designed to force the recognition of the country's sovereignty. This move, moreover, was critical for UFA and the entire German cinema industry. The League of Nations planned to get involved in international cultural affairs by establishing an organization resembling Film Europe, which would unify public and private agencies on the continent. As Richard Maltby points out, there were lobbyists who argued that 'the League should involve itself extensively in the motion picture's international affairs'.[22]

In early 1926, immediately after UFA sealed the Parufamet agreement and just before Germany's acceptance as a member of the League of Nations in September of that year, *Lichtbildbühne* called for the government's urgent intervention. 'After all', the paper stated, 'it is not only individuals who take an interest in UFA's well-being, but also the entire nation and the government that represents and attends to its [UFA's] wishes'.[23] This bold claim of national investment in the film industry was far from gratuitous. In fact, UFA had received government support since its inception in 1917 and throughout the 1920s, all of which contributed to the studio's advantage over other European production companies. In response, the German trade press repeatedly launched campaigns in favour of Germany becoming 'a keymodel for European resistance to Hollywood'.[24] For instance, *Film-Kurier*'s editor, Ernst Jäger, had appealed for unity on the part of film producers and, indeed, the entire industry in the belief that only national cohesion and a consistent protection of quotas could raise the reputation of German productions and ensure their wide distribution.[25] In other words, the very idea underpinning the notion of strong national European cinemas was largely based on the German dominance of other markets.

The national impetus behind the alleged European interest is evident from UFA's practical attempts to collaborate with French companies in order to support Germany's aspirations in joining the League of Nations. In working with the French, the largest European studio sought a practical solution to overcome the economic restrictions imposed by Germany's isolation. In the summer of 1924, UFA signed an agreement with the French company Aubert with the promise to help them expand their market. Shortly after that, in December, another distributor, Westi, formed an alliance with Pathé Cinéma. Although viewed as steps towards the creation of a European film association, these efforts point to Germany's expansionist aspirations. The most important of these attempts, L'Alliance Cinématographique

Européene – a joint distribution company set up by UFA and Svenska, with French investment – occurred just before the inclusion of Germany in the League of Nations. According to Kristin Thompson, the Alliance 'announced plans to produce in all three countries, but its main purpose was actually to serve as an outlet for UFA films in France, and as such it functioned very efficiently for the next few years'.[26]

DEFA's pursuit of French contacts in the 1950s in many ways resembles UFA's policies in the 1920s. Like the exclusion of Weimar Germany from the League of Nations, the West German Hallstein Doctrine was designed to limit economic trade, cultural exchange, and diplomatic relations with any countries in and outside of Europe that recognized the sovereignty of East Germany. In response, DEFA developed various strategies to conserve the image of an internationally acclaimed studio and to promote the socialist state abroad. Until the GDR's international recognition in 1973, DEFA relied largely on co-productions with other European countries, in order for their films to access the competitions at international film festivals based in Western Europe. This film cooperation involved primarily French, West German and Swedish partners and thus recalled the political goals of L'Alliance Cinématographique Européene.

In the mid 1950s, East German politicians sponsored collaborations with West European partners enabling DEFA to export a positive image of the GDR. Such films were predominantly adaptations of world literature that recycled the cinematic successes of the interwar years. By appropriating pre-socialist traditions, East German filmmakers sought to position their studio on the wider European market. This was evident, for instance, in the studio manager's pronouncement about a 1955 co-production with French partners in which he spoke of 'DEFA's first appearance on the world market' and insisted that such films demonstrated 'DEFA's international importance and particularly its impact on West Germany'.[27] Key politicians, especially from the Ministry of Culture, agreed with him and identified the potential of such co-productions to 'provide the important West German producers with a strong weapon in their struggle with Bonn to allow co-productions with DEFA'.[28] Such grand statements express less the GDR officials' hopes for the success of East German cinema on the world stage, but rather an exhortation of GDR filmmakers to cultivate the political and national agendas of the socialist state through their art. In other words, in the eyes of the functionaries, co-productions were first and foremost products of international solidarity, and as such, tools for political advancement.

In this context we should also elaborate on the various responses by UFA and DEFA to the expectations of their respective governments. Weimar producers and directors seem to have profited from national support for the development of ties to other European industries and expansion of their market. We should not forget that the UFA of the 1920s was not nearly as dependent on the state as it later became following the NSDAP rise to power. Accordingly, it can be concluded that in between the two world wars German filmmakers shared the national agenda in order to enhance their own opportunities for production and to increase their economic profit. In contrast, by citing international aspirations and simultaneously succumbing to the agenda for state recognition, their East German counterparts in the 1950s were concerned with professional – rather than economic – rewards. In such co-productions filmmakers saw an unparalleled opportunity for transnational exchange and artistic expression that otherwise might have remained extremely limited or even impossible.[29] The opportunity to explore both in private and in public the future of international cooperation and bilateral projects also provided the impulse for filmmakers' congresses. More often than not these congresses were outlets for utopian ideas that would never be realized; yet the value of the transnational contacts established at these events seems hard to overstate.

International Solidarity – Transnational Cooperation

'International friendship', 'unity' and 'solidarity' were the buzzwords at the 1920s film congresses in Paris and Berlin in the attempt to launch Film Europe as a viable organization. Although the latter never happened, these notions re-emerged in the early 1950s, and received ideological connotation in East German political discourse. Whereas filmmakers in the interwar and in the postwar periods saw themselves as internationalists for very different reasons, their conceptualization of cooperation among nations as well as among people within these nations was strikingly similar. Moreover, their internationalist ideas were supplemented by transnational projects relating to the planning, production and distribution of such films. While international solidarity remained for the most part a utopian ideal discussed at film congresses, transnational cooperation often resulted in practical exchanges that took the form of multinational crews making films at Babelsberg, the cross-border mobility of film workers and the supply of editing or copying services for partners. In this context, film co-productions offer a unique example of the intersections of both international and transnational models for collaboration.

Various UFA strategies for co-producing provided DEFA with functional models of working with multinational crews and director teams, as well as of winning partners, by offering technical expertise at competitive prices. In the late 1920s, co-productions functioned as star vehicles, boosted the market share of domestic films and kept alive the hopes for the creation of a European cinematographic union. Immediately after Germany's entry into the League of Nations, there was an unprecedented surge in the number of French–German co-productions: within only three years (between 1926 and 1928) seventeen such films were shot and distributed throughout Europe. This trend continued after 1929 when, for a decade, UFA and French partners co-produced some 186 films, a significant number by any yardstick.[30] As Joseph Garncarz has argued, these films 'provided a new answer to the long-standing problem of how to market films successful in a Europe marked by so many cultural differences'.[31] Although the early co-productions were initially produced in two identical versions of the same film (shot on different locations using either French or German actors), later on this practice changed. For example, from the early 1930s, Babelsberg recruited foreign actors speaking their own language or cast German actors speaking French or English while adapting the stories to mask poor linguistic performance.[32] Later on, with the growing popularity of dubbing, UFA started delivering a wide range of technical services relating to sound and image editing.

East German co-productions from the 1950s were large-scale prestige pictures or heritage films conceived as manifestations of German and European cultural traditions. Because they relied on previous contacts, these projects profited from established models for the management of multinational crews. For instance, French actors were frequently engaged to work with DEFA directors or, vice-versa, director duos from France and the Netherlands were invited to work with German or multinational crews at Babelsberg. Such was the case for most DEFA co-productions with France. For instance, Wolfgang Staudte attempted to adapt Bertolt Brecht's *Mutter Courage* [*Mother Courage*] in the early 1950s with French actress Simone Signoret and Bernard Blier, while *Die Abenteuer des Till Ulenspiegel* [*The Bold Adventure*, 1956] was originally a film directed by the duo Gérard Philipe and Joris Ivens.

By the late 1960s, DEFA had embarked on co-producing 'homegrown' genres, the so-called *Indianerfilme* or *utopische Filme* that recast the classical Hollywood Western or science fiction film, respectively. What motivated these projects was the trade in professional services, including the provision of exotic-looking extras or props and landscapes not found in the GDR, in exchange for DEFA's technical expertise. In some cases, socialist states even supported artistic exchange through travel grants and work visas. East German producers and directors thus had the opportunity to travel abroad and meet European colleagues of potential interest to DEFA whom the studio later would contract for prestige co-productions.

A major venue for such interpersonal exchanges in the 1920s and the late 1950s was a series of international congresses and conventions. Such meetings granted European filmmakers with opportunities to establish transnational ties, discuss common goals of the industry, and put their own understanding of cooperation and solidarity into practice. In addition, much like UFA's management, DEFA saw these conferences as an opportunity to attract partners for future projects, to build up the distribution network of their domestic products and to draw on expertise and innovations in film and sound technology.

The international film congresses of the 1920s not only provided a discursive space for the evolution of Film Europe as an idea, but they also proved to be of symbolic importance for the inclusion of German filmmakers in an international artistic community. Although not invited to the first Paris congress in 1923, UFA delegates attended the congress of 1926 that had been organized under the auspices of the League of Nations. In order to reinforce Germany's support of Film Europe, in 1928 Berlin hosted the First International Cinema Exhibitors' Conference, which discussed the organization of a European-wide trade body designed to ease the cross-border circulation of films. Two other conventions followed, in Paris in 1929 and in Brussels in 1930, where the focus was on combating the Hollywood invasion with dual- and multiple-language version productions and by reinforcing the restricted quota of film imports. All four conferences, Andrew Higson argues, failed to achieve any concrete results, insofar as their ideas remained theoretical reflections about the future of European cinema.[33] Yet, at the same time, as Higson confirms, these conferences provided a basis for further networks and promoted the idea of film as a cultural product with the potential to preserve a specifically European cultural heritage. These same two goals together with the establishment of 'a cultural discourse of international cooperation and understanding' – as Higson terms the lasting achievement of the 1920s congresses[34] – also informed the agendas of the Eastern European film congresses during the late 1950s.

The series of socialist filmmakers' conferences that took place in Eastern Europe between 1957 and 1960 addressed two agendas: first, the acknowledgement of a set of shared political and aesthetic values that differentiated socialist film art from capitalist Hollywood cinema; and second, the need for solidarity among artists in order to ensure a successful interaction with international audiences.[35] For DEFA's filmmakers, these conferences presented the opportunity to develop ties with a community of Eastern European artists in the wake of the Hallstein Doctrine, and to develop new projects for cooperation once the doors to the West were shut. In their efforts to distinguish socialist and capitalist cinemas, however, Eastern Europeans proposed strategies that closely resembled those debated at the congresses of the 1920s. For example, the Prague conference of 1957 underscored the necessity of creating new aesthetic styles and genres that drew on progressive movements such as Italian Neorealism – and that could compete with Hollywood and popular cinema for the attention of socialist audiences. The second film conference in Sinaia, Romania, met in 1958 and elaborated on the differences between socialist and capitalist filmmaking; it also introduced new models for efficient collaboration within state-sponsored studios. The proceedings of both conferences attest to the changing role of film as a medium for connecting and mobilizing viewers and to the need for defining socialist cinema in opposition to West European and Hollywood competitors. The resolutions at these conferences culminated in the decisions of the last international conference, of 1960, in Sofia, Bulgaria, regarding the development of new directorial styles and setting a new course in the practice of co-production and film exchange involving socialist countries. On the one hand, the emphasis on international friendship and cooperation as categories central to socialist political discourse since the 1940s suggest an approximation of the political and artistic agendas that had already happened in the 1920s. On the other hand, the practical outcomes of the socialist filmmakers' congresses also compare to those of the 1920s: many filmmakers became known outside of their national film industries, new styles in filmmaking emerged and co-productions as well as multinational casts become much more common.[36] The revived discussions of these practices at the congresses between 1957 and 1960 brought a new understanding of the necessity for European cooperation and it also drew on the recent renewal of these practices by DEFA. East German co-productions with French directors since the mid 1950s were to a considerable extent shaped by the legacy of Film Europe. At the same time, they were also based on their political commitment, as the following discussion demonstrates.

DEFA Co-productions with French Partners

When French producers first made contact with DEFA, in 1948, they initially proposed the production of five dual-language films per year to be distributed in both countries.[37] With the advent of sound, such co-productions had gained far-reaching acclaim among European audiences. Yet the new technology of dubbing had turned them into what was arguably an outdated model for postwar European industries and, understandably, DEFA, rejected the idea. Several years later, however, the French proposal was revived, together with the German hopes to rekindle the successes of the 1920s. The East Germans' involvement with French directors, as Marc Silberman suggests, was motivated partially by existing ties with former UFA directors and/or left-wing organizations such as the French Communist Party.[38] This resulted in a curious interplay between the French artists' political agenda and their producers, who saw DEFA primarily as a cut-price successor to UFA.

By the mid 1950s, DEFA renewed previous contacts with French film companies, notably UFA's largest former ally, Pathé Cinéma, as well as with Films Borderie (closely associated with Max Ophüls' dual-language productions of the 1930s), and with the left-leaning Films Ariane that since 1945 had specialized mostly in Franco-Italian co-productions. While the GDR was not yet recognized in the West and, therefore, had no bilateral agreements with France as far as cinema was concerned, private producers were able to sign 'co-participation' contracts with DEFA. As we shall see, the uncertain status of these joint projects would soon become problematic, but in 1955 both sides had hopes of a productive cooperation. For the French, the lucrative deal included access to one of the largest film facilities in Europe, together with a body of highly trained technicians and the economic advantage of being able to make films with a big-budget look that could compete with Hollywood. DEFA, for its part, also developed a complex agenda: on the one hand, the studio hoped to regain its place on the European scene, and, on the other, East German culture's visibility and support by Western artists could promote the recognition of the GDR. In short, DEFA's co-productions with French partners in the 1950s revolved around the three key concepts discussed earlier, namely anti-Americanism, promoting a national agenda as the impetus for international cooperation, and a call for international solidarity, which translated practically into the production of films with multinational casts.

The anti-American agenda is reflected first and foremost in the cooperative projects that drew on a common European cultural heritage and which were used to distinguish a highbrow *cinéma de qualité* from mass-produced Hollywood entertainment. As Marc Silberman discusses at length in 'Learning from the Enemy: DEFA-French Co-Productions of the 1950s', all four East German–French co-productions made between 1956 and 1960 were prestige films with an ideological twist. They revisited a historical past that was inevitably of appeal to European audiences, and, that simultaneously invited critique of contemporary social and political relations. Three of the films were adaptations of European classical literature, translating issues such as struggles for justice, class equality, and liberation from occupiers, into costume dramas and period films. The fourth was based on a theatre play critical of the 1950s' anti-communist movement in the United States. The first co-production, *Die Abenteuer des Till Ulenspiegel* [*The Bold Adventure*, 1956], directed by Gérard Philipe was a film adaptation of Charles de Coster's novel of 1867 about the legendary national hero whose adventures served as an allegory for the struggle for independence in the Netherlands. The second co-production, Raymond Rouleau's *Die Hexen von Salem* [*The Crucible*, 1957], was based on Arthur Miller's 1953 critique of McCarthyism, *The Crucible* and had been adapted for the screen by Jean-Paul Sartre. The adaptation of Victor Hugo's 1862 classic historical epic *Die Elenden* [*Les Misérables*, dir. Jean-Paul Le Chanois, 1958] addressed the lower classes' striving for social justice and better life. Similarly, the fourth film adaptation, *Trübe Wasser* [*Muddy Waters*, 1960] was a socially critical moral tale based on Honoré de Balzac's historical novel *La Rabouilleuse* from 1842 and directed by Louis Daquin. Over the five years of their production, these films, formally speaking, represented a rather conservative approach to cinema, where entertainment seemed secondary to the representation on screen of serious highbrow literature. But precisely because of their realistic narratives and attention to European historical struggles, these four projects contested the laughter and glamour of US productions.

Both the narrative content of these films, and the real-life struggles and political beliefs of the French artists involved, attest to the films' implicit anti-American programme. Since 1946, left-leaning authors, directors and technical personnel in

France had formed the Centre National de Cinématographie in order to counteract the Hollywood hegemony on the continent. As Thomas Lindenberger points out, most French directors who worked with DEFA were members of the Labour Union or the French Communist Party.[39] As such, they naturally developed strong nationalist and protectionist sentiments recalling those in the 1920s. Gérard Philipe, the director of the first DEFA–French co-production, for instance, became known for his vehement protest against the 1947 import agreements between France and the US and this protest informs his adaptation of the *Ulenspiegel* tale. Another left-wing director, Henri Aisner, contacted DEFA manager Albert Wilkening in 1955 with a proposal to collaborate with him on several pro-communist projects. Aisner had assisted Max Ophüls in French–German co-productions in the 1930s, and after World War II had made numerous efforts to become re-involved with the Babelsberg studio. Last but not least, Jean Gabin, a key actor in early German–French co-productions, had embraced communism and drawn on these in his characterization of his role as Jean Valjean in *Die Elenden*.

This cooperation with French filmmakers encouraged East German artists to perpetuate their national agenda and to protest against DEFA's exclusion from European venues of cultural exchange. Consequently, in March 1955, an East German delegation went to Paris to negotiate participation in the Cannes Film Festival. This move was designed to counteract the detrimental consequences of the Hallstein Doctrine and secure greater visibility for GDR film art. Three months later, one of the delegates, Rudolf Böhm, reported the mission's success: unofficial screenings of two DEFA films at the festival: *Der Teufel vom Mühlenberg* [*The Devil from Mill Mountain*, 1955] directed by Herbert Ballmann, and Slatan Dudow's *Stärker als die Nacht* [*Stronger than the Night*, 1954]. Accordingly, he argued that film relations with France were of primary importance for the GDR's efforts to gain political and cultural prestige. 'The struggle for Germany's democratic unification', Böhm advised, 'is to be undertaken more forcefully in the film sector so that relations to West Germany's film industry are secured and expanded; at the same time, securing relations to France and England and establishing new relations to Italy will have an impact on our West German film strategy'.[40] DEFA's delegation to Cannes, therefore, was a serious step towards confirming French filmmakers' patronage of East German cinema, and suggests that, for DEFA, political priorities defined the initiatives for co-producing. Indeed, in the eyes of East German politicians, the involvement of such celebrated European writers as Jean-Paul Sartre, and such renowned directors and stars as Jean-Paul Le Chanois, Gérard Philipe,

Simone Signoret, Yves Montand, and Jean Gabin, was seen as evidence of left-wing European intellectuals' support for the GDR's socialist project. More importantly, the widespread reception that the co-productions enjoyed in over ten countries (including Finland, Sweden, Hungary, West Germany, Poland, Spain, Italy, the USA and Greece), boosted – at least temporarily –DEFA's reputation at home and abroad.

The immediate publicity that DEFA received in French and other Western media initially confirmed the promising prospects of such co-productions and even encouraged projects of a more overtly political nature. Such was the case with the last French–East German co-production, *Trübe Wasser*, a gesture of international solidarity extended to Louis Daquin. A prominent communist filmmaker in France, Daquin had lost his position due to his political convictions. His career had started as assistant director at Babelsberg in the 1930s, where he participated in a number of early dual-language co-productions. Like many other young talents, he came to the studio following the French–German bilateral agreement of 1929.[41] During World War II, Daquin was active in the French Resistance and subsequently assumed leading posts in the communist union of filmmakers. He experienced increasing financial difficulties in France after a media scandal surrounding his 1954 adaptation of Guy de Maupassant's *Bel Ami* that was filmed in the Soviet sector of occupied Vienna and was critical of French colonial politics. Four years later, in 1959, the French Communist Party negotiated with their Berlin comrades Daquin's involvement in one of the DEFA–French co-productions. The decision to take the director on board during the last joint project before the building of the Berlin Wall in 1961 made such ventures impossible, was motivated purely by political concerns, as Daquin's letter of thanks to the GDR's Minister of Culture suggests.[42] In addition to the flair that international solidarity among comrades lent to such co-productions, the East German studio played the leading role in selecting the production team, including – in particular – actors from the Berliner Ensemble and Hans Eisler as the composer of film music. The last joint film project was only released in East Germany and France, but never in the Federal Republic and had much less acclaim than previous prestige films.

By 1960, DEFA's growing discontent with French partners eventually led to the end of the collaborations. The problems first emerged from the French companies' hesitancy to include DEFA in the credits of their film versions. Even in the case of *Die Elenden* in 1957, Pathé had downplayed DEFA's role by presenting the double-feature as a French–Italian co-production 'with the cooperation of DEFA'.[43] In

1958, the French went as far as erasing East Germany and DEFA from their promotional leaflets for the Cannes film festival.[44] In this context, the GDR officials' hopes of using co-productions to establish the *de facto* recognition of the GDR's sovereignty were shattered. Even though DEFA had initially tolerated the privilege of genre aesthetics over the political message in the literary adaptations, it became clear that their partners' view of such collaborations was becoming increasingly ambivalent. As a consequence, two further projects, Louis Daquin's film adaptation of Émile Zola's 1892 novel, *La Débâcle*, as well as another Arthur Miller adaptation addressing anti-Semitism, *Focus*, failed. With DEFA's decision following the events of 1961 to seek future collaborations exclusively with Eastern European and socialist partners, DEFA's joint projects with French partners were suspended indefinitely.

Conclusion

The difficulties that DEFA ran into while trying to develop their co-production agenda in the 1950s were not unlike those encountered by the proponents of a utopian ideal of a European-wide cinema union in the 1920s. Both were cultural projects rooted in prevailing ideas of internationalism that proved hard to realize, especially in the conditions of war-ravaged Europe. Likewise, the practice of co-production and developing a cultural policy shaped by political expectations in both the interwar years and in postwar Europe encountered similar obstacles and constraints. In both historical contexts, pragmatic forms of collaboration, such as co-productions and exchange of services, emerged from a need to compete with the American film industry and to strengthen the home market. In this sense, the resurgence of the ideals of Film Europe in postwar alliances between the East Germans and French can be seen not only as evidence of the enduring nature of previously successful transnational contacts, but also as evidence of the extent to which the ideal for a shared European culture developed from a desire to protect and promote national cinemas. Nonetheless, in both cases, the economic and political strategies underpinning the endeavours made to reach out to European partners and audiences were generally justified by means of ideology. This ideological motivation behind the impetus for cooperation and the competing interests of the state, the market and the filmmakers themselves posed insurmountable challenges to the long-term realization of the proposed ideals.

Mariana Ivanova is Assistant Professor in German Studies at Miami University in Oxford, OH. She has published on 1960s DEFA 'Wall' films, the memory of the GDR in contemporary German cinema, as well as on DEFA co-productions with West German partners in the 1950s.

Notes

1. Translated by Thomas J. Saunders, quoted in Andrew Higson and Richard Maltby (eds), 'Film Europe' and 'Film America'. Cinema, Commerce and Cultural Exchange 1920–1939, Exeter: University of Exeter Press, 1999, p. 334. All other translations from the German, unless noted otherwise, are by the author.
2. Similar agreements were signed in postwar Europe to counter the inflow of American imports. On the role of co-productions in postwar Europe, see Anne Jäckel, 'Dual Nationality Film Productions in Europe after 1945', Historical Journal of Film, Radio and Television 23.3 (2003), 231–43, as well as Tim Bergfelder, International Adventures. German Popular Cinema and European Co-Productions in the 1960s, New York, Oxford: Berghahn, 2005.
3. See Lenny Borger, 'Ufas Russen. Die Emigranten von Montreuil bis Babelsberg', in Hans-Michael Bock and Michael Töteberg (eds), Das Ufa-Buch. Kunst und Krisen – Stars und Regisseure – Wirtschaft und Politik. Die internationale Geschichte von Deutschlands größtem Film-Konzern. Frankfurt am Main: Zweitausendeins, 1992, pp. 236–39; Sybille M. Sturm and Arthur Wohlgemuth (eds), Hallo? Berlin? Ici Paris! Deutsch-französische Filmbeziehungen 1918–1939, Munich: edition text + kritik, 1996; Jörg Schöning and Johannes Roschlau (eds), Film im Herzen Europas. Deutsch-tschechische Filmbeziehungen im 20. Jahrhundert, Berlin: absolut Medien, 2007.
4. Andrew Higson, 'Film-Europa. Kulturpolitik und industrielle Praxis', in Sybille M. Sturm and Arthur Wohlgemuth, pp. 63–76.
5. See, for instance, David Bathrick, 'From UFA to DEFA. Past and Present in Early GDR Films', in Jost Hermand and Marc Silberman (eds), Contentious Memories. Looking Back at the GDR, New York: Lang, 1998, pp. 169–88.
6. Anonymous author, 'Europäische Monroe-Doktrin', Lichtbildbühne, 1 March 1924, translated by Brenda Benthien in Higson and Maltby, pp. 328–30 (p. 329).
7. Anonymous author, 'Amerikanisierung der UFA?', Lichtbildbühne, 9 January 1926.
8. Anonymous author, 'Europas Filme den Europäern!', Film-Kurier, 11 November 1925.
9. Anonymous author, 'Ufa's neuer Kurs', Lichtbildbühne, 15 September 1927.
10. Quoted in Albert Wilkening, Betriebsgeschichte des VEB DEFA Studio für Spielfilme, 3 vols., Berlin: VEB DEFA, 1981, vol. 1, p. 76.
11. Ibid., p. 78.
12. Bergfelder, pp. 24–25.
13. Cited in Christiane Mückenberger and Günter Jordan (eds), 'Sie sehen selbst, Sie hören selbst...'. Eine Geschichte der DEFA von ihren Anfängen bis 1949, Marburg: Hitzeroth, 1999, p. 375.
14. See Pommer's quote in Ursula Hardt, From Caligari to California. Erich Pommer's Life in the International Film Wars, Providence RI, Oxford: Berghahn, 1996, p. 180.

15. See Thomas Saunders, 'Hollywood in Berlin. American Cinema and Weimar Germany, Berkeley, Los Angeles, London: University of California Press, 1994, pp. 117–44 ('The Hollywood Invasion. Amerikanisierung and Amerikamüdigkeit').
16. Saunders, p. 127.
17. Anonymous author, 'Amerika, hörst du die Pfeife?', Film-Kurier, 10 September 1926.
18. Felix Henseleit, 'Film Europa', Reichsfilmblatt, 24 July 1926 (trans. Thomas J. Saunders, in Higson and Maltby, p. 340).
19. Mückenberger and Jordan, p. 25.
20. See Thomas Heimann, DEFA, Künstler und SED-Politik. Zum Verhältnis von Kulturpolitik und Filmproduktion in der SBZ/DDR 1945 bis 1959 [= Beiträge zur Film- und Fernsehgesellschaft, vol. 46], Berlin: Vistas, 1994.
21. This foreign policy doctrine received its name from the leading West German civil servant at the German Foreign Office, Walter Hallstein. The Hallstein Doctrine announced in September 1955 that the Federal Republic would not maintain diplomatic relations with any state that recognizes the GDR as a sovereign state.
22. See Richard Maltby, 'The Cinema and the League of Nations', in Higson and Maltby, pp. 82–115 (p. 82). Maltby provides an excellent account of the involvement of the League of Nations in the affairs of world cinema, ranging from European film producers' push for cultural resistance to the US industry to 'an engineering acquiescence' in the 1930s (p. 106).
23. Anonymous author, 'Amerikanisierung der Ufa?', Lichtbildbühne, 9 January 1926.
24. Thomas Saunders, 'Germany and Film Europe', in Higson and Maltby, pp. 157–80 (p. 165).
25. Ernst Jäger, 'Die Einkreisung Deutschlands', Film-Kurier, 9 June 1925.
26. Kristin Thompson, 'The Rise and Fall of Film Europe', in Higson and Maltby, pp. 56–81 (p. 61).
27. Letter by Albert Wilkening dated 1 June 1955 [= BArch DR 1 /4701], p. 14.
28. Letter by Fritz Apelt, State Secretary of the Ministry of Culture to the Central Committee of the SED, dated 1 June 1955 [= BArch DR 1 / 4701], p. 66. Cited in Marc Silberman, 'Learning from the enemy. DEFA-French Co-Productions of the 1950s', Film History 18 (2006), 21–45 (25). Translation by Marc Silberman.
29. Such examples provide not only these DEFA co-productions with French partners, but also films made with other socialist countries, such as Sterne (Stars, 1959). Made by DEFA director Konrad Wolf (at the start of his career) and the Bulgarian Jewish scriptwriter Angel Wagenstein, Sterne tells the story of Sephardic Jews being deported to Auschwitz through the territory of Bulgaria. This story seemed inconvenient to the Bulgarian socialist government at the time and the film was banned. Nevertheless, the East German filmmakers and studio insisted that the film would be shown at the Cannes Festival as a Bulgarian production. Sterne became the first film with DEFA participation officially shown in Cannes and won the 1959 audience's award for best film.
30. For a detailed account on prewar German–French co-productions, see Francis Courtade, 'Die deutsch-französischen Koproduktionen', in Heike Hurst and Heiner Gassen (eds), Kameradschaft-Querelle. Kino zwischen Deutschland und Frankreich, Munich: Institut Français de Munich, 1991, pp. 159–172.
31. Joseph Garncarz, 'Made in Germany. Multiple-Language Versions and the Early German Sound Cinema', in Higson and Maltby, pp. 249–73 (p. 250).
32. Garncarz, pp. 253–54.
33. Higson, 'Film-Europa', p. 74.

34. Andrew Higson, 'Cultural Policy and Industrial Practice. Film Europe and the International Film Congresses of the 1920s', in Higson and Maltby, pp. 117–31 (p. 128).
35. While the film industries of the 1920s were concerned about their market share falling into the hands of Hollywood, for the socialist state-owned studios, reaching out to the audiences had highest priority. In both cases we can observe a desire to convince the domestic viewers of the value of the 'homegrown' product and to cultivate their taste for European films.
36. On the 1920s practices for film co-production, see Thompson, p. 78.
37. 'Protokoll zur 23. DEFA Vorstandsitzung' signed Albert Wilkening and dated 14 April 1948 [= BArch DR 117 / 21701], p. 118.
38. See Silberman, 21–22.
39. Thomas Lindenberger, 'Terriblement démodée: Zum Scheitern blockübergreifender Filmproduktion im Kalten Krieg (DDR-Frankreich, 1956–1960)' in Antoine Fleury and Lubor Jilek (eds), Une Europe malgré tout, 1945–1990, Contacts et réseaux culturels, intellectuels et scientifiques entre Européens dans la guerre froide, Brussels: Lang, 2009, pp. 283–96.
40. Report from 6 June 1955 [= BArch DR 1 / 4644], cited in Silberman, pp. 40–41.
41. On Daquin's later career at Babelsberg in the 1930s, including directing the French version of Gerhard Lamprecht's *Der Spieler* [*The Gambler*, 1938] see Silberman, p. 37.
42. Louis Daquin, letter to Erich Wendt from 25 October 1959, quoted in Lindenberger, p. 295.
43. See also Marc Silberman's discussion of the production history of *Die Elenden*, pp. 35–37.
44. As in the case with *Die Hexen von Salem*, Pathé Cinéma and other French companies and distributors ran into difficulties with an exact definition of DEFA in the film credits. The reason was political, as the GDR was not yet officially recognized by France and an open collaboration with the East German state film studio brought bureaucratic problems. To avoid these, the French partners wanted to label the films as 'Franco-Italian co-productions with the collaboration of DEFA' and although initially accepting this fact, GDR functionaries later rejected further collaborations wholesale. See Silberman, 26.

CHAPTER 5

Betting on Entertainment
The Cold War Scandal of *Spielbank-Affäre* [*Casino Affair*, 1957]

Stefan Soldovieri

With its exotic Mediterranean locations, sumptuous casino interiors, gangsters, fashion models, and themes of drug smuggling and corruption, Artur Pohl's *Spielbank-Affäre* offered sights and stories that stand out among DEFA's often unspectacular subjects. In fact, *Spielbank-Affäre* was a troubled production from the start. Conceived as high-production-value vehicle for enhancing DEFA's image abroad, the film was produced in an inter-German partnership that promised access to an international market. In the end, the effort to package a critique of West German society in an entertaining story failed on a grand scale, provoking what was the most public inter-German film scandal of the 1950s. Released in two versions (widescreen colour for the West German market and black and white for GDR distribution) *Spielbank-Affäre* is an instructive example of the complex and conflicting interests of DEFA and film officials in negotiating an entertainment film strategy. At stake was more than the suitability of titillating material for socialist screens, but rather the status of the GDR as a modern society and alternative to the West.

If *Spielbank-Affäre* (released as *Parkplatz zur großen Sehnsucht* [*A Car Park Called Desire*] in the Federal Republic) touched on a number of controversial themes, the production itself was typical of DEFA's pragmatic entertainment film strategy for much of the decade before the construction of the Berlin Wall in August 1961. The GDR film industry pursued over the course of its history an array of strategies to address the entertainment demands of East German cinema-goers. Having inherited a vast repository from the UFA era of the 1930s and 1940s, film programmers had access to a seemingly unending supply of comedies, melodramas and musicals for GDR cinemas and, increasingly, television. Imports from a host of countries in East and West also played a shifting but significant role in supplying cinemas with entertaining content right up until the very end of the GDR and included a relatively wide range of films, from Hollywood blockbusters to popular West German features such as the Edgar Wallace film adaptations that played from the late 1950s to the early 1970s.[1]

In terms of domestic production, DEFA also took recourse to different approaches over its history; throughout most of the 1950s, for instance, the studio drew on a trans-border pool of film talent in mounting light entertainment. Until DEFA was compelled by the end of the decade to sever such employment relationships with film professionals not residing in Germany's eastern half, DEFA relied quite heavily on actors, directors and a range of film technicians and experts to ensure at least a baseline of popular subjects made in the GDR. The sealing of the inter-German divide in 1961 effectively ended this trans-border strategy, exemplified by films such as Hans Heinrich's *Meine Frau macht Musik* [*My Wife Sings*, 1958], a production that consciously sought to address a still-connected German audience.

The production of *Spielbank-Affäre* reflected not only the reality of mobile film talent, but the impetus of the Socialist Unity Party's (SED) 'New Course' (*Neuer Kurs*) in the wake of Stalin's death and the fallout over the domestic scandal of the worker's revolt of 17 June 1953. The New Course promised increased attention to the needs of GDR citizens in a variety of areas, including the production of consumer goods and the availability of leisure-time offerings, as well as new efforts to improve relations between the GDR and the FRG. In terms of film policy, the New Course meant a new openness with respect to the West German film industry, resulting in an increase of imports beginning in 1954 and the promise at least to remove barriers to economic and artistic exchanges. There would also be new initiatives to enhance DEFA's image abroad.[2]

Producing for Germany

The plan to mount *Spielbank-Affäre* as a German–German co-production arose early in the filmmaking process and was very much in keeping with the New Course's rhetoric of cooperation with the West. Reflecting the spirit of the new policy, DEFA dramaturges reacted to the first screenplay submitted by Artur Pohl in early July 1955 with guarded enthusiasm. DEFA dramaturges, who were responsible for ensuring that the films produced by the studio could pass the Ministry of Culture's licensing board, recognized immediately that the script was likely to draw scrutiny. Yet they also saw it as an exciting story with the potential to effectively deliver a political message. Film officials in the Ministry of Culture's *Hauptverwaltung Film* also endorsed the co-production gambit at an early stage, gaining an increasing stake in bringing the production of *Spielbank-Affäre* to a successful conclusion – even as massive pressure began to come down on the film from the Minister of Culture himself, Johannes R. Becher.

Based on a report by Hans von Oettingen, who had been a public relations officer for a casino in Wiesbaden and the managing editor of West German periodicals such as *Casino-Revue*, the story set in the casino milieu in the West combined social problem film conventions with melodrama.[3] Already in March 1955, DEFA had reached a tentative agreement on an option for Oettingen's story and sent a copy to the GDR's film bureau, the *Hauptverwaltung Film*, for a preliminary testing of the political waters. According to the studio, Artur Pohl, who had being working at DEFA for several years, was 'burning' to get to work on turning the material into a film treatment.[4]

In the versions ultimately experienced by German audiences, *Spielbank-Affäre* relates the story of a power struggle over a casino in a West German spa town. Gallinger is a wealthy casino owner and an influential man in the resort. Martinez, an equally rich, Marseille-based casino and drug cartel Mafioso, is bent on muscling in on Gallinger's business on the road to monopolizing the European casino industry. The plan is to smuggle counterfeit chips into Gallinger's casino as a way of compromising his business and making him vulnerable to a takeover. The film's romantic storyline is provided by Gerhard and Sybille, a young couple who become caught up in this power struggle for different reasons. She is a model and aspiring actress struggling to make ends meet. Although she is not a gambler out of passion, Sybille needs money for acting school – and to pay the monthly instalments on the new furniture she and Gerhard have bought for their apartment. Having met the smooth-talking Dr Busch in a chance encounter, she agrees to play with the bogus chips he gives her, naively believing his story that she is merely helping him test his gambling system. The conflict comes to a head when Martinez makes a swaggering appearance at Gallinger's casino, thinking that he is about to triumph over his West German rival. But Gallinger is able to turn the tables. Having squeezed Busch for information about Martinez's illegal operations in betting and drugs – and then having had him killed – Gallinger can diffuse the emerging counterfeiting scandal and outwit Martinez. Meanwhile, a call from Gallinger to the owner of the newspaper for whom Gerhard is working results in the quashing of his exposé. Without Dr Busch to provide testimony, Gerhard is unable to extricate Sybille from the clutches of Gallinger, who has become aware of Sybille's unwitting role in the counterfeit scheme. Now Gallinger can deny that any wrongdoings have occurred. In the GDR release of the film, the story ends here, with Gallinger's public proclamation that there will be no trial, since 'no one has been harmed'. The final message could hardly be clearer: in the restorative Adenauer state the corrupt escape justice as the press stands idly by. The West German version on the other hand contains two subsequent scenes in which Gerhard learns that Dr Busch's death is being investigated and that the evidence seems to be leading to Marseille, where Martinez has been arrested. Gerhard vows to follow this trail with Sybille at his side. And so a happy end has been rescued for DEFA's West German partner.

In her review of a first treatment of April 1955, Marieluise Steinhauer, managing dramaturge on the project, praised Pohl's rewrite of Oettingen's tantalizing material about the West German casino business.[5] According to Steinhauer, the story had obvious box office appeal and would be marketable in capitalist countries. She also endorsed the film's politics, which were not presented as a 'boring lecture', but took the form of an 'exciting power struggle' with an underlying 'humanistic and moral' message. Based on Steinhauer's positive view of the story's potential, Pohl's treatment, which had the working title 'Money is a Hard Business', was discussed among studio dramaturges at a story conference on 15 July 1955. Not all of those present at the July story meeting were as convinced that the dramatic gangster story could be the vehicle for launching a substantial ideological critique of the West, however. According to dramaturge Karl-Georg Egel, this was not going to be a film that could offer real social critique emanating from a realistic story.[6] Although the treatment at this point suggested the involvement of high-level personalities under Adenauer in a corrupt system, Egel argued that it was not suited to delivering a broadly humanistic and democratic message because it neither showed the roots of exploitation under capitalism, nor did it assume the perspective of the oppressed. In this way, Egel suggested, the story compared unfavourably with social dramas such as Edward Dmytryk's *Give Us This Day* (1949), which played in the GDR as *Haus der Sehnsucht*, or neorealist films like Giuseppe de Santis's *Roma ore 11* [*Rome 11 O'clock*, 1954]. The questions were also raised as to whether it made sense that nearly a quarter of the films currently being produced at the studio were set in West Germany, and why DEFA should be interested in a story about a battle between two gangsters. There were also more specific criticisms regarding the characterization of the young couple, particularly the actress, Sybille. While there was some sympathy towards the theme of Sybille's addiction, for instance, which could potentially be framed as a phenomenon of 'imperialist exploitation', this personal struggle was seen as too dominant in the story and thus an obstacle in terms of her potential as a character with whom viewers could identify. Sybille, it was argued, should appear as a figure more capable of love and turning her life around. In fact, the issue of her drug dependency eventually disappeared from her story. Although he 'need not be converted into a communist', Gerhard was to become a more active figure, both in helping Sybille, and in his quest to uncover the dark dealings at the casino. Egel also insisted that it was crucial that Gerhard's efforts ultimately fall short, shattering his illusions about the power of the media to combat corruption. The suggestion was also made to deepen the shallow reach of the screenplay's political critique by implicating 'important leading functionaries in the Adenauer system'. With the tentative backing of film officials already in place – Steinhauer referred in the meeting to previous consultation between the *Hauptverwaltung Film* and DEFA's head office – the project received the green light despite these and other criticisms. The results of the meeting suggest the extent to which the GDR film industry was willing to bet on genre and entertainment as a way of being present in West German cinemas in particular.

A number of these ideological considerations flowed into the subsequent screenplay that was reviewed again by DEFA dramaturges on 25 July 1955.[7] The ideological stage is set in the first scenes depicting the casino, which is described as a place whose days of splendour are long gone:

> *Under the low-hanging green shades of the roulette lamps there is nothing to recall the images of the glorious history of this room, no recollections of Russian nobility and its immeasurable wealth, no Babylonian confusion of languages, no ostrich feathers nodding on elegant hats, no bouncing skirts and frills, no sign of the feverish passion of a Dostoyevsky, not a single pale beauty with consuming fire in her eyes – only the sober faces of West German reality emerge in the dim light, people from the streets, offices and businesses, indistinguishable from a respectable movie audience.*[8]

In addition to casting an aura of decline upon the casino setting, this version more explicitly laid out the power dynamics surrounding the gambling industry. As early as the second scene there is reference to a protest of the town citizens regarding problems at the casino and the roles of the municipal government and minister in awarding the gambling permit to the shady casino proprietor (going by the name of Strakowsky in this screenplay). Strakowsky's rival is the Loewe AG of Munich – also a casino stakeholder – that is fronting a former government official, Kröger, to stir up damaging rumours about Strakowsky's business. In this scenario Kröger makes public trumped-up evidence that funds promised to the city by the casino are flowing into Swiss bank accounts instead of into the improvement of municipal facilities, a planned golf course and the renovation of the town concert hall. The meeting in this screenplay version also provided an opportunity for a more fundamental critique of the casino delivered by an everyday citizen who insists that the issue is not about who controls the casino, but the casino itself. In the end, this perspective is underscored when it is revealed that the Loewe AG bankrolls Kröger.

In later, less politicized versions of the screenplay, and the final film in both East and West versions, the civic airing of the scandal has been omitted and the Kröger character 'demoted' to the rank of a crooked croupier who is unable to extricate himself from the casino mafia.[9] In a similar bid to dissipate the story's ideological critique, the Loewe AG has been replaced by the foreign mobster Martinez. Designed to appease the West German partner, this change heightened the entertainment value of the story with attractive Mediterranean settings while simultaneously displacing the critique of corrupt business interests in West German society. This version also still contained the controversial subplot of Sybille's drug addiction – fed by a much more sinister Dr Busch than would appear in German cinemas – as well as her death in the final scenes. As in the final story, Gerhard eventually uncovers enough evidence to write his exposé, but his editor refuses to publish his work, citing the fear of lawsuits and the loss of advertising revenue from the casinos. Driven by his grief over Sybille's death, Gerhard remains determined to pursue the story, even as the headlines of the local papers trumpet the successes of the casino industry.

Commenting on the July 1955 version, Steinhauer reported that Pohl had generally accommodated the wishes of her department. Sybille was now softer and more sympathetically portrayed and clearly a victim of Dr Busch's perfidy and her social circumstances as opposed to her 'pathological desires'.[10] Gerhard, too, had become a more dynamic figure, yet without sacrificing any of his boyish charm. An effort had also been made to implicate the West German government in the casino scandal through the introduction of a state minister who makes an appearance at a shareholder's meeting. Reminiscent of the unresolved narratives of West German social problem films of the period – films like Georg Tressler's *Die Halbstarken* [*Teenage Wolfpack*, 1956] or Frank Wisbar's *Nasser Asphalt* [*Wet Pavement*, 1958] – the tragic ending with Sybille's death was still a matter of contention, as it would remain throughout. Despite a number of disputed issues, the *Hauptverwaltung Film* nonetheless gave the go-ahead to begin production in November 1955. A key factor for his office's approval of the screenplay, according to its head Anton Ackermann, was the fact that the film was to be made as co-production that would be released on the Western market and would be suitable for international festivals. At the same time, Ackermann reiterated the *Hauptverwaltung Film*'s expectations regarding the film's politics and expressed doubts about whether Pohl was the right man for the job.[11] Unsatisfied with the changes that had been made, the film official expected significantly more to be done to exploit the topic's potential for a critique of capitalism. Ackermann also insisted that the filmmakers transform the heroine into a figure with whom the audience can identify as she tragically succumbs to the social conditions in West Germany. Gerhard, too, ought to appear as a true opponent of the capitalist world. Ackermann complained that the reporter's investigations did not fundamentally question the casino as a capitalist phenomenon. Instead Gerhard's efforts merely aimed at keeping the casino out of the hands of outsiders. Finally, the *Hauptverwaltung Film* head criticized the absence of working-class opposition to the casino that would help expose the true class conflicts at work.

Casting for Germany

Work on the existing screenplay was diverted with the finalizing of the co-production agreement with West Berlin film businessman Erich Mehl, who was to act as co-producer.[12] A familiar face at DEFA, Mehl was the head of the Stockholm-based Pandora company, which was participating in the DEFA features *Leuchtfeuer* [*Signal Fire*, 1955] and *Das Fräulein von Scuderi* [*Mademoiselle de Scudéry*, 1955]. The agreement between Mehl and DEFA, which was signed in December 1955, shared many of the features of the co-production arrangements that the studio used to augment its entertainment film output and promote its films abroad. While the contract allowed that a writer hired by the co-producer would revise the screenplay written by Artur Pohl, DEFA maintained considerable editorial control with a veto right over the final version. As part of the financial terms of the contract, DEFA would pay the director, cinematographer, set designer and composer. Mehl, on the other hand, was responsible for providing actors for the principal roles of the romantic couple and competing casino gangsters, as well as casting smaller roles with actors that would appeal to a West German audience. DEFA retained the right to reject casting decisions made by Mehl and his associates. Also on Mehl's payroll were five experienced croupiers to man the casino tables on screen. In addition, the co-producer assumed the financial burden for a number of other aspects of the production designed to increase the film's overall entertainment value. These included location shooting outside the GDR – plus any special props and sets – as well as costumes. Finally, the contract permitted Mehl to produce a musical number, at his own cost, to be used in the version of the film displayed in the countries to which he had the rights. These countries were the Federal Republic and West Berlin, Switzerland, Italy, France, Sweden, Spain, Yugoslavia, South America, the United States and Japan. Sung by Eva May, a minor pop singer whose career peaked in mid 1950s, the 'Cha Cha Bim Bam Bum' number provides in both the Eastern and Western releases of *Spielbank-Affäre* little more than a backdrop to Gerhard's investigations at the bar where Kröger works. DEFA was able to secure special conditions in exchange for ceding distribution rights for these countries. If the final product was screened in the FRG, for instance – not a given in the light of DEFA's patchy record in accessing the West German market – DEFA would receive in exchange five foreign titles for free distribution in the GDR, including East Berlin. Here, too, DEFA retained a right of veto, in which case the studio would receive in lieu of the international films 15% of the net profits of the production in the FRG and West Berlin for a period of five years. Each of the partners would have the right to make cuts to the film to satisfy censorship regulations. Finally, the contract regulated DEFA's mention in the credits and set what would turn out to be a wholly unrealistic deadline of 1 September 1956 for distribution to begin.

The actors supplied by Mehl as a part of the co-production contract were intended to ensure that the film would fit into a pan-German film market, and the studio had every reason to be satisfied with its partner's casting success. In negotiating for Western currency to pay for the expensive Western actors, DEFA managing director Albert Wilkening emphasized that Mehl had been able to secure the services of actors of a stature unavailable in the GDR.[13] For the suavely sinister Dr Busch, Mehl had enlisted the services of the prolific Peter Pasetti, whose previous credits included Georg Jacoby's *Sensation in San Remo* (1951), *Eine Nacht in Venedig* [*A Night in Venice*, 1953], and Franz Antel's *Verliebter Sommer* [*Summer of Love*, 1954]. Typically cast in West German productions as the self-assured bon vivant, Pasetti was perfect for the role of Dr Busch, even if it would be his only one in a DEFA film. Mehl also showed a deft hand in arranging for the participation of the eminent Rudolf Forster, who had name recognition going back to the Weimar Republic and would enjoy a West German career stretching into the late 1960s. Most recently he had acted in the Harald Braun films *Regine* (1956) and *Der letzte Mann* [*The Last Laugh*, 1955], an update of F.W. Murnau's classic also featuring Romy Schneider and Hans Albers. An extremely familiar face in the German film landscape in everything from *Heimat* dramas and comedies to adventure stories and costume dramas, Forster was working on no fewer than five West German productions when he signed up for the role of casino boss Gallinger in *Spielbank-Affäre*, which would also be his only involvement with DEFA. Willi Kleinau, cast as the Mediterranean gangster Martinez, was no stranger in the Babelsberg studio. Already an established theatre actor when he began his film career at DEFA in 1949 with *Die blauen Schwerter* [*Blue Swords*], by the time shooting for *Spielbank-Affäre* began in the summer of 1956, Kleinau was featuring in West German productions as well. Between 1955 and 1956, he appeared in the revue film *Liebe, Tanz und 1000 Schlager* [*Love, Dance and 1000 Hits*, 1955], the *Heimatfilm*, *Waldwinter* [*Winter Forest*, 1956], the literary adaptation *Der Hauptmann von Köpenick* [*The Captain of Köpenick*, 1956], and the marriage drama *Wie ein Sturmwind* [*Like a Storm Wind*, 1957]. In fact, Kleinau was perhaps the only major actor to perform in lead roles in films produced in both German states during the height of the Cold War in the 1950s.[14]

Less-established actors were also a part of casting the film for all of Germany. The selection of Gertrud Kückelmann as the aspiring acting student, Sybille, points to the interests of Mehl's company in mounting a film that would fit into the landscape of West German genre films. In 1953, Kückelmann had appeared in Kurt Hoffmann's *Musik bei Nacht* [*Music by Night*], a comedy of errors with musical numbers, in which she played the owner of a rundown tavern. A year later she appeared in *Die goldene Pest* [*The Golden Plague*], set in the black-market milieu near an American army base. As Sybille, she reprises this latter role as an innocent in a degraded environment. At the time of her engagement for *Spielbank-Affäre*, she was embroiled in the scandal around *Frucht ohne Liebe* [*Fruit Without Love*, 1956], a film thematizing artificial insemination. The massive protest mounted by religious groups in West Germany in the wake of the film's release caused producers to shy away from the actress and may even have been the reason she accepted the part in Pohl's film. In any case, it would be her last major cinematic role.[15] Her partner in the film, Jan Hendriks in the principal role of journalist Gerhard Fischer, may also have had his reasons for taking a chance with the film company in the Eastern zone. Although he had a number of acting credits to his name, Hendriks had not had a breakthrough lead role. His first film credit was bound to have found favour with DEFA, namely *Sündige Grenze* [*Border of Sin*, 1951], a social problem film about cross-border smuggling directed by Robert A. Stemmle. Franz Arzdorf, in the minor role of the casino floor manager, played in both GDR and West German productions until the fortification of the inter-German border. His first feature-length DEFA films were *Der Ochse von Kulm* [*The Ox of Kulm*, 1955] and the biopic *Thomas Müntzer* (1955). *Spielbank-Affäre* was his last DEFA engagement.

The technical staff also included film professionals based outside East Germany who did not have long-term DEFA contracts. Costume designer Vera Mügge, for instance, worked on several DEFA films, starting with *Rat der Götter* [*Council of the Gods*, 1949] and *Die lustigen Weiber von Windsor* [*The Merry Wives of Windsor*, 1950]. Her last feature was Joachim Hasler's *Gejagt bis zum Morgen* [*Persecuted Until Morning*, 1957]. Her West German productions of the same period included films like *Mädchen mit Zukunft* [*Girls With a Future*, 1954], *Ist Mama nicht fabelhaft?* [*Isn't Mama Wonderful?*, 1958] and *Meine 99 Bräute* [*My 99 Broads*, 1958]. Berlin-based film composer Martin Böttcher was another commuter to Babelsberg whose participation in *Spielbank-Affäre* (his only DEFA collaboration) was facilitated by Mehl, according to the details of the co-production contract. Director Pohl was also on the DEFA payroll as an 'external' director, drawing, according to a 1954 DEFA foreign currency report, 1,500 West German marks monthly.[16]

Scripting the Scandal

Following the agreement with Mehl, Pohl drafted a new, 80-scene treatment reflecting the new context of the inter-German partnership. This 'intermediary treatment', written by Artur Pohl with the help of an outside writer hired and paid for by Mehl, was summarily rejected by the *Hauptverwaltung Film* as a kitschy crime story in which the heroine is reduced to an incurable drug addict destined to die at the end of the film. According to the *Hauptverwaltung Film*, Anne Pfeuffer, then a staffer in DEFA's script unit, had complained that Pohl's rewrite had been undertaken in utter disregard of the well-known recommendations of her office. Nothing had been done to unmask the workings of the casino business. Instead, 'Martinez's dark deeds and the life of luxury and comfort have become the most attractive things in the world'.[17] As opposed to the previous version in which the waning casino functioned as a metaphor for West German society at large, this latest screenplay begins in Monte Carlo with a lavish song and dance number with the theme 'Life is like Roulette'.[18] Instead of succumbing to injuries sustained when she runs into the path of a truck, Sybille survives to encourage Gerhard to do what he has to do to get the story about corruption out – regardless of the consequences for her. As the couple embrace, fireworks go off in the background to the sounds of an outdoor concert.

Negotiations between the DEFA Studio executives, director Pohl, co-producer Mehl, and the *Hauptverwaltung Film* continued unabated over the next four months following the rejection of the new treatment. By 5 April 1956 Pohl had completed what was being called the fourth screenplay version and submitted it to the dramaturgy department for scrutiny. In her assessment, Pfeuffer summarized a number of points that continued to trouble film bureaucrats in the Ministry of Culture. Pohl was once again taken to task for not taking full advantage of the story's 'possibilities for unmasking the capitalist system and for creating truly profound and real human conflicts'.[19] Pfeuffer characterized the fourth screenplay as an imperfect but acceptable attempt to balance the politics of the first screenplay version with the demands of the co-producer for a more exciting and attractive film. Once again, the film's denouement drew special criticism for trying to reconcile everyone and everything and failing to clearly identify the victors in the battle against the capitalist casino mafia. Particularly tacky, in Pfeuffer's view, was the characterization of Sybille, whose own experiences appear as little more than a bad dream from which she has awoken. At a subsequent meeting chief dramaturge Rudi Böhm and Steinhauer again put pressure on Pohl to address the ending, extracting the promise at least to consider an alternative ending. In fact, the next screenplay had not really resolved the issue between the West German producers and DEFA, but rather proposed two different finales. The first, which would ultimately form the unresolved, social-problem-film denouement of the East German release, ended with a triumphant casino head announcing to the press that the charges against him have been dropped and that no one has suffered any harm. The second ending offered a happy end in keeping with the wishes of the Mehl group.

Despite the ongoing uncertainty about how the film would actually end and continued revisions that would produce a fifth screenplay dated 16 May 1956, the *Hauptverwaltung Film* recommended confirming the production start. This 'final version' had in fact changed very little in terms of the content of the story, but efforts had been made to make the dialogue more lively. Reporting to the head of her office, Anton Ackermann, Pfeuffer noted that the controversial ending had not been affected by revisions due to the co-producer's insistence that the film conclude on a harmonious note. As a compromise, dramaturge Steinhauer had suggested reviving scenes that had been slated for removal but were still contained in both of the previous screenplay versions of 5 April and 16 May 1956.[20] According to Pfeuffer's report, the four scenes depicting the apprehension of Martinez by police could be easily cut for the East German release, and Steinhauer had already cleared this gambit with the director and the West German partner.[21] In both screenplays, the arrest of the casino gangster directly precedes the happy end in the final scene in which Gerhard, walking arm in arm with a convalescing Sybille, sees a poster promoting his sensational multi-part exposé of the casino affair. In a nod to the critics of this rosy outcome, the set directions indicated that the advertisement is half-concealed by more recent ones promising even more spectacular revelations.[22] Pfeuffer recommended accepting DEFA's solution instead of continuing to fight a hopeless battle for a different ending.[23] As it turned out, neither the arrest scenes nor the happy end promised in these screenplays would make it to German cinemas.

Shooting finally began on 4 June 1956, with the casino scene in Babelsberg's large south hall.[24] This major set had already been built and decorated by late December 1955 at the urging of director Pohl, who was impatient to get the delay-plagued production started. As the project's production head complained, continued haggling over the screenplay had delayed the production start, causing significant cost overruns for the rental of the studio space. Additional costs accrued due to preliminary tests with lenses and film stock as camera operator Joachim Hasler familiarized himself with the new Totalvision technology. Further costs and delays were caused by serious injuries sustained by actor Peter Pasetti (Dr Busch in the film) in a car accident en route from Berlin to Munich in mid July 1956. In late February 1957 Pasetti was finally in a condition that allowed him to be flown in to perform his remaining scenes. Still on crutches, Pasetti had to wear dark glasses due to an injury to his eyes. In the meantime, tragedy had struck again with another serious car crash that kept Pohl out of the director's chair and left the bulk of the work to camera operator Joachim Hasler, who completed shooting on 12 March 1957.

The Soft Power of Set Design

The production of *Spielbank-Affäre* as a German–German co-production conceived to popularize DEFA's brand abroad reflected the impetus of the New Course to actively engage the West. Still, the struggle for ideological ground continued unabated, and on various levels. One flashpoint for film administrators was the fear that East German audiences would be blinded by the film's visual attractions and the associated links to leisure, consumerism and mobility (Fig. 5.1). The causes for such concerns are evident in the opening sequences of the two release versions. The opening sequence in the widescreen colour version, for instance,

Figure 5.1: *Spielbank-Affäre* (1957). Sybille and Gerhard in their apartment. Too many comforts for East German eyes? DVD screen capture.

offers sweeping and unobstructed vistas of the unnamed Mediterranean city hosting the fashion show for which Sybille will do her turns as a model. This sequence in the East German release is of an entirely different quality. Shot in standard format from a different camera inside the bus transporting the models – cinematographers produced three different negatives in accord with the stipulations of the contract with Mehl – the panoramas are not only transformed by the transition to black and white, but are less immersive since they are framed by the bus windshield through which they have been shot.

It was not just the exotic resort locations that were the problem, but private and domestic spaces in the film that exuded an international modernism that would not be officially embraced in the GDR until well into the 1960s.[25] These included, among other scenes, Gerhard and Sybille's apartment, Gallinger's casino office, Martinez's penthouse suite (Fig. 5.2) and Dr Busch's villa. Officials and studio executives screening the film for the first time could not have been entirely

Figure 5.2: Mafioso Martinez in his Mediterranean penthouse. DVD screen capture.

prepared for the highly stylized, modernistic decor of Gallinger's executive suite, for instance.

During the development of the story, the casino boss's office had been intermittently described as a boudoir-like room full of rococo furniture and satin-hung lamps.[26] In the film, DEFA set designer Gerhard Helwig creates an explosion of modernist design, complete with a curvilinear desk, abstract paintings and wall ornamentation, whimsically shaped chairs, eye-catching lighting effects and a blue-grey and red colour scheme that oozes cool capitalist power. Gallinger's extravagant penthouse in Marseille is characterized by a similar modernist impetus – tubular steel furniture adorns his balcony with a view of the bay and liquor is dispensed from an abstract sculpture housing an expensive bottle (Fig. 5.3).

Even the chief editor's office at Gerhard's newspaper – an otherwise insignificant location in the film as a whole – is a model of sleekly transparent postwar design. Glass-block walls separate the workspace from the surrounding offices and, as Gerhard reports on his latest inquiries into the mysterious Herr Kröger, who

Figure 5.3: Casino boss Gallinger in his ultra-modern office. DVD screen capture.

seems to have inside knowledge of the affairs of Gallinger's casino, his boss prepares a coffee with a fashion-forward piece of glass barista-ware.

Perhaps the most controversial scenes in terms of set design involved Gerhard and Sybille's apartment. Over the course of the film's production, this domestic space experienced a veritable economic-miracle makeover. A shared apartment was missing from the first versions of the script as well as Pohl's rewrite in the wake of Mehl's entrance onto the scene. Conforming more closely to the conventions of the social problem film than the final film with its fully developed romance, these stories emphasized Sybille's low social status and troubles with addiction. The haphazardly furnished rooms she inhabits are sad, run-down, even 'nightmarish' places.[27] Reflecting calls to elevate Sybille's status and to create a context for Gerhard's initiative to help her, screenplays four and five gave more space to the development of Gerhard and Sybille's relationship. In these iterations, as in both the domestic and West German cuts of the film, the pair become a true couple and move in together. When we first encounter this domestic space in a representative house that has seen better days, the rooms are a shabby reminder of a Biedermeier past. Just a short time later, the space has been completely transformed. In the final version of the film, we learn that the young couple is making monthly payments on the modest, yet stylish mass-produced furniture. Where there were dingy corners of the past, there is now light and shades of pastel. When Sybille's acting school friends arrive with Coca Cola and music, the vision of a postwar utopia of consumption and leisure is complete. In an earlier version of the story contained in the second screenplay of 25 July 1955, the consumerist theme is developed even more explicitly. About halfway through the story, we find Gerhard and Sybille walking along a busy shopping boulevard and stopping in front of the display of a well-stocked furniture store. As Gerhard and Sybille gaze at the 'lovely living room set' in the window, a young woman standing next to them gushes, 'A dream, isn't it?'[28] For the watchdogs of East German film culture it was clearly more of a nightmare.

As scrutiny of the film continued to mount following the completion of shooting in March 1957, a report was commissioned to determine to what extent the film deviated from the last version of the screenplay. Throughout shooting, Pohl had added, deleted and rewritten scenes, reporting the changes retroactively to Steinhauer.[29] At stake was whether the current cut of the film represented an improvement, as had been argued by Steinhauer, and whether the changes and additional scenes added by the filmmakers were acceptable. The author of the document, dramaturge Hanns Julius Wille, found numerous discrepancies – some of which reflected cuts that had been demanded following the film's screenings before the *Hauptverwaltung Film*'s licensing board. Such abridgements included shortening the controversial scenes involving Gerhard and Sybille's apartment, which had been deemed far too attractive and unrealistic given the means of the young couple portrayed, allowing for dangerous assumptions about Western prosperity and the availability of consumer comforts to the masses. Wille also drew attention to a scene referred to in the screenplay as 'Hotel Room in Nice'. According to Wille, it was a 'perfect example of the architecture-based generality of many scenes in this movie, which presents all milieus (be they those of Gallinger or Busch or fashionable locations) in an extravagant style that is supposed to be Western and is so generalized as to prevent any artistic differentiation or functionalization of space'.[30] Wille's comments emphasize the failure to exploit the possibilities of set design to adequately demarcate the film's different locations, but they also describe the kind of modernist cosmopolitanism that continued to cause such political anxiety among culture bureaucrats. In addition to the decision not to screen the film in colour in the GDR, a number of cuts were made as compared to the film that would be released as *Parkplatz zur großen Sehnsucht* in West Germany. The primary two scenes post-renovation occur after we learn that Sybille and Gerhard have married. The first and longer scene in which the couple unpack and are eventually joined by Sybille's acting school friends for a spontaneous celebration of the wedding, runs approximately 20 seconds longer in the colour version. Missing in the GDR release is most of the opening shot in which the camera follows Gerhard walking the full length of the spacious apartment as Sybille hangs up an unending supply of fashionable dresses left over from her modelling jobs. Unlike the black-and-white version, the scene ends with the couple gushing about how much they love their new place. In the black-and-white version they comment instead on how nice it is that they have room to dance. A second scene following directly on the aforementioned one and cut by three-quarters in the black-and-white version, also prevents the eyes of the viewer from lingering too long on the apartment's modern furnishings. The limitations of the story in terms of a social critique of West Germany had been evident and tolerated from the beginning of story development at the studio, but in the end it was the fear of the soft power of set design that led to the decision to screen the film in normal format and black and white in the GDR.[31]

Divided Distribution

Spielbank-Affäre finally came before the licensing board on 27 April 1957, accompanied by an overwhelmingly approving report by Pfeuffer. Although critical of many aspects of the story during the course of screenplay development, she had become heavily invested in assuring that the film reached GDR cinemas. The film was now 'everything that we had hoped for' – an interesting and attractively arranged film with quality acting and a clear political statement.[32] Deflecting criticisms that too much of the social critique contained in earlier versions of the story had been eliminated, Pfeuffer argued that it was possible to get a message across without lecturing to the audience – although she also noted that the involvement of the West German co-producer had led the filmmakers to downplay certain themes, among them the presence of progressive forces in West German society that opposed the capitalist casino. According to the documentation of the screening, the film was approved in the colour version with the stipulation that it end with Gallinger's claims of innocence and that no one has suffered any injury through events at the casino.[33] The mandatory opinion section contained in the approval sought to frame the circumstances of the film's production as an 'experiment', claiming somewhat disingenuously that it was DEFA's 'first co-production with a West German film producer'. DEFA had of course worked with Mehl before, but had preferred to stress his Pandora company's legal status as a Swedish entity. It was also an experiment in the sense that it tried with very uneven results to wed 'a primarily entertainment-oriented story with a socio-critical agenda'.

Despite the ostensibly positive outcome of the meeting of the licensing board, discussion continued through the summer due to the intervention of the Minister of Culture himself. The film returned to the licensing board on 16 July in a meeting that included hardline State Secretary Alexander Abusch, Minister of Education Egon Freyer, and Arno Röder representing the Central Committee. At the meeting, studio head Wilkening reported that some additional 200 metres had been cut from the previous version, primarily scenes surrounding the apartment of Gerhard and Sybille, which had been criticized for promoting an image of the standard of living in West Germany that was too high. Wilkening also advised that the ending of the version that had been screened for the meeting would be cut to end instead with Gallinger's public declaration of his innocence, as had already been mandated at the previous meeting of the licensing board.[34] In the ensuing discussion, respected director Slatan Dudow criticized the film for its overly opulent sets worthy of an UFA production and the unrealistic, disingenuous story surrounding Sybille. Still, despite the depicted luxury and opulent sets more than worthy of UFA, according to Dudow, it would be more dangerous not to show the film than to show it. Abusch shared the opinion that the film could be released, pending additional cuts beyond those to the end of the film. Specifically, the minister recommended cutting the scene first introducing the West German resort as well as the previously shown musical number with Eva May. The feasibility of mitigating the film's impact by abandoning the colour and widescreen format were also discussed, but no definitive decision was made in this regard. The meeting ended with the scheduling of another screening in two weeks' time in order to compare the widescreen version with a colour version in standard format.

Spielbank-Affäre was ultimately approved for GDR release on 1 August 1957 in a black-and-white widescreen version – although it would in fact play in normal format.[35] Pohl fumed at the fate of his preferred ending at the hands of GDR culture bureaucrats and went public on Norddeutscher Rundfunk to announce his break with DEFA.[36] The scandal was widely reported in mainstream media in West Germany and in *Neues Deutschland*.[37] In the wake of such bad publicity, the principal actors boycotted the GDR premiere of the film on 13 September 1957 in Rostock – far from the major East Berlin cinema where it had initially been scheduled to appear months earlier. At a cost of some 3 million East German marks, double the cost of an average DEFA film at the time, *Spielbank-Affäre* turned out to be something of a disaster for the studio in the short term. While it would eventually turn a profit – the application to renew the film's screening licence based its favourable recommendation on the strength of returns of 3.1 million marks by 1961 – the film had produced a scandal in both German states that effectively ended any hopes of future German–German collaborations and only exacerbated DEFA's struggles in the area of entertainment.[38]

Stefan Soldovieri is Associate Professor of German at the University of Toronto. He has published on various aspects of GDR cinema, inter-German film relations and genre film during the postwar period. His current research focuses on remakes in Germanophone contexts and cultural explorations of futurity and sustainability.

Notes

1. See Rosemary Stott, *Crossing the Wall. The Western Feature Film Import in East Germany*, Oxford: Peter Lang, 2012.
2. On the impact of the New Course on the film industry, see Thomas Heimann, *DEFA, Künstler und SED-Kulturpolitik* [= Beiträge zur Film- und Fernsehwissenschaft, vol. 46], Berlin: Vistas, 1994, pp. 189–93. See also Stefan Soldovieri, 'Finding Navigable Waters. Inter-German Film Relations and Modernization in Two DEFA Barge Films of the 1950s', *Film History* 18.1 (2006), 59–72.
3. Thomas Koerber, 'Problemfilm', in Thomas Koerber (ed), *Sachlexikon des Films*. Stuttgart: Reclam, 2002, pp. 465–68; 'Problemfilme', in Thomas Elsaesser and Michael Wedel (eds), *The BFI Companion to German Cinema*, London: BFI, 1999, pp. 120–21.
4. Rodenberg to Ackermann dated 16 March 1955 [= BArch DR 1 / 4659], p. 1.
5. 'Stellungnahme "Spielbank-Affäre"' signed by Steinhauer dated 8 July 1955 [= BArch DR 117 / 32583]. All quotations are from this short document.
6. 'Dramaturgensitzung, Spielbankstoff "Geld ist eine harte Sache"' dated 15 July 1955 [= BArch DR 117 / 32358]. All quotations are from this document. Also cited at length in Wolfgang Jacobsen (ed), *Babelsberg. Das Filmstudio*, Berlin: Argon, 1992, p. 279–84.
7. '"Spielbank-Affäre" (Arbeitstitel), Fassung DII' dated 25 July 1955 [= BArch DR 117 / 2563].
8. '"Spielbank-Affäre" (Arbeitstitel)' dated 25 July 1955 [= BArch DR 117 / 2563], p. 6. All translations by the author unless otherwise noted.
9. Steinhauer reported on the change to the Kröger character in a report to production head Werner Dau. 'Drehbuchaenderungen "Spielbankaffaere"' signed by Steinhauer dated 23 June 1956 [= Barch DR 117 / 32358], p. 1.
10. 'Stellungnahme zu den Drehbuchänderungen "Spielbank-Affäre"' dated 25 July 1955 [= BArch DR 117 / 32358].
11. 'Ackermann to Rodenberg' dated 5 November 1955 [= BArch DR 1 / 4367], p. 1.
12. For an early account of Mehl's role in a DEFA co-production, see Stefan Soldovieri, 'Socialists in Outer Space. East German Film's Venusian Adventure', *Film History* 10.3 (1998), 382–98. For a broader view, see Mariana Ivanova, 'Die Prestige-Agenda der DEFA. Koproduktionen mit Erich Mehls Filmfirma Pandora (1953–1957)', in Michael Wedel, Barton Byg, Andy Räder, Skyler Arndt-Briggs and Evan Torner (eds), *DEFA International. Grenzüberschreitende Filmbeziehungen vor und nach dem Mauerbau*, Wiesbaden: Springer VS, 2013, pp. 217–33.
13. 'Wilkening to Schlotter' dated 23 May 1956 [= BArch DR 1 / 4659]. The subject of the letter was in fact DEFA's difficulties in meeting Rudolf Forster's wage demands.
14. See F.-B. Habel and Volker Wachter (eds), *Das Große Lexikon der DDR-Stars*, Berlin: Schwarzkopf & Schwarzkopf, 2002, pp. 189–90.
15. Hans Helmut Prinzler, 'Fern von jeder Realität: Über die Schauspielerin Gertrud Kückelmann', *FilmGeschichte* 11/12 (1998), pp. 54–57.
16. 'Valuta – Planung für das Jahr 1954' undated (circa November 1953) [= BArch DR 1 / 4597], p. 2.
17. 'Stellungnahme zu dem Drehbuch "Spielbank-Affäre"' signed by Pfeuffer, dated 20 March 1956 [= BArch DR 1 / 4731], p. 1.
18. '"Spielbank-Affäre" by Artur Pohl. Zwischentreatment' dated January 1956 [= BArch DR 117 / 10773], p. 1.
19. 'Stellungnahme zu dem Drehbuch "Spielbank-Affäre"' dated 20 April 1956 [= BArch DR 1 / 4731].
20. 'Aktenvermerk für den Genossen Ackermann' signed by Pfeuffer dated 25 May 1956 [= BArch DR 1 / 4731].

21. 'Spielbank-Affäre' dated 5 April 1956 [= BArch DR 117 / 2564], pp. 204–08.
22. Ibid., p. 209.
23. 'Aktenvermerk für den Genossen Ackermann' signed by Pfeuffer dated 25 May 1956 [= BArch DR 1 / 4731].
24. 'Bemerkungen zum Produktionsablauf', unsigned and undated [= BArch DR 117 / 33041].
25. On the set design for *Spielbank-Affäre*, see Annette Dorgerloh, 'Nachkriegsmoderne als Herausforderung. Konstrasträume zwischen West und Ost in DEFA-Filmen der fünfziger Jahre', *Kunsttexte.de* (January 2014) [= http://edoc.hu-berlin.de/kunsttexte/2014-1/dorgerloh-annette-2/PDF/dorgerloh.pdf], accessed 20 June 2016. See also Paul Betts, 'The Bauhaus in the German Democratic Republic – between Formalism and Pragmatism', Jeannine Fiedler and Paul Feierabend (eds), *Bauhaus*, Cologne: Könemann, 2000, pp. 42–49.
26. '"Spielbank-Affäre" by Artur Pohl. Zwischentreatment' dated January 1956 [= BArch DR 117 / 10773], p. 4.
27. '"Spielbank-Affäre" (Arbeitstitel), Fassung DII' dated 25 July 1955 [= BArch DR 117 / 2563], p. 49, and '"Spielbank-Affäre" by Artur Pohl. Zwischentreatment' dated January 1956 [= BArch DR 117 / 10773], p. 8.
28. 'Spielbank-Affäre' dated 25 July 1955 [= BArch DR 117 / 2563], pp. 139–41.
29. Steinhauer to Wilkening and Böhm dated 19 July 1956 [= BArch DR 117 / 32358], p.2. See also Ralf Schenk's description of Pohl's DEFA career, which includes the outlines of the production of *Spielbank-Affäre*, in Ralf Schenk (ed), *Das zweite Leben der Filmstadt Babelsberg. DEFA-Spielfilme 1946-1992*, Berlin: Henschel, 1994, pp. 139–42. A selective account of the film's production history referencing Western press reports is contained in Wolfgang Jacobsen, 'Cha Cha Bim Bam Bum', in Jacobsen, pp. 279–84.
30. 'Betr.: Abnahme "Spielbank-Affäre"' signed by J. Wille dated 19 June 1957 [= BArch DR 1-Z / 667].
31. I borrow this term, of course, from Greg Castillo, *Cold War on the Home Front. The Soft Power of Midcentury Design*, Minneapolis: University of Minnesota Press, 2010.
32. 'Betr.: Vorbereitung der Abnahme des Films "Spielbank-Affäre"' signed Pfeuffer and dated 26 April 1957, [= BArch DR 1-Z/ 248], p. 1.
33. 'Protokoll Nr. 248/57 "Spielbank-Affäre"' dated 7 May 1957 [= BArch DR 1-Z / 248], p. 1.
34. 'Protokoll über die Diskussion bei der Vorführung des DEFA-Films. "Spielbank-Affäre"' dated 22 July 1957 [= BArch DR 1-Z / 248], p. 1.
35. 'Zusatzprotokoll zum Protokoll Nr. 248/57 "Spielbank-Affäre"' dated 20 August 1957 [= BArch DR 1-Z / 248], p. 1.
36. 'Die gefährliche Farbe', *Der Spiegel* 44, 30 October 1957, 58. See also Schenk, p. 142.
37. Jacobsen, p. 283f.
38. 'Zusatzprotokoll zum Protokoll Nr. 248/57 "Spielbank-Affäre"' dated 2 August 1962 [= BArch DR 1-Z / 248], p. 1.

CHAPTER 6
'Operación Silencio'
Studio H&S's Chile Cycle as Latin American Third Cinema

Dennis Hanlon

It is autumn 1973. Chile's Salvador Allende, the world's first democratically elected Marxist president, is addressing a large and enthusiastic crowd at a ceremony to mark the handing-over of new housing blocks built by the Unidad Popular. At the end of his speech he gives the keys to some of the new occupants, and a woman asks if she can have her picture taken with him. Throwing his arms around her he jokes, 'a photo that will go all around the world!' His words are repeated twice on the soundtrack for emphasis, slightly overlapping with the next shot: a high-angle take of Chile's presidential palace, the Palacio Moneda, with flames coming out of its windows and bombs exploding on the roof. The sounds of detonations, gunfire and jets screaming overhead complete the soundtrack.

These dramatic images of the coup of 11 September 1973 led by General Augusto Pinochet (during which Allende was killed) did indeed travel all around the world and still do so today. Their origins, though, are largely forgotten. If the images are familiar to contemporary audiences, then that is because they are embedded within Patricio Guzmán's monumental *La batalla de Chile* [*The Battle of Chile*, 1975-1979], a three-part epic widely regarded as one of the masterpieces of New Latin American Cinema. The same images of the Moneda appear beneath the opening titles of all three parts and recur as a leitmotiv throughout parts one and two (Fig. 6.1).

The film described in the opening paragraph is *Krieg der Mumien* [*War of the Mummies*, 1974] by the East German documentary filmmakers Walter Heynowski and Gerhard Scheumann, known collectively as Studio H&S. It was their second film in a cycle about Chile that would eventually amount to some ten films in total. Although many of the films were awarded prizes at international film festivals, and

Figure 6.1: Studio H&S's footage of the bombing of the Palacio Moneda as seen in the opening titles of *La batalla de Chile*. DVD screen capture.

shown on television not only in North and South America but also on both sides of the Iron Curtain, few English-language studies of documentary filmmaking make detailed reference to Heynowski and Scheumann. Thomas Waugh, for instance, laments 'the scandalous neglect in the English-speaking world of these two important committed artists, honoured in 29 major retrospectives around the world since 1974'.[1] A recent article in the Mexican magazine *Proceso* recounting the story behind the images of the Moneda concludes by noting that the films are an important record of events that Pinochet attempted to suppress via his so-called 'Operación Silencio' (Operation Silence), and that although the films have survived the passing of time, their makers have long been forgotten.[2]

This essay seeks to address the relative neglect surrounding Heynowski and Scheumann by considering the extent to which their cycle of films about Chile should be regarded as an integral part of Latin America's Third Cinema. Their films remain key documents for understanding the response to the Pinochet coup on the part of both the Latin American and wider international left, not only because of the valuable testimony and evidence they contain, but also because their rhetoric and cinematic style both reflected and helped define international trends in militant filmmaking during the period. For contemporary audiences, the films remain essential viewing for anyone wishing to understand how and why the hegemonic ideology of today's world, sometimes referred to as 'neoliberalism', was so brutally tested out in Chile in 1973.

The History of Studio H&S

Walter Heynowski and Gerhard Scheumann began their collaboration in 1965, and it would continue in various forms (both with and without the involvement of DEFA) up until 1991. Prior to 1965, Heynowski had worked for the East German satirical magazine *Eulenspiegel* and for the state television (the *Deutscher Fernsehfunk*, or DFF).[3] Between 1963 and 1965, Scheumann produced *Prisma*, a current affairs programme intended to counter the propaganda put out by West German broadcasts such as *Panorama* and *Report*.[4] Initially Scheumann and Heynowski seemed an unlikely duo, on account of their very different orientations; Heynowski's early films were hard-hitting propaganda pieces about the Federal Republic and, in particular, the 'failings' of its capitalist economy and enduring legacy of the Nazi past, while Scheumann's television films addressed problems of everyday life in the GDR.[5]

In 1965 they started working under the auspices of DEFA as 'Studio H&S' with the aim of representing the GDR at international film festivals.[6] Their first major international success was *Der lachende Mann* [*The Laughing Man*, 1966], a film for which they had a camera team in the Federal Republic interview a German mercenary, Siegfried 'Congo' Müller, who had participated in the Congolese civil war, fighting against Patrice Lumumba, a hero of the international left. Films like *Der lachende Mann* and *400cm^3* (1966), a short film exhorting East Germans to donate blood for the Vietnamese cause, caught the attention of the staff in the North Vietnamese embassy in East Berlin and led to Studio H&S being invited to make a film in North Vietnam. The resulting film, *Piloten im Pyjama* [*Pilots in Pajamas*, 1967], was a four-part television documentary based on filmed interviews conducted with downed US pilots being held at the Hanoi Hilton in Saigon. In 1969, Studio H&S was taken out of DEFA and made an independent entity, answerable to the East German film bureau, the *Hauptverwaltung Film* within the Ministry of Culture; and the Ministry of Finance paid them directly from a different budget than that allocated to DEFA.[7] In addition to generous salaries well above the norm for East German citizens, they were also allowed to keep 60% of revenues generated by sales abroad of the prints and rights to their films.[8] Heynowski and Scheumann used their generous funding and the revenue generated abroad to buy state of the art post-production equipment from the West. They had the only subtitling machine in the GDR, and by 1982 were providing a range of specialist technical services to DEFA and the Ministry of Culture.[9]

The newly independent Studio H&S assembled a regular team that would go on to work on most of the Chile cycle; key members included the (West German) camera operator Peter Hellmich,[10] producer Mathias Remmert, editor Traute Wischnewski, publicists Robert Michel and Wolfgang von Peletz, and their own in-house film theorist, Günter Agde.[11] They quickly developed a house style, (even in such areas as the typography and design of the credits) and adopted a form of international branding that made their films instantly recognizable as Studio H&S products. As an autonomous entity in a socialist country, Studio H&S's practices were riven with contradictions. It was essentially a capitalist enterprise subsidised by a socialist state. Heynowski and Scheumann charged DEFA for access to their subtitling and dubbing equipment, all of which had been provided by the *Hauptverwaltung Film*, so that they could produce copies of their films in a range of languages and contribute to the GDR's efforts at cultural diplomacy. Because they did the work of dubbing and subtitling themselves, they were then in a position to sell the prints back to the government which, in 1980 alone, purchased some 500 prints of films from the Chile cycle to disseminate abroad.[12] Their publications, translated into multiple languages (all at government expense), doubled as marketing material promoting the sale of their films.[13] The foreign rights to their films were handled in two different ways: socialist countries could purchase the rights for the films in perpetuity, while capitalist states could only purchase screening rights for a limited period (usually five years).[14] Among their distributors in the West were Unidoc in Munich and Stanley Forman's Educational Television Films (ETV) in London.[15] Of the ten most popular Studio H&S films, in terms of sales, eight belong to the Chile cycle – evidence that this cycle was not only the most profitable for the production company but also the most widely distributed.[16] However, the prolonged phase of independence and privilege that dated back to 1969 came to an abrupt end in 1982 when Gerhard Scheumann, in a speech to TV and film professionals, advocated a return to *Prisma*-style programming and a sharper focus on the problems faced by ordinary citizens in the GDR (rather than by their counterparts in the West).[17] Studio H&S was subsequently threatened with the loss of half of its income if it refused to reintegrate itself into DEFA, and Scheumann had his passport confiscated.[18]

Chile and the GDR

Although Studio H&S was institutionally independent throughout much of its existence, the filmmakers themselves were not at liberty to choose the subjects of their films, but needed clearance from the GDR's Ministry of Culture and Ministry of Finance. The reason why Chile became the focus of so many of their films was closely bound up with the special relationship that existed between the GDR and Chile during the Allende administration. After the USSR, the GDR was the largest donor of foreign aid among the Eastern Bloc countries, and its leaders were motivated to do so by the pressing need to secure international recognition. Cultural diplomacy was an important part of this effort; Studio H&S was among its best-known cultural ambassadors, and Chile was one of the GDR's most important partners.

During his 1969–1970 presidential campaign, Salvador Allende promised visiting East German dignitaries that he would grant them immediate recognition (which he did in April 1971).[19] Chile became only the second Latin American country (after Cuba) to recognize the GDR's sovereignty, and the first in South America. The GDR opened an embassy in Chile in 1971, and the two countries developed close diplomatic ties. Salvador Allende regularly consulted with East German officials about foreign trade, banking and the establishment of universal education.[20] East German radio had daily reports about Chile, extolling such achievements as the nationalization of the copper mines and the introduction of land reform.

The Pinochet coup was a political catastrophe for the GDR, which responded with increasingly emphatic expressions of solidarity for the people of Chile (often presenting Pinochet's regime as a fascist organization, an approach Studio H&S would also adopt in a number of its films about Chile).[21] The GDR also took in around 2,000 Chilean refugees, many of them associated with left-wing political parties belonging to the Unidad Popular. Almost all were members of the Chilean intelligentsia, and there were many artists, journalists and filmmakers among their number. This influx of Chilean intellectuals led to contacts with East Germans active within the sphere of cultural production (including the filmmakers at Studio H&S) who received important material for their films and publications. The fruits of these interactions, including the Chile cycle, imprinted a positive image of the GDR on the minds of committed internationalists in Latin America and elsewhere. The Pinochet coup, which at first seemed an unmitigated disaster for the GDR, soon proved to be an opportunity for both it and Studio H&S, as it furnished it with a theme that would ensure their work received unprecedented international exposure.

The Chile Cycle of Studio H&S

Between 1974 and 1979, Studio H&S released nine films on Chile. The cycle can be subdivided into shorts and features that rely heavily on montage to promote a political analysis and films that are closer to *cinéma vérité* and devoted for the most part to conveying testimony of the victims of the junta. The cycle therefore replicates in miniature the span of Studio H&S's thematic concerns, which ranged from attacking the Federal Republic for supporting US neo-imperialism, to embracing a broader internationalist agenda that included identifying the class enemy at various flashpoints in the Third World during the Cold War. While the first feature in the cycle, *Krieg der Mumien*, contains several sequences highly critical of the Federal Republic, these become far less prominent over the course of the cycle, before eventually disappearing altogether as the films gained an international audience. This downward trend is matched by a concomitant increase in self-reflexive strategies designed to highlight Studio H&S's collective authorship of the works in question.

The first Studio H&S film about Chile, *Mitbürger!* [*Fellow Citizens!*, 1974] premiered at the 1974 Oberhausen Short Film Festival less than five months after the Pinochet coup, and (somewhat unusually) was subsequently broadcast on West German television.[22] *Mitbürger!* is short and simple; the soundtrack is a recording of Allende's final radio address given while the Moneda was under siege, and the images alternate between footage of throngs of people cheering for Allende and images of the coup and the subsequent mass arrests. The primitive dialectic created by the editing is less about analysis and more about generating repeated emotional states of loss and outrage.

The first feature film (and the longest in the cycle), *Krieg der Mumien*, premiered simultaneously on East German and Cuban television on 5 March 1974. If the structure of *Mitbürger!* is simple and calculated to have a predominantly emotional appeal, the dialectical montage of this feature film is complex and operates on multiple levels, to provoke an analysis of the political and economic forces, both national and international, that led to the coup. *Krieg der Mumien* shuttles back and forth in time, between Allende's presidency and the immediate aftermath of the coup. Within each period it alternates between Allende's supporters and the forces of reaction that were responsible for the coup, in an attempt to offer an analysis of the rival factions in the conflict. It also adopts a dialectical approach to *mise en scène*. *Krieg der Mumien* begins on a light note, with students hopping and chanting, 'Whoever doesn't hop is a mummy!' The sequence pauses several times, with titles appearing over it demanding to know what a mummy is. The answer is provided by a worker interviewed by the filmmakers: 'A mummy is an owner of capital'. The sequence with the students is shot at night, while the next with the workers is filmed in daylight, creating a contrast of light and dark, and suggesting that the latter are politically 'enlightened'. *Krieg der Mumien* concludes with a montage of people being taken prisoner, a darkly ominous denouement that contrasts starkly with the jubilant images at the beginning of the film. The contrapuntal, quasi-Eisensteinian use of sound and image is another distinctive characteristic of the film. The whole work is held together using a panoply of techniques (including associational montage), many of which date back to the Soviet documentaries of the 1920s and were still common in political cinema of the period (especially in Latin America). These techniques certainly enliven the film; but this virtuoso display of technical prowess also has the effect of giving it a propulsive energy that makes it almost impossible to evaluate the political analysis being presented; one is merely swept along by a bravura show of technique.

Ich war, ich bin, ich werde sein [*I Was, I Am, I Shall Be*, 1974], which was premiered on the first anniversary of the coup, begins with a technique familiar from *Krieg der Mumien*, namely the use of candid footage to make the forces of reaction and/or members of the junta appear foolish. For instance, we are treated to an endlessly repeated montage depicting a vainglorious Pinochet preening himself as he sits down in a chair waiting to be interviewed while an assistant hovers over him, picking solicitously at his jacket. After this brief section, though, we can discern a shift in Studio H&S's practice. For the first time in the cycle, they comment on their own presence, explaining how they tricked the authorities into letting them film in the concentration camps of Chacabuco and Pisagua before then dramatizing the dangers involved. *Ich war, ich bin, ich werde sein*, differs from the earlier features in other ways too. First, the film is shot in the tradition of *cinema vérité*. The camerawork in

Ich war, ich bin, ich werde sein is fluid and probing and the takes are long and seek to record as many faces as possible so that the prisoners could be identified and their families notified of their fate (Fig. 6.2). Another shift in style abandons rapid-fire montage in favour of a dialectical organization of much longer film segments. Between the sections on Chacabuco and Pisagua, historical footage is used to give a history of the labour movement in the saltpetre mines, suggesting that the transformation of the former mines into concentration camps is merely the latest in a long string of setbacks that workers have had to endure in their attempt to escape exploitation.

Studio H&S commemorated the second anniversary of the coup with the September 1975 release of *Geldsorgen* [*Money Troubles*] – perhaps the only film in the cycle which could be described as a comedy. The title refers to the problem the junta had with people writing slogans of resistance on the paper currency; in an on-camera interview, the general in charge of the central bank explains how people are required to exchange the bills with slogans for clean ones. Peter Hellmich

Figure 6.2: Capturing as many faces as possible for later identification in *Ich war, ich bin, ich werde sein* (1974). DVD screen capture.

brought some of the altered bills back to the GDR, where they were filmed by Studio H&S in colour on an animation stand.²³ The slogans include: 'The military junta is a bunch of crooks', 'Allende lives!', 'Enough with the gunfire!' and 'Our land will be like Cuba!' Slogans such as 'We've lost the battle but not the war!' appear in speech bubbles so they seem to be the words of a miner depicted on the back of the bill. *Geldsorgen* is the first film in the cycle to celebrate popular resistance to Pinochet, and its light tone, emphasized by the use of colour, reflects a sense of optimism common at that time among Chilean refugees, and a belief that the junta would soon be swept away. Subsequent films returned to the darker tone with which the cycle had begun; the final film in the cycle, *Im Feuer bestanden: die letzten Stunden in der Moneda* [*Steadfast in Fire, the Last Hours in the Moneda*, 1978], dissects the attack on the Moneda and repeatedly shows Allende's corpse being removed from the building and unceremoniously dumped in the back of a military truck.

The very last film Studio H&S shot in Chile, *Eine Minute Dunkel macht uns nicht blind* [*One Minute of Darkness Does Not Blind Us*, 1976], explores the situation in Chile two years after the coup and features ongoing resistance both at home and abroad. Extending the self-reflexive approach evident in *Ich war, ich bin, ich werde sein*, a pre-title sequence quotes the newspaper *El Mercurio*, the mouthpiece of the junta, reporting that *Der weiße Putsch* [*El Golpe Blanco/The White Coup*, 1975], had been shown on East German television and was made by the same team as *Krieg der Mumien* and *Ich war, ich bin, ich werde sein* – filmmakers who 'had betrayed the trust of Chilean officials'. The lead article the next day reports tightened scrutiny in respect of non-nationals entering Chile, followed up a few weeks later with new laws relating to foreigners. A title then announces that 'further filming seems unlikely'. This use of self-reflexivity (as opposed to a straightforward juxtaposition of the filmmakers' cleverness and daring and the officials' stupidity and timidity such as we find in *Ich war, ich bin, ich werde sein*) reflects the political impact that films and other cultural products made in solidarity with the people of Chile were having both at home and on the international stage. The same point is underscored in the next sequence, in which a press spokesman for the Foreign Ministry produces a pile of books, in multiple languages, denouncing the coup (including examples from both the FRG and the GDR). He claims that communists abroad (and above all in the USSR), are funding these books, and both threatening and tricking workers into supporting their cause. He challenges the filmmakers to interview anyone they like and to find out for themselves that ordinary Chileans do not believe these foreign-produced lies. After a brief shot of Pinochet and his fellow junta members – and before the film's title – we see the first in a series of interviews featuring people searching for their missing loved ones.

Eine Minute Dunkel macht uns nicht blind is particularly effective because it juxtaposes official pronouncements with the moving testimony of the families of the junta's victims, rather than relying on Scheumann's customary acerbic narration. It is a return to the *cinéma vérité* style of *Ich war, ich bin, ich werde sein*, with many extended handheld takes during which the camera probes its subjects; when the wife whose husband has gone missing talks about the chronic illness of her youngest child, the camera tilts down and zooms in on him just as he falls asleep exhausted. Perhaps the most extraordinary aspect of *Eine Minute Dunkel macht uns nicht blind* is the redaction of names and identities, which we first see in the opening titles when the names of the crew working in Santiago are covered with grey rectangles. There are two similar moments of redaction in the main body of the film. In the first, the camera suddenly pans left during an interview with workers, revealing the sound engineer whose face is hidden by a black square (Fig. 6.3), a

Figure 6.3: The redacted face of the sound engineer in *Eine Minute Dunkel macht uns nicht blind* (1975). DVD screen capture.

move that seems staged for effect, as it is the only time in the cycle in which a member of the crew inadvertently appears onscreen.

Near the end of the film, at a meeting of trade unionists discussing their strategy for resisting the junta, some of the speakers' faces are also covered with black rectangles, while others are not. No explanation is given for the apparent arbitrariness of this redaction. Were the redacted people 'disappeared' after the shooting of the film? Were they particularly susceptible to persecution by the junta? Were they communists? None of this is clear; however, the second use of the rectangles near the end of the film does suggest to viewers that Studio H&S's film crew faced as much potential danger as syndicalists fighting the junta.

Since sending crews to Chile was no longer an option after 1976, Heynowski and Scheumann decided to end the cycle that same year. However, in 1978, they attended a retrospective of their work in Mexico City, where the writer Gabriel García Márquez introduced them to the audience. In attendance were Hortensia Bussi (the widow of Salvador Allende) and Danilo Bartulín (Allende's personal doctor who had been in the Moneda the day of the coup and had been one of the last people to see the president alive). Both were then living in exile in Mexico, and through them the filmmakers were introduced to other members of the exile community there. This experience prompted Studio H&S to add two more films to the Chile cycle, namely *Die Toten schweigen nicht* [*The Dead Are Not Silent*, 1978] and *Im Feuer bestanden: die letzten Stunden in der Moneda*. In each case the bulk of the material was shot in Mexico.

Die Toten schweigen nicht is the testimony of Moy de Tohá and Isabel Letelier, who were living in the Chilean exile community in Mexico City. The former was the widow of José Tohá, Allende's Minister of the Interior, who had died in February 1974 from complications brought on by extended torture and interrogation. Isabel Letelier was the widow of Orlando Letelier, the highest-ranking member of the Allende government arrested on the day of the coup, who was murdered in Washington DC in 1976 when agents of the Chilean secret police (DINA) bombed his car. Of all of the films in the cycle, this seems the one most clearly targeted at North American audiences (especially those outside Chile-solidarity and activist circles), since it largely eschews ideological analysis and instead presents a number of moving personal stories. In an interview in a volume produced to accompany the film, Heynowski and Scheumann describe their motivation in making the film as follows: 'In several countries we have encountered people who were only reluctantly prepared, or not prepared at all, to accept broadly based arguments on the activities of international capital in Pinochet's Chile. ... We thus hope to win with this film, audiences which we have hitherto not been able to reach on the theme of Chile, and in this way strengthen the movement of solidarity'.[24] With its emphasis on 'human interest' rather than political analysis, it is hardly surprising that, according to Robert Michel, it became the US Chile Committee for Human Rights' film of choice from the cycle for fundraising and was reviewed in the *San Francisco Chronicle*, the *Los Angeles Times*, and the *Washington Star*.[25] The final film, *Im Feuer bestanden: die letzten Stunden in der Moneda*, closes the cycle with a visceral emotional appeal, very similar to that articulated in the opening work, *Mitbürger!*.

The Chile Cycle as Latin American Third Cinema

The Chile cycle was mostly filmed in Chile and Mexico and incorporates footage and photographs shot by numerous (often anonymous) Latin Americans. In addition, Studio H&S worked closely with Chileans in exile both in the GDR and in other countries. For this reason alone, its cycle must be seen as a contribution to Latin American Third Cinema, just as films made in Europe by Chileans in exile were. But the affinity Heynowski and Scheumann's films have with Latin American cinema goes further than just the content of their work or the provenance of the images assembled; Studio H&S emulated the filmmaking and promotional practices of their Latin American associates in several ways, just as Latin American filmmakers copied them in turn. Some of the most important similarities include: the cultivation of a series of myths about the dangers with which the filmmakers were confronted; the use of collective production practices; the use of film festivals to promote political ideas; the attempt to deploy cinema as a form of direct intervention in national and international politics; and the creation an aesthetic form that could address multiple audiences simultaneously.

The lead article in the May 1974 issue of *Film und Fernsehen* is devoted to *Krieg der Mumien*. It begins with a reminiscence about Leonardo Henrickson, an Argentine camera operator working for a Swedish television producer, who 'filmed his own death' during 29 June 1973, 'test coup' of the Chilean military. This dramatic footage of a soldier stepping down from the back of a truck and pointing a pistol at the camera, after which the camera falls to the ground, remains one of the iconic images of 1973 Chile, along with the bombing of the Moneda.[26] *Film und Fernsehen* portrays him as standing 'eye to eye with the putschists'.[27] In the next paragraph the very same phrase recurs in the context of a description of Studio H&S's work: 'A few weeks later, on 11 September, Peter Hellmich was pointing his camera at the Moneda presidential palace as it was heavily bombarded by tanks and fighter jets. This camera, as well as Heynowski and Scheumann and their co-workers stood eye to eye with the putschists'.[28] Pictures of bullet holes in the hotel windows, with the burning Moneda out of focus in the background, heighten the drama of the magazine's report. Another myth that bolstered Studio H&S's cultivation of a 'creative persona' was the suggestion that they were present at the interviews with Pinochet and in the Chacabuco and Pisagua. In reality, they had left Chile months before the coup, and Heynowski did not return until 2001. Whether these myths were created and perpetuated by the East German authorities, Studio H&S, or both, is unclear; but the filmmakers do not appear to have denied them (perhaps because they recognized their potential to promote the film). Moreover, these accounts of how they tricked Pinochet and sneaked into the concentration camps persisted for many years. As recently as 2001, British Third Cinema scholar Mike Wayne wrote, 'a classic example of guerilla cinema can be found in the documentary short *Inside Pinochet's Prisons* [sic] [...] It was into this situation of fascist dictatorship that an East German film group entered Chile on Western passports and got access to some of the prisons on the pretence that they were filming an anti-communist, pro-Pinochet film'.[29] This description suggests that the subterfuge somehow involved fake passports, but the reality was that the crews Studio H&S used were all from the West. It came as something of a bombshell when Heynowski admitted in a 2013 interview published in *Neues Deutschland* that he was not actually there during the coup and had told his camera operator, Peter Hellmich, that he would have to be his eyes and ears in Chile.[30]

Given that Jorge Müller Silva, the camera operator for *La batalla de Chile*, died filming in Chile (as did Leonardo Henrickson), it may seem unscrupulous for Heynowski and Scheumann to have allowed such myths about the supposed risks they took to continue circulating. However, like their Latin American colleagues, the East Germans understood that clandestine filming and the threat of danger (both to filmmakers and audiences in Latin American dictatorships who watched their films) made for a compelling narrative. The Bolivian filmmaker Jorge Sanjinés claimed he had to flee to Chile in 1971 because he was on a list of targets following a coup, and that he was forbidden from entering the United States because he had made a film that contributed to the Peace Corps being kicked out of Bolivia. The first claim may well be true, but there is no evidence for the second, and yet they persisted as powerful elements of his political persona. In 1986, the Chilean director Miguel Littín, who had fled to Mexico and then Spain after the coup, returned to Chile disguised as a Uruguayan businessman. Once there he contacted filmmakers and instructed them to film the anti-Pinochet resistance; subterfuge, secret operations, and dangerous exploits were all part of the romantic ethos of Latin American Third Cinema during the 1970s, and provided a model for the filmmakers at Studio H&S to emulate.

Studio H&S operated as a collective, much in the manner of the Grupo Cine de la Base and Grupo Cine Liberación in Argentina, Grupo Ukamau in Bolivia, Grupo Chaski in Peru and Grupo Tercer Año in Chile. The post-1968 era saw the formation of similar collectives in Western Europe, such as Chris Marker's Groupe Medvedkine and Jean-Luc Godard and Jean-Pierre Gorin's Groupe Dziga Vertov. Such filmmaking practices were international rather than national and linked by a common political ideology that transcended the local. The Latin American filmmaking collective most similar to Studio H&S was the newsreel section of the Instituto Cubano del Arte e Industria Cinematográficos [The Cuban Institute for the Cinematographic Arts and Industry, ICAIC] founded in 1960 by Santiago Álvarez, so it is unsurprising that Heynowski and Scheumann looked to him as a model. Like Studio H&S, ICAIC was state funded and answerable to the party leaders, although it was never as closely monitored as DEFA. Álvarez also travelled to North Vietnam to make films, and worked with a dedicated team that, like Studio H&S, could produce well-crafted films very rapidly. Heynowski and Scheumann also modelled their studio on Dziga Vertov's 'creative laboratory', and they distinguished between organising and directing films.[31] Álvarez, who was often compared to Dziga Vertov because of his editing style, claimed that he had never seen a Vertov film until the 1980s. If true, it is highly possible that he became familiar with Vertov's editing style via his frequent contact with Heynowski and Scheumann at the annual documentary film festival in Leipzig.

Like their Latin American counterparts, Studio H&S used international film festivals as a way of gaining recognition for its films and the political causes it sought to promote. Just as Jorge Sanjinés saw film as a political instrument able to bring about change (in his case, the expulsion of the Peace Corps from Bolivia), so too Heynowski and Scheumann saw their work as a direct intervention in Chilean politics, as evidenced by the prologue to *Eine Minute Dunkel macht uns nicht blind*, which seeks to give the impression that their earlier films were responsible for tighter controls on foreigners. If true, it might be argued that the filmmakers' political intervention led to greater repression; but this could have been justified at the time as potentially hastening the end of Pinochet's brutal dictatorship. Most significantly, Heynowski and Scheumann mastered the art of addressing multiple audiences at once by making films that were acceptable to an international left on both sides of the Iron Curtain and further afield in Latin America. Their films appealed to both the SED and solidarity groups in the United States – a key trait they shared with Latin American Third Cinema filmmakers (who in many cases were dependent on Europe and North America for income and often unable to screen their films at home due to political or commercial censorship).

The reception of Studio H&S's films in Latin America suggests that, at least to some extent, these films were regarded as 'Chilean' films in all but name. *Ich war, ich bin, ich werde sein* was the only film shot in post-coup Chile screened at the 1975 Pesaro Festival, an important venue for Latin American filmmakers; and the films were embraced by no less a figure than García Marquez, who had once been an aspiring filmmaker himself. *Krieg der Mumien* was shown on Cuban television the same day as it premiered on East German television; and the first part of *La batalla de Chile*, which also premiered in Cuba, would not be released until after the first three films in Studio H&S's cycle. Accordingly Heynowski and Scheumann's earliest films on Chile filled a void left on the one hand by those directors in Chile who were banned from film production and, on the other, by those who had gone into exile. Hortensia Bussi, the widow of Allende, went as far as to say that Studio H&S had written the first chapter in the history of the Pinochet coup, and that Chileans and other Latin Americans would write the rest. Articles on the films were published in *Cine Cubano*, a publication of ICAIC and the closest thing Latin American Third Cinema had to a dedicated journal.

Latin American filmmakers also valued Studio H&S's Chile cycle. The Bolivian filmmaker Alfonso Gumucio Dagron, in a manual for political Super 8 filmmaking commissioned by the Sandinista government in Nicaragua, cites the images of the Moneda, which he attributes to unnamed Europeans, as a model for guerilla filmmaking that demolishes the argument that cinema must be technically perfect to be effective.[32] When Patricio Guzmán returned to Chile in 1998 to curate FIDOCS (the International Documentary Film Festival of Santiago), he organized the first showing in Chile of *Ich war, ich bin, ich werde sein*; and the following year that same film was rescreened alongside *Mitbürger!, Geldsorgen, El Golpe Blanco/Der Weiße Putsch* and *Eine Minute Dunkel macht uns nicht blind*.

In 2001, Alfredo Barría, the director of the Valparaíso Film Festival, staged a complete retrospective of the cycle and invited Heynowski to attend (Scheumann had died in 1998). Rather than take his wife, Heynowski brought along Horst Pehnert, the last head of the GDR's *Hauptverwaltung Film*. Barrios introduced Heynowski as 'one of the greatest exponents of documentary of the second half of the twentieth century'.[33] Some 2,000 people (mainly university students) came to the opening event at which Heynowski himself was present, and subsequent screenings were well attended with an average audience of over 1,000.[34] After the screening, Heynowski travelled to Santiago, where Chilean President Ricardo Lagos gave him a personal tour of the Moneda. Ironically, *El Mercurio*, which had once been Pinochet's chief apologist in the private media, declared Heynowski the success of the festival.[35]

Perhaps the most compelling reason for considering Studio H&S's Chile cycle as a form of Latin American Third Cinema has to do with the film material itself. Just as the distribution, exhibition and reception of Studio H&S's films is inextricably bound up with that of other films from Latin America, so too is the footage its teams shot impossible to disentangle from that shot by Chilean crews. When Studio H&S returned to the GDR with footage shot in Chile, they also brought back film prints and undeveloped rolls given to them by Chilean filmmakers, prompting one member of the team to declare that 'the Chilean editing table is from now on in our studio'.[36] Studio H&S used a mix of this footage to construct the cycle, often combining other people's footage with their own – a desecration of sorts only partially mitigated by the speed at which they worked and the prohibitive costs of copying. At the same time, they were anything but careful as far as identifying the provenance of the film stock was concerned. When the Bundesarchiv returned this material to Chile in 2001, it was often impossible to distinguish what had been shot by Studio H&S crews and what had been shot by other teams.

Conclusion

While it is certainly true that Studio H&S films (and especially the Chile cycle) were of a piece with militant cinema of the late 1960s to early 1980s, and that they played a key role in the international circulation of films and footage upon which Latin American Third Cinema relied, the fact remains that their themes were, at least to some extent, determined by officials at the highest levels of the SED and its related ministries. Santiago Álvarez also worked for a dictatorship, namely that of the Castro brothers; but unlike the Castro dictatorship, the SED regime in the GDR for which Studio H&S worked, has few defenders today. This – and the often dogmatic tone of their work – has been a factor in the neglect of Studio H&S in English-speaking academic circles. But if we are prepared to look beyond the films' rhetorical and technical excesses then it is impossible to overlook the importance of their contribution to Latin American Third Cinema generally, and to Chilean cinema in particular.

Acknowledging their historical importance and formal brilliance does not, however, constitute a blanket endorsement of their practice; the films will forever appear dated due to their monovocal nature of their rhetoric. This has led to a certain ambivalence on the part of scholars writing on their work; in their monograph on Studio H&S, *Documentary Film – Between Evidence and Pamphlet*, Steinmetz and Prase include a section on *Der lachende Mann* with the revealing subtitle: 'Highpoint of Film or Demagogic Demontage?' Even Studio H&S's in-house film theorist, Günter Agde, gave his obituary of Scheumann a similarly ambivalent headline: 'Mal Wahrhaftigkeit und Manipulation, mal Anbiederung und Rebellion' ('A blend of truthfulness, manipulation, ingratiation and rebellion').[37] At an individual and personal level too, Heynowski and Scheumann remain contradictory figures: committed internationalists who furthered what were often cynical and hollow policies of solidarity on the part of the SED; communists who ran their studio along capitalist lines by hiring out their resources; artists and propagandists. While Heynowski only dealt with officials when their film careers required it, Scheumann was a willing Stasi informer since 1957. And yet, it was Scheumann whose denunciation of filmmaking practice in East Germany earned the wrath of the SED and led to the dissolution of the studio.[38]

Given the ambiguous status of these films and their makers, it is tempting to regard them, in the words of Rüdiger Steinmetz, as 'documents of the Cold War, mirroring tensions and arguments between opposing media systems'.[39] I have pointedly avoided doing this until now, preferring to emphasize their significance for and consonance with militant cinema of the period and Latin American Third Cinema more generally, both of which could accurately be labelled a 'media system', although that is not what Steinmetz intends. Yet there are very good reasons for treating the Chile cycle as Cold War historical artefacts. As David Harvey and others have argued, Pinochet's Chile, under the guidance of Milton Friedman and the other so-called 'Chicago Boys', became the testing ground for a political and economic ideology, now labelled neoliberalism, that would, within a few years, be introduced to the United States and the United Kingdom, and from there, to most of the rest of the world. Like the writings of the economic historian Andre Gunder Frank, who wrote his influential essays on 'el enemígo principal' ('the principal enemy', i.e. imperialism) while teaching at the University of Chile and while working as an advisor to Allende, the films of Studio H&S may seem dated, but they are nevertheless a vital tool for understanding a watershed moment in Latin American history and the depths of resistance levelled by Latin Americans, and Chileans in particular, against the first imposition of neoliberalism.

Dennis Hanlon is Lecturer in Film Studies at the University of St Andrews. His research interests include transnational approaches to Third Cinema, and he has published articles on the relationship between New Latin American Cinema and European Art Cinema.

Notes

1. Thomas Waugh, 'Introduction' to Pierre Vérroneau, 'The Children of Vertov in the Land of Brecht', in Thomas Waugh (ed), *'Show us Life'. Toward a History and Aesthetic of the Committed Documentary*, Metuchen, NJ; Scarecrow Press, 1989, pp. 417-30 (pp. 417-18).
2. Francisco Marín, 'La historia detrás de las imágenes', *Processo*, 10 September 2013.
3. Rüdiger Steinmetz, 'Heynowski & Scheumann. The GDR's Leading Documentary News Team', *Historical Journal of Film, Radio and Television* 24.3 (2004), 365-79 (366).
4. Steinmetz, 368.
5. Claudia Böttcher, Judith Kretzschmar and Corinna Schier, *Heynowski & Scheumann. Dokumentarfilmer im Klassenkampf. Eine kommentierte Filmographie*, Leipzig: Leipziger Universitätsverlag, 2002, p. 45.
6. Rüdiger Steinmetz and Tilo Prase, *Dokumentarfilm zwischen Beweis und Pamphlet. Heynowski & Scheumann und Gruppe Katins*, Leipzig: Leipziger Universitätsverlag, 2002, p. 62.
7. Steinmetz and Prase, p. 64.
8. Ibid., p. 71.
9. Steinmetz, 372.
10. This is important, as having a West German passport allowed Hellmich to enter and leave Chile freely without having the material he brought out of the country examined. Without such a passport, the interviews with coup plotters, junta members, fascist group leaders, right-wing businessmen, agents provocateurs of the right, and even Pinochet himself – in short most of the elements that make the Chile cycle such a unique and important document – would have been impossible.
11. Böttcher, Kretzschmar and Schier, p. 33.
12. Caroline Moine, *Cinéma et guerre froide. Histoire du festival de films documentaires de Leipzig (1955-1990)*, Paris: Publications de la Sorbonne, 2014, p. 222.

13. See, for example, Robert Michel (ed), *Politischer Film und politische Aktion: Chile-Zyklus des Studio H&S im internationalen Wirkungsraum*, Berlin: Solidaritätskomitee der DDR Chile-Zentrum, 1976.
14. Steinmetz and Prase, p. 70.
15. Steinmetz, 372.
16. Steinmetz and Prase, p. 71.
17. Steinmetz, 375.
18. Mónica Villarroel and Isabel Madrones, *Señales contra el olvido. Cine chileno recobrado*, Santiago: Editorial Cuarto Propio, 2012, pp. 143-44.
19. Sven Felix Kellerhof, 'Mit Pinochet machte die DDR beste Geschäfte', *Die Welt*, 5 September 2013.
20. Karlheinz Möbus, 'Die Beziehungen DDR-Chile' in Willi Baer and Karl-Heinz Dellwo (eds), *Diktatur und Widerstand in Chile* [= Bibliothek des Widerstands, vol. 29], Hamburg: Laika, 2013, pp. 209-21 (pp. 216-17).
21. Thomas P.M. Barnett, *Romanian and East German Policies in the Third World. Comparing the Strategies of Ceausescu and Honecker*, Westport, Connecticut: Praeger, 1992, p. 102.
22. Robert Michel, 'Kurzfilm machen: Mit Walter Heynowski und Gerhard Scheumann sprach Robert Michel', *Film und Fernsehen* 8/1974, 28-33 (29).
23. Ingrid Poss, Christiane Mückenberg and Anne Richter, *Das Prinzip Neugier. DEFA-Dokumentarfilmer erzählen*, Berlin: Das Neue Leben, 2012, p. 86.
24. Studio H&S, *Die Toten schweigen nicht (Los muertos no callan): Ein Film von Heynowski & Scheumann, Peter Hellmich*, Berlin: Studio H&S, 1978, p. ix.
25. Robert Michel, 'Geschichte schreiben, Geschichte machen', in Manfred Lichtenstein and Gerd Meier (eds), *Film im Freiheitskampf der Völker – Chile*, Berlin: Staatliches Filmarchiv der DDR, 1983, pp. 103-9 (p. 108).
26. Jorge Ruffinelli, *Patricio Guzmán*, Madrid: Ediciones Catedra, 2001, pp. 144-45.
27. Klaus Wischnewski, 'Analyse einer Klassenschlacht. Der Krieg der Mumien', *Film und Fernsehen* 5/1974, 2-7 (2). All translations are by the author unless otherwise indicated.
28. Wischnewski, 4.
29. Mike Wayne, *Political Film: The Dialectics of Third Cinema*, London: Pluto Press, 2001, p. 57.
30. Niels Siebert, 'Aufnahmen, die um die Welt gingen', *Neues Deutschland*, 11 September 2013.
31. Dziga Vertov, *Kino-Eye. The Writings of Dziga Vertov*, Berkeley: University of California Press, 1984, pp. 204-9.
32. Alfonso Gumucio Dagron, *El cine de los trabajadores*, Managua: Taller de Cine Super 8 de la CST, 1981, p. 74.
33. Siebert, 'Aufnahmen, die um die Welt gingen'.
34. 'Heynowski, el Suceso del Festival', *El Mercurio*, 1 September 2001.
35. Ibid.
36. Pierre Vérroneau, 'The Children of Vertov in the Land of Brecht', in Thomas Waugh (ed), *'Show us Life'. Toward a History and Aesthetic of the Committed Documentary*, Metuchen, NJ: Scarecrow Press, 1989, pp. 417-30 (p. 428).
37. Günter Agde, 'Mal Wahrhaftigkeit und Manipulation, mal Anbiederung und Rebellion', *Die Welt*, 5 June 1998.
38. Steinmetz, 368.
39. Ibid., 365.

CHAPTER 7

Deconstructing Orientalism
DEFA's Fictions of East Asia

Qinna Shen

When the German Democratic Republic (GDR) was founded on 7 October 1949, three states in East Asia had already embraced socialism – Mongolia, North Korea and China – and all three presented themselves as natural allies for the German newcomer in the Soviet Bloc. As early as 25 October 1949, the GDR established diplomatic relations with the People's Republic of China (PRC); and within less than six months this network was extended to include the Democratic People's Republic of Korea (7 November 1949) and the Mongolian People's Republic (13 April 1950).¹ Official recognition by the governments of these East Asian countries was all the more important because the Federal Republic of Germany (FRG) committed huge resources to a diplomatic blockade against the GDR, and in December 1955 declared that any formal relationship between a noncommunist country and the GDR would provoke punitive measures. The Federal Republic's policy of non-recognition – the so-called 'Hallstein Doctrine' – effectively deterred countries in the nonaligned world from making contact with the GDR at an official level.² Nevertheless, the East German government continually attempted to subvert this diplomatic blockade by soliciting recognition as an equal and sovereign nation wherever it could.

This essay considers the ways in which East Asian states were represented by DEFA's filmmakers, and the extent to which the aesthetics of these films – for the most part rooted in a concept of socialist realism – challenged quasi-orientalist notions of the culture and society of those states. Such notions included the suggestion that East Asian regimes were 'inherently inferior' to their Western counterparts and consisted of subservient peoples ruled over by cruel and villainous tyrants. To further justify the colonialist enterprise, East Asia was also seen as a huge threat to the security and wellbeing of Europe. The origins of the racist term 'Yellow Peril' (*Gelbe Gefahr*), a term used by Kaiser Wilhelm II in 1895,[3] extend well beyond late-nineteenth-century Germany and are rooted in the fear of Genghis Khan and Mongol invasions of Europe. In popular culture, the stereotype of the 'Yellow Peril' was reinforced via the Fu Manchu novels and films in both Europe and the United States and was deployed to legitimize colonial rule and domestic xenophobic exclusion.[4] During World War II, the Soviet Army was similarly depicted in terms of Asiatic hordes who, like Genghis Khan, were supposedly capable of all kinds of monstrous cruelty. Such stereotypes also informed the rhetoric of the Cold War, as exemplified by Robert Rigg's anticommunist treatise *Red China's Fighting Hordes*, which was published in 1951 at the height of the Korean War to support the American war effort. Rigg, a US lieutenant colonel, analyses the People's Liberation Army (PLA) – which he portrays as made up of backward, barbaric ochre hordes – its leaders and its organizational strengths and weaknesses.[5] By contrast, the DEFA films to be discussed here adopt a very different stance. They resonate with arguments against the ideology of 'Yellow Peril', suggesting instead that – as the colonial history of the region shows – it was not 'Yellow Peril' but rather '*White* Peril' that presented the real threat to world peace.[6]

Like the Middle Eastern and North African countries singled out for analysis in Edward Said's classic study *Orientalism* (1978),[7] East Asia also experienced a long history of imperialist interventions; these included a period of semi-colonial rule in China following the First Opium War between Great Britain and China (1839-1842), the establishment of colonial rule in French Indochina, American military support for Chiang Kai-shek, and the direct involvement of US combat troops in the Korean War. Although the depiction of technologically backward societies in films such as Walter Marten's *Vom Amnok-kang zum Kymgansan* [*From Amnok River to Mt Kumgang*, 1957] and Gottfried Kolditz and Rabschaa Dordschpalam's *Die goldene Jurte* [*The Golden Yurt*, 1961] would, at first sight, appear to echo such orientalist prejudices such as the supposed 'inferiority' of East Asian cultures, actually the reverse is true. The films argue instead that the reason why development in 'Third World' states lags behind that of first-world nations is a reflection of social, historical and economic forces. Put another way, if such nations are 'inferior' then that inferiority is not natural, but a direct consequence of earlier exploitation by capitalist/imperialist nations. Accordingly, the films make the case for a new type of relationship, namely one rooted in the concept of a global socialist partnership (as opposed to a dichotomy of the colony and the 'motherland'). These films suggest that orientals and occidentals are equals and there is no reason why – given the right kind of economic aid and national development – these East Asian states could not match their counterparts in the West.

By and large, the socialist realist style of DEFA's documentary films about East Asia is used to construct an unambiguously positive image of the fledgling socialist states, and one which runs directly counter to stereotypical notions of the Far East as either barbaric and cruel, or backward, exotic and sensual. For example, the tinker who walks the alleys of Beijing to mend cracked cast-iron pots in Joop Huisken and Robert Menegoz's *China – Land zwischen gestern und morgen* [*China – A Country between Yesterday and Tomorrow*, 1957] may strike non-Chinese viewers as an exotic example of East Asian 'backwardness'. However, the socialist realist aesthetic of this documentary ensures that the tinker is portrayed as a transitional figure whose activities link the historical milieu of small-scale manual labour with the modernity of contemporary large-scale industrial production (Fig. 7.1). Socialist realist documentaries of this kind not only challenged orientalist

Figure 7.1: The collision of Old and New in *China – Land zwischen gestern und morgen* (1957) © DEFA-Stiftung/Robert Ménégoz, Jean Penzer, Joop Huisken.

clichés, but also presented the struggle against imperialism and the drive to socialist nation-building as goals that East German citizens had in common with their counterparts in East Asia. The prewar colonialist projects of Britain, France, and the United States are continually subjected to criticism and those same nations are presented as enemies of socialism on account of their postwar political aspirations. Not surprisingly, the United States, because of its postwar occupation of Germany and its role in the Cold War, is almost always singled out for particular criticism.

As early as the 1950s (and thus well before the anticolonial struggles and national liberation movements that would unfold in Latin America, Africa and Asia during the 1960s), developments in East Asia provided East German filmmakers with a new non-European context in which (often familiar) messages designed to mobilize GDR citizens for national and international causes could be recycled. Films such as Bruno Kleberg's *Starke Freunde im fernen Osten* [*Strong Friends in the Far East*, 1956], Rudolf Schemmel's *Von Wismar nach Shanghai* [*From Wismar to Shanghai*, 1958], as well as the fairy-tale film *Die goldene Jurte* with its Mongolian setting, present an explicitly Marxist analysis of the legacy of colonialism and its capitalist underpinning. Although not all the films are entirely free from conventional orientalist tropes, they do nonetheless conceptualize the East–West binary in a radically new way. By underlining the solidarity between the GDR and East Asia, the films reposition the GDR as 'other' to the imperialist nations of the West (including not only Britain, France and America but also, and perhaps most importantly, the Federal Republic). At the same time, in a number of instances, the films' analysis of the political, economic and social structures of East Asian socialist states functions as a mirror in which contemporary political issues in the GDR, and the Soviet Bloc generally, are mediated. Of course, it might be argued that in exploiting the potential of such documentaries as a means of engaging with problems closer to home, East German filmmakers laid themselves open to the charge of instrumentalizing the East Asian 'Other', thereby underlining the old adage that the Self can never be entirely extricated from the discourse of the Other.

When these transnational productions are considered chronologically against the background of developments in diplomatic relations between the states, it can be seen that, geographically speaking, the films move from North Korea to China in the 1950s, then from China to Mongolia in 1961 (at the start of the Sino-Soviet split) before returning to China in the 1980s after tensions between the two nations subsided. However, each East Asian country configures a different set of problems and mobilizes a different ideological register. North Korea is the only one involved in a 'hot war' played out in the 'Third World', all of which made it a convenient ideological bridge to the situation in Vietnam later.[8] DEFA documentaries about Korea trace the causes of this 'hot war' to fascism and imperialism as manifestations of late capitalism. By contrast, the films about China that straddle the Sino-Soviet split place greater emphasis on revolutionary history, internationalism, solidarity, productivism, and the emancipation of women – all issues central to programmes of socialist nation-building during this period. For its part, Mongolia might be seen as an *ersatz* China after the Sino-Soviet split had rendered the production of films about the PRC problematic; and for that reason the films' praise of Mongolia's modernization during the 1960s (when the films were released) is not always wholly convincing.

North Korea

DEFA films about North Korea, such as Feodor Pappe's *Die amerikanischen Schandtaten in Korea – ein Tatsachenbericht* [*American Crimes in Korea – A Factual Report*, 1951][9] and *Vom Amnok-kang zum Kymgansan* concentrate predominantly on the 1950s and on the Korean War (1950-1953) in particular – the first armed conflict that mobilized ideological rivals on both sides of the Cold War divide. In these films, the entry of (US controlled) United Nations troops into the war to help the South Koreans is presented as a justification for the GDR's anti-American and anti-imperialist propaganda of the 1950s. DEFA's tendentious portrayal of the destruction of North Korea was designed to evoke sympathy from East German citizens for both Asian victims and (implicitly) for all victims of Western aggression (including East Germans). In passing, we might note that the films refer to the military aid Chiang Kai-shek received from the Americans and to the Chinese leader's visit to South Korea in 1949. In this way, DEFA's filmmakers highlighted China's vital role in assisting North Korea, while at the same time criticizing America's intervention in East Asian affairs. East German viewers would inevitably associate such military interference with the American occupation of Germany immediately after World War II and alliance with the Federal Republic soon afterwards. Seen from this perspective, films about divided Korea mirrored not only the division of Germany, but also the GDR's own efforts at postwar reconstruction.

Using considerable quantities of footage captured from the enemy (so-called *Beutefilme*), the short film *Die amerikanischen Schandtaten in Korea* focuses on 'war crimes' committed by Americans and South Koreans during the Korean conflict. The film begins with a definitive statement of authenticity: 'This film places a documentary record of indisputable facts before the world. Parts of it were made by the US information service and were captured at Seoul after its liberation on June 28, 1950, by the Korean People's Army' (English in original). Visceral images of mutilated corpses are shown while the voiceover explains that 'thousands of political prisoners were murdered when the South Korean troops retreated'.[10] Sequences showing North Korean cities such as Namp'o, Won San, Heung Nam, and An Joo in ruins after American bombardments highlight the civilian casualties and destruction of nonmilitary targets. As the camera captures images of these ruins, the voiceover points out that the Americans' assertion that 'only military targets were hit' was not true. The film does not, however, refer to the fact that the conflict was triggered by North Korea's invasion of the South on 25 June 1950, an acknowledgement that would, of course, have undermined its explicit solidarity with North Korea. Instead, the narrative and images accuse the American government of interfering in the internal affairs of a foreign state and waging an aggressive, imperialist war on North Korea. The film shows the arrival of the American fleet in South Korea in 1948 and the sending of some 500 American advisors to the country. It also includes a clip of Chiang Kai-shek's 1949 visit to Chinae, South Korea, to take part in a meeting with the South Korean president, Syngman Rhee.[11] In this way it sets up a contrast between, on the one hand, China's crucial intervention on behalf of North Korea and, on the other, America's former support of Chiang's nationalist forces in their struggle against the communists and its current support of South Korea in its struggle against the North. In *Die amerikanischen Schandtaten in Korea*, Feodor Pappe's emphasis is primarily on American (rather than South Korean) participation in the war; as a result the film's analysis of the Korean War also serves to justify the GDR's anti-Americanist stance in the wider context.

Also released during the first year of the Korean War, a bulletin from 1950 in the DEFA newsreel *Der Augenzeuge* [*The Eyewitness*, 1950/28] argues the case for continuity between fascism and imperialism before suggesting that it was the latter that prompted the US to engage in Korea. The newsreel shows street demonstrations by German workers alongside members of the Free German Youth (FDJ) and the Communist Party of Germany (KPD) in Hamburg, protesting against 'the criminal attack of the United States on the People's Republic of Korea'. In an attempt to solicit solidarity with North Korea from all quarters, the East German voiceover appeals to the sympathies of even West German viewers, pointing out that the Federal Republic too has a stake in this conflict as it might be the next victim of American aggression should the US decide to take care of 'unfinished business' from World War II. 'US strategists', he argues, 'would not hesitate to attack that which they had been unable to destroy during World War II thanks to the advance of the Soviet army'. Ostensibly a report about protestors demonstrating against the war in Korea, the bulletin shifts its focus on to the Allied bombing raids and the wartime suffering of Germans. This is just one example of how *Der Augenzeuge* exploited any opportunity to draw a parallel between American bombing raids in North Korea and the Allied bombing of Germany during World War II. Positing such an analogy was also typical of the Socialist Unity Party's (SED) political rhetoric about the Korean War.[12] The following bulletins in this newsreel go on to censure both America's alliance with Chiang Kai-shek and the arming of German legionnaires in the French colonial war in Indochina, thus making a sweeping condemnation of the West's collusion in the recent colonial history.

Four years after the Korean War ended, DEFA sent its own filmmakers to visit the war-torn country. Shot in Agfacolor, the documentary *Vom Amnok-kang zum Kymgansan* uses the river border in the north and the scenic Diamond Mountain in the south as territorial markers to symbolize North Korea's sovereignty. The film bears witness to the accomplishments of the GDR's socialist ally in postwar reconstruction, including the building of a hydroelectric power plant, a shipyard and a steel mill destroyed by American bombs. Sequences showing ordinary peasants growing food and going about their daily lives attest to the filmmakers' efforts to convey a sense of everyday life in North Korea. However, as the narrator points out, while the implements they use may still be primitive, the land now belongs to the peasants. The sparse images and short duration of the film (just nineteen minutes in total) suggest that there was little reconstruction in North Korea that could be filmed and singled out for special praise. Nonetheless, as the voiceover solemnly states – 'there is peace in North Korea' – normal everyday life had been restored. East German specialists helping North Korea's reconstruction are captured on camera in a manner that seems designed to remind East German viewers of the strength of the GDR's economy in 1957 – especially when compared to other socialist states in East Asia. Like the Soviet Union and Czechoslovakia, the GDR too, acting in a spirit of internationalist solidarity, sent experts to socialist countries in the 'Third World', and the images in the film serve to underline its status as an advanced European nation making its distinctive mark on the world stage.

The sequences of peaceful international cooperation are, however, disrupted by images of bomb craters and other painful reminders of the war. In addition to the craters, we are shown a cemetery where Korean soldiers are buried: '10,000 soldiers were buried here; they all could have lived if foreign tanks, cannons and aeroplanes had not attacked the country'. It is striking that the narrator does not say whether the soldiers are from the North or the South. Yet it would appear that the graves contain the bodies of soldiers from both sides, thus realizing the 'unity' of Korea in an especially macabre way; it is the 'foreign tanks, cannons and aeroplanes' that have caused their death. For East Germans watching the film, the allusion to 'foreign' war machines would, no doubt, invoke memories of the Allied bombing of Germany and the subsequent division of Germany into occupation zones. *Vom Amnok-kang zum Kymgansan* ends at the Military Demarcation Line between the two Korean states. The war machines may be on display in museums, but American troops continue to patrol in the Korean Demilitarized Zone (DMZ). As the narrator points out, 'foreign troops are still stationed here' because, according to the armistice agreement, Americans are South Koreans' partners in negotiation, a statement implying that the Korean conflict was an internal matter that did not warrant US intervention. Likewise, in the eyes of East Germans, Americans could be regarded as 'negotiation partners' stationed on the foreign territory of the Federal Republic. The film draws a parallel between the national divisions of the two Korean and German states to condemn America's role in both. However, while *Vom Amnok-kang zum Kymgansan* highlights South Korea's lack of sovereignty, it is diplomatically silent about the extent of foreign control in North Korea. Although shot in 1957 – some four years before the construction of the Berlin Wall – it is hard to imagine that the film and its analysis of the situation in Korea did not prompt East German viewers to reflect on the continuing presence of Allied forces in their own divided nation.

China

There are more DEFA documentaries about China than about all the other East Asian countries put together, a statistic that had much to do with China's ideological and political status at the time.[13] Between 1956 and 1961, DEFA produced six documentaries about China: *Starke Freunde im fernen Osten* (1956), *China – Land zwischen gestern und morgen* (1956/1957), *Von Wismar nach Shanghai* (1958), as well as three films by Gerhard Jentsch – *Wir berichten aus Pan Yü* [*We Report from Pan Yü*, 1959], *Wir sangen und tanzten in China* [*We Sang and Danced in China*, 1959] and *Genosse Sziau erzählt* [*Comrade Xiao Narrates*, 1960/1961]. In addition, Joris Ivens's *Lied der Ströme* [*Songs of the Rivers*, 1954] and his film *Die Windrose* [*The Compass Rose*, 1956] have significant references to the Chinese revolution and post-revolution construction as part of the international socialist struggle.[14]

Most of these films begin by depicting the semi-colonial era of China in order to convey a sense of the liberation and freedom from oppression that the PRC has provided for its population. For example, when historic sites such as the Forbidden City and the Temple of Heaven in Beijing are shown in *Starke Freunde im fernen Osten*, the voiceover points out that these imperial places were inaccessible to ordinary Chinese until the founding of the PRC; in *Wir sangen und tanzten in China*, viewers are also told that buildings visible from the Forbidden City were not allowed to be higher than the palace itself; but all this has now changed. A deep-seated admiration for the long, hard-fought – but ultimately successful – communist revolution in China runs through all of the films about the PRC. The price that Chinese communists paid for their revolution instils an affective quality in the voiceover: 'Our path is covered with blood!' and 'The victims of the revolution will never die!' we are told in *Starke Freunde im fernen Osten*. It would not have taken long for East German filmmakers and viewers alike to draw parallels between the suffering of the Chinese communists and that which the German communists endured under the Nazis, as well as the similarities between the cults of Mao and Stalin. Likewise, praise of revolutionary achievements in the 'new China' can be read, during the early 1950s at least, as coded praise of Stalinism in the 'new Germany' that was the GDR. In this way, these international documentaries could also be integrated into the GDR's own antifascist foundational narratives.

The narration in these films strikes an unmistakably anti-imperialist and anti-capitalist tone. Shanghai's colonial past is invariably invoked when the famous promenade, the Bund with its Western architecture, is shown. For example, the narrator in *China – Land zwischen gestern und morgen* states: 'Shanghai, a seven-million-strong city, with skyscrapers and gigantic hotels, with parks and avenues; once a symbol of foreign rule, with foreign concessions, child labour and a flourishing opium trade. After liberation, this major port is China's gateway to the world'. As *Wir berichten aus Pan Yü* shows, visits to military bases (often part of the official agenda for guests from the GDR) remind the viewer of the need for China to remain vigilant: 'Never forget', the voiceover warns, 'that socialist China is a thorn in the eyes of imperialists!' The travel reportage *Von Wismar nach Shanghai* about the maiden voyage of a 10,000-ton freighter, *Friendship*, to Shanghai does not focus on international trade or tourism. Instead, the narrator exploits the travelogue format to lament the continuing colonial status of Algeria and Yemen: 'Over there lies the coast of Algeria. A French gunship; how much longer will it be stationed there? The most beautiful island of Malta; how much longer will the island be the bomber base for the US fleet and NATO's marine headquarters?' When passing Indonesia, the voiceover hails Indonesia's recent independence from 'Dutch imperialism'. Clearly, DEFA took every opportunity to comment on the colonial policies of Western Europe, and the former colonies in Africa, the Middle East and Asia provided many opportunities for it to re-emphasize the ideological divide between the GDR and the FRG. Sailing into the port of Shanghai, the narrator exclaims that, for the first time, the crew of a ship sailing under the GDR flag has set eyes on the 'China that is now our friend'. Hardworking Chinese dockers load 'gifts of friendship' such as silk, spices, tobacco, nuts, tea and valuable ores onto the ship.

While the Federal Republic used both carrots and sticks to prevent other developing nations from forming relationships with the GDR, for its part the SED attempted to discredit its Western neighbour by implicating it in the history of colonialism, fascism and imperialism. In this way the GDR was able to assume the moral high ground and, at the same time, bolster its own antifascist narratives.[15] The SED promoted the GDR's image as the 'revolutionary' Germany, so as to avoid being seen as the 'poor' Germany 'that could not match its rival's much larger aid programs'.[16] As *Starke Freunde im fernen Osten* documents, during his state visit to China in December 1955, Otto Grotewohl, the GDR's first Prime Minister, handed back to China that which, as he put it, had been 'looted by German imperialists': a number of volumes of the *Yongle Encyclopaedia* compiled during the Ming Dynasty as well as flags taken during the Boxer Rebellion. The seizing of the encyclopaedia and flags was, of course, trivial compared to the wholesale exploitation of the country undertaken by the Western powers since the end of the First Opium War in 1842. However, China's first Premier, Zhou Enlai, regarded this as the start of a process of retrieving treasures lost during China's semi-colonial period: 'It won't be too long before all the spoils looted by imperialists will be returned to China'. The narrator construes the return of the Boxer flags as a diplomatic event inspired by genuinely progressive political convictions: 'As German socialists, descendants of Marx and Engels, we hand the flags back to you'. Grotewohl's symbolic gesture reflected the GDR's sympathetic view of the Boxer Rebellion as a peasant revolution against feudal and imperialist oppression.[17] On the one hand, it demonstrated the GDR's dissociation from German imperialism because of the role Wilhelminian Germany played in quashing the Boxer Rebellion. On the other hand, the return of the Boxer flags also suggested that it is the GDR – not the Federal Republic – that was the legitimate successor to prewar Germany; and that only it had the right (and responsibility) to correct the mistakes of the past.

These 1950s films routinely represent China as a nation in transition. The best example of this is the DEFA-French co-production *China – Land zwischen gestern und morgen* – a film that was supported by China's Ministry for Culture and Filmmaking. Shot in Agfacolor, the film was praised as a masterpiece of the documentary genre in numerous newspaper reviews.[18] The two directors, Joop Huisken and Robert Menegoz, also won a state film and television award – the Heinrich Greif Prize – in 1957.[19] Huisken and Menegoz's film captures the huge economic and social upheavals that the 600 million Chinese have undergone since the founding of the new socialist republic. Old and new stand in constant contrast: massive dams are built not far from the Great Wall; a column of trucks drive alongside loaded camels; an itinerant tinker carrying his traditional tools passes through a modern steel plant; a couple in the countryside celebrate their wedding in accordance with traditional custom, but their marriage is no longer arranged; peasants continue to grow and harvest rice, but now they can own land and exchange rice for money; and while boats have to be hauled upstream using a system of men and ropes, a railway network is being built with the help of a female engineer. Accompanied by nondiegetic Chinese music and a cinematography that, at times, seems inspired by Chinese watercolours, the narrator (Wolfgang Kieling with a script by Bodo Uhse) often resorts to a metaphorical language that brings out the contrasts between old and new in a manner that is by turns both lyrical and sentimental: 'The plough sows new seeds in the old soil'; 'A new life pulses through the old gates of Beijing'; and 'The old city of Beijing has a young heart'. The film depicts China's endeavours in the drive to socio-economic development and modernization and emphasizes the diligence and work ethic of the Chinese people who carry the nation's hopes for the future.

By contrast, all three of Gerhard Jentsch's documentaries – *Wir berichten aus Pan Yü, Wir sangen und tanzten in China* and *Genosse Sziau erzählt* – bear witness to the unprecedented and (in hindsight) catastrophic developments in China during the 1950s: the Great Leap Forward (1958 to 1961) and the People's Commune. The films enthusiastically support the People's Commune as an example of the concerted and efficient utilization of collective power that is not unlike the Agricultural Production Cooperatives (LPGs) established in the GDR. The fact that Walter Ulbricht led a delegate to the CCP's Eighth Party Congress in October 1956 to learn about Chinese approaches to agricultural collectivization suggests that, in addition to following the Soviet model, the GDR of the 1950s was also eager to learn from China.[20]

Wir berichten aus Pan Yü visits the district of Pan Yü in the city of Canton with the aim of familiarizing East German viewers with the collectivist operations and achievements of the People's Commune there. Against a background of Chinese propaganda songs praising the Party, the German voiceover relays the Chinese government's official rhetoric emphasizing its ambition to match – and surpass – the achievements of Western countries. The film includes sequences showing the production of steel from scrap metal in backyard furnaces (in the manner that Mao – with subsequently disastrous consequences – had advocated). The brevity of these sequences depicting such backward technology hints at a lack of faith in, or perhaps even disapproval of, such primitive methods on the part of the German filmmakers. Be that as it may, it is striking that the film fails to offer an explicit critique of the political, economic and cultural campaigns waged in Red China; and the lack of any genuine criticism in this and other DEFA documentaries about China merely serves as a reminder of the constraints under which its teams had to operate when working in other socialist countries.

Friendship between China and the GDR is a central feature in almost all these documentaries. As Weijia Li notes, the roots of this friendship can be traced back to the Weimar Republic, when Chinese communists and other leftist activists living and studying in Germany collaborated with their German counterparts before the Nazis came to power.[21] Such transnational friendships were the very opposite of the kind of anti-oriental prejudice embodied in Kaiser Wilhelm II's rhetorical references to the Chinese as 'Yellow Peril'. A similar evocation of such international friendship is reflected in the film *Wir sangen und tanzten in China,* a film that covers a tour of China in late 1958 by the GDR's Erich-Weinert-Ensemble. As we watch the ensemble visiting a warship in southern China in the wake of the Second Taiwan Strait Crisis in August 1958, the narrator cautions against the threat from (noncommunist) Taiwan that, as he puts it, could 'disrupt our celebrations of friendship'. Here too, what starts off as a report about a cultural exchange between

Germans and Chinese soon becomes a series of reflections about the vicissitudes of the Cold War (Fig. 7.2).

This friendship between the GDR and China, however, proved to be a fragile arrangement and one that depended on good relations between the Soviet Union and China. Due to irreconcilable differences on ideological and socio-economic issues, such as the People's Commune, the process of de-Stalinization and Khrushchev's policy of peaceful coexistence with the US, the Sino-Soviet relations deteriorated around 1960 leading to a recall of all Soviet experts stationed in China and the interruption of a great number of collaborative projects. As a Soviet satellite state, the GDR had little choice but to follow Moscow's lead.[22] Tensions between China and the GDR built up in 1960 as the SED's policy shifted in accordance with Moscow's condemnation of the People's Commune. The public break with China came during the SED's Sixth Party Congress in January 1963.[23] DEFA documentaries such as *Wir berichten aus Pan Yü* and *Wir sangen und tanzten in*

Figure 7.2: The ensemble sings songs that echoed the Chinese government's rhetoric about overtaking England and America in *Wir sangen und tanzten in China* (1959) © DEFA-Stiftung/Peter Barthel, Peter Sbrzesny.

China that had depicted the Great Leap Forward and the People's Commune in a positive light came to be regarded as historically erroneous. By the same token, the celebrations of Sino-German friendship, in such films as *Starke Freunde im fernen Osten*, had been overtaken by events on the political stage and appeared equally out of place.

The Sino-Soviet split, which lasted for two decades, curtailed DEFA's interaction with China, since the making of transnational documentaries was heavily contingent upon political relations between the two nations. However, when the tension between the Soviet Union and China eased during the early 1980s, the GDR immediately resumed economic and cultural exchanges with China. During the GDR's final years, DEFA made a number of China-related films – for the most part ethnographic travel reportages commissioned by East German state television. The best known is Uwe Belz's eight-part series, *Stromabwärts nach Shanghai* [Downstream to Shanghai, 1987]. These films visualize a rapidly developing China and provide a much broader and more detailed coverage of Chinese landscapes, people, culture and traditions (including martial arts, acrobatics and local operas). The film team flew into Beijing, which is the focus of the first instalment in the series. This episode notes that, among other achievements, China has built more apartment blocks in Beijing since 1981 than in the thirty years before that, and that the government is planning to continue its programme of housing development so that by 2000 every family would have its own flat.[24] The informative report on the housing situation in Beijing was prompted by a similar policy on the part of the SED designed to solve housing shortages in the GDR. These and other cultural connections between China and the GDR were always highlighted whenever a suitable opportunity presented itself, such as the student exchange programme for those studying at Peking University and the Humboldt University in East Berlin.

Although the overtly Marxist-Leninist rhetoric of this 1987 television series is toned down, the ideological paradigm remains similar to that in earlier documentaries dating back to the 1950s. Each episode explores one city along the Yangtze river, except for the one on Beijing. The episode on Chongqing, at that time a major city in the province of Sichuan, has much in common with reports from the 1950s in terms of its ideological positioning. After the Qing Dynasty was defeated in the first Sino-Japanese War (1894-1895), Chongqing and a number of other Chinese cities were forced to become treaty ports for capitalist powers: 'Chongqing, 1895. After the First Sino-Japanese War, the city had to be opened to capitalist powers for their business branches and semi-colonial exploitations'. The city still exhibits indelible traces of the Communist revolution: 'There were twenty such prisons in Chongqing at that time. Two of them have been kept as memorials. Here, revolutionaries were tortured and murdered barbarically. Mao's handwriting commemorates those who no longer live to see the victory of the revolution'. The creation of the PRC liberated a city of coolies from misery: 'The Monument of Liberation in sight at the market place calls to mind of a time when Chongqing was a city of coolies and misery. Since the establishment of the People's Republic many new things have been built and, since the beginning of modernization, faster and more generously than ever before'. A massive quarry, with the noise of hammers and chisels, is compared to a concert that the manual labourers play: 'It seems as if we have walked into a concert with hammers and chisels in huge fields. Heavy rocks are still carried manually. There are still no machines. But the work is important for the country'.

The anti-imperialist rhetoric abated in the 1980s – a change that was essential given the new developments in international geopolitics. The belligerent discourse of the 1950s now sounded outdated, detrimental, and politically incorrect. Chinese officials openly encouraged this change of tone following Deng Xiaoping's new economic and foreign policy and his willingness to embrace Western capitalism. During Erich Honecker's visit to China in 1986 – a visit that took place after the two states had reasserted their friendship – the then General Secretary, Hu Yaobang, promised that China would never damage the close relationships that existed between socialist countries in Eastern Europe and the Soviet Union. Hu also recommended abandoning the use of certain terminologies, such as 'US imperialism, Japanese militarism or West German revanchism'.[25]

As in the 1950s, DEFA films of the 1980s such as *Stromabwärts nach Shanghai, Zwischen Großer Mauer und Perlfluss – Begegnungen in der Volksrepublik China* [Between the Great Wall and the Pearl River – Encounters with the People's Republic of China, first aired on 20 October 1986] and Uwe Belz's *Ni hao – heißt Guten Tag* [Ni Hao – Means Hello, 1989] did not engage critically with China's policies and, despite over thirty years of strained relations, the Chinese government's rhetoric was adopted as the dominant GDR narrative about China. The fact that the Chinese government often co-sponsored East German film projects goes some way to explaining the filmmakers' need to adopt the discourse of the Chinese government. These films repeatedly affirm improved living standards and go out of their way to show an abundance of consumer goods in China. At a time when Eastern Europe was facing a period of economic stagnation on account of outdated technology and collapsing industries, DEFA filmmakers seem to have appealed to China's economic success in an attempt to reassure GDR citizens that socialism was still capable of creating high standards of living. However, whereas China created a hybrid communist/capitalist model to achieve political stability as well as economic growth, this was impossible for the GDR due to its dependence on the Soviet Union.

Mongolia

After DEFA had discontinued its film projects in China in 1961 following the Sino-Soviet split, it turned its attention to Mongolia and, that same year, joined forces with Mongolkino in Ulan Bator and released two feature-length co-productions: a fairy-tale film titled *Die goldene Jurte* and an ethnographic documentary *Mongolia* (directed by B. Daschdortsch). The reason for releasing both films in 1961 was that this year marked the fortieth anniversary of socialist Mongolia. On 9 November 1921, with the backing of the Soviet Union, Outer Mongolia gained *de facto* independence from the Republic of China. After the Sino-Soviet split began, Mongolia continued to align itself closely with its Soviet sponsor. Given that the films were made in 1961, the quality of the colour films was something that the Mongolkino alone would not have been able to achieve technically.

Shot primarily in Mongolia, *Die goldene Jurte* adapts a traditional Mongolian tale that emphasizes the importance of kindness, diligence, honesty and filial piety. In the film, the Wise Herdsman (Der weise Arat) gives the shepherd Pagwa a magic chest on the condition that no one opens it. In fact, the chest serves as a magical duct that channels water from the sea to a nearby pond. As long as the chest is full of water, the Valley of Red Blossom will be protected from drought. Pagwa initially believes that the chest contains gold, and the Wise Herdsman reprimands him for making a dangerous secret out of it. Pagwa's two older sons, both of them greedy and lazy, try to steal the key to the chest. Pagwa suffers from depression as a result because a catastrophic drought is looming. The youngest son, Dawadorshi, goes to seek advice from the Wise Herdsman, who offers him solutions to three problems: Pagwa's melancholy, the dried-out condition of the river and the blindness of a Mongolian girl (whom he subsequently marries). After Dawadorshi rescues a fish that turns out to be the daughter of the Water-Khan (*der Wasserkahn*) he receives three gifts – a magical hat, a sheepskin that can summon up rain, and a small hammer that conjures up a golden yurt (Fig. 7.3). His two brothers also redeem themselves (somewhat unconvincingly) by plugging a hole in the reservoir. The entire family lives happily ever after under the tender care of the daughter-in-law in their golden yurt.

Die goldene Jurte contains a number of extended sequences that are simply designed to showcase the Mongolian landscape (including the steppe and Gobi desert) and local customs (including traditional games and dances, and markets with people buying and selling carpets and furs). These sequences were included primarily to satisfy the curiosity of East German viewers who had virtually no possibility of travelling there in person. What is particularly striking about the film is the way in which it casts German actors in the role of the Water-Khan and his daughter; all other roles are played by Mongolian actors. Because of their otherworldly origins, the roles of the Water-Khan and his daughter would appear to be the most suited for 'foreign' (i.e. non-Mongolian) actors. Nonetheless it is hard to ignore the possibility that casting an East German actor (Kurt Mühlhardt) in the

Figure 7.3: Dawadorshi passes the Water-Khan's test and receives three magic gifts in *Die goldene Jurte* (1961) © DEFA-Stiftung/Peter Blümel.

deus-ex-machina role of the Water-Khan was a means of highlighting the contribution of the GDR and its citizens in the modernization of Mongolia and other (socialist) countries in the 'Third World'– for ultimately it is the Water-Khan's magical gifts that bring happiness to the region. That is to say, by shifting the focus away from the (Mongolian) Wise Herdsman to the (German) Water-Khan, the film adaptation of the original Mongolian tale highlights the crucial role that (East) German assistance plays in building a better and more prosperous Mongolia as symbolized by the golden yurt.

By contrast, the more prosaic documentary *Mongolia* (also released in 1961) provides a sober reality check on the fairy-tale commentary on Mongolian life and argues that a yurt – even a golden one – is no longer a desirable home in socialist Mongolia. A yurt, according to their government, represents a backward, pastoral and nomadic existence that Mongolians today should no longer embrace: 'The People's Republic has declared the end of the yurt'. The government has ambitious plans for building 'proper' houses in order to ensure that the population has a stable, modern existence: 'Another generation will pass, and then yurts will be nothing more than holiday homes for herdsmen'. Viewed from the perspective of the documentary *Mongolia*, the fairy-tale solution proposed at the end of *Die goldene Jurte* is old-fashioned and impractical in the context of the state's modernization. Nonetheless, there are moments where the documentary's German narrator seems reluctant to back the Mongolian government's disapproval of the yurt: he claims that yurts 'should only be on display in the museum and serve as a warning of the terrors of the past', and yet he is clearly infatuated with their artistic and architectural beauty and admires them as 'proof of the industriousness and artistry of the Mongolian people'. Although ostensibly endorsing the official policy of renouncing the yurt, even a film like *Mongolia* – which remains ambivalent in its evaluation of the ethnic traditions and cultural values of the yurt – retains the potential to make East German viewers question what is entailed by progress and what new forms of socialist living they should aspire to. Seen from this perspective, the fairy-tale ending of *Die goldene Jurte* invokes a nostalgia for a way of life that is both utopian and yet outdated, and hints at a plea not to abandon long-held national traditions too quickly and too radically.

As might be expected, both of the films dealing with Mongolia eulogize socialism, though this is more obviously the case in the documentary *Mongolia* – which is infused with Cold War rhetoric – than in the multi-facetted fairy tale *Die goldene Jurte*. The narrator in *Mongolia* reminds us that 'in forty years, the

People's Republic has led a small nation out of the dark Middle Ages into the bright dawn of a new era'. As we observe the Mongolian landscape and customs, the narrator heaps praise on the 'beautiful Mongolian *Heimat*', before going on to anticipate a critical response from viewers in the West: '"But this is all very primitive" – that's what some snobbish NATO-Germans will say'. However, blame for the lack of modern consumer goods in Mongolia and difficulties the state is experiencing is placed firmly at the feet of the reactionary lamas. The narrator then goes on to set up a contrast between the political choices of the Mongolian people and those of (politically reactionary) Germans: whereas the former have embraced Lenin, Khrushchev and world peace, the latter have elected Hindenburg, Hitler, and – in the year of the film's release – the CSU chairman, Franz-Josef Strauß. The inference is clear: however backward Mongolia may be in terms of its GDP and material standards of living, all of this is more than compensated for by the strength of its ideological commitment to progressive (socialist) politics – a message that, no doubt, resonated with East German viewers in 1961 as they reflected on the economic and ideological gulf between the GDR and the FRG.

Both films also have an antireligious and antifeudal thrust. *Die goldene Jurte* is set in a feudal society where the laws of the lamas forbid farming. The Wise Herdsman breaks that taboo and sows corn seeds in order to relieve the prevailing famine. When the youngest son Dawadorshi reminds him of the law, the Wise Herdsman answers, 'Yes, but who has issued such an absurd ban? It was the powerful. They want people to starve'. As the documentary underlines, the socialist government in Mongolia carried out antireligious and antifeudal campaigns designed to divest the lamas of their former power: 'With cunning, deceit and violence, the lamas used to exclude the people from having power; now they must do productive work and no longer own serfs. Land and livestock have been seized from the monasteries'. The Wise Herdsman's anti-authoritarian attitude casts him in the role of a proto-typical socialist leader who rebels against the old rule. Ultimately, however, real authority in the fairy tale is conferred not upon the Wise Herdsman but rather upon the figure of the Water-Khan, whose intervention renders Dawadorshi's search for water finally successful.

What distinguishes *Die goldene Jurte* from the more dogmatic documentary *Mongolia* is its aesthetic form (which is perhaps best described as a provocative blend of socialist and magic realism). The golden yurt, with which the fairy-tale adaptation closes, embodies a successful conclusion to the struggle for a better future and the establishment of a utopian socialist realm in which virtuous members of the collective can live together in harmony and prosperity as a big and happy socialist family. At one level, the film presents a vision of a future in which the obstacles to political progress caused by the reactionary lamas have been swept aside; but at another, directors Gottfried Kolditz and Rabschaa Dordschpalam exploit the discursive *naiveté* of the fairy-tale form to address the increasingly urgent problem of the deterioration of relations between the Soviet Union and the PRC since the late 1950s. While for most filmmakers in 1961 the Sino-Soviet split was, in effect, a taboo subject (and thus one quite beyond the scope of conventional socialist-realist documentaries such as *Mongolia*), in the closed moral world of *Die goldene Jurte*, underpinned as it is by the naïve logic of the fairy tale, Mongolia functions as an exotic location – far removed from the harsh geopolitical reality of Sino-Soviet relations – with a hope that future socialist harmony can be articulated.

Conclusion

Analysing DEFA films on East Asia reveals that, while investigations of East Asian societies allowed a new and sympathetic image of East Asia to emerge on European screens, they also often doubled as a commentary on both the role of the GDR in the 'Third World' and on the development of German-German relations during the Cold War. Now that the GDR and the socialist states in East Asia were united in their ideological opposition to British, French and American imperialism, East German filmmakers set about rejecting clichéd orientalist images of the Far East and foregrounding instead the revolutionary and anticolonial accomplishments of the fledgling socialist states in East Asia. By and large, these East German productions served dual functions: they assisted in promoting the ruling SED's foreign policy in respect of East Asia, and at the same time they used East Asia as a way of reflecting on pressing issues relating to the contemporary political situation in the GDR and in the Soviet Bloc generally. Reports on the Korean War and on the emergence of new socialist states in East Asia could be cited as evidence of the GDR's commitment to, and active involvement in, an antifascist, anticolonial and anti-imperialist agenda. Moreover, such reports underlined not only the international dimension of the struggle for socialism, but reminded (East German) viewers of their own nation's contribution to this global undertaking.

Qinna Shen is Assistant Professor of German at Bryn Mawr College (Pennsylvania). Her book, *The Politics of Magic. DEFA Fairy-Tale Films*, appeared in 2015. She is also the co-editor of *Beyond Alterity. German Encounters with Modern East Asia* (2014).

Notes

I would like to thank the following archives for making this project possible: Bundesarchiv-Filmarchiv in Berlin, Deutsches Rundfunkarchiv in Potsdam-Babelsberg, Pressedokumentation at the Hochschule für Film und Fernsehen (*HFF*) 'Konrad Wolf' in Potsdam-Babelsberg, and the DEFA-Stiftung. I am also indebted to the DEFA Film Library at the University of Massachusetts Amherst for hosting the 2011 DEFA Summer Film Institute with a thematic focus on 'Cold War/Hot Media: DEFA and the Third World' that provided me with an expertly compiled reader and a week of inspiring discussions. I thank Benjamin Robinson, Evan Torner and Skyler Arndt-Briggs for reading my essay and offering insightful suggestions for revision.

1. Japan was the first nation to become the victim of atomic bombs and thus fulfilled a specific function in the GDR's peace program. The few documentaries about Japan during this time are dominated by concerns for security issues and disarmament. For example: Fumio Kamei's *Bedrohte Menschheit* [*Endangered Mankind*, DEFA-Studio für Synchronisation, 1958]; Karl Gass's *Zwei Tage im August: Rekonstruktion eines Verbrechens* [*Two Days in August. Reconstruction of a Crime*, 1982]; and *Tele-Atlas: Japan* [1974]. However, as Japan is a nonsocialist state, it is beyond the scope of the present discussion.
2. William Glenn Gray, *Germany's Cold War. The Global Campaign to Isolate East Germany, 1949-1969*, Chapel Hill: University of North Carolina Press, 2003; Thomas Barnett, *Romanian and East German Policies in the Third World. Comparing the Strategies of Ceausescu and Honecker*, Westport, CT: Praeger, 1992.
3. The murder of two German Catholic missionaries in 1897 provided Wilhelm II with the desired excuse to seize Kiaochow Bay in order to expand economic exploits in China. The subsequent murder in 1900 of the German diplomat in Beijing, Clemens von Kettler, during the Boxer Rebellion prompted the Kaiser to send 10,000 German troops to China. See David M. Crowe, 'Sino-German Relations, 1871-1917', in Joanne Miyang Cho and David M. Crowe (eds), *Germany and China. Transnational Encounters since the Eighteenth Century*, New York: Palgrave Macmillan, 2014, pp. 71-96.
4. Gina Marchetti, 'From Fu Manchu to M. *Butterfly* and *Irma Vep*. Cinematic Incarnations of Chinese Villainy', in Murray Pomerance (ed), *Bad. Infamy, Darkness, Evil, and Slime on Screen*, Albany, NY: State University of New York Press, 2004, pp. 187-200.
5. Robert B. Rigg, *Red China's Fighting Hordes*, Westport, CT: Greenwood, 1951.
6. See Yu-Chien Kuan and Petra Häring-Kuan, *Die Langnasen. Was die Chinesen über uns Deutsche denken*, Frankfurt am Main: Fischer, 2009, pp. 78-9.
7. Edward W. Said, *Orientalism*, New York: Pantheon Books, 1978.
8. The term 'hot war' is borrowed from Mark Atwood Lawrence's 'Hot Wars in Cold War Africa', *Reviews in American History* 32.1 (2004), 114-21. It is a review of Piero Gleijeses, *Conflicting Missions. Havana, Washington, and Africa, 1959-1976*, Chapel Hill: University of North Carolina Press, 2002.

9. The film has an alternative title: *Greueltaten amerikanischer Aggressoren* [*Atrocities of American Aggressors*].
10. All translations are by the author unless otherwise indicated.
11. Scott T. Price, 'The U.S. Coast Guard's Role in the Korean Conflict', 26 November 2012 [= http://www.uscg.mil/history/articles/Korean_War.asp], accessed 20 June 2016.
12. Robert G. Moeller, 'The Politics of the Past in the 1950s. Rhetorics of Victimisation in East and West Germany', in Bill Niven (ed), *Germans as Victims. Remembering the Past in Contemporary Germany*, New York: Palgrave Macmillan, 2006, pp. 26-42 (pp. 29, 36 and 37).
13. Along the same lines, the diplomatic missions to North Korea and the Democratic Republic of Vietnam after 8 December 1954 operated from Beijing with the same GDR ambassador to China, Johannes König.
14. See Dennis Hanlon, '*Die Windrose*', *DEFA Film Library Newsletter* (Jan 2012).
15. Gray, p. 102.
16. Barnett, p. 105.
17. Joseph W. Esherick, *The Origins of the Boxer Uprising*, Berkeley: University of California Press, 1987.
18. See, for example, 'Filmschaffen in Wahrheit und Gemeinsamkeit', *Sächsisches Tageblatt*, 6 November 1956; W. J., 'Am Jangtse steht ein Riese auf', *National Zeitung*, 26 March 1957; 'China – Land zwischen gestern und morgen', *BZ am Abend*, 26 March 1957; 'Die Lotosblüten und der neue Stahl', *Neue Zeit*, Berlin – Ostsektor, 27 March 1957; Hans Bergmann, 'Jahrhunderte verbrüdern sich', *Neues Deutschland*, 28 March 1957; 'Bilddokumente vom neuen China: Ein Gemeinschaftsfilm der Defa und Procinex, Paris', *Das Volk*, Erfurt, 3 April 1957.
19. Alexander Abusch, 'Reale Perspektiven unserer sozialistischen Filmproduktion', *Deutsche Filmkunst* 7/1957, 193-94.
20. Werner Meißner (ed), *Die DDR und China 1949 bis 1990: Politik – Wirtschaft – Kultur. Eine Quellensammlung*, bearbeitet von Anja Feege, Berlin: Akademie Verlag, 1995, pp. 83-91; Harald Möller, *DDR und Dritte Welt. Die Beziehungen der DDR mit Entwicklungsländern, ein neues theoretisches Konzept, dargestellt anhand der Beispiele China und Äthiopien, sowie Irak/Iran*, Berlin: Köster, 2003, pp. 112-14.
21. Weijia Li, 'Otherness in Solidarity. Collaboration between Chinese and German Left-Wing Activists in the Weimar Republic', in Qinna Shen and Martin Rosenstock (eds), *Beyond Alterity. German Encounters with Modern East Asia*, New York: Berghahn, 2014, pp. 73-93.
22. Lorenz M. Lüthi, *The Sino-Soviet Split. Cold War in the Communist World*, Princeton: Princeton University Press, 2008.
23. Meißner, pp. 14-15.
24. See also Mimosa Künzel, 'Abenteuer in China', *Neue Zeit*, 19 January 1988.
25. Meißner, pp. 56 and 369ff.

CHAPTER 8
Transnational Stardom
DEFA's Management of Dean Reed

Seán Allan

'Do we need stars?', asks an article of 1955 published in the East German youth magazine *Neues Leben*.[1] The answer, as audience polls conducted by publications such as *Filmspiegel* underlined, was that stars were indeed needed and East German cinema-goers held strong opinions regarding their favourite actors and actresses (not all of whom were from the GDR). As a result, during the mid 1950s DEFA increasingly relied on international co-productions featuring foreign stars to boost the flagging popularity of the studio's output. Yet for many cultural theorists in the GDR, the concept of stardom, bound up as it was with the prewar traditions of both Hollywood and UFA, remained inherently problematic. Writing in the introduction to a volume published in 1962 entitled *Unsere Filmsterne* [*Our Filmstars*], the then Deputy Minister of Culture, Hans Rodenberg, noted 'Although this volume is entitled "film stars" it should not be seen as an appeal for stars with overinflated egos and dressed up like the kind of idols we unfortunately come across all too often in "blockbusters" from the West'.[2] The concept of stardom, however, did not simply conjure up images of decadent excess; and in *Mach dir ein paar schöne Stunden* [*Make Some Time For Yourself*], a highly polemical survey of cinema in the West published the year before, the emphasis was instead on stars as victims of exploitation; for, as we are told 'the economic mills of capitalist film production crush not only existing stars, but stars in the making too'.[3]

As Stefan Soldovieri has argued, many aspects of Western stardom (notably the dynamics of desire, identification and ideology) could be adapted to suit the very different context of socialist film production in the East.[4] DEFA's turn to more popular film genres during the 1960s, a period that Sabine Hake has termed 'the golden decade of the socialist star system',[5] was accompanied by the emergence of a new discourse of stardom. At its heart was the so-called *Publikumsliebling* (darling of the masses), a distinctively East German concept designed to capture the popularity of individual performers while at the same time avoiding the negative connotations of excess associated with Hollywood. The concept of the *Publikumsliebling*, as Claudia Fellmer has demonstrated, was predicated above all on notions of 'ordinariness' and social 'immobility'.[6] In popular magazines such as *Filmspiegel, Neue Berliner Illustrierte* and *Für Dich*, DEFA stars were often shown visiting factories and remaining firmly in touch with the everyday lives of GDR citizens. Instead of homing in on salaries, scandal and the intimate details of stars' private lives, the GDR's popular press focused on restrained consumption and, where appropriate, included endorsements of goods produced in the GDR. Yet, as Soldovieri argues, 'on the whole, star discourse in East Germany was both heterogeneous and contradictory, with anti-Western posturing coexisting uneasily with the publicity put out by DEFA's distributor for its own films and imports'.[7]

One possible resolution of this paradox presented itself in the form of the American-born singer and actor Dean Reed who, in 1972, had emigrated to the GDR.[8] Reed's status in the GDR was quite different from that of Erwin Geschonneck, Armin Mueller-Stahl or Manfred Krug, not least because he was already firmly established as a popular entertainer in the Eastern Bloc when he first visited the GDR towards the end of 1971. Like Gojko Mitic, his Yugoslavian-born co-star in *Blutsbrüder* [*Blood Brothers*, 1975], Reed had the bonus of being an 'exotic' outsider; and his non-German origins and striking good looks could not but appeal to an East German audience whose desire to identify with international stars was only partially satisfied by limited exposure to West German television and to films imported from the United States and Western Europe. However, what made Reed stand out so markedly from other international stars was the fact that he was an American who had turned his back on the United States and swapped sides during the Cold War. The radical nature of Reed's politics, coupled with his wide appeal across Eastern Bloc audiences, presented DEFA with a unique opportunity to combine the popular and the political; but, as we shall see, this same combination also made him a liability in the eyes of the studio management and the GDR's Ministry of Culture.

When Reed first visited the GDR, in November 1971, as a guest of the Fourteenth International Documentary Film Festival in Leipzig, he had already completed his second tour of the Soviet Union. His credentials as a left-wing activist had been bolstered in the autumn of 1970 not only by his support for the

Allende regime in Chile, but also by his symbolic washing of the American flag before the US Consulate in Santiago: 'This North American flag', he declared 'is stained with the blood of the North Vietnamese... dirty with the blood of the Negro race... with the blood and pain of the American Indians... of millions of people in South America, Africa and Asia who are forced to live in misery and injustice because the US government supports the dictatorships that keep these people in bondage'.[9] Although this act of protest attracted relatively little coverage in the international press at the time, it featured prominently in the construction of Reed's star personality in the GDR from 1971 onwards, above all in a four-page feature on Reed published in *Filmspiegel* in December 1971.[10] In addition, Reed's political reputation in the eyes of GDR citizens had been further enhanced by his participation in an event staged in support of the black American activist Angela Davis.[11]

At the Leipzig festival, Reed's role was to promote a documentary (directed by José Roman) about his support for Allende and the Unidad Popular in Chile. During the course of his stay he met Wiebke Dorndeck, an English teacher from Leipzig, and the couple married in January 1973. Reed's decision to settle in the GDR was an enormous coup for the East German government and, from the point of view of the DEFA studio, the timing could hardly have been better. By the end of 1971, discussions regarding a film adaptation of Joseph von Eichendorff's Romantic novella *Aus dem Leben eines Taugenichts* [*From the Life of a Good-for-Nothing*] were at an advanced stage. In a memo dated 1 December 1971, the director, Celino Bleiweiß, had alerted the studio to the difficulty of recruiting an East German actor for the title role and raised the possibility of looking outside the GDR.[12] As a discussion that same month between representatives of DEFA and the GDR's Deputy Minister of Culture, Günter Klein, reveals, Bleiweiß's project was seen as a potentially prestigious production that could make an impact on the wider European market. Like a number of literary adaptations released in the early 1970s in the GDR, it was also seen as a further opportunity to exploit what Klein termed 'the progressive aspects of German Romanticism' – loosely defined as the love of one's homeland (*Heimat*), a deep-rooted relationship with ordinary people (the *Volk*) and a high regard for femininity – and thereby to further the GDR's claim to be the true guardian of Germany's nineteenth-century cultural heritage.[13] Given the film's potential to appeal to the international TV market (and to compete successfully alongside the other adaptations of highbrow works of German literature by directors associated with the New German Cinema in the Federal Republic) the studio was not only allowed to use highly expensive (Kodak) colour filmstock, but also to engage the services of Reed and the West German star Hannelore Elsner.

Reed was an experienced screen actor and had already featured in a number of spaghetti westerns. Performing in German, however, proved particularly challenging, and as a handwritten note of 17 July 1972 from the production files indicates, his initial recordings of the musical numbers were deemed unusable and would require re-recording once he had 'a genuinely accent-free command of German'.[14] For the dialogue, Reed's voice was overdubbed using the distinctive voice of Peter Reusse, an actor best known from his role as the rebellious pupil, Peter, in *Denk bloß nicht ich heule* [*Just Don't Think I'll Cry*, 1965], a highly controversial film that had been banned in the wake of the infamous Eleventh Plenum of 1965. Reed's poor command of German was by no means the only difficulty with which the studio was confronted during the making of the film. Looking back at her experiences of working with DEFA, Reed's co-star, Hannelore Elsner, complained that she felt isolated on set because no one trusted her on account of her West German origins (and following a dispute with the GDR authorities she did not attend the premiere in East Berlin).[15] In addition, perhaps prompted by the knowledge that both Elsner and Reed were already receiving large payments in Western currency, the Polish actress, Anna Dziadyk-Dymna, succeeded in extracting a considerable increase in her fee, much to the displeasure of the studio management.[16]

Like Eichendorff's novella, Bleiweiß's film adaptation recounts the adventures of the Taugenichts, a happy-go-lucky figure whose reluctance to abandon the realms of music and the imagination renders him ill-suited to the prosaic demands of bourgeois society and the world of work symbolized by his father's mill. (As the studio was careful to point out, however, what he objects to is not work per se but alienated labour that is 'contrary to the harmonious and all-round development of the individual'.)[17] Inspired by the beauty of a German countess he meets on his travels, the Taugenichts resolves to pursue his female Ideal wherever she may lead him and embarks on an episodic journey of self-discovery punctuated by a series of folk songs. Ultimately he discovers that the woman he worships is not, as he thought, a German aristocrat, but rather the orphaned niece of the lowly porter; and with this discovery all obstacles to their marriage are miraculously dissolved. By showing how the central character is led astray by an imagination that is caught up in the ritualistic chivalric fantasies of an outdated class, Bleiweiß's adaptation of the novella strives to remind the spectator that true happiness is to be found in the real world of the here and now.

Wera and Claus Küchenmeister's script offers a conventional Marxist reading of Eichendorff's Romantic novella whereby the central character's encounters with representatives of both the aristocracy and bourgeoisie reveal the repressive aspect of a hierarchical class-bound system that is ripe for reform. In keeping with this agenda, we are presented with a series of songs that eschew the subtle lyricism of the novella's original texts in favour of a more overt radicalism that was regarded as likely to appeal to contemporary audiences and better suited to Reed's singing style; accordingly, in place of Eichendorff's 'Wohin ich gehe und schaue' ('Wherever I go and look'), we are treated to a rendering of 'Die Gedanken sind frei' ('Thoughts are free') popularized by the author of the German national anthem, Hoffmann von Fallersleben, in the mid 1840s. The film's critical thrust is further amplified by the stylized cinematography of Bleiweiß and his cameraman Günter Jaeuthe who, as the numerous visual references to well-known works of Biedermeier painting underline, invite us to view the Taugenichts's world through the critical lens of Carl Spitzweg and his contemporaries.[18]

Figure 8.1: Dean Reed on the set of *Aus dem Leben eines Taugenichts* (1973) © DEFA-Stiftung/Wolfgang Ebert, Alexander Kühn.

Not surprisingly, the production of the film was eagerly followed in the East German press (Fig. 8.1). While the popularity of Reed's concert appearances in the Soviet Union was beginning to attract the attention of the press in the United States,[19] his casting in the role of the Taugenichts provided East German journalists with an opportunity to explore the singer's conversion to Marxism in more detail.[20] From mid 1972 to mid 1973, the magazine *Filmspiegel* presented its readers with a steady stream of updates from the set of *Aus dem Leben eines Taugenichts*; and these reports were complemented in mainstream newspapers such as *Neues Deutschland* by articles alluding to Reed's pro-Vietnam sympathies.[21] In an article for the August 1972 edition of the youth magazine *Neues Leben*, the film's scriptwriters Wera and Claus Küchenmeister went out of their way to draw attention to Reed's political activism, pointing out: 'He's not like most stars, who are simply happy to remain within the confines of their own world'.[22] Six months later, the same magazine used the film as a pretext to present its readers with a brief account of Reed's political odyssey while at the same time providing him with a platform to argue against the alleged incompatibility of politics and popular entertainment: 'No one who ignores such vital things in life as love', he observed, 'can hope to persuade people politically'.

Critics were far from impressed, however, when *Aus dem Leben eines Taugenichts* premiered at East Berlin's Kosmos cinema on 10 May 1973. Writing in *Neues Deutschland* Horst Knietzsch suggested that the scriptwriters had failed to find an 'adequate aesthetic form' and that the film 'lacked clear plotlines'.[23] Heinz Hofmann's review for the *Nationalzeitung* went even further, complaining that at certain points in the film it was impossible to follow what was happening.[24] Yet these and other reviewers who judged the film primarily in terms of its oblique relationship to its literary source failed to see what was really at stake; as the film's success at the box office confirms, what cinema-goers were interested in was not the nineteenth-century author Eichendorff, but the twentieth-century star Dean Reed. Not surprisingly, the critics were taken to task by irate cinema-goers such as one who, having seen the film no less than four times, wrote to the editors of *Filmspiegel* complaining that, such negative reviews 'would discourage Dean Reed from working in the GDR', and pointing out that 'it is precisely because Reed's interpretation of the Taugenichts is rooted in his own view of life that it comes across so genuinely, so convincingly and as a true role model for young people today'.[25]

As with Reed's much later film, *Sing, Cowboy, sing* (1981), the professional critics' desire to promote cinema as an essentially highbrow art form explains not only their reluctance to acknowledge Reed's capacity to attract mass audiences to films which, aesthetically speaking, had many shortcomings, but also their failure to grasp the role of popular cinema in the GDR generally. In contrast to those critics who often struggled to recognize the role of the *Publikumsliebling* in their conceptualization of cinema, Reed – perhaps because of his American origins – was far more attuned to the complex relationship between stars and their publics. In this context it is striking that in almost all the interviews he gave during the shooting of *Aus dem Leben eines Taugenichts*, he goes out of his way to blur the distinction between his own star personality and that of the fiddle-playing protagonist of Bleiweiß's film. In keeping with his self-presentation as a man of action, most at home when riding through open countryside on horseback, he confesses to the *Neue Berliner Illustrierte* that 'time and again I noticed that the Taugenichts and myself share many important traits – above all a love of nature'.[26] Likewise, when Erica Gromnica writing for *Neues Leben* refers to 'this art-loving, humorous young man who vigorously defends the right of Romantic sentiment in the face of prosaic objections', there is a delicious ambiguity as to whether her description refers to the fictional figure of the Taugenichts or to Reed himself.[27] However, the most extreme form of identification between fictional role and star personality is to be found in the outline for the film's trailer (directed by Heinz Thiel). There Reed – in Taugenichts costume – addresses the camera directly, making fun not only of himself, but also of his poor German: 'Thoughts are free; who can guess what they are? I'm a sort of good-for-nothing, I don't speak English – that's right. Before I came to the GDR I used to be known by the name Dean Reed', adding perhaps for the benefit of those who followed the developments of his personal life and marriage to his Leipzig-born wife, 'Maybe you think I have a slightly Saxonian accent when I speak German?'[28] Nonetheless, behind the facade of Reed's self-deprecating humour, we can catch a glimpse of the internationalist agenda that was so crucial a part of his star personality, when he suggests: 'I believe that love is the greatest international language – it's something everyone understands'.[29]

The release of *Aus dem Leben eines Taugenichts* took place during what was one of the most tolerant periods in the GDR's cultural history. Only a few weeks earlier the hugely popular *Die Legende von Paul und Paula* [*The Legend of Paul and Paula*, 1973] had been released, another film that drew upon the spirit of 1968 and the attitudes of the flower-power generation in its presentation of its female protagonist's quest for self-fulfilment. On the wider political stage, the signing of the Paris Peace Accords in January 1973 seemed to presage the end of the Vietnam War, while Brezhnev's visit to the Federal Republic in May ushered in a new climate of détente. In the GDR itself, the tenth *Weltfestspiele der Jugend* (Festival of Youth and Students), a resounding success that was retrospectively dubbed the 'Red Woodstock', reflected this newly found feeling of optimism and international cooperation. Nevertheless, Reed was a staunch critic of what he regarded as the sentimentality of flower-power activism. When asked in December 1971 about his view of the hippies, in an interview for *Freie Welt*, he replied, 'In my view a hippy is a more politically progressive individual than an American who goes to Vietnam and commits murder there. But the hippies don't get the next stage in the argument – they don't really know what they want and what is at stake in the global struggle'.[30] Seen in this context, Reed's idiosyncratic interpretation of the title role in *Aus dem Leben eines Taugenichts* can be read both as a warning to those whose activism was confined to colourful protest against an oppressive social order and as a reminder of the need for an active commitment to the construction of a new and better world of the kind that he believed he had discovered in the GDR of the 1970s.

Reed's rejection of pacifism as an adequate response to the political conflicts of his time finds its fullest expression in *Blutsbrüder* of 1975. 'I used to think that peace and love were just the same then / I learned that life was / not only a game, each man must fight, and fight again', he announces in the introductory song 'Love Your Brother'. Although *Blutsbrüder* was the first DEFA film for which Reed had written the script, it was not the first western he had made with the studio. Some eighteen months earlier, he had featured alongside three of the GDR's best-known stars, Armin Mueller-Stahl, Rolf Hoppe and Manfred Krug, in the comic cowboy film *Kit & Co.* (1974) directed by Konrad Petzold. Based on a series of short stories by Jack London, *Kit & Co.* is set in 1896 during the Alaskan Gold Rush. Yet in keeping with DEFA's re-invention of the genre, it is a film that not only eschews violence, but also – as the studio was at pains to emphasize – encourages the audience to sympathize with Kit (Reed), Shorty (Hoppe) and Wildwater Bill (Krug) on the grounds that their desire for loyalty, love and friendship rather than mere gold sets them apart from the other representatives of capitalism in this Wild West setting. Nevertheless, as the studio noted, 'Reed's performance as the main character is overshadowed by Manfred Krug's composure and control'.[31] In part this may have been a reflection of the tension between the two stars; Krug made no secret of his distaste for Reed's support for the SED party line, and matters would come to a head some two years later when the American refused to sign a petition protesting against the expatriation of the singer Wolf Biermann. Yet for all the studio's concerns about the stars' individual performances and the fact that, in contrast to Petzold's earlier films, *Kit & Co.* did not sufficiently emphasize 'the demoralizing and destructive impact of capitalism on individuals and their relations with others', the film was – like all Reed's films – a huge hit with GDR cinema-goers.[32]

While the DEFA studio management struggled to come to terms with what they saw as the ideological limitations of *Kit & Co.*, Reed's next film, *Blutsbrüder*, was far closer stylistically to the well-established traditions of the classic DEFA *Indianerfilm*. This time Reed's co-star was the well-known Yugoslavian-born actor Gojko Mitic (who had declined to take part in *Kit & Co.*). As Reed himself noted in the original treatment, the film draws its inspiration from the massacre of the Cheyenne Tribe at Sand Creek in 1864.[33] It tells the story of Harmonika, a US cavalryman who, having witnessed the massacre of the Cheyenne tribe at Sand Creek, becomes a deserter and, having saved the life of the injured squaw Rehkitz and survived a duel with her brother, Harter Felsen (Gojko Mitic), marries into the tribe. Yet the mutual understanding at which Harmonika and the tribe arrive is shattered when he returns to the village to discover that, once again, the Cheyenne – including his wife Rehkitz – have been the victims of yet another unprovoked attack. However, having discovered Rehkitz's killer, Harmonika finds that he is incapable of exacting individual revenge and sinks into a state of drunken depression. Nonetheless, at the end of the film, the sight of Harter Felsen and the Cheyenne being led in chains to a reservation inspires him to join them in their armed struggle for freedom.

Although based on a historical incident dating back to the nineteenth century, *Blutsbrüder* was also in part inspired by more contemporary events, notably the Wounded Knee incident of 27 February 1973 in the United States. This incident, in which a group of Native American Indians occupied the town of Wounded Knee in South Dakota in protest at the abuse of their civil rights, was widely reported in the East German press and cited as an example of ongoing racial discrimination in the United States.[34] Just how close the plight of the American Indian Movement in the 1970s was to Reed's heart is also evident in his later efforts to promote his (ultimately unrealized) film project *Bloody Heart*.[35] In the case of *Blutsbrüder*, Harmonika's decision to renounce individual revenge in favour of a guerilla-type campaign against the US soldiers could not but conjure up images of anti-American resistance in both Chile and, in particular, Vietnam. At one level, *Blutsbrüder* is a film that argues for a rejection of pacifism and a recognition that, as the studio put it, 'searching for truth always means fighting for the truth as well';[36] and here too the hippy-style decoration of Harmonika's teepee – complete with a crudely drawn dove of peace – can be read as a critique of the peace and love ethics of the flower-power generation of 1968. At another level, however, *Blutsbrüder* is a film about the political conversion of Reed himself, and one calculated to inspire faith in the possibility of an alternative, and more politically progressive, faction in the United States. In an interview with Marlis Linke for *Neues Leben*, Reed confesses: 'The thoughts and emotions I ... perform are my own. That makes it my most straightforward role to date. Harmonika – he's virtually identical to Dean'.[37] During the attack on the Cheyenne village, Harmonika's snapping of the US flag conjures up memories of Reed's washing of the same flag some years earlier, before the American consulate in Santiago; and during the sequence in which Reed proposes to Rehkitz, the woman whose life he has saved, her answer 'Ich sage Ja, Ja, Ja!' ('I say yes, yes, yes!') is an unmistakable allusion to the hit 'Wir sagen Ja' that, since the tenth *Weltfestspiele der Jugend* of 1973, had become Reed's personal signature tune. In the circumstances, it is hardly surprising that Gojko Mitic, unaccustomed as he was to having to share the limelight in a DEFA western, should have been a reluctant participant in the film.[38]

From the point of view of the Socialist Unity Party (SED), Reed's value lay not so much in the quality of his acting (indeed Reed's insistence on performing all his own stunts and his physical prowess and skills as a rider were often used a means of compensating his limitations as an actor); his real ideological capital was a star personality built up around his rejection of the United States and emigration to the GDR, a state he almost always refer to as his 'second home' ('zweite Heimat'). Not only did the then secretary of the FDJ organization, Egon Krenz, go out of his way on a number of occasions to pacify a disgruntled Reed in order to keep him onside,[39] but he also received a steady stream of letters urging him to intervene when the American was arrested and imprisoned in Minnesota after participating in a political demonstration. At the same time, coverage of the Minnesota incident in the East German press underlined the extent to which, for the general public, Reed had the right credentials to extend Angela Davis's legacy as the representative par excellence of 'an alternative America' ('das andere Amerika').

Reed's non-German origins and highly unusual biography, however, meant that most attempts to present him using the conventional categories of the star discourse with which East German *Publikumslieblinge* were presented to their fans usually missed the point. Articles such as 'Ein Tag mit den "Reeds"' ('A Day Out With The Reed Brigade') for the regional newspaper *Freie Presse* that showed Reed (with rolling pin in hand) meeting the members of a workers' collective named after him, tapped into the well-established GDR tradition of the so-called *Patenbrigade* (adopted brigade).[40] Yet, as the authors of such articles must have realized, images of Reed dressed up as a baker were hardly what his East German fans wanted to see. Accordingly, in a feature of 1974 for the *Freie Welt* (Fig. 8.2) entitled 'Haus-Besuch bei Familie Reed' ('At Home with the Reed Family') the

Figure 8.2: At home with the Reeds © Jo Gerbeth.

title page shows him in the garden standing behind his wife, Wiebke, with what looks like a rake in his hand; at the same time, however, the composition of the photograph contains an obvious allusion to Reed's role the year before in *Aus dem Leben eines Taugenichts* and to the sequence in which he guides the countess and her troupe of aristocrats across the lake by boat (Fig. 8.3).[41]

Similarly, the coy smile on the face of Reed's wife acts as a typically ironic commentary on the contradictory roles she temporarily assumes in the photograph – an ordinary high school teacher from the *Volk* and yet wife of a superstar. Inside the magazine itself, in what is her only contribution, she reassures readers that, despite the volume of love letters from adoring fans she is not jealous and that 'Dean's fame isn't something that bothers me'. Moreover, while she is depicted hanging up Reed's jeans on the washing line, he is shown water-skiing on the lake near their house in Berlin-Schmöckwitz. This tension between the demands of the conventional East German star discourse and the desire on the part of GDR

Figure 8.3: Dean Reed in *Aus dem Leben eines Taugenichts* (1973). DVD screen capture.

audiences to see Reed in the typically all-action postures that were so much part of the star personality of 'the man from Colorado' – a man accustomed to entering the GDR television studios on horseback to host his own show – runs through almost all the publicity materials associated with him during his career in the East. Sometimes this aspect of Reed's personality could be exploited in the form of a subtle product placement designed to boost the GDR's self-image, such as those photographs where he is shown riding an MZ motorcycle (produced in the East German town of Zschopau), or trying out guitars produced in the GDR by Musima Klingenthal. But more often than not, editors sought to emphasize precisely that which set Reed apart from the average GDR citizen, and homed in on what, at least in their imagination, was typically American about Reed: rodeos, cowboy hats and horsemanship all set against a quasi Wild West setting. In this context, Reed's signature trait when interviewed by the press was to include a personalized handwritten letter (often in English) to his East German fans – a gesture that came across as typically American.

Reed's appeal to young people in both the Soviet Union and the GDR also meant that his biography could be used as a tool for ideological education. In 1980 Hans-Dieter Bräuer's biography *Dean Reed erzählt aus seinem Leben* [*Dean Reed Talks About His Life*] was released by the Verlag Neues Leben, a publishing house more obviously associated with the FDJ organization than with the biographies of performing artists. The volume itself offers the reader extended passages of Reed's memories (ostensibly compiled by the singer himself in a first-person narrative) and these are interspersed with more descriptive passages by Bräuer, which, arranged thematically rather than chronologically, provide a political context for these reminiscences. While the lavishly illustrated volume offers an insight into the singer/actor's life and career, the titles of individual chapters 'Bekanntschaft mit dem Lande Lenins' ('Getting to know the Land of Lenin') and 'Zu Haus in einem anderen Land' ('At Home in a Foreign Country') hint at the biography's underlying agenda, namely a simplified introduction to the course of world history as viewed through Reed's Marxist-Leninist eyes.[42] Yet as his career began to stall in the GDR during the early/mid 1980s, Reed's role as a political icon was increasingly called into question. Despite sales of some 15,000 copies of the 1980 edition, plans for a new edition met with considerable opposition. In February 1984, the director of the Verlag Neues Leben wrote to the FDJ complaining that publishing biographies of pop singers was not part of their programme and that if they produced a new edition of Reed's biography they would be under pressure to publish books about other pop idols such as the star of *Heißer Sommer* [*Hot Summer*, 1968], Frank Schöbel.[43] Some readers (even Reed's own fans it was claimed) had objected to what they saw as an over-simplification of the political context of the American's life. Moreover, as Chowaretz noted, 'the existing edition and any future edition revolves around a cult of stardom [*Starrummel*] that we don't really endorse'. Finally, the publishers argued that 'all the various children, wives, weddings in his life' (Reed had in the meantime divorced Wiebke and married the DEFA star Renate Blume) meant that any new edition that included details of Reed's love life would have the character of a trashy tabloid. Ultimately, a solution was found by assigning the publication of the second edition to the musical publishers Edition Peters on the grounds that the text was accompanied by the music for Reed's songs.

By 1984, Reed's standing both in the eyes of his fans and the SED leadership was beginning to wane. But even as early as 1978 there is clear evidence that both the DEFA studio and the Ministry of Culture were beginning to see Reed as a liability. During the *Weltfestspiele* of 1973, Reed had been introduced to Yasser Arafat, and in 1977 he had flown to Lebanon as a guest of the PLO leader.[44] What he saw there inspired him to write a screenplay about the Tel al-Zaatar massacre of 12 August 1976 and, to the obvious consternation of the studio director Hans Dieter Mäde, he submitted a treatment not only to DEFA but also to Arafat in person. As Mäde's letter of 5 June 1978 to Politbüro member Hermann Axen underlines, the singer's propensity to see this (and other) complex political conflicts in simplistic black-and-white terms posed a challenge for the studio management.[45] Following the response from the Politbüro's Department of International Affairs, Mäde was left in no doubt that Reed's project was doomed from the start. First, as the letter pointed out, the treatment ignored the role of the Syrians (who the GDR had been supplying with arms for some time) in the massacre, and noted that 'at the present moment the GDR has absolutely no interest in tackling this problem and attacking the Syrian government'.[46] In addition, the letter makes it clear that, despite its openly professed hostility to Israel, the SED leadership considered the PLO far from blameless and regarded it as 'indirectly responsible for the destruction of the Tel al-Zataar refugee camp'. Finally, the letter pointed out that the Phalangist leaders Gemayel and Chamoun, who Reed accused of being primarily responsible for the massacre, were set to assume important roles in Lebanese politics, and that it would be inadvisable ('politisch falsch') if the GDR soured its relations in the Middle East by singling them out for criticism.

While much of Reed's appeal, at least in the eyes of Krenz and the FDJ, stemmed from an ability to reduce the complexities of US foreign policy during the Cold War to a set of statements that could be easily assimilated by his fans, when it came to the GDR's own system of alliances and often bizarre diplomatic arrangements with the emerging states in the Arab world, the singer was, understandably, quite out of his depth. Reed's political naivety is evident in a letter of 13 October 1981 addressed to Erich Honecker, where he writes: 'I believe that the Palestinian People are today for the world what the Vietnamese people were yesterday .... It is such a tragedy that many Jewish people who lived through the horrors of Nazism, today have become, through the racist theory of Zionism – the new fascists of our time'.[47] As the letter shows, however willing Reed may have been to embrace the GDR's 'anti-Zionist' stance, he remained blissfully unaware of just how ambivalent the SED-leadership was regarding the PLO and the plight of the Palestinian people. In part, Reed's innocence was a crucial part of his star image: not only did he speak a simplified style of German that, precisely because it seemed so far removed from the forked tongue of GDR political rhetoric, imbued his discourse with an aura of authenticity; but the seemingly endless series of photographs depicting him surrounded by animals and at home in natural settings gave him the appearance of a modern-day 'noble savage' whose innate sense of what is morally right had led him to his 'second home', the GDR.

Reed's capacity to appeal to cinema audiences in the GDR was beyond doubt; yet, paradoxically, it was his popularity that the studio management found so challenging, precisely because it was one of the few aspects of film production that lay beyond their immediate control. With the possible exception of the TV movie *El Cantor* (1978), most of Reed's films were heavily criticized in the East German press; but, in terms of box office, the popularity of the films themselves could not be ignored. In a poll to find the best DEFA actor of the year conducted by *Neues Leben*, Reed came fourth in 1974, second in 1975 and third in 1981; likewise, in 1975, *Blutsbrüder* was voted the best film of the year and, in 1981, the comedy western *Sing, Cowboy, sing* came second. With over one million viewers, *Sing, Cowboy, sing* was by some way DEFA's most popular release of 1981; yet the misgivings at both pre- and post-release screenings underline the extent to which the studio management, for all its professed desire to reach a broader cinema-going public, struggled to come to terms with Reed's conceptualization of popular cinema within a socialist context.

Sing, Cowboy, sing was a comedy western written and directed by Reed and was the last DEFA production in which he starred. The film recounts the adventures of the two penniless cowboys, Joe (Dean Reed) and Beny (Václav Neckář) who, despite their best intentions, find themselves implicated in an elaborate scheme to thwart the evil intentions of the unscrupulous land-grabber Dave Arnold. While Arnold tries to increase his property portfolio by means of a loveless marriage with the widowed Maria, her young daughter Susan has other ideas and attempts to engineer a marriage between Joe and her mother. Following a comedy shoot-out involving Arnold's men and the inhabitants of Liebenthal, a caricatured German-style community in the mid West, the film ends happily with Arnold banished and Joe seemingly set to embrace family life. Very different in tone from the more politically engaged *Blutsbrüder*, *Sing, Cowboy, sing* built on the comic elements of *Kit & Co.* and took these to a level which East German film critics clearly found intolerable. Rosemarie Rehan was one of the very few reviewers who, despite finding little to admire in the film, nonetheless acknowledged its mass appeal: 'I'm sitting in a cinema that is sold out,' she writes, 'and I'm the only one not enjoying herself; everyone else is convulsed with laughter'.[48]

For DEFA, the difficulty in assigning the film to any recognized genre was unsettling, even if, as some argued, the production should be seen as an encouragement to experiment with new forms of popular entertainment.[49] However, the muted enthusiasm of both film critics and studio management prompted Reed to deliver a scathing attack on the studio at a post-release discussion of the film on 30 April 1982. Tackling the question of popular entertainment head on, he reminded those present that there must be more to cinema than simply the production of political films that no one wanted to see, adding: 'life is a complex phenomenon and I think that there are times when laughter is just as important as love, work and fighting your corner ... . Everybody living under socialism has the right to be entertained, to forget their problems so that the next day they can work better in their factories'.[50] And in an attempt to justify popular entertainment he turned Lenin's definition of cinema against the studio: 'It's one of the most obvious truisms of politics that having an empty cinema makes no sense and is actually a crime against ordinary people. Film is an art for the masses, it's a plebeian art as Konrad Wolf once said – and that is something that no one in the GDR seems to have quite grasped'. In the course of his diatribe, Reed accused the studio of making films not for the masses but for a 'privileged group of elitist critics'. Seen from the perspective of Reed's outburst, it is tempting to interpret the depiction of Liebethal in *Sing, Cowboy, sing* – a petty bourgeois German-style community in which nothing is decided before being subjected to a process of interminable debates – as both a satirical commentary on the structures of decision making in both the GDR and the DEFA hierarchy itself. While representatives of the studio attempted to downplay the mixed reception the film enjoyed in terms of a mismatch of American and German attitudes to humour, Reed went back on the attack, claiming that because the style of *Sing, Cowboy, sing* was rooted in an American concept of popular cinema, the GDR's Ministry of Culture had instructed the magazine *Filmspiegel* not to run its usual feature on the most popular film of the year.[51]

As the belligerent tone of the discussion suggests, Reed's relationship with DEFA was becoming increasingly strained, and the situation was not helped by the studio's reluctance to back Reed's next project, *Bloody Heart* about the 1973 incident at Wounded Knee. Reed's growing disenchantment with his life in the GDR is also reflected in an interview of 1 August 1984 with Marlies Menge for the West German broadsheet *Die Zeit*: 'I have an incredible longing for the Rocky Mountains [...] I feel out of place here, the mentality of those around me is so different. I burst into tears very easily, or start shouting. The Germans find that disconcerting. That bothers me'.[52] Yet Reed's attempt to return to the United States and relaunch his career was also torpedoed by his refusal – or perhaps even inability – to abandon straight-talking in favour of political tact and guile. In a catastrophic interview with Mike Wallace for the CBS television show *60 Minutes*, broadcast in the United States on 4 April 1986 to some sixteen million viewers, Reed was provoked into defending the Berlin Wall, praising the actions of the PLO, drawing a parallel between Ronald Reagan and Joseph Stalin, and finally declaring his intent to run for the US senate as a socialist delegate for Colorado. On 13 June 1986, following a series of furious rows with his third wife Renate Blume, Reed was found drowned in Lake Zeuthen near his home in Berlin-Schmöckwitz.

The star image, as theorized in Richard Dyer's classic study, is 'an intertextual construct produced across a range of media and cultural practices, capable of intervening in the working of particular films, but also demanding analysis as a text in its own right'.[53] Few figures in GDR cinema have embraced such a wide range of diverse media practices as Dean Reed and, to a large extent, much of the media work surrounding the construction of his star image was designed to demonstrate a congruence between his on- and off-screen personalities as a fighter for the freedom of oppressed peoples all around the globe. While other DEFA stars such as

Erwin Geschonneck, Manfred Krug and Armin Mueller-Stahl have, as Sabine Hake has argued, 'come to personify the continuities and ruptures of postwar history and today function as vessels of generational memory',[54] Reed's non-German origins meant that he occupied a rather different place within the economy of socialist stardom. Although often referred to in the East German press as a Hollywood star, a description that flew in the face of a decidedly mediocre career in the United States, his star image could hardly be contained within the discourse of ordinariness to which other home-grown *Publikumslieblinge* in the GDR were subject. Unlike Geschonneck, Reed could not draw on the legacy of antifascism; unlike Armin Mueller-Stahl, Reed was not a classically trained actor; and unlike Krug, Reed's 'rebelliousness' was not directed against the structures of authority in the GDR, but those in the United States.

Some – above all those who see him as a figure ruthlessly manipulated by the SED leadership – have portrayed him as the victim of a Stasi plot to have him murdered before he could expose, at first hand, the deficiencies of the GDR to an international press conference he had convened for the following week. Others – those who seem him as a Romantic rebel – regard his death as the consequence of a deep-seated depression exacerbated by a realization that the stagnating GDR of the mid 1980s was a far cry from the more optimistic country of the early 1970s during which Reed was at his most productive. But what contributed to Reed's enduring popularity in the GDR and other Eastern Bloc countries was precisely his ability to embody an alternative version of the American Dream – 'das andere Amerika' – in which the spirit of adventure held sway in a world in which socialism had succeeded in overcoming the contradictions of capitalism and the conflicts of race and class.

Seán Allan is Professor of German at the University of St Andrews. He is co-editor (with John Sandford) of *DEFA. East German Cinema, 1946-1992* (1999), and has published widely on the films of Konrad Wolf, Kurt Maetzig and Jürgen Böttcher, and on East German identity in post-unification cinema.

Notes

I would like to acknowledge the help of the following in preparing this article: Frau Ute Klawitter (Bundesfilmarchiv, Berlin), Frau Birgit Scholz (Filmmuseum, Potsdam), Tim Storch (Bundesarchiv, Berlin), Hans Jürgen Furcht (www.filmstadt-quedlinburg.de), and Frank-Burkhard Habel.

1. Heinz Linde, 'Sind Stars gefragt?', *Neues Leben* 9/1975, 7–9. All translations are by the author unless otherwise indicated.
2. *Unsere Filmsterne* [= Jahrbuch Neues Leben], Berlin: Verlag Junge Welt, 1962, p. 5.
3. Joachim Hellwig and Claus Ritter, *Mach dir ein paar schöne Stunden... Filmkunst contra Wirtschaftswunder*, Berlin: Kongress Verlag, 1961, p. 8.
4. Stefan Soldovieri, 'The Politics of the Popular. *Trace of Stones* (1966/89) and the Discourse of Stardom in the GDR Cinema', in Randall Halle and Margaret McCarthy (eds), *Light Motives. German Popular Film in Perspective*, Detroit: Wayne State University Press, 2003, pp. 220–36 (p. 222).
5. Sabine Hake, 'Public Figures, Political Symbols, Famous Stars. Actors in DEFA Cinema and Beyond', in Marc Silberman and Henning Wrage (eds), *DEFA at the Crossroads of East German and International Film Culture*, Berlin, Boston: de Gruyter, 2014, pp. 197–220 (p. 205).
6. Claudia Fellmer, 'Stars in East German Cinema', unpublished PhD Diss., University of Southampton, 2002. See esp. Ch 2.
7. Stefan Soldovieri, 'Managing Stars. Manfred Krug and the Politics of Entertainment in GDR Cinema', in Barton Byg and Betheny Moore (eds), *Moving Images of East Germany. Past and Future of DEFA*, Washington: AICGS, 2002, pp 56–71 (p. 61).
8. The best – and most comprehensive – biography of Reed is that by Frank-Burkhard Habel, *Dean Reed. Die wahre Geschichte*, Berlin: Neues Leben, 2007.
9. Dean Reed, *Aus meinem Leben*. Aufgeschrieben von Hans-Dieter Bräuer, 2. aktualisierte und erweiterte Auflage, Leipzig, Dresden: Edition Peters, 1984, p. 87.
10. 'Ich singe für den Frieden', *Filmspiegel* 26/1971.
11. Since 5 January 1971, Davis had been imprisoned in the United States, and there had been a prolonged and intensive campaign for her release in the GDR, where she enjoyed an almost cult-like status as a victim of US racial discrimination.
12. Celino Bleiweiß, Memo of 1 December 1971. 'Aus dem Leben eines Taugenichts' [= BArch DR 117 / 29502]. A note in pencil in the margin indicates that Dean Reed was already under consideration for the role.
13. 'Aktennotiz über ein Gespräch bei stellv. Minister, Gen. Klein am 8.12.71 über das Projekt "Aus dem Leben eines Taugenichts"' [= BArch DR 117 / 29502].
14. 'Aktennotiz' dated 17 July 1972 [= BArch DR 117 / 29502].
15. See Jana Haase, 'Dean Reed zum 70. Geburtstag', *Potsdamer Neueste Nachrichten*, 20 September 2008.
16. See 'Telegramm Acker Thiess' dated 23 August 1972. Dean Reed's fee is recorded as 30,000 (East German) marks plus US$ 10,000. Hannelore Elsner's fee is not specified as such, and is recorded as paid via an agency in West Berlin [= BArch DR 117 / 30619].
17. 'Drehbucheinschätzung des Films *Aus dem Leben eines Taugenichts*. 1.8.1972' [= BArch DR 1-Z / 194].
18. This approach is evident even in a much earlier treatment submitted to the studio on 10 March 1962 by Wera Küchenmeister, where she argues 'The sentimental aspects of the story need to be countered by a sense of irony grounded in today's world'[= BArch DR 117 / 26294].
19. 'The Red Dean', *Newsweek*, 20 March 1972.
20. See, for example, Ilse Jung, 'Künstlerporträt Dean Reed', *Treffpunkt Kino* 4/1973.
21. See, for example, 'Vietnam ist nicht allein', *Neues Deutschland*, 16 March 1972 and 'Filmschaffende solidarisch mit dem kämpfenden Vietnam', *Neues Deutschland*, 23 November 1972.
22. Wera and Claus Küchenmeister, 'Ein Arbeitstag mit Dean', *Neues Leben* 8/1972.

23. Horst Knietzsch, 'Blumen der Romantik. Der DEFA-Film *Aus dem Leben eines Taugenichts*', *Neues Deutschland*, 18 May 1973.
24. Heinz Hofmann, 'Filmische Reise in die Beschaulichkeit', *Nationalzeitung*, 16 May 1973. The same complaint had been levelled at the film by the studio's senior dramaturge, Walter Beck, in a letter of 24 August 1972 to Bleiweiß.
25. E. Sch., 'Zu *Aus dem Leben an dem* [sic] *Taugenichts*. Kritik an der Kritik', *Filmspiegel* 14/1973.
26. 'Gespräch über einen Taugenichts', *Neue Berliner Illustrierte* 21/1972.
27. 'Aus dem Leben keines Taugenichts', *Neues Leben* 12/1972.
28. 'Werbespann: Aus dem Leben eines Taugenichts' [= BArch DR 117 / 27102].
29. Ibid.
30. Barbara Nix and Jutta Voigt, 'Singen so laut, daß Angela es hört. Treffen mit dem amerikanischen Protestsänger Dean Reed', *Sonntag*, 12 December 1971.
31. 'Stellungnahme der HA Kulturpolitische Arbeit mit dem Film *Kit & Co*. 9. Oktober 1974' [= BArch DR 1-Z / 432].
32. HA Künstlerische Produktion. Abt Dramaturgie. Stellungnahme zum staatlichen Zulassungsverfahren "Kit & Co." am 9.10.1974' [= BArch DR 1-Z / 423A]. After Manfred Krug emigrated to the Federal Republic the *Hauptverwaltung Film* ordered the film to be withdrawn from circulation from 30 June 1977.
33. Dean Reed, 'Blood Brothers. Treatment' [= BArch DR 117 / 13469].
34. See for example 'Im Geiste der großen Tecumseh', *Neues Deutschland*, 10 March 1973. In an earlier version of the script ('Originaldrehbuch von Dean Reed') [= BArch DR 117 / 3521], the issue of racial discrimination is widened when Harmonika is confronted by a former slave from his father's plantation.
35. As early as 1982, however, the studio criticized Reed's script on the grounds that it lacked 'artistic quality' and that the parallels drawn with Vietnam were 'very forced' ('stark überstrapaziert'). See 'Letter from A. Scheinert to Dean Reed' dated 12 April 1982 [= Film Museum, Sammlung Dean Reed / No78].
36. 'Stelllungnahme zum Film *Blutsbrüder*, 8.4.1975' [= BArch DR 1-Z / 216].
37. '*Blutsbrüder*', *Neues Leben*, 6/1975.
38. Norbert Diener in conversation with Gojko Mitic [= www.deanreed.de/deutsch/index.html], accessed 20 June 2016.
39. See, for example, Krenz's letter to Reed of 16 November 1976 in which Krenz writes, 'I want to reassure you once again, my dear Dean, that we on the Central Council of the FDJ enjoy working with you very much and have every intention of continuing to do so in the future' [= BArch DY 24 / 22979].
40. 'Ein Tag mit den "Reeds". Vom Besuch Dean Reeds in der Großbäckerei Pasewalk', *Freie Erde*, 7 March 1980. See also the account of Reed's visit to a clothing factory in Leipzig in the works newspaper: 'Dean Reed bei den "Vestis"-Frauen zu Gast', *Vestis-Forum*, November 1972.
41. 'Hausbesuch bei Familie Reed', *Freie Welt* 25/1974, 1, and 10–11.
42. Essentially the same approach underpinned the five-year pedagogical plan of the Potsdam secondary school that had adopted Reed's name. See 'Konzeption zur Arbeit mit dem Namen unserer Schule "Dean Reed" im Rahmen der Traditionspflege 1987-1991' [= Film Museum, Sammlung Dean Reed / No78].
43. Letter from Rudolf Chowaretz to Eberhard Aurich of 10 February 1984 [= BArch DY 24 / 14291].
44. 'Der Feddajin mit der Gitarre', *Neue Berliner Illustrierte*, 11/1978.

45. Letter from Hans Dieter Mäde to Hermann Axen of 5 June 1978 [= BArch DY 30 / IV B2 / 2.024 / 105].
46. The response is included in the same file [= BArch DY 30 / IV B2 / 2.024 / 105].
47. Letter of 13 October 1981 from Dean Reed to Erich Honecker [= Filmmuseum Potsdam, Sammlung Dean Reed, N078].
48. Rosemarie Rehan, 'Mildwest in Babelsberg', *ESP*, 21/1981.
49. 'Progress Film-Verleih. Stellungnahme des Verleihs zur staatlichen Zulassung des Films 'Sing, Cowboy, sing. 06.04 1981' [= BArch DR 1-Z / 236A].
50. 'Protokoll des Auswertungsgesprächs "Sing, Cowboy, sing" vom 30.4.82' [= BArch DR 1-Z / 236C], p. 5.
51. Ibid. p. 23.
52. Marlies Menge, 'Revolutionär im Ruhestand. Ein amerikanischer Cowboy-Sänger, der in der DDR heimisch wurde', *Die Zeit*, 10 August 1984.
53. Christine Gledhill (ed), *Stardom. Industry of Desire*, London, New York: Routledge, 1991, p. xiv. See also Richard Dyer, *Stars*, London: BFI, 1998.
54. Hake, p. 219.

PART III
GENRE AND POPULAR CINEMA

CHAPTER 9
Walter Felsenstein and the DEFA Opera Film

Sabine Hake

Opera in the twentieth century has always relied on other forms of dissemination – live radio broadcasts, telecasts, opera films and, most recently, high definition broadcasts – to reach its audience and assert its relevance. These formats confirm media convergence as the predominant mode of cultural production and consumption today, including for a musical genre regularly declared dead or dying. Indeed it might be argued that sustaining this notoriously elite entertainment, with its aristocratic origins and bourgeois pretentions, would be impossible without recourse to intermediality as an aesthetic, technological and institutional model. Not surprisingly, the question of media specificity continues to haunt the opera film on account of its hybrid status – neither film nor opera, but a strange amalgamation marginal to the grand narratives of film form and style. In order to understand its remarkable staying power, it might therefore make sense to turn to the long history of media convergence and focus not on what the opera film should or should not be, but on what functions it has in fact served in specific national cinemas and musical cultures; this, however, requires some introductory comments on methodology.

For some time now, the technical, cultural and social possibilities of media convergence have brought into sharp relief the limitations of traditional approaches to film and the other arts.[1] Their conceptual hierarchies can still be found in close readings that rely on categories such as authorial intention or truthfulness to the original to evaluate the adaptation of novels or plays to the screen. It is partly due to the privileging in film studies of the image over the soundtrack that opera adaptations have rarely been studied in this way, and that is despite the long history of the film-opera interface since the early days of cinema. The contested status of the opera film as either a mixed form of questionable value or as the mere documentation of a musical performance has prevented sustained scholarship beyond the exceptional cases. Here, developing a critical vocabulary that makes productive use of recent scholarship on media convergence is important but not sufficient. As a closer look at the opera films of Walter Felsenstein will confirm, this process must also involve some historical contextualization if we want to understand the central role of opera both in the making of national cinema (especially in countries with a rich musical culture) and in the making of socialist culture (especially as regards the intense preoccupation with the classics in the building of socialism).

Opera and Film

In responding to such desiderata, we are likely to end up in Germany, the country most strongly defined through the historical configuration of classical music and the nation-state in its emancipatory as well as hegemonic effects – a dynamic that assumed heightened relevance in the German Democratic Republic (GDR). The opera films made in East Germany from the 1950s to the 1970s build on these long traditions but also complicate them in ways that cannot be separated from the larger project of socialism. Noticeably different from Western productions, these films have little in common with the celebration of musical genius and auteurist style that informs the filmic adaptations of Mozart operas by Joseph Losey or Ingmar Bergman. They lack the visual spectacle and material excess found in the screen and stage oeuvre since the 1970s of Franco Zeffirelli, whose mentor Luchino Visconti developed the formula in the 1950s and 1960s. Yet they also eschew the kind of experimentation that, during the 1990s, inspired the postmodern re-stagings of Mozart popularized for television by Peter Sellars and the minimalist look cultivated by Götz Friedrich in his Strauss opera films. Last but not least, while the revisions of opera in the old Federal Republic are inseparable from efforts to come to terms with the 'Wagner problem' – with Hans-Jürgen Syberberg's *Parsifal* (1982) a filmic contribution to that process – East German opera film directors, and Walter Felsenstein in particular, remained focused on those works in the repertory considered uncontroversial, accessible and enduringly popular.

How could the form of classical music most closely aligned with feudalism and capitalism assume such an elevated function in GDR society, namely as a force of democratization? How could film, that great liberator of the artwork from its aura, according to Walter Benjamin, be enlisted in the popularization of music as the very embodiment of aura according to Theodor W. Adorno?[2] And, to continue with Frankfurt School pronouncements on this problematic, how could Siegfried Kracauer's assertion that 'opera on the screen is a collision of two worlds detrimental to both'[3] be reconciled with the broad range of practices – from films and filmic effects on the operatic stage, to arias and singers in feature films, to opera films and filmed operas – that defy any simplistic distinction between realism and illusionism? A first answer can be found in the shared ambitions of opera and film as exemplars of the *Gesamtkunstwerk*: multimedial, intertextual and defined by their collective modes of production and reception.[4]

However, it is the productive difference between both models that allows us to conceive of the film–opera interface as a mutually productive dialogue and to consider the specific contribution of the modern mass medium to the ongoing transformation of this established art form. To quote Jeremy Tambling:

> *Through film, operatic texts are opening up for a new kind of examination that cannot assume the simple hierarchical structure of the opera house .... And in that way, it [cinema] can make the musical-dramatic text show itself as it cannot in the opera house, make it apparent what is being articulated here .... The differences of opera from film are crucial, yet the switching of codes involved in moving from one to the other, may prove enabling.*[5]

As defined by Tambling, the heuristic function of the film–opera interface is based on the recognition of the opera as text, and of adaptation as interpretation. Accordingly, the opera film (broadly defined) always involves acts of translation: on the level of musical and dramatic performance, through the presence/absence of the body and from the performative rituals of the opera house to the different spatialities and sociabilities of cinema and television. This process of translation also includes the changing cultural prestige associated with opera and operetta across the range of traditional and modern media and, as the case of Felsenstein confirms, is inseparable from the aesthetic and ideological mobilization of their differences.[6]

Confirming Tambling's observation, Felsenstein's earliest and most important opera film, *Fidelio* (1956), which is based on Beethoven's only opera, played a key role in the development of his vision of *Musiktheater* (music theatre), a theatricalization of opera aimed at the equal treatment of musical and dramatic elements. This connection will be reconstructed on two levels: Felsenstein's own comments on his film and television work as a laboratory for his work on the operatic stage; and the formal qualities, especially point of view, shared by his opera films and filmed operas (i.e. recordings of Komische Oper productions). Moreover, both will be evaluated within the historical conditions that aligned opera with film as the quintessential mixed medium and created the competing demands on opera as *Volksoper* (people's opera) and *Nationaloper* (national opera). As the essay's second section shows, *Fidelio* brought together all of these aspects in almost ideal-typical ways.

Austrian-born, Felsenstein was the founder, director and *Intendant* (artistic director) from 1947 to 1976 of the Komische Oper in East Berlin and a pivotal figure in the history of twentieth-century European opera culture. His media experiments beyond *Fidelio* can be grouped into filmed operas based on Komische Oper productions and live performances recorded for television. The filmed operas include Leoš Janáček's *Das schlaue Füchslein* [*The Cunning Little Vixen*, 1965], Verdi's *Othello* (1969), as well as two productions based on Offenbach operettas, *Hoffmanns Erzählungen* [*The Tales of Hoffmann*, 1970] and *Ritter Blaubart* [*Bluebeard*, 1973]; the latter two were shot in colour for GDR state television. While of limited interest from an artistic perspective, the two recordings of live performances of Mozart's *Don Giovanni* (1966) and *Die Hochzeit des Figaro* [*The Marriage of Figaro*, 1975] contributed to the larger project of popularizing opera which, as I argue, is key to Felsenstein's uniquely filmic conception of music theatre as the full integration of musical and dramatic elements. Confirming the importance of digital media in preserving the East German operatic tradition, the Walter Felsenstein Edition released by Arthaus in 2009 has made restored versions of these films available to new audiences.[7] Together with the growing number of publications on Felsenstein (monographs, dissertations, collected writings) that assess the legacy of music theatre within contemporary debates on the postdramatic in theatre and opera, these films not only bring belated recognition to, in the words of the *New York Times*, 'one of 20th-century opera's most influential and creative geniuses',[8] but also offer clear proof of the significance of opera in defining the cultural legacy of the GDR today.

Such international recognition should not distract from the fact that Felsenstein's film and television work developed in the highly politicized atmosphere that haunted Cold War Berlin and culminated in the battle of the opera houses in East and West prior to the building of the Wall.[9] Conceiving of opera as a social and sensory experience, Felsenstein found in media convergence an aesthetic and ideological model for the desired reconciliation of folk, national and socialist culture. Committed to using modern mass media in the democratization of high culture, he would have agreed with Jean Kurt Forest's praise of opera as 'the great democratic folk play [*Volksschauspiel*], the great interplay of the arts'.[10] However, whereas that composer, together with Hanns Eisler and Paul Dessau, was actively involved in the conception of a socialist *Gegenwartsoper* (opera with contemporary themes), Felsenstein set out to liberate the classics from the class-based practices surrounding them. Thus the repertory at the city-financed Komische Oper (built on the grounds of the Metropol Theater) remained reliably traditional, with a clear emphasis on opera buffa in line with the old Metropol's commitment to the *leichte Muse* (light entertainment) and a strong preference for eighteenth- and nineteenth-century German operas by Mozart, Beethoven, Offenbach, Lortzing and von Weber; there was little room for the kind of twentieth-century works showcased at the neighbouring Staatsoper Unter den Linden.

Felsenstein was not the only one who believed that opera provided an ideal model of integration and unification for the *Gesamtkunstwerk* of socialist culture. Accordingly, the opera film was to reproduce the totality (in the Lukácsian sense) through which to overcome the division between the immediacy of aesthetic experience and the mediations of history, and do so through the most advanced media technologies available. The SED party newspaper *Neues Deutschland* in 1952 defined the parameters early on when it concluded that 'opera belongs as an inseparable component to the national culture of a people. During the period of development of the nation, the unity of poetry, theatre, acting, dance and staging make this genre like a point of crystallization of the artistic life of a nation'.[11] The fact that the language of all productions at the Komische Oper was (and still is) German played a key role in this ambitious and problematic project.

Like Bertolt Brecht at the Berliner Ensemble, Felsenstein belonged to the country's cultural and political elites and enjoyed considerable travel privileges and material rewards – in his case a historical country estate in Glienicke that in 1967 lured him permanently from West to East Berlin. And, like Brecht, Felsenstein provided the regime with cosmopolitan flair in exchange for ideal working conditions in a fully subsidized socialist culture industry. The *Intendant* had complete artistic and administrative control over a major opera house (and one that would be extensively renovated during the 1960s). Felsenstein was known as a perfectionist – demanding, despotic and driven by the desire to make his favourite theatrical form usable for, and relevant to, the present.[12] His bureaucratic struggles with the

Berlin Magistrate were an integral part of this arrangement; so were his numerous public honours and awards, including the coveted Order of Karl Marx. Evidence of Felsenstein's elevated status as a public figure is reflected in his regular appearances in the GDR's *Augenzeuge* newsreels, for instance in No. 1959/99 featuring a guest performance in Moscow and in No. 1965/17 about the laying of the foundation stone for an extension of the Komische Oper.

In their conception of theatre, the bourgeois humanist Felsenstein and the modernist socialist Brecht could not have been more different – notwithstanding their shared distaste for all historicization on the stage. Associated with epic theatre, Brecht experimented with the technique of defamiliarization to promote an attitude of critical detachment in the audience; these modernist sensibilities made him the subject of official rebukes during the formalism debates of the 1950s. By contrast, Felsenstein believed in immersion, empathy and catharsis and developed his realist music theatre in line with an idealist bourgeois aesthetic, including the Schillerian belief in the stage as a moral institution.[13] His call for clarity and honesty in relation to the work remained inextricably linked to the goal of addressing 'the totality of the working people'.[14] He insisted on the relevance of this utopian project even as he occasionally wondered 'why music theatre is not yet a matter of the people and how it could become a matter of the people'.[15] Not surprising, Fabian Bien calls the Komische Oper under Felsenstein a '*Musterbühne* [model stage] of socialist realism' and, by extension, of the new socialist state.[16]

Felsenstein developed his concept of music theatre in opposition to the tradition of *Sängeroper* and its focus on the virtuoso performances of famous singers. Like the classical Hollywood narrative style, his realist music theatre entailed a definition of realism based on the seamless incorporation of all elements, a strong emphasis on psychological motivation and character identification, and a direct appeal to the audience (via point of view) to experience the work's emotional truth. In line with these goals, Felsenstein's mode of working at the Komische Oper involved extensive textual and historical research, with equal attention paid to dramatic and musical elements, a thorough study of the libretto and existing German translations that sometimes required retranslations, and intensive rehearsal times with the singers that drew on the psychological methods developed by Konstantin Stanislavsky. But the kind of realism produced through practices first developed in the film studio remained beholden to what it was – and was not – meant to signify. Thus against the threat associated with formalism in music, literature and film, *Werktreue* (or rather, the claim of 'truthfulness to the work') promised a commitment to the classical musical heritage. The opposition to modernist experimentation implied a validation of German idealist notions of art and form. Meanwhile the goal of bringing high culture to the masses signalled a continuation of early debates about art under socialism. Finally, the emphasis on psychological motivation, in line with Stanislavsky's theories of acting, provided evidence of the compatibility of socialism and humanism.

Yet how could these ideological positions and institutional perspectives be translated into the very specific formal registers required for adapting operas to the screen? By appropriating formal techniques developed in classical narrative cinema. Felsenstein's most original solution to what Robert Braunmüller calls the inherent contradictions of realism on the stage was the privileging of character identification.[17] He was well aware of the challenges faced by opera films that aspire to be more than mere recordings, beginning with the difficulty of reducing monumental scores to acceptable film lengths and of adapting the musical and dramatic elements to the different experiential modes associated with live performance, theatrical projection and television viewing. Unlike literary works whose narratives are fundamentally changed through translation into the filmic registers of showing and telling, operas put considerable constraints on the adaptation process because of the status of music as raw material, that is: its immediacy and temporality. This may be one reason why *Fidelio* proved so important as a testing ground for the theatricalization of opera – namely as an exploration of identification as the most important emotional mechanism for closing the gap between music and drama. Under these conditions credibility and authenticity are no longer a problem of media specificity but of communicability; to quote Felsenstein:

> *The heart of music theater is to turn music-making and singing on the stage into a communication that is convincing, truthful and utterly essential ... Music theater exists when a musical action with singing human beings becomes a theatrical reality that is unreservedly believable. The dramatic happening must take place on a level where music is the only means of expression.*[18]

In addressing the challenges faced of the opera film, Felsenstein proposes limiting screen adaptations to operas that in all the musical aspects 'serve the story and express the story-based relationships among the acting human beings'.[19] While admitting a personal preference for film over television, he makes no qualitative distinction between opera and new media:

> *I do not believe that film and the opera differ fundamentally from each other in respect to dramatic structure and continuity. Film has its own techniques for emphasis, such as cutting, montage, and so on, and music provides opera with equivalent possibilities, so that in both forms of art we have a great deal of leeway. The inappropriate use of film devices can change and even distort the original concept of an opera production. On the other hand, these devices make possible certain aspects in the film for which there is no opportunity on the stage because of technology limitation but which the interpreter would like to stress. Thus film can sometimes afford us greater clarity.*[20]

Recalling his experiences on the set of *Ritter Blaubart* Felsenstein was particularly intrigued by the filmic possibilities of close-up and point of view, a point to be pursued in greater detail in the next section:

> *During shooting I took more and more pleasure in the project and discovered opportunities to realize my conception more unambiguously in the other medium. Because of the many attractions on the stage, even an attentive audience cannot always get every detail, while in film I have the possibility to set accents through close-up, editing and all the other technical possibilities (which are, of course, entirely untheatrical) and emphasize aspects of the conception that I find valuable.*[21]

Fidelio

Fidelio, Felsenstein's first and only true opera film, was the product of the fluid political borders in postwar Europe during the early 1950s. Shot by the Austrian Akkord-Film at Vienna's Rosenhügel studios in the last year of the Soviet occupation, the film allowed him to work with the Vienna Symphony Orchestra, the Vienna State Opera Chorus, and well-known singers Magda László as Leonore/Fidelio, Richard Holm as Florestan, and Heinz Rehfuss as Don Pizarro. They gave their voices to the film actors who played their characters on the screen in a first manifestation of the principle of dramatization that would henceforth preoccupy his work across venues and media. The film was not the director's first foray into filmmaking. Working at the Schiller Theater in Berlin during the early 1940s, he had been asked to direct *Ein Windstoß* [*A Gust of Wind*, 1942], a minor Tobis film comedy about tenants in an apartment building. This experience possibly helped him cut down *Fidelio*'s average duration of two-and-a-half hours to less than ninety minutes. For the screenplay Felsenstein collaborated with Eisler, then in the middle of his controversial *Johann Faustus* project. In the context of the times, the choice of *Fidelio* made perfect sense, with the emphatic calls for freedom from tyranny conceived by Beethoven against the backdrop of the Napoleonic Wars obviously resonating in contemporary Cold War discourses. In fact, the Soviet occupation contributed to many delays during the three-year production, and the film's denunciation as Soviet propaganda greatly complicated its reception in the West.

The story of Leonore, who, disguised as a young man named Fidelio, seeks employment in the prison where her husband Florestan is held by the tyrannical Don Pizarro, has been described as a paean to uxorial love; but has also been understood as a call for political resistance. Already the overture defines the core conflict between the human desire for freedom and the conditions of oppression, by cutting between the poor, frightened peasants and the soldiers spreading terror in the name of the governor. Most important for my purposes, the opening sequence is shot like a feature film, with the freely moving camera re-enacting the hierarchies between those above (the castle) and those below (the village) and introducing the main characters as intermediaries between both worlds. Filmed in the high-contrast style of neorealist filmmaking, the settings are reminiscent of both the Weimar expressionist film and postwar rubble film and their use of *mise en scène* in visualizing emotional turmoil and social tension. The staging of the famous prisoner chorus 'Oh welche Lust in freier Luft', with the men emerging emaciated from their cells, bears an uncanny resemblance to the atrocity films about the liberation of the concentration camps; indeed camera operator Walter Tuch had worked in a German army propaganda unit during the war. At the same time, the depiction of blooming meadows and trees as symbols of life reveals the influence of the postwar *Heimatfilm* (homeland film) for which Tuch provided idealized images of nature and *Volk*.

These intertextual references are important for understanding Felsenstein's dramatization of music and visualization of emotion in uniquely filmic terms. Time and again long dialogue scenes lead to moments when emotions overwhelm the characters; at that point, the (unseen) singers take over as the actors fall silent. Throughout, the disjuncture between image and sound is used to foreground the difference between external and internal worlds, between tyranny and freedom, with any changes in their relationship an indication of the shifting balance of power. The power of emotions as a conduit from speaking to singing, and the importance of nature metaphors in visualizing their transgressive force, are evident already in Marcelline's 'Oh wär ich schon mit dir vereint'. Presented as the expression of a woman's longing for her beloved, the scene (via superimpositions) moves from a close-up of her face to a montage of images of blooming trees. Similarly, Fidelio's heartfelt rendition of 'Abscheulicher' facilitates the transition from remembrance (of happy days with her husband) to resistance (to the inhuman treatment of the prisoners) and ends with her demanding the prisoners' immediate release. This dynamic continues in Florestan's 'Gott, wie dunkel hier', his own flashback to scenes of marital love as well as struggles for freedom. Significantly, the act of singing in the narrative is always introduced through psychological motivation; yet as inner monologue turns into song, the world of the diegesis begins to change.

The division between exteriority and interiority corresponds to that between diegetic and nondiegetic music, with their eventual convergence signifying the empowerment of the oppressed. For those in power, singing is invariably a public act. Pizarro's assertive 'Ha, welch ein Augenblick' triggers a spectacle of violence, with his face superimposed with images of storms, floods and landslides. But for those fighting for freedom, the interiority of singing offers a hidden source of strength first made visible through the nature metaphors. Here dark skies exploding in thunder and lightning suggest a groundswell of anger that initially cannot be verbalized, except through the emotional performativity of songs. Finally, the clearing of the sky in the final chorus of 'Heil sei dem Tag' announces the possibility that the voice of the people can finally be heard. In the triumphant finale Florestan is freed by the enlightened king, Don Fernando, and the couple carried along by the empowered *Volk* during a torchlight parade. Shown singing on the screen, they have found their political voice, with public and private desire now experienced as identical.

The Opera Film at DEFA

Felsenstein's contribution to the phenomenon of media convergence beyond *Fidelio* can only be assessed in relation to the cultural and political project of the DEFA opera film.[22] The East German film studio released thirteen opera films for the big and small screen during the forty or so years of its existence, with the vast majority made during the 1950s and 1960s. Together these films represent a well-defined genre that proved surprisingly resistant to changing tastes – even in the face of the genre's growing marginalization and eventual demise during the 1970s. Influenced by longstanding debates on culture and society, studio heads and party leaders strongly believed in aesthetic *Bildung* (education) and cultural heritage as essential forces in the building of socialism. Like the heavily promoted historical films, the opera films were big-budget productions that took full advantage of the studio's extensive collection of costumes and props inherited from the old UFA studio. *Die lustigen Weiber von Windsor* [*The Merry Wives of Windsor*, 1950] became one of the ten top-grossing DEFA films of all times; *Figaros Hochzeit* [*Figaro's Marriage*, 1949] and *Die schöne Lurette* [*Belle Lurette*, 1960] also proved popular with audiences.[23] Yet critical assessments of the DEFA opera film were not always favourable, with Wolfgang Thiel in 1986 describing the overall results as 'meagre' and the genre's influence on GDR music culture negligible.[24]

The DEFA opera films broadly fall into the same categories (opera classics and popular operettas) which defined the repertory of the Komische Oper. Four adaptations of famous operas belong to the first group apart from *Fidelio*: Mozart's *Le nozze di Figaro*, directed by Georg Wildhagen under the title *Figaros Hochzeit* in 1949 (and with Felsenstein calling his later version *Die Hochzeit des Figaro* [*The Marriage of Figaro*]); Wagner's *Der fliegende Holländer* [*The Flying Dutchman*], the formally most ambitious project completed by Joachim Herz in 1964; and two nineteenth-century works in the German opera buffa tradition – Otto Nicolai's *Die lustigen Weiber von Windsor*, directed by Georg Wildhagen in 1950 and Albert Lortzing's *Zar und Zimmermann* [*Tsar and Carpenter*], directed by Hans Müller in 1956. The operettas chosen for screen adaptations include reliable favourites such as: Johann Strauss's *Die Fledermaus*, called *Rauschende Melodien* [*Resounding Melodies*, 1955]; Carl Millöcker's *Der Bettelstudent* [*The Beggar Student*], called *Mazurka der Liebe* [*Mazurka of Love*, 1957]; as well as two Offenbach operettas – the above-mentioned *Die schöne Lurette*, directed by Georg Kolditz in 1960 and Horst Bonnet's *Orpheus in der Unterwelt* [*Orpheus in the Underworld*, 1974].

All the films represent abbreviated and revised versions of original operas, with arias deleted and sequences changed, recitatives turned into dialogues, side stories added and endings sometimes reworked in line with socialist ideology (for example, the critique of the aristocracy in *Die Hochzeit des Figaro* or the empowerment of the people in *Die schöne Lurette*). The transformation of librettos into screenplays required the addition of extensive dialogue scenes in order to strengthen character identification; justifying the films' often theatrical style, framing narratives set in theatres sometimes showcased the orchestras featured in the productions. It was common practice to prerecord the music and have singers or actors lip-synch to playback, which accounts for the double casting of actors and singers in the leading roles. On two occasions, opera films also functioned as a showcase for new technologies, with the 1956 production of *Zar und Zimmerman* chosen to promote the Agfa Wolfen colour film technology and Bonnet's sumptuous, irreverent version of *Orpheus in der Unterwelt* selected for an experiment with the 70mm widescreen format.

Before the building of the Wall, the pursuit of international prestige repeatedly propelled studio executives to invest in transnational forms of production involving performers from the West. As an indication of the relative openness of German borders, the 1949 film *Figaros Hochzeit* featured internationally known coloratura soprano Erna Berger as Susanne and the 1956 *Zar und Zimmermann* baritone Josef Metternich from the Bavarian State Opera in the role of Czar Peter I. In the 1950 production of *Die lustigen Weiber von Windsor*, the world famous soprano Rita Streich gave her voice to *Heimatfilm* star Sonja Ziemann in the role of Frau Fluth, whereas the young Martha Mödl prior to her Wagner career as a dramatic mezzo sang the role of Frau Reich performed on the screen by Camilla Spira; both singers soon thereafter left East Berlin for the West.

If the East and West German competition over the classical legacy produced a vibrant and rich musical life after World War II, the building of the Berlin Wall in 1961 brought growing conservatism and provincialism as well as short-lived efforts at artistic experimentation. The brief period of liberalization after Honecker's 1971 'no taboos' speech allowed younger composers to discover the classical avant-garde and Western neo-avant-garde and explore the different sensibilities of *Kammeroper* (chamber opera) and *szenische Kammermusik* (scenic chamber music).[25] Indicative of its essentially conservative nature, the DEFA opera films reproduced the class-based tastes, whether called 'bourgeois' (in the case of opera) or 'petty bourgeois' (in the case of operetta), that had come to define the reception of classical music since the early postwar years and to preserve musical sensibilities (or, rather, their interpretation) with a particular investment in questions of Germanness.

Meanwhile, the German-German opera wars continued to dominate the airwaves, first through programming for classical stations on public broadcasting, and later on public television in the form of opera telecasts. The 1949 DEFA *Figaro* adaptation most likely prompted Bayerischer Rundfunk (BR) to air a television production of the same opera in 1956 (again with Rita Streich). West German public television continued this practice by broadcasting von Weber's *Der Freischütz* [*The Marksman*] and *Fidelio* in 1968, *Zar und Zimmermann* in 1969 and *Orpheus in der Unterwelt* in 1973; all were based on productions at the Hamburg State Opera under Rolf Liebermann. But whereas later opera films made in the Federal Republic, as well as opera productions by leading directors of New German Cinema (Volker Schlöndorff, Werner Schroeter and so on), incorporated new art film sensibilities, the last filmed operas made in the GDR affirmed their commitment to tradition and convention by reproducing the aesthetics of classical narrative cinema. In that sense, the productions from the 1970s must be seen as part of a larger crisis of socialism that contributed to the abandonment of early visions of socialist mass culture and the fragmentation of the public sphere – captured in the term *Nischengesellschaft* (niche society) – that, rather ironically, brought a retreat to forms of entertainment more typically associated with the prewar period. This point is confirmed by a closer look at Felsenstein's later film and television work.

Opera and Television

Roughly two decades after directing *Fidelio*, Felsenstein reshot two successful Komische Oper productions, *Hoffmanns Erzählungen* and *Ritter Blaubart*, as filmed operas on the Babelsberg sound stage. Compared to the innovative *Fidelio*, the two latter works represent a retreat from filmic experimentation in favour of the familiar television aesthetic of medium shots, close-ups and shot/reverse shots. However, from the perspective of identification as the most effective conduit to the emotional power of music, Felsenstein's turn to theatricality can also be read as a necessary adjustment to the different possibilities available in the medium of television. Only now, in the musical register of comedy and farce, identification is no longer limited to characters, but extends to the entire musical *mise en scène* as a visualization of what might be called the Offenbach musical habitus of surface splendour and mild mockery.

The filmed versions of *Hoffmanns Erzählungen* and *Ritter Blaubart* start with a man entering an opera house for a performance and with singers arriving at a Babelsberg sound stage during a set change. However, this foregrounding of theatricality is achieved through uniquely filmic means such as point of view, with camerawork and editing inviting forms of engagement not possible on the proscenium stage. Contributing to these self-referential qualities, the episodic structure of both operas reduces identification with any particular character or narrative in favour of identification with an overall mood or attitude. Thus Hoffmann's retelling of his three loves (the automaton Olympia, the singer Antonia and the courtesan Giulietta) and the stories surrounding Bluebeard's seven wives invite an indulgent, ironic view of human desire and its inevitable disappointments. Under such conditions, social commentary and political critique are possible as long as they are contained within the terms of performativity: in the play with disguise, in the pleasure of exaggeration and in the form of farce (for example the figure of King Bobêche). The ending of *Ritter Blaubart* is very telling in this regard as Boulotte exclaims, 'Once again, the powerful win' and walks off the set, declaring the end of the performance. When another woman protests, 'We have to finish the film!' the peasant woman asks, 'But how? With a happy ending? ... Mind you, we're not in an operetta!' In lieu of an answer, the performers decide to pretend that they are living in an operetta world in order to force a happy ending.

The fact that three Offenbach operettas were adapted to the screen in the 1970s calls for some consideration of the hidden affinities between Second Empire Paris and late socialist East Berlin and the conditions under which Felsenstein's contribution to the opera–film interface served an increasingly superficial notion of 'the people' far removed from early pronouncements about opera as an instrument of democratization. Petty bourgeois tastes had remained an integral part of socialist opera culture despite efforts to promote the great works and develop a contemporary (i.e. post-class) opera. Offenbach's operettas, in particular, responded to a desire for luxury and sensuality not only unsatisfied by socialist consumer society, but also left unaddressed by the functionalist aesthetics known as socialist modern. Packaged in beautiful sets and costumes, the composer's hyperbole and his affinity for parody and the grotesque produced an atmosphere of illusionism that made the critique of sociosexual mores and power structures both possible and inconsequential.

The fluid terrain marked by the dramatization of music and the theatricalization of film is even more apparent in Felsenstein's telecasts of two Mozart operas, the 1966 production of *Don Giovanni* and the 1975 production of *Die Hochzeit des Figaro*. At first glance, they seem representative of a high-culture model of media convergence in which the medium of distribution (television) has no influence on the style of the production. In that sense, the difference between the documentary style of the Mozart telecasts and the sumptuous sound studio aesthetic of the Offenbach films could not be greater. In marked contrast to the two Offenbach productions, which revel in types and clichés, the two Mozart productions also attest to the director's lifelong interest in the human condition and the problem of individuality. Thus the problem of (male) sexuality shared by the figure of the compulsive seducer in *Don Giovanni* and the scandal of the *droit du seigneur* in *Die Hochzeit des Figaro* offers Felsenstein an opportunity to probe the complexities of desire without recourse to political interpretations. The difference from the critique of class society in Wildhagen's 1949 *Figaro* adaptation and the people's fight against tyranny in his own *Fidelio* could not be greater, suggesting considerable changes in the politics of opera from the 1950s to the 1970s.

The formal characteristics shared by his film and television work confirms such impressions as they substitute individual identification with the camera for the models of collective spectatorship and social agency still present in *Fidelio*. The live recordings of Komische Oper productions attest to Felsenstein's continuing efforts at making opera more accessible to mass audiences – or, to phrase it more critically, to cater to a particular segment (i.e. older, educated viewers) of the television audience. Yet as televisual versions of music theatre, these recordings also reveal the degree to which filmic modes of character identification have already become an integral part of his staging of opera – exactly at a time when the critique of classical narrative cinema associated with the European New Waves produced new models of film narrative and spectatorship in the cinema. Meanwhile, in the continuous development of the opera–film–television interface, the adaptation to the small television screen is achieved through the close-up as the most effective filmic means of creating both emotional intimacy and musical intensity; but in a way, the close-up is already incorporated in the spatial choreography of performers, sets and props on the stage. This emphasis on emotional realism is confirmed by the sparse use of props in *Don Giovanni* and the half-finished walls and scaffolding in *Die Hochzeit des Figaro* as well as the psychologically nuanced, restrained performance of the singers. Felsenstein's demand that a singer 'must make emotionally believable that he has no other form of self-expression at his disposal than singing'[26] thus allows him not only to redefine realism for music theatre without recourse to physical or social reality, but also to reframe the meaning of audiences and publics in purely individual terms; the televisual aesthetic is the perfect vehicle and venue for this process.

Accordingly, the camerawork in both Mozart telecasts follows the conventions of the television play, with several cameras recording the performance from the wings and making extensive use of zooms and pans to follow the movement of the actors or capture facial expressions. Long takes prevail in the duets and trios, whereas the back and forth between medium shots and close-ups is most pronounced during individual arias. The point of view of the audience is essential to the success to these filmic effects across the opera-television divide. Both productions align the perspective of the live audience with the spatial logic of the proscenium stage at the beginning and end of each act and, in so doing, establish a model for its miniature reproduction in the living rooms of the so-called peasants' and workers' state. Shown applauding, the opera-goers no longer embody the utopia of mass reception or the fantasy of a unified socialist collective; instead, in their attire and demeanour, they serve as a stand-in for the television audiences and their cultural tastes and aspirations. When Felsenstein moves the perspective to the wings on the stage, where the viewers can (almost) become part of the dramatic events and experience opera in ways not available to the people in the theatre, the promise of a democratization of opera seems to have been fully realized – with the need for such illusory scenarios of immersion and participation inseparable from the crisis of legitimacy during the last two decades of the GDR.

The underlying shift from socialist re-readings of famous operas to the preservation of opera culture through modern media technologies can only be explained through the changing function of media convergence and the politics of opera during the Cold War. The ideological enlistment of well-established filmic and musical traditions and the political functionalization of the seemingly apolitical discourse of humanism are especially apparent in the opera films of Walter Felsenstein and, by extension, his work at the Komische Oper. They show the formative influence of his film and television work on the continuous evolution of his music theatre, with the dramatization of music achieved through uniquely filmic means, including character identification and psychological motivation. As we have seen, his film work not only allowed Felsenstein to explore ideas for and work out problems in his stage work; it also enabled him to pursue early ideas about the democratization of opera at the interface of old and new media and to hold on to these ideas despite the persistence of a high-low culture divide. In the larger context of DEFA cinema, his contribution therefore allows us to gain a clearer sense of the complicated institutionalized constellations of high culture, socialist culture and mass culture in the GDR.[27] Especially relevant for future studies is the contribution of these opera films – namely as exemplars of media convergence – to the reconciliation of two competing cultural paradigms – bourgeois high culture and socialist mass culture – and their enlistment in the making of the socialist culture industry, including its growing social and cultural fragmentation beginning in the 1970s. Intermediality played a key role in this process; and its aesthetic and political effects can be seen with particular clarity in the film and television work of the GDR's most famous opera director.

Sabine Hake is the Texas Chair of German Literature and Culture in the Department of Germanic Studies at the University of Texas at Austin. She is the author of numerous books on German mass culture, including *German National Cinema* (2008), and *Screen Nazis: Cinema, History, and Democracy* (2012).

Notes

1. This version has much benefited from comments by Joy Calico, Stephen Brockmann and members of the film study group at University of Texas at Austin, especially Jim Buhler. Most studies on opera film are historical surveys in the style of Richard Fawkes, *Opera on Film*, London: Duckworth, 2000; or close readings such as Marcia J. Citron, *Opera on Screen*, New Haven, CT: Yale University Press, 2000; and Jeongwon Joe and Rose Theresa (eds), *Between Opera and Cinema*, New York: Routledge, 2002.
2. Theodor W. Adorno, *Introduction to the Sociology of Music*, trans. E.B. Ashton, New York: Continuum, 1988. Adorno writes: 'Benjamin's word about the decay of the aura suits opera more exactly than almost any other form. Music in which dramatic events are a priori doused in atmosphere and exalted is aura pure and simple. And where that character is abruptly abandoned [i.e. by avant-garde composers, S.H.], the combination of music and action becomes illegitimate' (p. 77).
3. Siegfried Kracauer, *Theory of Film. The Redemption of Physical Reality*, with an introduction by Miriam B. Hansen, Princeton: Princeton University Press, 1997, p. 154.
4. This point is made in Adorno's 'Bourgeois Opera', in David Levin (ed), *Opera through Other Eyes*, Stanford: Stanford University Press, 1993, pp. 25–44, esp. p. 32.
5. Jeremy Tambling, *Opera, Ideology and Film*, Manchester: Manchester University Press, 1987, pp. 5–6.
6. Indicative of the difficulty of academic disciplines in dealing with the phenomenon of media convergence, scholarship on the DEFA opera film has been limited to a brief general overview published in the GDR, two unpublished dissertations on Felsenstein productions and one scholarly article on Wagner and cinema. This lack of interest among film scholars is more than compensated for by the extensive research of historians and musicologists on the importance of opera to German identity, from the enlistment of classical music in the making of nineteenth-century German nationalism and the politicization of German music during the Third Reich to the continuation of these projects in the East German debates on a national opera during the 1950s. Joy

Calico, Fabian Bien and Katrin Stöck have documented the instrumentalization of opera in the ideological battles of the Cold War, traced the resonances of the East German operatic tradition after unification and acknowledged Felsenstein's role as an important mediator between East and West. However, Felsenstein's specific contribution to the opera film and, more importantly, his reliance on media convergence as a model of aesthetic and political reconciliation has remained unexplored. Formal aspects of Felsenstein's opera films are discussed in two musicological studies: Konrad Körte, *Die Oper im Film. Analysen des Produktionsapparates anhand von Guiseppe Verdis 'Othello' in der Inszenierung von Walter Felsenstein*, Frankfurt am Main: Lang, 1989; and Alison M. Furlong, 'Georg Wildhagen's *Figaros Hochzeit*. How an Italian Opera Based on a French Play Became a German Socialist Film', MA thesis, The Ohio State University, 2010. For a historically contextualized reading of a DEFA opera film directed by Felsenstein's successor at the Komische Oper, see Joy H. Calico, 'Wagner in East Germany. Joachim Herz's *Der fliegende Holländer*', in Jeongwon Joe and Sander L. Gilman (eds), *Wagner and Cinema*, Bloomington: Indiana University Press, 2010, pp. 294-313. For the larger political context, see Joy H. Calico, 'The Politics of Opera in the German Democratic Republic, 1945-1961', unpublished PhD Diss., Duke University, 1999. And for a Berlin-based historical overview, see Elizabeth Janik, *Recomposing German Music. Politics and Musical Tradition in Cold War Berlin*, Leiden: Brill, 2005.

7. Five operas were screened in Berlin's Babylon Kino in 2010/11, and another five in 2016, evidence of the continuous movement of mediality from the theatrical, filmic and televisual to the digital and back to the theatrical. See: http://www.babylonberlin.de/walterfelsenstein.htm, accessed 16 June 2016.

8. See: http://www.operatoday.com/content/2009/01/walter_felsenst.php, accessed 16 June 2016, and http://www.nytimes.com/2008/05/18/arts/music/18davi.html?pagewanted=all&_r=0, accessed 16 June 2016. Today Felsenstein is sometimes falsely credited, together with Wieland Wagner, with having invented the *Regieoper*, a director-driven approach that privileges staging as a form of reinterpretation. If we had to construct patterns of influence, it would have to be through the work of his protégés Götz Friedrich of the Deutsche Oper Berlin (1981-2000) and Harry Kupfer, his successor at the Komische Oper (1981-2002), as the most influential proponents of *Regieoper* today.

9. Cold War Berlin had three opera houses: the Deutsche Staatsoper Unter den Linden, the Komische Oper and, after 1961, the Deutsche Oper in West Berlin.

10. Jean Kurt Forest, quoted by Katrin Stöck in 'Die Nationalaperndebatte in der DDR der 1950er und 1960er Jahre als Instrument zur Ausbildung einer sozialistischen deutschen Nationalkultur', in Helmut Loos und Stefan Keym (eds), *Nationale Musik im 20. Jahrhundert. Kompositorische und soziokulturelle Aspekte der Musikgeschichte zwischen Ost- und Westeuropa*, Leipzig: Gudrun Schröder, 2004, pp. 521-39 (p. 521). All translations from the German are mine unless noted otherwise. On the national opera debate, also see Joy H. Calico, '"Für eine neue Nationaloper". Opera in the Discourses of Unification and Legitimation in the German Democratic Republic', in Celia Applegate and Pamela A. Potter (eds), *Music and German National Identity*, Chicago: University of Chicago Press, 2002, pp. 190-204.

11. Quoted by Calico, '"Für eine neue Nationaloper"', p. 201.

12. These qualities are clearly in evidence in the many extras (photos, sketches, interviews, recordings) included in the Felsenstein DVD box.

13. On the effects of Brecht's defamiliarization and Felsenstein's hyperrealism on contemporary *Regieoper*, see Joy H. Calico, 'The Legacies of GDR Directors on the Post-Wende Opera Stage', in

Elaine Kelly and Amy Wlodarski (eds), *Art Outside the Lines. New Perspectives on GDR Art Culture*, Amsterdam: Rodopi, 2011, pp. 131–54.
14. Felsenstein in Ilse Kobán (ed), *Die Pflicht, die Wahrheit zu finden. Briefe und Schriften eines Theatermannes*, Frankfurt am Main: Suhrkamp, 1997, p. 267.
15. Felsenstein in Kobán, p. 33.
16. Fabien Bien, *Oper im Schaufenster. Die Berliner Opernbühnen in den 1950er-Jahren als Orte nationaler kultureller Repräsentation*, Vienna: Böhlau, 2011, pp. 258–77.
17. See Robert Braunmüller, *Oper als Drama. Das 'realistische Musiktheater' Walter Felsensteins*. Tübingen: de Gruyter, 2002; and Werner Hintze, Clemens Risi and Robert Sollich (eds), *Realistisches Musiktheater. Walter Felsenstein: Geschichte, Erben, Gegenpositionen*, Berlin: Theater der Zeit, 2008.
18. Walter Felsenstein, 'Method and Attitude', in Peter Paul Fuchs (ed), *The Music Theater of Walter Felsenstein. Collected Articles, Speeches and Interviews by Walter Felsenstein and Others*, New York: Norton, 1975, pp. 15–26 (p. 15).
19. Wolfgang Thiel, 'Opernverfilmungen der DEFA', *Oper heute* 9 (1986), 276–90 (270).
20. Felsenstein, 'Opera in Films and on Television', in Peter Paul Fuchs, pp. 126–29 (pp. 128–29).
21. Dieter Kranz, *Gespräche mit Felsenstein. Aus der Werkstatt des Musiktheaters*, Berlin: Henschel, 1977, p. 72.
22. In Germany, opera made its earliest appearance in the films of early pioneer Oskar Messter who in the 1910s created so-called *Tonbilder*, short sound films with synchronous sound projection that featured famous arias performed by singers from the Berlin stage. Robert Wiene's much discussed film treatment of Richard Strauss's *Der Rosenkavalier* [*The Knight of the Rose*, 1926], performed with live music, confirmed the importance of opera in bringing middle-class audiences into cinemas during the 1920s. Not surprisingly, the 1932 adaptation of Smetana's *Die verkaufte Braut* [*The Bartered Bride*] by Max Ophüls was chosen to showcase the new sound technology and establish a filmic model for integrating music and dialogue into the narrative. By contrast, the so-called *Sängerfilme* of the 1930s emphasized the star phenomenon and built their stories around the lives of famous opera singers such as Richard Tauber and Jan Kiepura. More contemporary formats inspired by American musicals prevailed in music films in the style of *Die Drei von der Tankstelle* [*The Three from the Filling Station*, 1930]. During the Third Reich, operetta films set in the capital of the waltz, and so-called genius films about classical composers, were promoted as viable compromises between elite and popular tastes. The Americanization of postwar Europe accelerated the marginalization of these musical traditions in favour of contemporary *Revuefilme* and *Schlagerfilme* featuring singers/actors such Peter Kraus or Catarina Valente. With DEFA launching their socialist equivalents with Frank Schöbel and Chris Doerk, the artistic coupling of film and opera by the 1960s had become a niche phenomenon – at least for younger audiences.
23. See: http://www.insidekino.de/DJahr/DDRAlltimeDeutsch.htm, accessed 16 June 2016. The different titles of the two DEFA adaptations of Mozart's *Le nozze di Figaro*, Wildhagen's *Figaros Hochzeit* and Felsenstein's *Die Hochzeit des Figaro*, are reflected in the English translations *Figaro's Marriage* and *The Marriage of Figaro*.
24. Thiel, 288.
25. See Katrin Stöck, *Musiktheater in der DDR. Szenische Kammermusik und Kammeroper der 1970er und 1980er Jahre*, Cologne: Böhlau, 2013.
26. Felsenstein in Stephan Stompor (ed), *Schriften zum Musiktheater*, Berlin: Henschel: 1976, p. 70.
27. For comparative purposes, it would be interesting to look at the work of Ulrich Plenzdorf in literature, theatre, film and television under this same aspect of socialist media convergence.

CHAPTER 10

Dreams of 'Cosmic Culture' in *Der schweigende Stern* [The Silent Star, 1960]

Sonja Fritzsche

> The rocket is absolutely necessary. If any other power gets one out into space before we do, we'll no longer be the United States, we'll be the disunited world ... The first country that can use the moon for the launching of missiles will control the Earth.
>
> Destination Moon, 1950

Science fiction films in the GDR were from the outset transmedial and transnational phenomena. The desire for an exotic setting, the level of special effects, the international casting and the overall expense of film production led to a number of co-productions in this genre. The best known of these films is the East German–Polish film *Der schweigende Stern* (Fig. 10.1) directed by Kurt Maetzig. Collaboration within the 'friendly' socialist states and also across the Iron Curtain with Western Europe brought with it both challenges and advantages, as studies of archival documents have demonstrated.[1]

While existing research has focused on the co-production history of *Der schweigende Stern*, this chapter seeks to understand the film within the international, comparative framework of other contemporary Eastern Bloc science fiction films. The quote above from the American-made film *Destination Moon* (dir. Irving Pichel, 1950) attests to the highly volatile, Cold War context in which the East German film was released. The Soviets successfully launched Sputnik in 1957 and, as French historian Joël Mak Dit Mack observes, *Der schweigende Stern*, in conjunction with other Eastern Bloc films that appeared between 1958 and 1965, act as a cluster that established a communist presence in celluloid space that had been dominated by Hollywood and Japanese titles of conquest and strife such as

Destination Moon (1950), *War of the Worlds* (1953), *Gojira* [*Godzilla*, 1954] and *Forbidden Planet* (1956).[2] The films appeared in the post-Stalinist/post-Sputnik era at a time when the Soviet space program was a taboo topic, but the Soviet achievements in space were not. That there had been virtually no science fiction films from Eastern Europe since the late 1930s makes this even more noteworthy.[3] The Soviet titles in this cluster include among others: Pavel Klushantsev's documentary film *Doroga k zvezdam* [*Road to the Stars*, 1958], Victor Morgenstern's *Ya byl sputnikom solntsa* [*I Was a Sputnik of the Sun*, 1959], Mikhail Karzhukov's *Nebo zovyot* [*The Heavens Call*, 1959], Pavel Klushantsev's *Planeta Bur* [*Planet of Storms*, 1962] and Karzhukov and Otar Koberidze's *Mechte navstrechu* [*A Dream Come True*, 1963].[4] Additional films appeared in Czechoslovakia: of interest here is an adaptation of Stanislaw Lem's story *The Magellanic Cloud* (1955) that was released under the title *Ikarie XB-1* [*Voyage to the End of the Universe*, 1963] and directed by Jindřich Polák.[5]

Figure 10.1: *Der schweigende Stern* (1960) with Professor Saltyk, Professor Harringway Hawling and Raimund Brinkmann (top row) and Professor Sikarna (below) © DEFA-Stiftung/Waltraut Pathenheimer.

There are many common themes that *Der schweigende Stern* shares with the above films. Dina Iordanova has written of the 'forced togetherness' of the Eastern Bloc that led to more closely linked influences and cultural interactions.[6] In the film industry, this led not only to numerous co-productions among Soviet satellite countries, but also to the common practice of screening each other's films. Marsha Siefert describes a 'well-developed system of cinematic barter between Bloc countries' that promoted cultural exchange, but also helped distributors fill gaps in their programming with films from other socialist countries. Numerous film festivals promoted these productions as well as the regularly scheduled 'film weeks' that screened the newest releases from other Bloc countries.[7] Indeed, Iordanova writes of the 'intricate part' that GDR culture played within the Eastern Bloc and that 'its cinema had correspondingly shared similarities in terms of ideology, style and thematic interests with the film traditions of other Bloc countries'.[8] Accordingly, this chapter first places *Der schweigende Stern* in terms of the broader 'cosmic culture' that existed in the Soviet Union and Eastern Europe.

Like the fascination with the 'space race' in the United States, so too the Soviet 'space age' was an essential part of the country's history and culture. Not surprisingly, the Soviet Union also exported this Cold War phenomenon to its satellite countries, many of which shared in the fascination and celebration via official and unofficial channels. These technological achievements seemed to validate a system that had promised not only a political revolution but a scientific one too.[9]

Der schweigende Stern has much in common with its Eastern Bloc cousins. Like such films, its narrative is driven by the adventure of a scientific expedition, and it reflects an obsession with rocket technology that is underlined by the prominent role afforded to special effects in it and other contemporary releases. In addition, it also emphasizes the importance of the so-called 'socialist personality' (*sozialistische Persönlichkeit*), a figure who, in this genre, often assumes the form of the heroic scientist-engineer. Yet, *Der schweigende Stern* also stands out from other films that were released around this time: despite presenting a vision of a peaceful, international communist future, it was the only film to use its portrayal of an international crew and its message of peace in an atomic world as a raison d'être. Moreover, while the Soviet films brought past heroes of Soviet rocket science to life on screen, the East German film was eager to distance itself from the most infamous name in German rocket science – Wernher von Braun.

Der schweigende Stern

Compared to the Federal Republic, the GDR made relatively few science fiction films. Between 1949 and 1989 the Federal Republic of Germany (FRG) generated over one hundred science fiction titles, a sizeable number of them co-productions, while the GDR released just nine, six of which were co-productions. Still, the East German film studio, DEFA, was responsible for a number of notable films in this genre during its existence from 1946-1992.[10] The best known is Kurt Maetzig's *Der schweigende Stern*. The film was a co-production with Poland and was based on Stanislaw Lem's novel *Astronauci* [*The Astronauts*, 1951]. The film was first released in the United States in a form made suitable for the B-film market under the title *First Spaceship on Venus*.

The film itself chronicles an exploratory trip to Venus to discover the source of a mysterious communication from the planet. An international crew on the spaceship *Kosmokrator* travels to Venus to investigate. When the crew arrives on the planet, they discover the remnants of a highly advanced civilization that had planned to obliterate life on Earth with nuclear weapons, but destroyed themselves in the process. The Japanese doctor compares the shadows of the Venusians to the shadows of the Japanese at Hiroshima and Nagasaki.

Mariana Ivanova points to the fantasy of a future international community in the film. While this was certainly a crucial element in the Marxist-Leninist conceptualization of global politics, it also had a particular resonance in a Germany where many people believed in the possibility of reunification at some level, up until 1961.[11] Film scholars have outlined the message of peace embedded not only in the film's content but also in its extended production process that included a screenplay of Polish origin, help from the Soviet Union with special effects, an international cast and concrete plans to co-produce with the French studio Pathé. While the latter agreement dissolved due to the Berlin Crisis (1958-1961), the cast did remain international and included actors from Japan, China, Czechoslovakia, the Soviet Union and Kenya as well as the GDR.[12]

Der schweigende Stern demonstrates what I have termed the 'utopian realism' that is characteristic of many East German science fiction novels of the 1950s and 1960s.[13] The term evokes a point of ideological tension. In the 1950s and 1960s, socialist realism, the politically driven, official aesthetic of East Germany and the Eastern Bloc, required the illustration of an ideal socialist 'reality'. For science fiction, the 'real' consisted of current scientific knowledge, enlightened notions of the rational, and compliance with the most recent ideological and economic plans. 'Utopianism', on the other hand, was considered to be irrational and escapist, this term often being used for works labelled fascist or capitalist. Practically, this term was applied to those narratives that did not correspond to the officially sanctioned vision of the future. For instance, Ernst Bloch's utopian philosophy laid out in his three-volume work *Das Prinzip Hoffnung* [*The Principle of Hope*, pub. 1938–47] had too much subversive potential to be accepted in a time when socialist realism was the dominant aesthetic of East Germany.

Technology, however, played a vital role in the GDR's idealistic conceptualization of Marxism-Leninism. According to its tenets, true communism, which represented the culmination of historical and societal evolution, would be reached most quickly through what Marx and Engels termed 'scientific socialism'.[14] For this reason, the Socialist Unity Party (SED) tolerated science fiction as a means by which to envision this technologically based socialist future. The utopian was restrained by the 'real', i.e. the ideological real and by what was scientifically possible. The warp drives, bug-eyed monsters or megalomanic onboard computers (HAL), so common in Western science fiction film, were perceived to be immoral, impossible, imperialist elements that exploited the fears of their audience. Consequently, East German science fiction films, like their literary counterparts, tended to be more philosophical and slow moving. Not worse than Hollywood, but with quite different goals.

Genre Film and 'Cosmic Culture'

Der schweigende Stern came out in a period in East Germany when the literary genre of science fiction began to regain its political legitimacy and also resurged in popularity among German audiences.[15] This phenomenon was not an isolated occurrence if one looks to other Eastern Bloc countries as well. Russia had a long tradition of revolutionary utopia and science fiction that the Soviet Union encouraged to a greater or lesser degree. In the Soviet Union itself, prominent writers of the postwar period include Ivan Efremov or Boris and Arkady Strugatsky. Czechoslovakia boasted Karel Čapek and later Josef Nesvadba. Poland had Stanislaw Lem. Yet, after the war, science fiction film remained too expensive and politically risky for such a closely monitored industry. This would change with the public successes of the Soviet space program, beginning in 1957 with Sputnik.

Science fiction was very popular in the Eastern Bloc. In East German bookstores, science fiction titles – both Eastern European works in translation and a growing number of home-grown publications – regularly sold out. Eastern European works in translation and a growing number of home-grown publications. The GDR developed a strong science fiction literary tradition, and its fans were eager to see their own country's science fiction film. Before the Wall was built in 1961, viewers crossed over the border to watch matinees in West Berlin, which screened many Western genre films. As science fiction films from other countries of the Eastern Bloc became available, they were quickly subtitled and screened in the GDR. For instance, an internal memo at DEFA stated that *Der schweigende Stern* would be screened in the GDR two and-a-half-months after the release of *Ya byl sputnikom solntsa* [*I was a Sputnik of the Sun*]. Five months later, viewers there were treated to *Nebo zovyot* [*The Heavens Call*].[16]

Not only was interest in science fiction growing, but a not unrelated enthusiasm for the 'space race' and space exploration was also a key factor in the sudden surge of science fiction film production. This phenomenon, so unique to Cold War history and the period leading up to the moon landing on 20 July 1969, had a lasting effect on the films of the period. Several recent books in Russian studies have documented the substantial popular interest in and Communist Party management of 'cosmic' or 'space culture' in the Soviet Union.[17] Russian historian James T. Andrews has detailed a substantial tradition of 'Russian cosmic popularization' that was begun by rocket engineer Konstantin Tsiolkovsky, capitalized upon by Lenin, nationalized by Stalin and then redoubled by Khrushchev in the run-up to the launching of Sputnik.[18]

In Russia, 'cosmic culture' coincided with a long tradition of revolutionary utopian literature that reached back to the nineteenth century and had continued on the silver screen in the first half of the twentieth century with Yakov Protozanov's *Aelita* [*Aelita. Queen of Mars*, 1924] and Vasili Zhuravlyov's *Kosmicheskiy reys* [*Cosmic Voyage*, 1935]. A variety of groups and individuals in the 1920s contributed to the popularization of space exploration with a particular fascination with rocketry. These included members of the Russian Futurist and Constructivist movements, including Vladimir Mayakovsky as well as leading natural scientists and Bolsheviks. In addition, the popular press published article after article devoted to developments in rocket technology and to Lenin's scientific-technological revolution; it also serialized science fiction stories.[19] For some, fascination with the cosmos included a philosophical and spiritual dimension.[20]

Under Stalin, utopian dreaming became politically risky and the fascination with technology focused on the more earthly pursuit of aviation and the hero cult of the pilot. Yet after Stalin's death, Khrushchev did not hesitate to proclaim a 'new cosmic era of man' with the success of Sputnik. Yuri Gagarin's flight in 1961 was celebrated as the coming of the Soviet 'new man'.[21] Formulated during 1958-1961, the new programme accepted by the Congress of the Communist Party in 1961 outlined a new Soviet utopia according to Khrushchev. At the centre of this techno-utopia was the space program. While its details were top secret, Soviet space travel was openly and ubiquitously celebrated. Again this was reflected in the popular press, in consumer goods and in public spaces.[22] Petr Vail´ and Aleksandr Genis even go as far as to equate ascension into the cosmos with a feeling of 'total liberation'. Stalin was gone and had been exposed; Khrushchev had 'relaunched' socialism; works by the dissident author Solzhenitsyn appeared in print. Russians could vicariously experience this liberation through the cosmonaut.[23]

Importantly, the propagation of a 'cosmic culture' did not stop at the borders of the Soviet Union.[24] It was very much a fascination in East Germany as well, both as a popular interest and within official policy. Germany too had its own past versions of a 'cosmic culture', with visions of rocketry combined with German nationalist and then national socialist dreams of the V-2 rocket. Yet, not all technological fascination was right wing, as Fritz Lang's *Metropolis* (1927) and *Frau im Mond* [*Woman in the Moon*, 1929] demonstrate. The propagation of 'cosmic culture' continued in East Germany, but this time was modelled on the Soviet version and was done with the intention of creating a new scientist hero. *Der schweigende Stern* helped to remould German V-2 nationalism to that of East German 'cosmic culture'.

The GDR public sphere reflected this cosmic policy. After 1957, mini-Sputniks dotted the architectural landscape of East Berlin, including atop the Café Moskau and in its indoor mural; an East Berlin cinema on Karl-Marx-Allee was aptly named the Kosmos Kino; and children's and young adults' literature was full of dreams of space exploration. The popular GDR comics *Atze* (1955-1991) and *Mosaik* (1955-) each contained a number of editions that featured space exploration. For instance, the September 1958 edition of *Atze* was entitled *Start in den Weltraum* [*Take off into Space*]. *Mosaik* characters the 'Digedags' embarked upon an interstellar adventure in the initial *Weltraum-Serie* (Space Series, 1958-1960).[25] Given to students at the GDR's secular coming-of-age ceremony, the *Jugendweihe*, from

1954–1974, the book *Weltall – Erde – Mensch* [*Space – Earth – Human*] contained extensive material on communist achievements and future plans in space.[26] All of this culminated not only with the string of celebrated Soviet successes, the highlights of which included Sputnik in 1957, Yuri Gagarin's space flight in 1961 and Valentina Tereshkova, the first woman in space, in 1963, but also with the first German astronaut in space – Sigmund Jähn – in 1978, as part of the Soviet *Interkosmos* programme. Indeed, cosmonaut visits played a vital symbolic role in the East. In her analysis of the media narrative surrounding the closing of the East-West German border on 13 August 1961, Heather Gumbert points to the enormous publicity surrounding the successful flight of cosmonaut Gherman Titov, also in 1961. On 6 August 1961, almost the whole of the GDR state TV's evening broadcast was dedicated to his return and he became an instant star in East Germany. He visited East Berlin as a hero on 1 September, on a tour of Eastern Bloc countries. This media event functioned as a counterweight to the political turmoil of the time.[27]

Dreams of Rockets to the Stars

Within the GDR context, there were several reasons why *Der schweigende Stern* appeared when it did. First, 'utopian realism' became an accepted socialist realist genre. Film officials were eager to fill a 'painfully conspicuous absence of futuristic films and adventure stories in [their] studio's production schedule'.[28] The desire to make such a film was so great that *Der schweigende Stern* had originally been scheduled to be released in 1959 in celebration of the tenth anniversary of the founding of GDR.[29] Yet, there were also external influences that led to the film's production. The success of writer Stanislaw Lem in Poland served as an importance precedent for science fiction in the Eastern Bloc. *Der schweigende Stern* was certainly helped by Lem's significance in that it was based on his book, which had appeared in the GDR as *Planet des Todes* [*Planet of Death*] in 1954, three years after it was published in Poland. Indeed, the wave of science fiction films from the Eastern Bloc in the late 1950s together helped to legitimize the science fiction film further as a valid socialist genre.

Still, DEFA's primary motivation to make a science fiction film almost certainly came from East Germany's neighbour to the West, with which it was continually in dialogue. In the 1950s and early 1960s, quite a few German titles appeared there despite the flood of Hollywood B-films. In cooperation with Carlton Film and Deutsche Styria Film, Arthur Maria Rabenalt directed *Alraune* [*Unnatural*, 1952] with the star-studded cast of Hildegard Knef, Erich von Stroheim and Karlheinz Böhm. The film was another contribution to the trope of the scientist who creates an artificial femme fatale. Universal Studios made the television series *Flash Gordon* (1954–1955), which was first filmed in Berlin-Spandau with producers Gruskin and Wenzel Lüdecke and later in Marseille with producer Gunther von Fritsch. From Rapid-Film Munich, Victor Trivas's *Der Nackte und der Satan* [*The Head*, 1959] of the severed-head subgenre had a plot remarkably similar to the science fiction story *Zaveshchaniye professora Douelya* [*Professor Dowell's Head*, 1925] by Alexander Belyayev, which the Soviets filmed in 1985. Finally, Fritz Lang continued his masterful Mabuse series with *Die 1000 Augen des Dr Mabuse* [*The Thousand Eyes of Dr Mabuse*, 1960]. Two additional Mabuse films subsequently followed, which Harald Reinl directed just before *Winnetou* (1963). Clearly there was significant pressure here for DEFA and the Eastern Bloc to provide a socialist alternative to these films.

Mariana Ivanova has established that *Der schweigende Stern* was, in part, a response to the plans of West German producer Friedrich A. Mainz at Fama Film to make a biography of German rocket scientist Wernher von Braun in 1958. Efforts to adapt Lem's book for film had continued since 1956 in a variety of drafts by Polish and German screenwriters. None had been able to produce a politically viable script. The project was about to be cancelled by both the GDR deputy Minister of Culture, Erich Wendt, and Hermann Schauer, head of the *Hauptverwaltung Film* – the board overseeing film production in the GDR – who objected to the involvement of the French Pathé film studios in the production.[30] A new policy precluded DEFA from working with any Western partners, something it had done productively, albeit to a limited extent, up to that point. To save the film, the studio head Albert Wilkening and Kurt Maetzig dropped the planned Western collaboration and put two trusted GDR screenwriters on the project, Wolfgang Kohlhaase and Günther Rücker.[31] But this last-minute substitution was not the only act that saved the film. Ivanova describes Maetzig's knowledge of a film documenting the life of Wernher von Braun being planned by the Hamburg-based studio Fama Film and suggests that this news was used to argue for the continuation of support for *Der schweigende Stern*. She cites evidence as well that Maetzig consulted von Braun's work as a source for the film, in addition to Soviet sources.[32]

Ivanova also argues convincingly that a scene that was added to *Der schweigende Stern* and is not in Lem's book came about precisely because of the potential for the Western film on von Braun.³³ In *Der schweigende Stern*, the American physicist Harringway Hawling has been invited to take part in the *Kosmokrator* expedition to Venus. He travels home to the United States to consult with his colleagues on the matter. There he meets with members of the 'consortium' who all dissuade him from embarking on the trip. But his mentor, the physicist Weimann, encourages Hawling to follow his own personal dream. The film characterizes Weimann as a victim of both the Nazis and the Americans: the former drove him from his teaching position in Göttingen and the latter exploited his knowledge of nuclear physics to construct the atom bomb; neither allowed Weimann to follow his own desired career path.

Due to the film's antinuclear message, this scene has often been interpreted as Hawling's meeting with members of the Manhattan Project, a scene in which his superior and mentor appears to be modelled on Oppenheimer. Archival sources support such an interpretation, as there are several references to Oppenheimer as the intended referent in film correspondence.³⁴ Yet, for a German audience, the additional relationship between von Braun and the United States cannot be overlooked. Known not only as the man behind the German V-2 rocket, von Braun had also recently published his own visions of space travel entitled *Die Eroberung des Mondes* [*Conquest of the Moon*, 1953] and *Die Erforschung des Mars* [*The Exploration of Mars*, 1957] in both the Federal Republic and in the United States. He became a household name after his highly successful short film *Man in Space* (1955) with Disney.³⁵ There can be no doubt that, without von Braun, the United States would not have been able to put Alan Shepherd in space on 5 May 1961, just several weeks after Yuri Gagarin's historic flight on 12 April. The references to Oppenheimer in *Der schweigende Stern* and the presence of von Braun, also suggest that the scene was designed to portray the German rocketry past in a negative light by associating this past with fascism, and the American atomic present with capitalism. In its place, the film suggests new scientist-heroes, particularly the dashing German pilot Raimund Brinkmann, who was played by Günther Simon of *Ernst Thälmann* film fame.

This strategy worked in tandem with the historical narrative of rocket science propagated by 'cosmic culture' and specifically by the Soviet film *Doroga k zvezdam* [*Road to the Stars*, 1958].³⁶ The first part of this film is a biography of the scientist and science fiction writer Konstantin Tsiolkovsky. In particular, it casts

Tsiolkovsky as the Soviet scientific hero who discovered the rocket and imagined travelling to the stars in his story *Na lune* [*On the Moon*, 1893] and his subsequent *Vne Zemli* [*Beyond the Planet Earth*, 1920]. The latter title includes a dedicated international team of famous scientists throughout history who concentrate on developing a super-fuel to take humanity to the stars.[37] Tsiolkovsky is also referenced in the 1962 Soviet film *Planeta Bur* [*Planet of Storms*] by the cosmonauts on Venus, in a discussion of humanity's necessary next step to travel to the stars. Their conversation seems to come straight from Tsiolkovsky's *Vne Zemli* (Beyond the Planet Earth).[38] Tsiolkovsky also routinely appeared as an illustration or was quoted on the inside cover in a number of early GDR science fiction books as a means to tie ideologically controversial East German science fiction publications to the Soviet Union. The Soviet Union was, after all, seen to be 'the land in which tomorrow is already today'. Indeed, the East German book *Auf dem Weg zu fernen Welten. Ein Buch von der Weltraumfahrt* [*On the Way to Distant Worlds. A Book on Space Travel*, 1958] quotes Tsiolkovsky ('Humans will not always stay on the Earth') immediately before it quotes Lenin on the human ability to discover the absolute truth about nature. The release of *The Road to the Stars* in the GDR reinforced efforts to cast Tsiolkovsky as a Soviet hero and visionary of space travel, and this is reflected in the title of the August 1960 issue of the comic *Mosaik: Ziolkowski weist den Weg* (Tsiolkovsky Shows the Way Forward).[39]

While Tsiolkovsky represented the scientist hero of the past, the scientist as socialist personality dominated the future in post-Sputnik science fiction film. In general, these fictional men and women dedicated and even sacrificed themselves to further humankind's inevitable progress out into the stars. While doing so, they proved their peaceful superiority over the American astronauts who were continually overcome by greed, egoism and fear. For instance, the cosmonauts of *Ikarie XB-1* discover an abandoned and derelict capitalist ship, *Tornado*, from the 'ancient' twentieth century, which had been manned by gamblers who had killed each other fighting over the last gasps of oxygen. The ship's nuclear weapons are activated accidentally and destroy the ship and the cosmonaut crew in the process. When the American astronauts in the Soviet film *The Heavens Call* realize that the Soviets are going to Mars, they recklessly attempt their own trip before their rocket is ready. Consequently, their lives are endangered and the Soviet cosmonauts must risk their own mission and lives to save the Americans. In *A Dream Come True*, it is the American scientist Laungton who believes that the aliens are coming to attack Earth. All of the others know that they will be peaceful and that this is Earth's historical chance at first contact. In *Der schweigende Stern*, Hawling's American colleagues are all sceptical about his proposed participation in the journey to Venus. The rest of the world is on board; only the American scientists are mistrustful. Yet, Hawling still chooses to return to continue the project he had been working on with his international colleagues. This is not a political choice, but rather one of personal interest and a desire to be part of the expedition. He may not be as committed as Los in the film *Aelita*, who converts to socialism; but he does, nonetheless, make a choice that is in defiance of his American associates.

As the Cold War progressed into the 1960s, films continued to integrate the problematic subject of Wernher von Braun into the narrative of Western 'cosmic culture'. As mentioned, the German Fama film production was cancelled in the late 1950s. However, director J. Lee Thompson released the US–West German co-production *I Aim at the Stars* [*Wernher von Braun – Ich greife nach den Sternen*] in 1960.[40] In this film, von Braun's activities in National Socialist Germany are played down. He is first portrayed as an apolitical sympathizer who dislikes Nazi arms policy and ultimately questions the use of his rocket technology; the second half of the film then focuses on his important work in the United States as a founder of NASA and great contributor to the American space program. Several years later, Stanley Kubrick's *Dr Strangelove* (1964) most famously stylized Peter Sellers' character of the same name in part after von Braun. Interestingly, Dr Strangelove was just called Dr Seltsam (strange, odd) in German. The 'love' of the bomb did not appear until the latter part of the film's title. In 1965, the British film *Operation Crossbow* (also released under the title *The Great Spy Mission*) appeared, directed by Michael Anderson and starring Sophia Loren and George Peppard. The film does not focus on von Braun, but is rather a spy thriller that extols a British-led effort to infiltrate and halt the production of the V-series rockets at Peenemünde and later in the Harz Mountains.

In an interview, dramaturge Dieter Wolf commented on the high standard set by *Wernher von Braun – Ich greife nach den Sternen* and *Operation Crossbow* for DEFA's own subsequent spy film on the subject: *Die gefrorenen Blitze* [*Frozen Lightning*] in 1967.[41] Directed by the Hungarian born János Veiczi, the two-part docudrama runs almost three hours and was the most expensive film made that year. It was written by Julius Mader and Harry Thürk. The latter was a highly successful GDR author of over sixty books, many of which were adventure and spy thrillers, or children's fiction.

Figure 10.2: *Die gefrorenen Blitze* (1967) with Wernher von Braun and the V-2 rocket in the background © DEFA-Stiftung/Roland Dressel.

In *Die gefrorenen Blitze*, von Braun (Dieter Körner) is an important but not central figure (Fig. 10.2). He is not even called by name throughout, but is referred to consistently as 'der Raketenbaron' ('the rocket baron'). Dieter Wolf stated that they did not intend to make an 'anti-von Braun film'.[42] Von Braun is not demonized, but objectified and portrayed as an opportunist who believes science and politics to be two separate worlds. The film is far more interested in highlighting the widespread efforts, particularly on the part of the British, Americans, French resistance and Polish communist partisans, to sabotage efforts at Peenemünde and also at the testing facility near the labour camp Mittelbau-Dora. To this end, von Braun takes a backseat to the film's main protagonist, his assistant Dr Grunwald (Alfred Müller). Initially, he had joined von Braun hoping to work on a mission to the moon. In this film, it is Dr Grunwald (not von Braun) who questions the purpose of their research and actively works to halt Nazi use of the V-series rockets. He is not a communist. Still, he sabotages production, aids the communists and ultimately surrenders to the Americans as part of Operation Paperclip. The film finishes with von Braun at Los Alamos, seated together with several high-ranking US officers. Again, von Braun is a silent, but clearly significant presence in the room. Instead, it is an American who comments, as they watch an atomic bomb explode on screen: 'We have built this bomb as a final barrier against one type of barbarism. When we use it to build a new type of barbarism, then others will build a new barrier against us'. This unstated reference to the Soviet Union is one of the very few in the film. The film is very much an East German one about German scientific ethics and the combined Western Allied and Polish efforts to undermine the development of the V-2 rocket.

Conclusion

Popular cinematic traditions have long borrowed and been in dialogue with each other in ways that exceed national boundaries. This is particularly the case for science fiction films in which exotic settings, international casts and expensive special effects often led to collaboration between countries in the Eastern Bloc. Yet, not only does a transnational approach illuminate new aspects of production, it also reveals new thematic and stylistic influences. As Iordanova writes, 'by looking regionally we see trends that otherwise remain neglected'.[43] This is particularly the case with DEFA cinema, the study of which has so often looked to the East German cinematic discourse with the West, but has only in recent years begun to investigate the interplay with the equally significant and influential films from its Slavic neighbours to the East.

Science fiction films from the early Cold War era captured the imaginations of viewers with dreams of travelling to the moon and beyond. At the same time, these films played an important role in linking visions of technological progress with space-race nationalist discourses and Cold War ideologies. This 'cosmic culture' present in both East and West greatly influenced the popular imagination that was captivated by space travel, from the fictional cosmonauts who escape the oozing sludge on Venus in *Der schweigende Stern*, to the interstellar voyage in *Ikarie XB-1*, to the complicated biography of the most celebrated and controversial rocket scientist, Wernher von Braun.

Sonja Fritzsche is Professor of German at Michigan State University. She is the editor of *The Liverpool Companion to World Science Fiction Film* (2014) and the author of *Science Fiction Literature in East Germany* (2006) as well as other articles on DEFA science fiction, fairy tale, 70mm and disco film.

Notes

I wish to thank Frau Renate Göthe and her assistant in the library at the Filmuniversität Babelsberg Konrad Wolf, Frau Ute Klawitter and the staff of the Bundesfilmarchiv and Frau Sabine Söhner at the DEFA-Stiftung for their assistance. In addition, I would like to thank Illinois Wesleyan University for a research grant that made this chapter possible.

1. See Stefan Soldovieri, 'Socialists in Outer Space. East German Film's Venusian Adventure', *Film History* 10.3 (1998), 382–98, Mariana Ivanova, 'DEFA and East European Cinemas. Co-Productions, Transnational Exchange and Artistic Collaborations', unpublished PhD Diss., University of Texas

at Austin, 2011, pp. 96-107, and Evan Torner, 'Casting for a Socialist Earth. Multicultural Whiteness in the East German/Polish Science Fiction Film *Silent Star*', in Sonja Fritzsche (ed), *The Liverpool Companion to World Science Fiction Film*, Liverpool: Liverpool University Press, 2014, pp. 130-49. See also my analysis of the East German films *Signale - Ein Weltraumabenteuer* [*Signals - A Space Adventure*, 1970] and *Eolomea* (1972) in the context of *2001. A Space Odyssey* (1968) and *Solaris* (1972) in 'The Natural and the Artificial. East German Science Fiction Film Responds to Kubrick and Tarkovsky', *Film & History* 40.2 (2010) [= Special issue on 'Visions of Science and Technology in Film'], 80-101.
2. Joël Mak Dit Mack, 'La conquête spatiale à travers le cinéma de science-fiction de la guerre froide (1950-1990)', *Gavroche, revue d'histoire populaire* 155 (2008), 4-11.
3. An exception to this includes Otakar Vávra's excellent *Krakatit* (1948) from then Czechoslovakia.
4. *Road to the Stars* appeared in the GDR as *Der Weg zu den Sternen*; *I Was a Sputnik of the Sun* as *Ich war ein Sonnensatellit*; *The Heavens Call* as *Der Himmel ruft* and also as *Battle Beyond the Sun* in 1962 in a re-edited US-version with Francis Ford Coppola as the director. *Planet of Storms* was *Planet der Stürme* in the GDR and had two different remix versions for the US market: *Voyage to the Prehistoric Planet* (1965) and *Voyage to the Planet of Prehistoric Women* (1968). *A Dream Come True* appeared as *Begegnung im All* in the GDR (1964) and as *Queen of Blood* in the United States (1966).
5. Also of note is *Cesta do pravěku* [*The Journey to the Primeval Age*, 1955] by the well-known director of puppet films Karel Zeman. It premiered in the GDR as *Die Reise in die Urzeit* (1955), in the FRG as *Reise in die Urwelt*, and in the United States (1966). *Ikarie XB-1* was the same in the GDR. Polák directed the famous Czech TV-series *Pan Tau* (1970-1978).
6. Dina Iordanova, *Cinema of the Other Europe*, London: Wallflower, 2003, p. 13.
7. Marsha Siefert, 'East European Cold War Culture(s). Alterities, Commonalities, and Film Industries', in Annette Vowinckel, Marcus M. Payk, and Thomas Lindenberger (eds), *Cold War Cultures. Perspectives on Eastern and Western European Societies*, New York, Oxford: Berghahn, 2012, pp. 23-54 (p. 35).
8. Iordanova, p. 13.
9. Eva Maurer, Julia Richers, Monica Rüthers and Carmen Scheide, 'Introduction. What Does "Space Culture" Mean in Soviet Society?' in Eva Maurer, Julia Richers, Monica Rüthers and Carmen Scheide (eds), *Soviet Space Culture. Cosmic Enthusiasm in Socialist Societies*, New York, NY: Palgrave Macmillan, 2011, pp. 1-9 (pp. 3-4).
10. Detlef Kannapin notes that science fiction film made up only one percent of the total feature film production by DEFA. See Detlef Kannapin, 'Peace in Space – Die DEFA im Weltraum. Anmerkungen zu Fortschritt und Utopie im Filmschaffen der DDR', in Frank Hörnlein and Herbert Heinecke (eds), *Zukunft im Film* [= Reihe Bildwissenschaften, vol. 6], Magdeburg: Scriptum Verlag, 2000, pp. 55-70 (p. 58). There were a number of DEFA science fiction films that were co-productions. The popular science film *Die Reise nach Kosmatom* [*The Trip to Cosmatom*, 1961], directed by Manfred Gussman and Janusz Star, was a co-production with the Wytwórnia Filmów Oświatowych in Łódź, Poland. The East German-Polish co-production *Signale – Ein Weltraumabenteuer* was directed by Gottfried Kolditz in 70mm. Yugoslavian-born actor Gojko Mitic starred as one of the cosmonauts. *Eolomea* (1972) directed by Herrmann Zschoche was an East German, Soviet, and Bulgarian production in 70mm. Kolditz's *Im Staub der Sterne* [*In the Dust of the Stars*, 1976] was made in cooperation with Romania. Egon Schlegel directed the children's film *Abenteuer mit Blasius* [*Adventures with Blasius*, 1975] as a co-production with Barrandov-Filmstudio in Prague.

11. Ivanova, p. 106.
12. See Soldovieri, 96–107, Torner, p. 130, and Ivanova, pp. 101–2.
13. See Sonja Fritzsche, *Science Fiction Literature in East Germany* [= DDR Studien/East German Studies Series 15], Bern; Oxford: Lang, 2006.
14. Friedrich Engels, 'Socialism: Utopian and Scientific', in Robert C. Tucker (ed), *The Marx-Engels Reader*, New York: Norton, 1978, pp. 683–717 (p. 687).
15. See Erik Simon and Olaf Spittel, *Die Science-fiction der DDR. Autoren und Werke*, Berlin: Das Neue Berlin, 1988, pp 28–40. Patrick Major maintains that science fiction was more popular in the Soviet Union and the Eastern Bloc than anywhere else. See Patrick Major, 'Communist Science Fiction in the Cold War', in Rana Mitter and Patrick Major (eds), *Across the Blocs. Cold War Cultural and Social History*, London, Portland, OR: Frank Cass, 2004, pp. 56–74 (p. 73).
16. Ivanova, pp. 106–7.
17. See James T. Andrews and Asif A. Siddiqi (eds), *Into the Cosmos. Space Exploration and Soviet Culture*, Pittsburgh: University of Pittsburgh Press, 2011; and Maurer, Richers, Rüthers and Scheide; and Andrew Thomas, *Kul'tura kosmosa. The Russian Popular Culture of Space Exploration*, Boca Raton: Dissertation.com, 2010, p. 109.
18. James T. Andrews, 'Getting Ready for Khrushchev's *Sputnik*', in Andrews and Siddiqi, p. 29.
19. Andrews and Siddiqi, pp. 33–43.
20. Victoria Smolkin-Rothrock, 'Cosmic Enlightenment', in Andrews and Siddiqi, pp. 159–94.
21. Richers and Maurer, 'Introduction to Part I', in Maurer, Richers, Rüthers and Scheide, pp. 23–25.
22. Iina Kohonen, 'The Heroic and the Ordinary. Photographic Representations of Soviet Cosmonauts in the Early 1960s', in Maurer, Richers, Rüthers and Scheide, pp. 103–20 (p. 105).
23. Petr Vail' and Aleksandr Genis, *60-e, Mir sovetskogo čeloveka*, 3rd edn, Moskva Novoe literaturnoe obozrenie, 2001, p. 25, quoted in Maurer, Richers, Rüthers and Scheide, p. 4. This same association of space with the attainment of personal freedom was parodied in the popular novel by Victor Pelevin, *Omon Ra*, Moscow: Tekst, 1992.
24. Certainly, 'cosmic culture' also had its own particular variant in the United States on the other side of the Iron Curtain.
25. See Thomas Kramer, *Micky, Marx und Manitu. Zeit- und Kulturgeschichte im Spiegel eines DDR-Comics 1955-1990. Mosaik als Fokus von Medienerlebnissen im NS und in der DDR*, Berlin: Weidler Buchverlag, 2002, pp. 216–20.
26. The *Jugendweihe* was a secular coming-of-age ceremony in East Germany held at fourteen years old that was meant to replace the Christian tradition of Confirmation. *Weltall – Erde – Mensch*, (Berlin: Das Neue Leben, 1954-1974) was a type of was a type of handbook written for a young adult on the history and future of the world according to Marxism-Leninism.
27. Heather Gumbert, 'Cold War Theaters. Cosmonaut Titov at the Berlin Wall', in Andrews and Siddiqi, pp. 240–62 (pp. 252–54).
28. 'Stellungnahme zum Antrag auf Aufnahme in den Thematischen Plan für den Stoff "Planet des Todes"', undated [= BArch DR 1 / 4433], n.p., qtd. in Soldovieri, 383.
29. Soldovieri, 382.
30. Ivanova, pp. 101–2.
31. Soldovieri, 392.
32. Ivanova, p. 101.
33. The Fama Film production was later cancelled after the success of Sputnik.
34. Soldovieri, 393 and 'Brief an Wolfgang Langhoff', in Günter Agde (ed), *Kurt Maetzig. Filmarbeit. Gespräche. Reden. Schriften*, Berlin: Henschel, 1987, pp. 276–77, as quoted in Burghard Ciesla,

'Droht der Menschheit Vernichtung? *Der schweigende Stern – First Spaceship on Venus*: Ein Vergleich', in Ralf Schenk and Erika Richter (eds), *apropos: Film 2002* [= Jahrbuch der DEFA-Stiftung, 2002] Berlin: Bertz + Fischer, 2002, pp. 121-36 (p. 131).

35. According to an MDR-Kultur report entitled 'Wernher von Braun als Pop-Figur', this film was the second most popular TV broadcast of all time in the United States. 'Wernher von Braun als Pop-Figur. "Ich greife nach den Sternen, aber manchmal treffe ich auch London"', *MDR-Kultur*, Mitteldeutscher Rundfunk, 2014 [= http://www.mdr.de/zeitreise/wernher-von-braun-erbe100.html], accessed 18 Jan 2015.
36. James Blackford states that the film was very popular in the Soviet territories. See James Blackford, 'Red Skies. Soviet Science Fiction', *Sight & Sound* 21.7 (2011), 44-48 (45).
37. Dominic William Esler, 'Soviet Science Fiction of the 1920s: Explaining a Literary Genre in its Political and Social Context', *Foundation* 109 (2010), 27-52 (30).
38. The dinosaurs in *Planet of Storms* – while they seem like a rip-off of Godzilla or other Western monster films – can also be traced back to Russian science fiction sources as well as the Czech film by Karel Zeman, *The Journey to the Primeval Age*. See the discussion of Vladimir Obruchev *Sannikov's Land* (1926) and *Plutonia* (1924). See Esler, 30-31 on this and Tsiolkovsky.
39. Interestingly, Klushanzev's documentary *The Road to the Stars* was released in the United States as well. Walter Cronkite showed portions of this film on television that left the American audience stunned. See, Blackford, 45.
40. Ivanova, pp. 102-3.
41. '"Die DEFA auf der Spur eines Geheimnisses." Gespräch mit Dieter Wolf.' Dir. Patryk Brodowiak and Kevin Weiß. *Die gefrorenen Blitze*. Dir. János Veiczi. Icestorm Entertainment GmbH, 2008. DVD. I would also like to thank Barton Byg for bringing this film to my attention.
42. 'Die DEFA auf der Spur eines Geheimnisses'.
43. Iordanova, pp. 12-13.

CHAPTER 11
The DEFA *Indianerfilm*
Narrating the Postcolonial through Gojko Mitic

Evan Torner

Race and capitalism, as many have recently argued, are ineluctably intertwined.[1] Yet feature films in the GDR – which actively sought both political and economic support from predominantly nonwhite countries in the 'Third World' – rarely addressed this interrelation. DEFA cinema instead unintentionally defended a notion of socialist whiteness that reflected the GDR's adherence to a seductive Western Eurocentric discourse of agency and progress.[2] One of the few forums where interracial conflict and cooperation could be thematized, however, was the genre of the *Indianerfilm*. As a response to the wildly popular West German Karl May-Winnetou Westerns of the early 1960s, seventeen *Indianerfilme* – so-called 'Easterns' or 'Red Westerns' – were produced by the two DEFA working groups, Roter Kreis and Johannisthal, and were huge box office successes. Of these films, thirteen feature the Yugoslavian-born actor/stuntman Gojko Mitic portraying an American Indian:[3] for example, a Dakotan chief in *Die Söhne der großen Bärin* [*Sons of Great Bear*, 1966], *Spur des Falken* [*Falcon's Trail*, 1968] and *Weiße Wölfe* [*White Wolves*, 1969]; a Shawnee in *Tecumseh* (1972); an indigenous Argentinian shepherd in *Severino* (1978); and a Nez Percé survivor in *Der Scout* (1983). In the films, muscular American Indians are oppressed by American expansionism and actively resist it. The films were also well received in Eastern European states such as Poland, Bulgaria and Romania. Tim Bergfelder writes that, rather than offering mere spectacle and easy resolutions, the *Indianerfilme* 'aimed more for ethnographic authenticity and the depiction of social realities'.[4] Indeed, these films were not ironic appropriations of the Westerns, but proceeded – as Jaimey Fisher puts it – to 'leave the genre's semantics mostly intact'.[5] Mitic's face and body thus became metonymic for the defiant indigenous warrior in the minds of East German and Eastern European audiences, with the *Indianerfilm* seen as an allegory of the postcolonial struggles of 'Third World' countries, such as Vietnam, Cuba and Angola, against Western European states and the United States. This allegory proved politically useful for all parties involved: film producers could present their entertainment fluff as ideologically important to functionaries in the ruling Socialist Unity Party (SED); these same functionaries could be assured that cinema-goers were consuming state-produced content; and audiences had an assemblage of state-approved, moralistic and consumption-driven alibis for seeing the films. Other East German products about Native Americans, such as Anna Jürgen's 1949 novel *Blauvogel* [*Blue Bird*] and Liselotte Welskopf-Henrich's 1951 novel *Die Söhne der großen Bärin*, proved to be bestsellers, using incessant claims of 'authenticity' to certify their status as a solidarity-raising vehicle.[6] But dismissing the cynical nature of these appeals casts aside the important public relations work they accomplished: the *Indianerfilm* helped market the GDR to its own citizens as a globally conscientious power.

By focusing on the productive entanglement of Mitic's figure in narratives of postcolonial resistance within Eastern Bloc discourse, I will argue that Mitic's openly fake performances of 'American Indians' – 'playing Indian' as I shall term it[7] – created an affective space of unplaced solidarity against white Euro-American imperialism. The *Indianerfilme* allowed white, Eastern Bloc consumers to reimagine themselves as concerned audiences in a position of political agency with respect to the 'Third World' – both within and outside of the official party line – whilst never abandoning the guilty pleasures of homegrown fantasies about American Indians.

As numerous essays on the DEFA *Indianerfilm* attest – including notable work by Norbert Wehrstedt, Gerd Gemünden, Henning Engelke and Simon Kopp, Vera Dika, Friedrich von Borries and Jens-Uwe Fischer, Annette Deeken, Dennis Broe, Holger Briel, Sebastian Heiduschke, Madeleine Casad, Jennifer Michaels, and Franz Birgel[8] – there has been a growing interest in both the *Indianerfilm* and its importance for throwing light on the GDR's distinctive social imaginary. Most scholars approach these films as a blend of genre kitsch and still-extant German *Indianthusiasm*, with serious geopolitical critiques of capitalism and Western crimes against indigenous peoples in the nineteenth and twentieth centuries. But the points where they diverge are telling.

Wehrstedt, Gemünden, Borries and Fischer, Heiduschke and Birgel focus on the historical context of the genre and its inflection of specific ideologies. Engelke and Kopp, by contrast, focus on the formal analysis of the films themselves, interrogating the market-driven notions of 'authenticity' that – with no little irony – underpinned the Euro-Western genre.[9] As the authors note, there is a tension in the films between the successful cinematic implementation of Western genre tropes – the daring horse rescue, the dying squaw, the final fight amidst cliffs and boulders – and the acceptance of a given representation of Native Americans as 'authentic'. The better the Western, apparently, the easier its emotional resonance could be applied to other – often quite different – situations including, in particular, postcolonial conflicts.[10] For her part, Deeken argues for a degree of continuity between the sympathetic portrayals of Native Americans in early Westerns such as D.W. Griffith's *The Red Man's View* (1909) and those in the DEFA-*Indianerfilme*. On this point, she writes:

> *The interesting thing about the DEFA-*Indianerfilme *is that they, in their filmic realization, clearly raised the audience appeal of the Western to the level of behavioural dictum, despite all the ideological padding in the press. It is often eagerly emphasized in the contemporary literature [on the films] that they somehow reveal the American 'politics of extermination of "native peoples"' and that the Indians stand as a case study for the fate of those who have been subordinated under imperialism, the victims of expansionist capitalist politics. You can already see this sort of historical writing about genocide for the sake of early capitalist interests ... in Karl May and in the first* Indianerfilm *– it was not exclusively a GDR 'class viewpoint'.*[11]

Deeken holds the DEFA *Indianerfilme* to be isomorphic to earlier films made as expressions of white-capitalist guilt at the dawn of the twentieth century. Michaels takes up this continuity with earlier 'soft' racism to state that the films' 'supposed anthropological authenticity was, therefore, filtered through romanticized versions of American Indians that perpetuated the stereotypes'.[12] It has recently become more interesting to talk about the *use* of these *Indianerfilme*, rather than their genealogy and surprising popularity, as indeed Dika, Briel, Broe and Casad have done.[13]

But it is H. Glenn Penny's *Kindred by Choice. Germans and American Indians since 1800* that offers the most productive contextualization of the DEFA *Indianerfilm* for my analysis.[14] Penny sees these films among a slew of cultural products that are not only in a continuum with the Karl May phenomenon – as Deeken does – but against the backdrop of a long history of positive, self-aware German affinity towards their mental construct of the American Indian (*Indianer*)'.¹⁵ In Penny's eyes, we should care not about the strangeness of the German fascination with Native Americans, but what persistent needs this obdurate stereotypy actually fulfils and how 'long-term American Indian resistance and resurgence gave many Germans ... the hope that they too might overcome challenges in the modern world'.¹⁶ The cultural-level emotional appeal of the fake tribesman, coupled with its suitability for didactic repurposing, gave the GDR a constellation of fictions it had to reckon with, one way or another. The DEFA *Indianerfilm* – and its star, Gojko Mitic – could take advantage of the ambiguities behind the fertile German national obsession with American Indians so as to come across as both artless and self-aware, as both harmless kitsch and earnest solidarity. It is from this position that Mitic's body, roles and star image tell postcolonial solidarity narratives.

The Self-Reflexive *Indianerfilm*

The second East German *Indianerfilm* – *Chingachgook, die große Schlange* [*Chingachgook, the Great Snake*, 1967] – begins with titles superimposed over a roaring campfire, with Wilhelm Neef's brass-laden symphony blaring a Max

Figure 11.1: Dancers perform fabricated choreography in *Chingachgook* (1967). DVD screen capture.

Steiner-esque Romantic melody. An entirely fabricated 'traditional' dance follows this sequence, performed by East Germans in masks playing Delaware tribespeople in the 1740s who are celebrating the recovery of their chief (Fig. 11.1). Upon the conclusion of this drum-fuelled dance, Chingachgook (Gojko Mitic) appears onscreen for the first time: he is topless; the camera tracks out as he rises, a doe-eyed expression on his face as he glances off-screen at his soon-to-be-kidnapped bride Wahtawa (Andrea Drahota); a gentle flute memory accentuates the tenderness of the moment. The bride is prepared for the ceremony. Later, a voiceover narrator introduces us to the Delaware village and its historical circumstances:[17] 'The Delaware, like other tribes, were in trade relations with the white men. The Indians had no basis for comparison for the value of their furs. ... The red men (sic) did not realize that they were losing their freedom and that their relations with other tribes would fatally deteriorate'. The Delaware have been rendered economically vulnerable by the Europeans and pitted against the Huron. Nevertheless, they are holding their celebratory ritual and Chingachgook/Mitic gives an acrobatic performance of how he helped the chief to recover. The village establishing shot appears pseudo-ethnographic in nature, done with a handheld camera and juxtaposed with the carefully controlled tracking shot a few moments later, when Chingachgook/Mitic takes

Figure 11.2: *Chingachgook* (1967): Mitic pretends to knife-fight with the audience. DVD screen capture.

centre-stage in a group ritual to demonstrate how he saved the chief's life. He runs towards the camera, which shoots him from a low angle, and he leaps up a tree. From the tree, he mimes keeping watch with his arms covering his eyes. Then he leaps to the ground, tackles a fictional assailant, and then gazes straight into the camera as he approaches with a mimed knife (Fig. 11.2). We then spend considerable time watching Chingachgook/Mitic roll around in the dirt with pretend assailants until he finally finishes them off by effectively stabbing the camera lens with the invisible knife in his fist.

The sequence above connotes a degree of self-reflexivity regarding the *Indianerfilm* genre, although its cues can be easily missed. The campfire doubly signifies the Indian hearth as well as the German campfire around which one would relate tales of American Indians, while the accompanying music functions as an intermedial reference to earlier Hollywood Westerns. It enunciates the village as a time set in stories and a place one would call home. The dance section, meanwhile, constitutes a site of what Philip J. Deloria calls 'mimetic action', in which nonindigenous people physically incarnate what they consider to be indigenous 'Native American' behaviour: '[Modernist] Indians imitated and appropriated the Other viscerally through the medium of their bodies'.[18] Dynamic editing reminds the viewer that this is not ethnographic footage, but intended for our entertainment. Rising up from the floor after the dance, Mitic performs the ultimate fan service: exhibiting both his naked torso and his mimicry of innocent love. Later, we watch Mitic self-reflexively play the consummate tribesman for the gathered Delaware, an act which also levels several faked attacks against us, the 'Other' audience. What does this all mean? Though one is tempted in an East German context to draw on Brechtian theories of alienation and cognitive activation of the viewer, a simpler answer presents itself. The self-reflexivity here signals that the viewer can relax and enjoy the film as mere spectacle (for example, the fire as storytelling space, the dance, Mitic's body in motion), while at the same time having a healthy alibi for this enjoyment: one is watching the rebellious acts of indigenous people as an allegory for contemporary struggles (for example, the ethnographic camera, the articulation of the historical troubles). As it turns out, self-reflexivity is easily co-opted,[19] with it only attaining a measure of political effectiveness when it '[stretches] the mediality of the medium of its limits ... ripping off the medium's clothes, as it were', as Rey Chow has recently argued.[20]

In fact, Dennis Broe sees a certain aesthetic of resistance to the state in the self-reflexivity of the *Indianerfilme*. He argues that these films constitute sites of active, working-class counterhegemonic resistance, be it against an oppressive state or neoliberal market forces, a move comparable to the New German Cinema of the 1960s and 1970s.[21] In essence, Broe sees this act of East Germans performing the American Indian onscreen as creating the kind of alternative socialist imaginary that would make the fall of the Berlin Wall possible. Interpretations that seek and validate the subversiveness of both high- and lowbrow DEFA film like Broe's, however, often succumb to two fallacies. The first would be ignoring recent research in GDR history that refuses the subversion/complicity dichotomy.[22] Rather, GDR citizens who participated in public society *in any form* (especially artists) found themselves in constant negotiations between intertwined personal loyalties and political structures. *Indianerfilm* director Gottfried Kolditz, for example, was able to direct at DEFA until the end of his life because his film sets had little internal or political discord – nor any overt aesthetic taboos. The second fallacy is the juxtaposition between individual auteurs and a perceived indifferent and/or hostile system that received their work. Systems do not exist as monolithic entities, but exist only between individual actors across networks, who behave in accordance with – and against the grain of – specific institutional values. In many respects, the *Indianerfilme* were one of the least controversial genres ever produced by the DEFA. They experienced virtually no censorship and were actively promoted by the party media apparatus, particularly at the open-air summer film festivals (*Sommerfilmtage*) where they were shown. At some level, these films had to be expressions of state ideology, while at the same time also containing some necessary level of apparent subversiveness to be at all relevant, something already acknowledged by contemporary film theory of the blockbuster.[23] The *Indianerfilme* can be construed as being 'about' the 'Third World', because this is both an institutionally established position (through newspaper and radio critiques, and so on), as well as one that contains the acceptable level of subversiveness towards the state and its apparently oppressive apparatuses.

Much of the genre's power was derived via the specific affective investment in the films from a targeted demographic: viewers found a reason to both pay substantive attention to the *Indianerfilm* as well as brush it off as mere kitsch. The broader the demographic that can invest itself in this way, the more 'universal' the film is. In the case of the *Indianerfilme*, Tamar Szabó Gendler's concept of 'alief' – the subconscious feeling that something may be true even if we do not really believe it – may be helpful. Whereas 'belief' deals with what we hold to be true and what is factual and probable, the term 'alief' deals with how we innately or habitually respond to what are clearly fictional stimuli.[24] Gendler writes: 'To have an alief is [...] to have an innate or habitual propensity to respond to an apparent stimulus in a particular way'.[25] Viewers of *Indianerfilme* may or may not for a second 'believe' that these Central and Eastern Europeans are really Native Americans, and yet 'alieve' that the film portrays the indigenous struggles in a historically accurate fashion and resonant with the 1960s and 1970s postcolonial struggles. Fiction proposes a truth, and we 'alieve' it with almost no scepticism. The act of partaking in a century-old tradition of 'playing Indian' can thus be cinematically mobilized to achieve political objectives, namely the vilification of the United States (and the moral exaltation of the Eastern Bloc.) Overall, one can see DEFA films for the affective responses they require, the truth claims they make and the specific subject positions they promote. It is from these that we can infer what 'ideology' looks like, rather than fall into the trap of projecting our own idealized images of Marxism-Leninism onto these films.

GDR, Film and the 'Third World'

Throughout its forty-year lifespan, the GDR proved a site of many contradictions, many of which could be found in the nation-state's project of solidarity. Solidarity constituted the programmatic support of other countries, often with nonwhite majorities, in their postcolonial struggles against capitalism and imperialism worldwide. I define 'postcolonial' as the condition of predominantly nonwhite nations emerging from the enslaving strictures of long-term colonial dominance to reckon with the threat of neocolonialism, i.e. financial and military dependence on the West. It is crucial in this space to note that, in Native American studies, the term 'postcolonial' has been rejected as a framework because, as Louis Owens posits, the United States of America has always remained a colonial power without a 'colonial aftermath' and 'never became postcolonial'.[26]

Solidarity took place at two different levels. One level was state directed, and included diplomatic missions, foreign aid, the welcoming of international students and even arms deals. The GDR brought Fidel Castro to East Berlin, rebuilt the North Korean city of Hamhung, sent FDJ missionaries to Mozambique and sold weapons to both sides of the Iran-Iraq War. Such solidarity efforts were largely in reaction to the meeting of African and Asian states at the Bandung Conference of 1955 and its articulation of a growing sense of discontent at the treatment of 'Third World' states by the two rival superpowers. The other level was genuinely grounded in the populace, insofar as particular countries captured the GDR national imaginary at certain points in time and prompted outpourings of letters, children's drawings, folk songs, mass demonstrations and, of course, films. These countries included Cuba, Chile and Vietnam, but also abstract entities such as 'oppressed' African populations. Native Americans as fictional *Indianer* were lumped together within the popular conception of the 'Third World', and were regularly deployed as allegorical figures of resistance against oppression everywhere.[27]

In stark contrast to the *Indianerfilme*, earlier productions dealing with the problems of 'Third World' resistance in the face of European military-colonial domination had been a failure – both at the box office and in terms of ideology. Such films included Erich Engel's *Geschwader Fledermaus* [*Bat Squadron*, 1958] – a screen adaptation of Rolf Honold's play about Americans fighting on the side of the French who eventually defect to the side of the Vietnamese resistance – and Kurt Maetzig's *Preludio 11* (1964), a thriller that dealt with the threat posed to Cuba by invading US-backed forces. Although both Engel and Maetzig were shooting contemporary features about 1950s' and 1960s' struggles against oppressive neocolonial powers, contemporary reviews underline that few regarded these films as effective popular vehicles for solidarity work. The audience sought, as illustrated above, 'dramatic action', 'proper heroes', and 'the compelling impression of authenticity'. Mitic's distinctive contribution to the genre of the *Indianerfilm* filled this void precisely, suturing together increased action with the seductive alibi that these films bespoke the experiences of oppressed people worldwide. He became a projection surface for feelings of solidarity and global resistance through the convincing portrayal of various American Indian chiefs in nineteenth-century America.

Gojko Mitic

Gojko Mitic can be seen as a nexus of interests and paradoxes. Yet regardless of any tensions – or perhaps precisely because of them – his star image has continued on, virtually unchanged, for the last half-century.[28] The so-called 'Chefindianer der DEFA' (DEFA's number one American Indian) actor Mitic has provoked curiosity and amusement from his 1966 entry into the East German cultural imagination as the star of *Die Söhne der großen Bärin* to the present. Mitic's biographical peculiarity and the kitsch at the centre of the *Indianerfilme* he popularized remain fixed points of fascination as his star image progresses. This star image can be broken down into its component semantic, syntactic and pragmatic dimensions in order to re-evaluate it within a context of discursive fantasy consumption. In so doing, my intention is to depict the biographical and physical exigencies that allowed Mitic his stardom, as well as the noble savage/indigenous socialist portrait that would emerge from most of his oeuvre. The sum total of his capabilities and fan discourse produced a star that appeared to be so 'authentic' that it threatened to expose the artificial foundations of the star system within the GDR, as well as the folk imaginary of what postcolonial struggle appeared to be.

Reproducing Mitic's biography is, of course, a discursive cliché and part of the narrative apparatus that already 'others' both the actor himself as well as his overstated lifetime profession of playing Native American chieftains for German and Eastern European audiences. Yet it could also be said that he had the 'right' kind of biography to achieve this semi-subversive star image in the first place. Mitic was raised during World War II in Strojkovce, near Leskovac: provincial farmland in Central Serbia with horses, poultry and a vineyard. His father ran logistics for Tito's resistance against the Nazis, and became disillusioned with established communist channels because of postwar politicking among Yugoslavs who claimed to have been in the resistance too. Nevertheless, Mitic and his family emerged somewhat unscathed by the ravages of mid-twentieth-century Europe, such that the actor recalls his childhood farm as a kind of 'Garden of Eden'[29] where he learned the unique athletic and animal-handling skills that would later prove decisive in his career.[30] He also devoured Karl May's famous *Winnetou* Indian stories at this time, which he associates with his childhood to this day. Initial cinema roles were due to the intervention of a famous Serbian actor who occasionally visited Mitic's school and who got him bit parts in Cornel Wilde's *Sword of Lancelot* (1963), several Italian sword-and-sandal epics, West German Winnetou pictures such as *Unter Geiern* [*Frontier Hellcat*, 1964] and a version of *Uncle Tom's Cabin* (1965), all filmed against the sweeping landscapes of Yugoslavian tourist locales. The arrival of Hans Mahlich's East German DEFA Group, Roter Kreis, in 1965 to shoot *Die Söhne der großen Bärin* with Mitic in the starring role of Chief Tokei-ihto signalled his shift from physical-education student and occasional mounted extra in assorted genres, to full-time actor-stuntman in the *Indianerfilme*.

These *Indianerfilme* were intended to address the Vietnam issue from a different angle than a film such as *Geschwader Fledermaus*. Producer Mahlich, dramaturge Günter Karl and screenwriter Hans-Joachim Wallstein, the key figures behind these films, made explicit statements in public interviews declaring their affinity with the oppressed people of Vietnam and other countries, and the press ruminated continuously on the topic. Günter Karl's justification for approving the release of *Osceola* (1971) – an account of Seminole rebellion and slave revolts against Florida plantation owners somewhat allegorical of the American civil rights movement – was underpinned by the notion that: 'The discrimination suffered by people of colour is not only part of the USA's unreflected past, but one of its burning contemporary problems. ... The demonstration for equal rights for people of colour merges with the demonstrations against the dirty war in Vietnam'.[31] Mitic had been, in theory, recruited as the stunt body for a very important Eastern Bloc solidarity project.[32]

Mitic's instant stardom among the twelve-million-plus GDR viewers who saw *Söhne der großen Bärin* took the world by surprise. The 'emissary of their lust for adventure' ('Sendbote ihrer Abenteuerlust'),[33] as one journalist describes him, Mitic instantly connected with Central and Eastern European fans and never lacked work in acting again. His retirement in 2006 from playing fictional Apache chief Winnetou, at the Bad Segeberg Festspiele, marked the end of forty-one years of ethnic performance to a devoted fan base that still addresses him as 'Ol Gojko' ('Olle Gojko') and 'our Indian chief' ('unser Chefindianer') to this day.

Mitic's career encompasses several contradictions salient to his distinctiveness as a DEFA star and apparent embodiment of indigenous socialism (in the sense of a grassroots socialist praxis shaped by pre-capitalist traditions and catalysed by rudimentary Marxist-Leninism). His own family had actively resisted the totalitarian regimes of both Hitler and Stalin. The farm allowed him to ride horses, a premodern ability that would produce a lasting career in a modern socialist state. He retained his Yugoslavian passport, allowing him freedom of travel, while maintaining honorary GDR citizenship in the eyes of the people. His tanned white skin would be accepted as nonwhite on account of his Slavic heritage, but he was otherwise granted 'honorary whiteness' as a highly cultured 'elective Berliner'

(*Wahl-Berliner*). Sheltered but exposed, complicit but opinionated, free but tethered, 'nonwhite' but honorarily white, naïve but professional, handsome but modest: these contradictions became the engine that drove a smooth career as an actor in an otherwise shaky German entertainment industry. Gerd Gemünden's description of Mitic's star persona as 'the Yugoslav partisan, the model German, the Native American tribal hero and the displaced Jew, but also the American'[34] offers national and ethnic labels to a star image specifically cultivated to attain transnational universality.

Figure

Mitic's body as a semantic object invokes discourses about beauty, athleticism and race. Films and publications in which he appears emphasize these characteristics. His body is as homegrown and firm as his antifascist convictions. As Mitic himself notes with regard to the 1960s, 'body culture, later called "bodybuilding" took hold of all the young people',[35] such that he consciously emulated movie musclemen like Steve Reeves to achieve the beefcake body in vogue at the time. Yet Mitic's bodybuilding routine was not unusual, consisting of basic weightlifting, squats, cycling, free swimming and a healthy diet (that excluded both cigarettes and alcohol). In contrast to ideals of masculine beauty in capitalist economies, Mitic's cultural capital was predicated on acquiring such a body not only through sports but also through labour.[36] His oft-exposed upper torso and biceps, however, receive more than their fair share of coverage in the press. Some past phrases that describe his sun-reflecting physique include: 'the pretty boy of cinema with the taut chest',[37] 'athletic like an Indian with looks like an Apache',[38] 'an eagle-eye gaze and biceps',[39] and 'Yugoslav hunk'[40] to name a few. The semantic field of these comments implies sex appeal (both for women and gay men), an objectified body without a character and an understood kinship between his athleticism and the native characters he played. But none challenge the physical prowess he is said to exhibit, nor his 'fit' for the part of a Native American brave.

The fact that Mitic did his own stunts – but not his own voice – adds a kinetic dimension to his eroticized body. Paul Willemen describes action movies as 'fantasies of labor power'[41] in which agency and effort are measured against their effect on transnational capital; in Mitic's protagonists' case, on his own speedy transport by horse and destruction of white capitalist structures such as oil wells (as in *Tödlicher Irrtum* [*Fatal Error*, 1970]) or riverboats (*Osceola*). Such fantasies become central in a postindustrial society where old capital must be razed for new capital and consumption replaces physical labour as one's primary economic activity. Mitic's physical interventions – jumping from horse to horse, navigating a herd of 1,200 horses (as in *Der Scout*, 1983), realistically wrestling a fake crocodile in a Cuban river, even bearing the weight of a heavy cosmonaut suit in *Signale – Ein Weltraumabenteuer* [*Signals – A Space Adventure*, 1970] – thus become a way of signifying and dignifying labour prowess presently valued only as spectacle, but historically branded as 'decisive' in its own fashion. The so-called 'body genres' – specifically horror, kung fu and pornography – found no place in the GDR mediascape, and so Mitic's *Indianerfilme* become a kind of politically sanguine substitute for the above. His physicality forms a constitutive relationship with historical progress: Mitic's star image must physically confront and overcome the obstacles of an era, whether they be greedy Confederate soldiers or zero-gravity movement. Mitic's often-improvised stunt work secures the star's presence on the screen as a focal point of tension; not only his character is in danger, but the star's body itself. As Ehrentraud Novotny states: 'What would Gojko Mitic be, if he were to let himself be stunt-doubled?'[42] A moving image of Mitic on a horse, such as in *Der lange Ritt zur Schule* [*The Long Ride to School*, 1982], always recalls the actor's star image first and the character second.

Mitic's body can be considered unmarked nonwhite, an 'ideal' combination for 'ethnic drag', which is Katrin Sieg's concept of excluding material bodies of cultural Others for their blank appropriation into white German typologies.[43] The Serbian Mitic's transformation into Native American or other non-North European ethnicity (Mexican, Greek, Italian, Russian) is effected through makeup, black wigs and costuming that offer him as a blank parody of the Other. In Vera Dika's words, 'his image is a picture of a picture, one that refers to the history of the North American Indian in film, yet to no one image in particular'.[44] Even as an Italian gas attendant in Peter Welz's *Burning Life* (1994), in which he plays against type by asking for the protagonist's autograph, the film's target audience would recognize him as the DEFA-*Indianer*. An ethnic performer of the greatest common denominator, he joins a long list of actors typecast in a similar fashion, such as Irish-Mexican Anthony Quinn and Italian-American Iron Eyes Cody. Mitic's 'eagle-eye gaze' and other typecast characteristics tell us mostly about European expectations of the body branded as 'ethnic'.

Hero

Gojko Mitic is narratively coded as an indigenous socialist through his *Indianerfilme*, with the rest of his acting work depicting him as a reliable warrior for the global Left. Mitic's presence in a film usually signifies a linear, simple narrative in which characters' outer actions outweigh their psychological interiority. This narrative serves as an allegory of what indigenous (i.e. nonwhite European) socialism would theoretically look like – that is, armed local resistance by nonwhites against whites conspiring to take their land, and other whites who deliberate until it is too late. The story arc for most *Indianerfilme*, often recounted in overview articles on the genre,[45] looks something like this: the tribe is portrayed at peace but uneasy, resources at stake come to the foreground, an initial violent incident generates tension between the tribe and whites, whites push the incident to their advantage, Mitic reduces or negates that advantage, the whites muster more power and Mitic overcomes some aspect of that power – usually by killing some white men – but a bittersweet ending reminds us that history would eventually squash that resistance. It is a closed system, an allegory with few open ends other than that which the dynamism of Mitic's body can provide. In some ways, Mitic's body in narrative affirms an old anti-vitalist tendency extant since Karl Marx. As Amy E. Wendling explains, capital itself 'supplants the [bodily] ideal with ... technophilic embrace of progress that loses sight of human beneficence; on the other hand, [it promotes] a corresponding Romantic and conservative demonization of technization. Both capitalist discourses ... treat technology as having a fixed nonhistorical essence'.[46] Effectively, Mitic can only exist and be physically successful within a specific temporal scope, before being effectively swallowed by history itself. Accordingly, the *Indianerfilme* might be conceptualized as ethnographic stunt shows, purporting to provide an ethnohistorically accurate image of America's earlier inhabitants while interrupting said realism with the stunts that move the narrative forward. Mitic is the stunt performer and, when excluding his scenes from an *Indianerfilm*, one finds the narrative to be primarily 'about' white cowboys, generals and officials in saloons and war rooms talking amongst themselves. So while the physical defence of indigenous socialism against these persistent white conversations often results in an unhappy ending, such as Mitic's dramatic death as Ulzana in *Weiße Wölfe*,[47] it is necessary to portray such a helpless defence against historical treachery as skilled, honourable and absolute (Fig. 11.3). Such narratives are then held up as

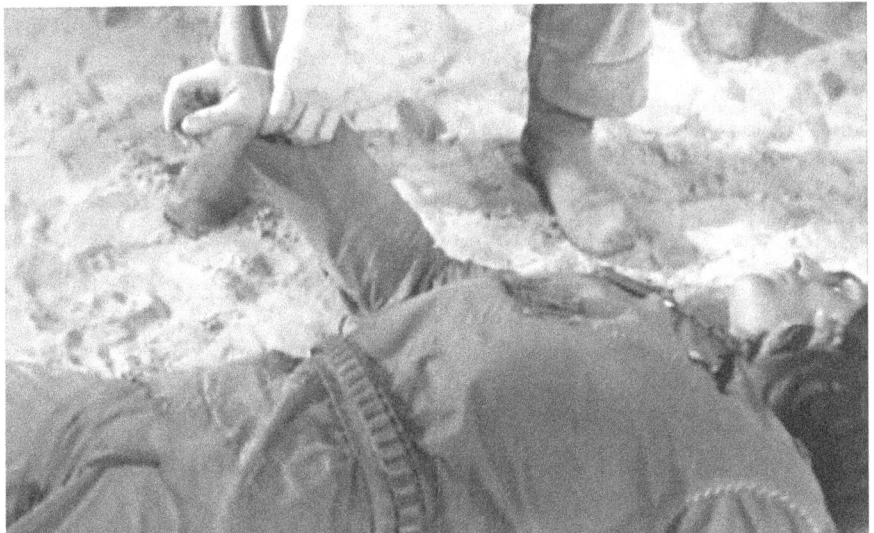

Figure 11.3: Farseeing Falcon (Mitic) lies dead at the conclusion of *Weiße Wölfe* (1969). DVD screen capture.

evidence of European gains as a product of history, unintentionally reproducing Mitic as a version of the noble savage stereotype so familiar in Western societies. On an allegorical level, the atrocities in Vietnam constituted both sites where resistance was possible, and an already foreclosed loss against the forces of capitalism.

Legend

Die Söhne der großen Bärin had already millions of fans as a bestseller novel by Liselotte Welskopf-Henrich before Mitic had even left junior school. This was largely due to what Penny interprets as a 'consensus among East and West German readers that Welskop-Henrich had successfully portrayed American Indian masculinity'.[48] Such a successful portrayal in the source material was then projected onto the star who would embody that very masculinity. The film version of *Die Söhne der großen Bärin* was also by far Mitic's most popular film to date,[49] and catapulted him from obscurity into the arms of millions of fans, particularly in Eastern Europe. The contradictions in the plot noted by contemporaries did not dissuade viewers since – as pointed out earlier – they watched the film in order to fulfil specific fantasies. A relatively quiet individual and non-native speaker of German, Mitic adopted an outgoing and cheerful public personality in order to please the young children who idolized his star image. Though his sincere appreciation of the fans' attentions kept him in the GDR, this sincerity cost him his leisure time. Biographer Ehrentraud Novotny writes that 'Gojko lives for his work. In private, he is a prisoner of his popularity'.[50] Answering fan mail and signing autographs became an onerous part of his job as socialist star and part spectacle, as young fans surrounded him at the open-air summer film festivals in the GDR, while cartons of mail poured into the Babelsberg studios for weeks after a film's release. This real work contributed to Mitic's image of authenticity, as the public role he created for basic crowd management was reinforced by following through on correspondence afterwards. And since few other DEFA stars, such as Manfred Krug or Armin Mueller-Stahl, received the same amount of attention, it can be said that Mitic led in the attention economy of the GDR – perhaps even over the SED itself – in terms of how many fans cared about his wellbeing. Novotny's book displays images of Mitic exploring all his hobbies – photography, guitar, diving – as if to ward off fans who thought he existed only for them.

In all his public appearances, Mitic finds himself both confronted by questions about real Native Americans, their plight, and why it is 'We' (white Germans) should continue to consume simulacra of 'Them' (nonwhite indigenous peoples of the Americas). This point of contradiction seems the final test for his authenticity, and his star image continues to pass it. In an interview, Mitic ponders the burden of representation: 'I find that it is our duty to interpret history exactly as it really was'.[51] Not only does this position obviously resemble that of nineteenth-century arch-historian Leopold von Ranke, but it also conflates the act of interpretation – the hermeneutic engagement with representation – with some predetermined notion of truth. An interview with René Römer has him lamenting his attention-grabbing media handle – 'Indian chief' – out of respect for those real chieftains whom he imitates.[52] This public display of sympathy only models the kind of solidarity his films otherwise marshal. Other roles that he has played on the stage over the many decades – Robin Hood, Spartacus, Zorba the Greek – do not incite such curiosity and are seen as a natural extension of his skillset and appearance. But his jeremiads for the always-absent natives continue to model the kind of empathy between 'First World' (United States/ Federal Republic), 'Second World' (GDR) and 'Third World' ('Indians', Vietnamese, and so on) that one would laud as authentic humanitarianism. At his 2 March 2010 fan event at the Urania Palast, his response to a question about whether he keeps in regular contact with the Native Americans he met during a trip to the United States in 1997 – 'No one can bring real justice to the Indians' – pricked the consciences of all white Germans present. His persona as antifascist fighter onscreen and (post)colonial sympathizer off-screen secures him as an embodiment of so many East German ideals. If there is one thing Mitic knows, it is his audience.

What can we glean from Mitic's functional star image when taking his figure, hero and legend as part of a total constellation of meaning? Central and Eastern European audiences revelled in the fantasies of disciplined physical action against overdetermined capitalist imperialism in a historical setting insulated from the murky present. Mitic's physique, prowess, professionalism and appearance of leisure point to 'real existing socialism's' successes and failures: a cultivator of strong, disciplined bodies that can only deploy them in far-removed fantasies of motoric labour power. His national origin made him a quasi-outsider in the GDR, and his lack of real legitimation by the State only enhanced his 'authenticity'. His vast fan following swayed both the mobility of his labour and his public temperament, such that he can continue to espouse a naïve humanitarianism. In short, Gojko Mitic trumps the GDR's overt and subversive 'triumph of the ordinary'[53] schema in favour of a triumph of the authentic, a real live professional-yet-openly fake Indian in a genre and social location where no one from the Party could touch him. When Stefan Kolditz calls him perhaps the DEFA's 'only true star',[54] he elevates Mitic to the status of folk hero of a country whose heroes were otherwise carefully chosen, hyped and then – on occasion – expatriated (*ausgebürgert*). The GDR itself chose Mitic, and he was the deity who chose them in return.

Conclusion

DEFA produced plenty of films about postcolonial struggles, but none of these films had very much traction at the box office, nor did they inspire many public conversations about the Vietnam War, which are only allegorically implied by Mitic's films. By bridging the so-called 'Second World' and 'Third World' with his athleticism, Mitic found himself with perhaps undue authority over what such conflicts 'looked' and 'felt' like. Ticket sales and fan discourse tell us that the search for 'authentic solidarity' ended with the one actor who could best resolve all of the contradictions that such a concept produces. The *Indianerfilm* cycle petered out with the end of the Vietnam War, but Mitic lives on in a fantasy space regarding the kind of good fight that good indigenous socialists apparently brought to the capitalists: a clean healthy male body directly combating the colonizers as they come, and a pure soul who answers fan mail with messages of solidarity.

Nevertheless, the *Indianerfilm* also toyed with audience expectation.[55] The opening clip from *Chingachgook* resonates here: Jean Rouch-style handheld camera proposing that we are watching ethnographic footage of a real ceremonial gathering, the narration explaining the political economy underlying the Delaware-Huron conflict, followed by Mitic's beautiful body athletically performing a concocted hunting ritual that would have him repeatedly break the fourth wall. We are intended to 'alieve' that we are watching history unfold as it happened, a process interrupted by Mitic aggressively 'playing Indian' before the camera. It is very difficult not to read these images ironically, but there we, as film scholars, tend to find nothing new to say about them when we do so. Gendler's concept of 'alief', and the formulation of Mitic as a star image amidst several networks, get closer to a less clichéd reading of the *Indianerfilme* generally and Mitic's performances in particular. Viewers 'alieve' Mitic is a Native American, and presume then that the contrived storyline has some historical merit, at which point the ideology – that of a tragic 'doomed' race martyred by capitalism – comes to rear its head. Nevertheless, Mitic embodies – also in the media archive – a long-term, physical resistance to global systems of domination that more or less receive little pushback from film protagonists today. In that reading, we can view these films in a less cynical light and see their potency for a certain future-oriented aesthetic of active resistance which, in some vain hope, will draw on the strategies and avoid some of the mistakes of its predecessors.

Evan Torner is Assistant Professor of German Studies at the University of Cincinnati. He has published articles on East German science fiction cinema, *Indianerfilme*, and the transnational cinema of Jörg Foth and Gottfried Kolditz.

Notes

1. Edward Baptist, *The Half Has Never Been Told. Slavery and the Making of American Capitalism*, New York: Basic Books, 2014; Greg Grandin, *The Empire of Necessity. Slavery, Freedom, and Deception in the New World*, New York: Metropolitan Books, 2014.

2. See Evan Torner, 'The Race-Time Continuum: Race Projection in DEFA Genre Cinema', unpublished PhD Diss., University of Massachusetts Amherst, 2013.
3. The term 'Native American' can be contested in this context, as Philip J. Deloria has argued that the 'Indians' in such products have little to do with the indigenous peoples of the Americas. Nevertheless, the term 'Indian' can also readily mean people from the South Asian country as well. For the sake of semantics I will use the formulation 'American Indian' when referring to the figures specific to the imaginaries of white people, and 'Native American' to refer to people with generalized indigenous American heritage. Philip J. Deloria, *Playing Indian*, New Haven: Yale University Press, 1998.
4. Tim Bergfelder, *International Adventures. German Popular Cinema and European Co-Productions in the 1960s*, New York, Oxford: Berghahn, 2005, p. 209.
5. Jaimey Fisher, 'A Late Genre Fade. Utopianism and its Twilight in DEFA's Science Fiction, Literary and Western Films', in Marc Silberman and Henning Wrage (eds), *DEFA at the Crossroads of East German and International Film Culture*, Berlin, Boston: de Gruyter, 2014, pp. 177–96 (p. 180).
6. H. Glenn Penny, 'Elusive Authenticity. The Quest for the Authentic Indian in German Public Culture', *Society for Comparative Studies in Society and History* 48.4 (2006), 798–819, esp. 801–4.
7. Cf. Deloria.
8. Norbert Wehrstedt, 'Indianerwestern made in GDR', in Ingelore König, Dieter Wiedemann and Lothar Wolf (eds), *Zwischen Marx und Muck: DEFA-Filme für Kinder*, Berlin: Henschel Verlag, 1996, pp. 55–69; Gerd Gemünden, 'Between Karl May and Karl Marx. The DEFA *Indianerfilme* (1965–1983)', *Film History* 10.3 (1998), 399–407; Henning Engelke and Simon Kopp, 'Der Western im Osten. Genre, Zeitlichkeit und Authentizität im DEFA- und im Hollywood-Western', *Zeithistorische Forschungen* 1.2 (2004) [= http://www.zeithistorische-forschungen.de/16126041-Engelke-Kopp-2-2004], accessed 16 June 2016. Vera Dika, 'An East German Indianerfilm. The Bear in Sheep's Clothing', *Jumpcut* 50 (2008) [= http://www.ejumpcut.org/archive/jc50.2008/Dika-indianer/], accessed 16 June 2016. Friedrich von Borries and Jens-Uwe Fischer, *Sozialistische Cowboys. Der Wilde Westen Ostdeutschlands*, Frankfurt am Main: Suhrkamp, 2008; Annette Deeken, 'Die Erfindung des DEFA-Indianers. Eine deutsch-deutsche Mediengeschichte', in Thomas Koebner (ed), *Indianer vor der Kamera*, Munich: edition text+kritik, 2011, pp. 158–80; Dennis Broe, 'Have Dialectic, Will Travel', in Terri Ginsberg and Andreas Mensch (eds), *A Companion to German Cinema*, Malden, MA: Blackwell, 2012, pp. 27–54; Holger Briel, 'Native Americans in the films of the GDR and Czechoslovakia', *European Journal of American Culture* 31.3 (2012), 231–247; Sebastian Heiduschke, *East German Cinema. DEFA and Film History*, New York: Palgrave Macmillan, 2013; Madeleine Casad, 'Rescreening Memory Beyond the Wall', *The Germanic Review* 88.3 (2013), 320–38; Jennifer Michaels, 'Appropriating the "Other" for the Cold War Struggle. DEFA's Depiction of Native Americans in its Indianerfilme', *Frames Cinema Journal* 4 (2013) [= http://framescinemajournal.com/article/appropriating-the-other-for-the-cold-war-struggle-defas-depiction-of-native-americans-in-its-indianerfilme/], accessed 16 June 2016; Franz Birgel, 'The Only Good Indian is a Good DEFA Indian. East German Variations on the Most American of all Genres', in Cynthia J. Miller and A. Bowdoin Van Riper (eds), *International Westerns. Relocating the Frontier*, Lanham, MD: Scarecrow Press, 2014, pp. 37–62.
9. Engelke and Kopp, 8–10.
10. Ibid., 11.
11. Deeken, p. 177. Translated from the German by the author.
12. Michaels.

13. These arguments are addressed more thoroughly in Evan Torner, 'The DEFA Indianerfilm as Artifact of Resistance', *Frames Cinema Journal* 4 (2013) [= http://framescinemajournal.com/article/the-defa-indianerfilm-as-artifact-of-resistance/], accessed 16 June 2016.
14. See Penny.
15. Ibid., xi–xiii.
16. Ibid., 21.
17. Shot on location in Bulgaria.
18. Deloria, p. 120. It should also be noted that this physical imitation is one of the main reasons why indigenous American tribes will not screen the *Indianerfilme*: such representation is seen as a mockery of sacred practices.
19. Rey Chow, 'When Reflexivity Becomes Porn. Mutations of a Modernist Theoretical Practice', in Jane Elliot and Derek Attridge (eds), *Theory After Theory*, New York: Routledge, 2011, pp. 135–48 (p. 143).
20. Ibid., p. 146.
21. Broe, pp. 47–49.
22. Dolores Augustine, 'The Power Question in the GDR', *German Studies Review* 34.3 (2011), 633–48; Andrew Port, *Conflict and Stability in the German Democratic Republic*, Cambridge, New York: Cambridge University Press, 2007.
23. Brian Price, 'Art/Cinema and Cosmopolitanism Today', in Rosalind Galt and Karl Schoonover (eds), *Global Art Cinema: New Theories and Histories*, Oxford: Oxford University Press, 2010, pp. 109–124.
24. Tamar Szabó Gendler, 'Alief in Action (and Reaction)', *Mind & Language* 23.5 (2008), 552-585.
25. Gendler, 557.
26. Louis Owens, 'As If an Indian Were Really an Indian. Native American Voices and Postcolonial Theory', in Gretchen M. Bataille (ed), *Native American Representations*, Lincoln, NE: University of Nebraska Press, 2001, pp. 11–25 (p. 14).
27. Cf. Evan Torner, 'The Red and the Black: Race in the DEFA Film *Osceola*', *New German Review* 25.1 (2011), 61–81.
28. Richard Dyer famously defines one's 'star image' as a 'complex configuration of visual, verbal and aural signs … [functioning] crucially in relation to contradictions within and between ideologies, which they seek variously to 'manage' or resolve'. Richard Dyer, *Stars*, London: BFI, 1998, p. 34.
29. Gojko Mitic, *Erinnerungen*, aufgezeichnet von Alex Wolf, Frankfurt am Main: Ullstein, 1996, p. 9.
30. Ehrentraud Novotny, *Gojko Mitic*, Berlin: Henschel, 1976, p. 13.
31. Günter Karl, 'Osceola Skizze', 1. Fassung, dated 4 July 1967 [= BArch DR 117 / 6639], p. 5. Translation by the author.
32. One should note that the left-wing appropriation of the Native American as Indian allegory for the Viet Cong was not unique to East Germany. Penny describes leftist movements of the 1970s also drawing similar comparisons to those of Karl and his compatriots in the 1960s. Penny, 180–81.
33. Hans-Dieter Schütt, 'Nun Grieche', *Neues Deutschland*, 4 August 2009.
34. Gemünden, 404.
35. Mitic, p. 12.
36. This contrasts with Dyer's assumptions about a capitalist star dynamic: 'Activities such as sport or the arts are not pursued for health or enlightenment but for the sake of displaying the leisure time and money at one's disposal. Thus a man's athletic body may be much admired, but only on condition that it has been acquired through sports not labour'. Dyer, p. 43.

37. Cited pejoratively in Rainer Wengierek. 'Das Terrain ausschreiten – nicht verlassen', *Filmspiegel* 15, 1982.
38. The words of Bad Segeberg Festspiele head Ernst Reher, 'Alle Stunts selber machen. Der neue Winnetou von Bad Segeberg', *Leipziger Volkszeitung*, 15 November, 1991.
39. E. Gerst, 'Adlerblick und Bizeps?', *Freie Erde*, 26 May 1983.
40. Ute Lischke and David T. McNab, *Walking a Tightrope. Aboriginal People and Their Representations*, Ottawa, CA: Wilfrid-Laurier University Press, 2005, p. 297.
41. Paul Willemen, 'Fantasy in Action', in Nataša Durovicová and Kathleen Newman (eds), *World Cinemas, Transnational Perspectives*, New York: Routledge, 2010, pp. 247–86, (p. 249).
42. Novotny, p. 10.
43. Katrin Sieg, 'Ethnic Drag and National Identity. Multicultural Crisis, Crossings and Interventions', in Sara Friedrichsmeyer, Sara Lennox and Susanne Zantop (eds), *The Imperialist Imagination. German Colonialism and Its Legacy*, Ann Arbor: University of Michigan Press, 1998, pp. 295–319 (p. 297).
44. Dika, p. 1.
45. Cf. Birgel, Heiduschke, and Briel.
46. Amy E. Wendling, *Karl Marx on Technology and Alienation*, New York: Palgrave Macmillan, 2009, p. 97.
47. This particular death resulted in a problem for Mitic's star image, as fans disagreed with Mitic's decision to have 'himself' killed. It is not coincidental that Mitic began to expand his career into television and theatre at this point.
48. Penny, p. 226.
49. 3,458,513 tickets were sold to the GDR populace within the first thirteen-week run in the summer of 1966, meaning over one-fifth of all GDR citizens saw the film. The film also ran successfully in Romania, Czechoslovakia, Bulgaria the USSR and Poland. 'Schlußbericht - Die Söhne der großen Bärin' 8 June 1966 [= BArch DR 117 / 23290].
50. Novotny, p. 10.
51. Quoted in Schenk, *Ein Leben als Indianer – Hintergründe aus dem Leben von Gojko Mitic*. Interview mit Gojko Mitic. DVD. Berlin: Icestorm Entertainment GmbH, 2005. Translation by this author.
52. René Römer, 'Von Tokei-ihto bis Winnetou', *Junge Welt*, Berlin, 1 February 1992.
53. Joshua Feinstein, *Triumph of the Ordinary. Depictions of Daily Life in the East German Cinema 1949–1989*, Chapel Hill, NC: University of North Carolina Press, 2002, p. 199.
54. Stefan Kolditz, 'Gojko Mitic', in Ralf Schenk (ed), *Vor der Kamera. Fünfzig Schauspieler in Babelsberg*, Berlin: Henschel, 1995, pp. 168–71 (p. 168).
55. Torner, 'DEFA Indianerfilm as Artifact of Resistance'.

CHAPTER 12

Defining Socialist Children's Films, Defining Socialist Childhoods

Benita Blessing

Although scholarship on DEFA's children's films (*Kinderfilme*) often claims that the GDR was the first country to establish this particular genre of film production in the German-speaking world, young people and their stories have been part of German cinema since the Weimar Republic.[1] Nevertheless, as Ulrike Odenwald has argued, it is to the GDR that we must look for the first example of a 'sustained programme of children's film production' (and one that was put in place much earlier than that in the Federal Republic).[2] Feature-length films for young audiences became a calling card for the GDR – a means of showing its own society and the world at large how important a role the cinema played in the socialist, antifascist education of children and young people.

Given the importance that the GDR assigned such films in the education of young people, it is not surprising that some of the most serious debates in East German cinema revolved around the very definition of a *Kinderfilm*. This was not simply a question specific to the GDR; children's films have always occupied an ambiguous space in the history of cinema, and it is often hard to identify what a children's film actually is, or whether or not a studio has designated a given film as appropriate for young audiences. What does it mean, for instance, for a film to be age appropriate, and who makes such decisions? Are children the only target audience? Beyond merely appealing to children, these films must also satisfy a number of (adult) expectations at private, public and political levels. Typically, films made for children should be well made, entertaining, educational, not (too) facile and not (too) violent. As Noel Brown and Bruce Babington note, 'in the majority of cases, the children's film remains an abstraction, a theoretical category seldom unambiguously realized'. Moreover, a feature film that is designated specifically as a children's film 'embodies more centrally the tension between pedagogy and pleasure which is inherent in all films for children'.³ In the case of East German *Kinderfilme*, these abstract and theoretical considerations were compounded by the need to explain what it meant to be a good socialist through the presentation of antifascist humanist values.⁴ The ideal socialist personality was not a static concept during the course of the GDR's existence, and DEFA's *Kinderfilme* reflect attendant societal, political and even cinematographic changes. Indeed, filmmakers faced considerable difficulties in making a *Kinderfilm* that both the GDR's film bureau, the *Hauptverwaltung Film*, and the ruling Socialist Unity Party (SED) could endorse as appropriate for children in DEFA's depiction of socialist values. Three films – examples of quite different kinds of East German *Kinderfilme* from three distinct different time periods – illustrate these tensions: Herbert Ballmann's fairytale adaptation *Der Teufel vom Mühlenberg* [*The Devil from Mill Mountain*, 1955], Heiner Carow's film about everyday life, *Ikarus* [*Icarus*, 1975] and Jörg Foth's historical drama *Das Eismeer ruft* [*The Arctic Sea Calls*, 1984]. In addition to highlighting differences between the kinds of *Kinderfilme* that DEFA produced, each film offers insight into the evolution of the genre over time. *Der Teufel vom Mühlenberg* demonstrates the uncertainty surrounding the production of an appropriate *Kinderfilm*, while *Ikarus* showcases the ways in which children began to star in roles that acknowledged the difficulties of growing up in the socialist society of the 1970s. Finally, *Das Eismeer ruft* shows a new kind of young socialist personality: one who believed in universal values that actively transcended the GDR.

Defining *Kinderfilme*

DEFA began its tradition of making films for and about children immediately after World War II (and well before the founding of the GDR in 1949). In 1946, DEFA produced its first film about children – Gerhard Lamprecht's *Irgendwo in Berlin* [*Somewhere in Berlin*, 1946]. The film's focus on antifascist humanism echoed other political programmes, such as those educational reforms designed to create a foundational myth for the emerging state.⁵ Indeed, film production at this point was itself initially overseen, alongside schools, as part of a general programme of socialist education – a practice that anticipated a school/cinema partnership in the (re-)education of young people that would endure long after the administrative arrangements of the early postwar years changed. Focusing on the predicament of a shell-shocked father returning home to his wife and son, *Irgendwo in Berlin* also set the stage for passionate debates about *Kinderfilme* that would persist throughout the history of the GDR.

The 1950s were an ideological melting pot for educational and pedagogical discussions about the place of these films in East German society and cinema. In part, the resulting debates were triggered by the plan to create a separate, permanent children's film studio. Although this larger project was never realized, a 'children's and youth film production unit' was established in 1953, within DEFA at Babelsberg, which ensured that *Kinderfilme* comprised a regular percentage of the studio's output.[6] With the production unit now established and a mandate to make films for children and young people part of the annual production plan, the need to define this unique film genre became a central point of discussion in the DEFA studio. Since other production units, such as Johannisthal, could also produce *Kinderfilme*, some agreement as to how to approach this category of production was important not only for filmmakers but also for the *Hauptverwaltung Film* and the SED. This discussion was more than mere bickering about film styles or empty claims about film being the most important art. What was really at stake was the question of whether *Kinderfilme* might be read as simple entertainment features for children or whether a genuine *Kinderfilm* had to be essentially a pedagogical work that embodied socialist ideology and did so in a form that could be assimilated by children independently of adults. It was a complex debate led by renowned film and educational experts who, backed by the SED, the *Hauptverwaltung Film* and pedagogical functionaries, established some guidelines and laid the groundwork for decades of ongoing discussions. Two of the most important interventions were published in 1954 in the periodical *Deutsche Filmkunst. Zeitschrift* für *Theorie und Praxis des Filmschaffens*. The first, by the then Minister of Education Hans-Joachim Laabs, differentiated between two types of film for children that filmmakers and educators should never allow to overlap: the *Kinderfilm* and the so-called *Unterrichtsfilm* (instructional film), the narrower purpose of which was to 'illustrate that which has been taught, clarify that which is complicated, and bring closer that which is distant. [The instructional film] instructs and informs'. A *Kinderfilm*, by contrast, represented a unique art form that had a direct educational influence on young people and did so without the intervention of a third party, such as a teacher or parent.[7] A child watching such a film should need nothing beyond the work itself in order to understand its antifascist humanist message. Similarly, Hellmuth Häntzsche, the pedagogical director of the children's and youth film production unit, insisted that *Kinderfilme* needed to embrace the same socialist realist aesthetic as films for adults.[8] If filmmakers took seriously the need to produce socialist humanist films for young people, then nothing shown on screen could harm children's less-developed sensibilities. Given the power of Häntzsche's veto at the level of the studio itself, this statement was more than a suggestion; it was a directive.

The production of DEFA children's films was also characterized by practices that differed markedly from those in the wider world of filmmaking. At first sight it might seem paradoxical that even directors who did not plan to make a career in children's films were often obliged to complete a *Kinderfilm* as a test before being assigned other projects – a practice which frustrated some directors and permanently embittered others.[9] Generally speaking, scholars and filmmakers themselves have viewed this practice as an indication that the SED and/or the *Hauptverwaltung Film*, did not really believe in the importance of *Kinderfilme*. But it is equally plausible that these films occupied such an important place in the annual programme of production that directors needed to demonstrate their mastery of the genre. Directors who made unsuccessful feature films did not suddenly find themselves restricted to the production of just *Kinderfilme* – something that might have pointed to their being demoted – they simply did not receive any further commissions at all. In addition, not all of these films made it to the screen, a fact that suggests that the practice of censorship on the part of the SED and the *Hauptverwaltung Film* (and self-censorship on the part of filmmakers themselves) was no less pronounced in this sphere than it was for other categories of feature films. It is thus plausible that either first-time directors of children's or youth films were actually being judged by the same (or possibly higher) standards as their colleagues, or that the SED and the *Hauptverwaltung Film* simply did not recognize or care about the unpopularity of such a policy.[10]

Despite a lack of clarity regarding the defining characteristics of *Kinderfilme* and the changes in both plot and cinematography that can be discerned in them over time, it is possible to identify a few common features that I will draw on in this essay. First, following the establishment of a dedicated production unit, their primary target audience was, following the *Hauptverwaltung Film's* orders, children – even when the studio suggested that they were suitable for an audience made up of both children and adults. On occasion, particularly in the postwar era, *Kinderfilme* included films about children that, while suitable for young people, had been conceived without any particular thought about a differentiated audience (as was the case with *Irgendwo in Berlin*).¹¹ Nonetheless, even before the production unit was established, critics and audiences could (and did) differentiate between feature films for adults and children, even if it was often the case that each group went to separate screenings. Second, these films contained everyday, historical and even fantasy elements designed to stimulate young cinema-goers to follow the protagonists' actions and ideals.¹² Third, usually they were made either by specialists in the production of children's and youth films or they tended to be the first film that many directors were assigned before being allowed to make conventional feature films. In no instance – at least as far as the SED and the *Hauptverwaltung Film* were concerned – was a *Kinderfilm* initially conceived as a film for adults; that is, a film never started off as an adult film only to be turned into a children's film. Nonetheless, some films crossed genres, so that a film not designated or evaluated as a *Kinderfilm* might nonetheless have a mixed audience. Fourth, *Kinderfilme* were shown either in conventional cinemas (usually during a showing exclusively for children) or in film clubhouses (although many of them appeared later on television). Fifth, scholarly estimates suggest that the total number of *Kinderfilme* made is somewhere between 160 and 200; here I will use the lower figure, which excludes those films such as science fiction productions that often had young audiences but were not intended to be subsumed under the genre of the *Kinderfilm* with its socialist pedagogical messages for children.

When a Children's Film is not a Children's Film

Nowhere are the debates about the aesthetic and pedagogical objectives of socialist children's cinema better illustrated than in the production and reception of Herbert Ballmann's *Der Teufel vom Mühlenberg* (1955). Based on an array of fables from eastern Germany's Harz forest, Ballmann's fairy-tale adaptation became an instant success among GDR cinema-goers and attracted large audiences of young people and adults.¹³ This reception did not coincide with the way that the SED and DEFA regarded the film, and both institutions embarked on protracted discussions (both during and after its production) about the genre to which it should be assigned and why it both was and was not a *Kinderfilm*. During production *Der Teufel vom Mühlenberg* had initially been advertised as a fairy tale for young people.¹⁴ Numerous problems accompanied the making of the film, including criticisms of the screenplay and questions regarding the story's appropriateness for a young audience. Still, its eventual release as an ordinary feature film confused critics, who had anticipated reviewing a *Kinderfilm*.[15]

Der Teufel vom Mühlenberg had much to recommend it. First, it was a fairy-tale film, a category that had already established itself as guaranteeing success among children with films like *Das kalte Herz* [The Cold Heart, dir. Paul Verhoeven, 1950] and the even more popular *Die Geschichte vom kleinen Muck* [The Story of Little Mook, dir. Wolfgang Staudte, 1953].[16] In addition, *Der Teufel vom Mühlenberg* was, aesthetically speaking, a beautiful film.[17] Filmed in part on location in the Harz mountains, the juxtaposition of the forest's brown and dark green hues with the simple bright colours of the villagers' clothes made it, in the words of one reviewer, a 'colourful extravaganza'.[18] The music (composed by Joachim Werzlau) provided a dynamic accompaniment to scenes of angry peasants confronting the wealthy town administrators, and at the same time served to differentiate the two groups by associating them with different musical registers; the peasants work in the fields singing traditional folk songs about the beauty of the land, while the mayor and his friends drink to excess at the local inn to the accompaniment of raucous drinking songs. Set against this charming background of an imaginary German past, the storyline is based around the town leaders' plot to force the inhabitants of a nearby village to use the mill in the town rather than the one close to where they live. The villagers uncover the scheme and, with the help of local forest spirits, rebel so that they can return to using the old mill in the forest. Having reclaimed their means of production they are no longer reliant on their feudal masters.

Yet not even this classic fairy-tale scenario was sufficient to persuade DEFA to release *Der Teufel vom Mühlenberg* as a *Kinderfilm*. In part this reluctance was a reflection of the director's recent success with *Das geheimnisvolle Wrack* [The Mysterious Wreck, 1954] – one of the first *Kinderfilme* to emerge from the children's and youth film production unit. That film had been a lively children's detective-adventure tale. In the case of *Der Teufel vom Mühlenberg*, Ballmann had been instructed to produce a 'reactionary romantic' fairy-tale film.[19] It was an entirely different kind of project and one accompanied by high expectations on the part of critics and audiences alike. Ballmann approached the task by setting up a conflict that would prompt the villagers to rise up against their oppressors, and by rooting the film even more deeply in German history and memory through the addition of elements of Romantic-era myths of benevolent forest spirits who would only help the virtuous. The kind of virtue that the spirits demanded was, of course, effectively identical to that required in socialist society. And who better to be the anointed figure who leads the peasants out of their misery (Fig. 12.1) than that 'child of the people', the parentless Anne?

Although the film met with a mixed critical reception – celebrated as a success by some critics and condemned by others as a failure – such a broad spectrum of reviews is not in itself unusual. In this case, however, while reviewers were able to identify what they did or did not like about it, they were far from being able to agree whether what they had just seen was in fact a *Kinderfilm* or a film targeted at adults. Those who argued that the film was not a *Kinderfilm* or youth film still praised its presentation of a truth that had been handed down through generations and that remained equally relevant today ('people fighting against need and danger need to be clever, courageous and united') – a reading of the film which underlines its educational dimension but which stops well short of explaining why it should not be regarded as a *Kinderfilm*.[20] Other reviews clearly saw the younger generation as the film's target audience and praised Ballmann for a work that satisfied the needs and

Figure 12.1: Anne and Jörg plot how to free the villagers from the enforced use of the town mill in *Der Teufel vom Mühlenberg* (1955). DVD screen capture.

desires 'of young people starved of adventure'.²¹ Similarly, the socialist youth magazine *Junge Welt* expressed its approval of Ballmann's innovative approach in creating new ways of looking at 'our German history' and praised him for having made a film that 'embodies genuinely national characteristics: those are real German landscapes, German people... Those are real people of flesh and blood, dependable, industrious, serious, clever and caring, embodying the best characteristics of our *Volk*'.²² Ballmann had made a film that extended Germany's national heritage, worked within a Marxist historical dialectic that included the failure of the feudal system, and was also enjoyable to watch. It would appear that, at the level of the general public at least, most people did regard *Der Teufel vom Mühlenberg* as a *Kinderfilm*.

Why was it then, that in the most incisive critiques of the film, the question was repeatedly raised as to why the film had not been designated a *Kinderfilm* when it was released? The prolific reviewer Charlotte Ewald, in her lengthy essay of 1955 in *Deutsche Filmkunst*, offers what is perhaps the clearest analysis of the problem. After listing a number of reasons why the film had not been designated a *Kinderfilm* by the production company, she concluded that, even so, it was one in all but name. Her complaints centred on the messages imparted to children in the film's plot. Most importantly, she found fault with the male protagonist Jörg, who could rouse a crowd to action but who also acted spontaneously and without thinking of possible consequences. She compared him to the more conventionally feminine heroine, Anne, who planned her actions deliberately. There was no clear guide for children as to which of these two characters – the more masculine Jörg or the feminine Anne – should be emulated or even if one was created specifically for boys and the other for girls. The lack of a clear answer to such a question should not be tolerated in films for adults, Ewald complained, let alone in a *Kinderfilm*.²³ She went on to note that *Der Teufel vom Mühlenberg* would have been acceptable as a *Kinderfilm* had the characters embodied a more positive concept of masculinity rather than greed, gluttony and malevolence. She further listed a series of problems that 'need to be addressed for the sake of future *Kinderfilme*' – a remark that suggests that the genre's future was by no means certain. One problem that she highlighted was that the antagonistic figures were too heavy-handed in their viciousness and not credible as medieval characters; the presence of virtuous protagonists was too limited; the protagonists did not display the same degree of passion as the evil characters. Despite claims on the part of the producers (both at the premiere and at subsequent press conferences) that no one had ever set out to create a *Kinderfilm*, Ewald concluded that 'the film is indeed a *Kinderfilm*, even if in many respects it remains unsatisfactory', and that in future the filmmakers would do well to present their films to critics as they are rather than hide behind formal statements as to how their film should or should not be received.[24]

Ewald's concerns went much further than simply demanding better *Kinderfilme*; rather she argued that films for young people should be judged on their own merits by external reviewers, and that they should not be re-designated as films for children *and* adults during the production process or following their release. Such directives couched in the form of reviews were to shape the future development of *Kinderfilme* and contributed to the genre being regarded as a continually evolving work in progress that remained under the scrutiny of the SED, the *Hauptverwaltung Film* and professional critics in the GDR. Perhaps not surprisingly, in subsequent *Kinderfilm* productions (particularly fairy-tale films), good and evil characters were more clearly delineated, and plots were streamlined to exclude any potentially ambiguous pedagogical messages that might otherwise confuse a child's understanding of his or her role in a socialist society. Ultimately, a *Kinderfilm* – whether appreciated by adults or not – remained a *Kinderfilm* as defined by its pedagogical objectives.

The 1970s: New Directions in Children's Films

The 1970s heralded the start of a new era for *Kinderfilme* insofar as they became a safe means for filmmakers to mount a limited criticism of East German society. In contrast to more strictly regulated feature films for adults, *Kinderfilme* offered a cinematic space in which certain seemingly negative aspects of modernity could be discussed alongside their impact on children. Changing demographic trends typical of almost all postindustrial societies in the developed world – a decreasing birth rate, changing roles for women and men, and a rise in the number of non-nuclear families – were the drivers behind many of the new themes in the *Kinderfilme* of the 1970s. Whereas in the same decade Hollywood turned out predominantly entertaining fantasy films for family consumption, such as *Willy Wonka and the Chocolate Factory* (1971) and *Freaky Friday* (1976), which celebrated a safe world with perfect adults and a utopian view of childhood, DEFA turned to the messy everyday lives of children, where endings were not always happy and children did not always get what they wanted or even needed. This focus on the – at first sight – mundane issues of children and young people called for new ideas about protagonists, aesthetics and interpretation and the kind of topics that were acceptable and could be explored without provoking the ire of the SED or the *Hauptverwaltung Film*.

The GDR was no longer trapped in the exigencies of the postwar period. Following a period of détente and the official recognition of its status as a sovereign state in the *Grundlagenvertrag* (Basic Treaty) of 1972 between it and the neighbouring Federal Republic, the GDR had become a society beset by new anxieties – including those that accompanied what was probably the most successful phase of its economic development. Equally importantly, the horizons of the parental generation no longer extended beyond the borders of the GDR itself, and their children had grown up behind the Berlin Wall. Filmmakers turned their attention to new themes such as love, divorce, changing gender relations – and the impact of these on children and childhood. Suddenly *Kinderfilme* belonged to everyone, and were regarded as a national treasure and as a commodity for export that everyone should be able to enjoy. *Kinderfilme* were made for children, but adults watched them as well (although the tradition of separate showings for young and adult audiences remained the norm).

This was particularly the case with Heiner Carow's *Ikarus*, which prompted some reviewers to ask what exactly its target audience was,[25] while others were left fuming that Carow seemed to have forgotten about adults altogether.[26] At its most basic level, *Ikarus* deals with the challenges of growing up as seen through the eyes of a young boy; but at another level it is a morality tale about the relationship between fathers and sons. The focus on a young boy's disappointment at his father's repeatedly broken promises made *Ikarus* one of the outstanding films of the 1970s – and one that criticized East German society with a degree of sensitivity that stopped short of apportioning blame. Articulating a social critique of this kind was a task increasingly adopted by other DEFA children's films of the 1970s such as Hannelore Unterberg's *Konzert* für *Bratpfanne und Orchester* [*Concerto for Frying Pan and Orchestra*, 1976] and Herrmann Zschoche's *Philipp der Kleine* [*Philipp the Small*, 1976], all of which demanded that adults celebrate childhood but did so without romanticizing away its difficulties. *Ikarus* tells the story of the eight-year-old Matthias, whose parents (like those of many of his classmates) are divorced and who struggles to come to terms with the changing family constellations. His mother's request shortly before his ninth birthday that he should start calling her new lover 'Uncle Jochen' does not help his attitude. His final break with the adult world comes when his father promises him a plane ride around Berlin and then buys him a train set instead.

Carow's film, however, is not simply just another film about insensitive parents. He deploys the metaphor of transportation to discuss the problems of family life. The father has told Matthias the tale of Icarus, leaving the viewer to wonder how, after that intense moment of father-son bonding, the father could imagine that his son wants to remain rooted to the ground. Matthias tramples the toy train and dreams instead of transcending the limits of the world he inhabits – the world of childhood and, by implication, the GDR – in the guise of Icarus (Fig. 12.2). In the GDR, with travel restricted not only between East and West but in all other directions as well, the possibility of flight, and of soaring above the state's borders, must have been the dream of more than one child.

Few children's films received as much praise in the East German press as *Ikarus*. One reviewer admitted to the difficulty of writing about a film that is just 'simply

Figure 12.2: Matthias 'flies' around his neighbourhood in *Ikarus* (1977). DVD screen capture.

good. Simple and good'.²⁷ Two aspects of Carow's film make it particularly compelling: first, a refined *mise en scène* based on imaginative camerawork whereby – in an obvious reference to the Icarus myth – Matthias is consistently framed by the sunlight; and second, a storyline that went further than most other *Kinderfilme* insofar as it neither shied away from harsh criticism of the parents nor insisted on a happy end. Carow uses the camera to comment on the characters and their interactions, and almost every scene is akin to a snapshot, framing Matthias in the centre of the chaos created by the adults around him. He gives full reign to a range of emotions that embarrass his parents and – at least within the limits that would have been acceptable to the *Hauptverwaltung Film* – is shown to rebel as much as an eight-year old boy can. In a daring move, Carow included a final sequence in which Matthias defiantly screams that all adults are liars – a statement that could easily have been interpreted as an allusion to the SED – before mitigating this critique in the closing scene by showing the young boy's reconciliation with his stepfather. Without doubt, the 1970s had opened a door for explorations of the everyday conflicts of childhood, and this focus would continue right up to the very end of the GDR with films like Karl Heinz Lotz's *Rückwärts laufen kann ich auch* [*I Can Run Backwards as Well*, 1990] and Rolf Losansky's *Abschiedsdisco* [*Farewell Disco*, 1990].

The Presence of the Past: Children's Historical Films of the 1980s

If the 1970s had been a time of critical introspection for the *Kinderfilm*, the films of the 1980s began to look at new topics, such as the environment, and children's gender roles, or else at new ways of approaching otherwise well-worn themes. One of the most impressive examples of reworking a traditional storyline is Jörg Foth's historical *Kinderfilm* of 1984, *Das Eismeer ruft*. Unlike other historical films in which successful German antifascist resistance against Nazis predominates, Foth's film offers a radically different perspective on the National Socialist period by moving the story to Prague in 1934, some five years before Nazi troops invaded Czechoslovakia. In this manner Foth captured what he later referred to as a 'political moment'²⁸ – one that addressed the delicate issue of Germany's occupation of its neighbours – without naming it outright. His decision to recount a historical vignette from the point of view of children allowed him to broaden the geopolitical range of National Socialism for contemporary audiences both in and beyond the GDR, and, implicitly at least, to point out the deficiencies of adults. The Nazi period is not ignored; but, for the first time in a DEFA *Kinderfilm*, it is contextualized in a time and space quite different from that which young viewers (and their parents) were used to. Perhaps for this reason contemporary commentators stumbled when identifying its intended audience; in Ralf Schenk's seminal volume *Das zweite Leben der Filmstadt Babelsberg*, the tag 'Filme nicht nur für Kinder' ('Films not just for children') accompanies the photos of *Das Eismeer ruft* as well as two other well-known *Kinderfilme*, namely, Helmut Dziuba's *Sabine Kleist, 7 Jahre* [*Sabine Kleist, 7 Years Old*, 1982] and Hannelore Unterberg's *Isabel auf der Treppe* [*Isabel on the Stairs*, 1984]. Like many of DEFA's children's films, *Das Eismeer ruft* is a smart, cinematographically complex film that is aesthetically satisfying in its use of colour and targeted at children and audiences interested in stories with juvenile protagonists.

Das Eismeer ruft brings together two common tropes in the DEFA *Kinderfilm*: history and adventure. Based on a story about a band of children from Prague who, in 1934, set out to save the Soviet ship *Tscheljuskin*, which is trapped in the Arctic Sea, *Das Eismeer ruft* addresses the ways in which the Nazi seizure of power impacted the lives of everyday people and wider political questions. The film begins much like a stage drama as the actors and musicians take their places: a dizzying 360-degree pan of a housing complex in Prague is accompanied by music that sounds like an orchestra tuning up with the intermittent noise of a transistor radio mixed in.[29] As the melody slowly develops, there is also the occasional hint of a military march – a reference to the Nazi presence that is vaguely felt but (at least at this point, and for these people) not yet entirely tangible. The first sequence shows children playfully indulging in a series of scientific experiments: making an improvised transistor radio; rolling down a hill in a barrel, as a test of courage in imitation of the American who rolled over the Niagara Falls; and experimenting with a self-made compass that will point to the North Pole. The fact that the leg of the eldest child, Anton, is in a plaster cast suggests that these sorts of (mis) adventures and experiments are all part and parcel of their daily life. Everything changes when the transistor radio reports on the attempts to save the *Tscheljuskin*, as suddenly their 'experiments' assume a more practical significance: they propose to travel to the 'North Pole' to save the crew members and passengers on the sinking ship (Fig. 12.3), but to do so without telling anyone, especially the adults, since 'when it comes to helping they [the adults] haven't got a clue'. Other children – those who do not take part in their scientific experiments – are excluded from their

Figure 12.3: The band of children set off in disguise to save the *Tscheljuskin* crew at the North Pole in *Das Eismeer ruft* (1984). DVD screen capture.

expedition. Rosi, however, is the exception because she offers to cook for the small band of five children, aged between six and ten, during their travels.

The film's juxtaposition of, on the one hand, international solidarity with the Soviet ship and, on the other, several allusions to a growing Nazi presence in Germany, make for a compelling plot. Numerous references in the film to the Soviet Union suggest a desire not to alienate Soviets politically, but rather to engage with them as part of the international socialist movement. Just how dangerous the children's idealism is, however, is underlined by the sequences in which they plan their route through Nazi Germany, and decide to travel at night and to use a series of escape tunnels. Foth's montage of overdubbed archival footage from newsreels succeeds in explaining the plight of the Soviet ship without the need for distracting explanations; it shows just how near the ship's crew and passengers were to perishing. Even if the children were to make it there, their brief experiment of sitting for several moments in a walk-in freezer would not have prepared them for the actual weather conditions they would have to endure. It is not that they do not understand the challenges ahead of them; it is rather than they simply have no sense of the sheer scale of their undertaking. Their perception of how perilous this trip could be is best summed up by the offhand comment that one of Rudi's German uncles used the tunnels to escape Germany. If his uncle could do it, it is suggested, then anyone can. Nor are the children worried about the practicalities of travel; once they have reached the Soviet Union, one of them claims, they will be travelling for free. 'That's how it is in communism' – a dual reference both to the prevailing ignorance about communism in the 1930s, and to contemporary representations of communism in many (non)-communist countries.

At the same time, the adults' general lack of interest in what the children are up to reflects another well-established trope in the DEFA *Kinderfilm* about the importance of adults respecting the needs of children, and helping them to fulfil their dreams and fantasies. In *Das Eismeer ruft*, the constant refrain that the children hear while playing or plotting their trip is their own names being shouted by their parents, who are demanding that they return home (sometimes for no other reason than to put an end to their supposedly frivolous activities). Perhaps the most blatant example of the lack of respect children have in the eyes of the adult world occurs when the young explorers try to fund their trip. A pawnshop owner does not blink when the children approach him to sell their watch and stamp collection and offers them a pittance in exchange. This is not an act conditioned by desperate political times; rather it is simply greed on the part of an adult who takes advantage of children, without any concern for their welfare. However, it is not only children that the adults do not care about; adults are often presented as heartless and uncaring in their treatment of other adults, as in the sequence, for example, where the local bar owner makes a bet with his patrons that the Soviets will not survive. While he derides all rescue attempts for being hopelessly misguided, the children are in another room putting on disguises to make sure they are not arrested when traversing Nazi Germany. It is a sequence in which we see how the youthful protagonists are transformed from children playing at saving the victims of the *Tscheljuskin* into adolescents who want to do good and who – in what is a tacit critique of the world of adulthood – believe they have the capacity to succeed where adults are failing.

Although the group makes it as far an aunt's house near the German border, manages to elude the police who are trying to bring them home and reaches the tunnel once used by Rudi's uncle, ultimately the children do not succeed. Once in the tunnel, they realize that the ground is uneven and find their passage disrupted by multiple crevices that appear impossible to negotiate. Discouraged, they turn around and lie down on the banks of the Vltava (Moldau). Two rafters discover them and gently help them on board, the first real kindness shown to them by adults. But the rafters are heading to Prague, and it becomes clear to the children (and to the audience) that their journey has been in vain. Even so, when they enter the city the children are hailed as heroes, and there they learn that the members of the *Tscheljuskin* have all been saved. Their own spontaneous (children's) march to victory is intercut with scenes of the victory parades in the Soviet Union in honour of the returned crew members, making the children appear as a visible and vital part of the rescue effort, even if they took no actual part in it. As we watch clips and newsreels about the *Tscheljuskin* embedded in *Das Eismeer ruft* it becomes clear that numerous other rescue efforts also failed; yet, at the same time, the logic of film suggests that these 'failures' were all part of the final successful outcome. Why should children from Prague be denied their place in the worldwide effort to resolve a moment of crisis?

Released at a crucial point in the Cold War – the period between the late 1970s and early 1980s when there were renewed militaristic tensions in US-Soviet relations – Foth's film had an additional resonance. That is to say, setting the film in the politically unstable world of the 1930s – and one that would soon be on the brink of all-out war – served as a warning of the dangers of global conflict in the present. DEFA's *Kinderfilme* were not alone in reflecting the fear of a possible World War III; John Badham's American youth film *War Games* (1983) focused on a Seattle high-school hacker whose actions nearly result in a nuclear war. Likewise, Steven Spielberg's blockbuster *ET* (1982), about an alien whom the children must protect from adults, also traded on the anxieties of global conflict and sought to reassure children that alien beings did not necessarily present an aggressive threat. Similar fears about modernity can also be found in Tim Burton's short feature of 1984, *Frankenweenie,* which gives a child the ability to bring his dog back to life (Disney shelved it after deeming it too violent for children).[30] But as *Das Eismeer ruft* – with its subtle message regarding the need for international solidarity in the face of impending disaster– underlines, East German *Kinderfilme* were different from their Western counterparts insofar as they seldom resorted to scare tactics in the service of pedagogy.

It is important not to underestimate the power of the message in *Das Eismeer ruft*: everything is possible if enough people work together. It is easy to read this simply as an expression of the socialist party line; but Foth's film suggests that there is more to the message. At the end of Das Eismeer ruft, radio announcers from around the world announce the successful rescue, reminding us that the Tscheljuskin catastrophe was one that many countries (of varying political ideologies) rallied around. And yet, as Foth shows, not everyone wanted to become part of an unofficial campaign of hope. The insight into workers' lives in Prague that the film offers highlights their concern about the accident; but there is also a degree of resignation that Foth's metaphorical language portrays as damaging to a shared sense of humanity. To find fault with a group of children who, though poorly equipped, are nonetheless willing to take risks in an attempt to save another group of seemingly doomed individuals, is to fail to recognize their capacity for fantasy and empathy.

By the 1980s, DEFA's children's films, as the studio management recognized, had captured the attention of children's film critics beyond the GDR. Much of this international reception was the result of screenings at international film festivals where its *Kinderfilme* were consistently awarded top prizes. Although lauded for their quality, as in the case of *Das Eismeer ruft*, West German critics often found ways of criticizing the films' allegedly socialist characteristics – even though viewers in the Federal Republic had become such devoted consumers of DEFA that, as Klaus-Dieter Felsmann has suggested, there is a case to be made for considering these *Kinderfilme* as part of a German–German cinematic heritage.[31] Foth's debut film and the book it was based on received considerable praise with its accurate reflection of life in 1980s East Germany.[32] Perhaps unconsciously, reviewers for the Munich-based trade magazine *Kinder und Jugendfilmkorrespondenz* echoed this sentiment in part by noting that it had all the characteristics of a typical socialist film insofar as it displayed an 'optimistic tendency', although they complained that it equated 'a good intention with a good deed'.[33] East German critics, on the other hand, found that there was more depth to Foth's film than was obvious at first viewing.[34] Lauding it as a tale for children and adults alike, reviewers latched on to the film's message of solidarity and its attempt to bring out the human qualities of all individuals regardless of the ideological systems they inhabited.[35] With so much at stake both in the world of *Das Eismeer ruft* and the political world of the 1980s, DEFA's *Kinderfilme* constituted a powerful attempt to articulate what it meant to act morally and politically, and to do so in a way that benefited not just East German society, but indeed all of humanity.

Conclusion

Taken together, these three films help explain the evolution of DEFA *Kinderfilme* as a key part of both the history of East German cinema and national debates in the GDR about children's antifascist humanist education. They also reflect the changes in the defining characteristics of *Kinderfilme* over time, as well as some typical characteristics of the genre and how the sub-genres of the fairy-tale film, historical film and films about everyday life were integral to *Kinderfilm* productions. If children were to be protected from potentially confusing political messages in the postwar period, then it would also be necessary to protect them from their parents' capriciousness and, at times, near-ignorance of their activities. In this way, DEFA's *Kinderfilme* also reflect the lives of adults. Through the mid-1950s, their primary concern was on rebuilding the country, physically as well as mentally, and this task included exploring how best to communicate the importance of socialism to children using the medium of film. By the 1970s, there was a substantial shift in focus onto the impact of a rapidly changing society in which divorce was no longer taboo, and children had to come to terms with feelings of disappointment and neglect as their parents began dating again or were busy with work. Finally, the *Kinderfilme* of the 1980s reaffirmed the need for parents to be there for their offspring, while at the same time highlighting the ways in which the fantasy of children – and their capacity to create a micro-moral universe within the macro-reality of the adult world – could be deployed to convey a transnational message of humanism that extended far beyond the limitations of the GDR.

Benita Blessing teaches in the School of Language, Culture and Society at Oregon State University. She is the author of *The Antifascist Classroom: Denazification in Soviet-occupied Germany, 1945–1949* (2006) and numerous chapters on the German Democratic Republic, education and DEFA children's films.

Notes

1. Andy Räder, 'Der Kinderfilm in der Weimarer Republik', in Horst Schäfer and Claudia Wegener (eds), *Kindheit und Film. Geschichte, Themen und Perspektiven des Kinderfilms in Deutschland*, Constance: UVK, 2009, pp. 21–38.
2. Ulrike Odenwald, 'Aufbruch zur Kontinuität', in Ralf Schenk and Erika Richter (eds), *apropos: Film 2001*[= Jahrbuch der DEFA-Stiftung, 2001], Berlin: Das Neue Berlin, 2001, pp. 296–327 (here

p. 296 and p. 321); Horst Schäfer, 'Höhen und Tiefen – Der Kinderfilm in der Bundesrepublik Deutschland in den 1950er-, 1960er- und 1970er-Jahren', in Schäfer and Wegener, pp. 73-109. All translations are by the author unless otherwise indicated.

3. Noel Brown and Bruce Babington, 'Introduction. Children's Films and Family Films', in Noel Brown and Bruce Babington (eds), *Family Films in Global Cinema. Beyond Disney*, London: Tauris, 2014, pp. 1-16 (p. 2 and p. 4).
4. Anon., 'Kritische Gedanken nach der Kinderfilmtagung', *Deutsche Filmkunst* 2 (1960), 38-41.
5. See Benita Blessing, *The Antifascist Classroom. Denazification in Soviet-occupied Germany, 1946-1949*, New York: Palgrave Macmillan, 2006.
6. Although the SED had actually called for a separate children's and youth film studio, it never explained why the original plans to establish the studio as an independent entity never came to fruition. See Odenwald, pp. 296-97 and p. 313.
7. Hans-Joachim Laabs (Minister für Volksbildung der Deutschen Demokratischen Republik), 'Pädagogische Bemerkungen zum Kinderfilm', *Deutsche Filmkunst. Zeitschrift für Theorie und Praxis des Filmschaffens* 5 (1954), 5-7, (5).
8. Hellmuth Häntzsche, 'Erste Erfahrung aus der Arbeit der Kinder- und Jugendfilmproduktion', *Deutsche Filmkunst. Zeitschrift für Theorie und Praxis des Filmschaffen* 5 (1954), 7-11.
9. Interview with former DEFA director Jörg Foth, November 2010. Interview notes in possession of author. See also Odenwald, p. 325.
10. In no archival material or in oral history interviews could I find proof that children's films carried less status within the *Hauptverwaltung Film*.
11. Although reviewers occasionally referred to families as appropriate audiences, the category of the 'family film' was not part of DEFA's production programme.
12. Dieter Wiedemann, 'Der DEFA-Kinderfilm: Zwischen Resteverwertung und Politikdiskursen. Überlegungen zum Umgang mit einem Kulturerbe', in Schäfer and Wegener, pp. 111-24.
13. 'Der Teufel vom Mühlenberg', in Ingelore König, Dieter Wiedemann and Lothar Wolf (eds), *Zwischen Marx und Muck. DEFA-Filme für Kinder*, Berlin: Henschel, 1996, pp. 89-91.
14. Hermann Martin, 'Der Teufel vom Mühlenberg', *Berliner Zeitung am Abend*, 12 April 1955.
15. Charlotte Ewald, 'Weshalb wurde "Der Teufel vom Mühlenberg" kein Kinderfilm?' *Deutsche Filmkunst* 3 (1955), 111-13.
16. See Qinna Shen, *The Politics of Magic. DEFA Fairy-Tale Films*, Detroit, MI: Wayne State University Press, 2015.
17. 'Der Teufel vom Mühlenberg', in Eberhard Berger and Joachim Giera (eds), *77 Märchenfilme. Ein Filmführer für jung und alt*, Berlin: Henschel, 1990, p. 37.
18. Ulrich Blankenfeld, 'Der Teufel vom Mühlenberg', *Sonntag* 16 (1995).
19. 'Der Teufel vom Mühlenberg', in König, Wiedemann and Wolf, p. 90.
20. Hermann Martin, 'Der Teufel vom Mühlenberg', *Berliner Zeitung am Abend*, 12 April 1955.
21. Ursus, 'Der Teufel vom Mühlenberg', *Tägliche Rundschau*, 13 April 1955.
22. Hermann Kähler, 'Der Teufel vom Mühlenberg', *Junge Welt*, 15 April 1955.
23. Ewald, pp. 111-12.
24. Ewald, p. 113.
25. Rosemarie Rehan, 'Ikarus', *Die Wochenpost*, 19 September 1975.
26. Fred Gehler, 'Ikarus', *Sonntag*, 26 October 1975.
27. Friedrich Dieckmann, 'Ikarus vielfach umgedeutet. Zu dem neuen Film von Heiner Carow', *Film und Fernsehen* 11/1975, 17-21 (18).

28. Wolfgang J. Fuchs, '"Sie haben ja den Film ganz gut ausgedacht." Gespräch mit Jörg Foth', *Kinder- und Jugendfilmkorrespondenz* 21.1 (1985) [=http://www.kjk-muenchen.de/archiv/index.php?id=727&sausgabe=19], accessed 14 March 2016.
29. Interview with Jörg Foth, Sept. 2010. Interview notes in possession of the author.
30. Ian Wojchik-Andrews, *Children's Films. History, Pedagogy, Ideology, Theory*, New York: Garland, 2000, pp. 100-2. Burton remade *Frankenweenie* as a feature-length stop-motion production in 2012.
31. See Klaus-Dieter Felsmann and Bernd Sahling, *Deutsche Kinderfilme aus Babelsberg. Werkstattgespräche – Rezeptionsräume*, Berlin: DEFA-Stiftung, 2010, pp. 9-12.
32. 'Das Eismeer ruft', in König, Wiedemann and Wolf, pp. 326-27.
33. Bernt Linder, 'Das Eismeer ruft', *Kinder und Jugendfilmkorrespondenz* 19 (March 1984) [=http://www.kjk-muenchen.de/archiv/index.php?id=699&sausgabe=19], accessed 14 March 2016.
34. S. Kaiser, 'Ein 'Mehr' unter der Oberfläche', *Film und Fernsehen* 5/1984, 12-13.
35. Horst Knietzsch, 'Erkundungen der Wirklichkeit für Kinder und für Erwachsene', *Neues Deutschland*, 28 April 1984; and R. Stolze, 'Ein Debüt wird zur Entdeckung', *Junge Welt*, 6 April 1984.

PART IV
DEFA'S LEGACY

CHAPTER 13

DEFA's Last Gasp
Ruins, Melancholy and the End of East German Filmmaking

Nick Hodgin

The view is from below. The camera looks up at the top, fourth floor balcony of a crumbling turn of the century building from which a cat tries to negotiate its exit. The base of the balcony has partly subsided, the railings are rusting, the building's surface is fatigued – bricks are visible where the plaster has shelved away. From a further vantage point, the view moves down the building to the right to reveal graffiti written across the side wall of the detached building. It reads: SAVE US! Graffiti is daubed across the front of the building, too: WE CAN STILL BE RESCUED... CITIZENS, HELP US!' The soundtrack hums, a droning note that does not augur well for the content of Peter Rocha's final DEFA documentary film, though the title has already indicated the mood we should expect: *Schmerzen der Lausitz* [*The Pain of Lusatia*, 1990]. The documentary, little under an hour long, and made between October 1989 and the spring of 1990, was the third (after *Hochwaldmärchen* [*High Forest Fairy Tale*, 1987] and *Leben am Fließ* [*Life Along the Rivulet*, 1989]) of Rocha's forays into the Lausitz, the eastern region of the GDR, home to the country's indigenous Sorbs, and serves as a particularly bleak portrait of a region that suffered under the GDR's open cast brown coal (lignite) mining projects.

Rocha's film shows a region rent by an economic policy that privileged industry over people, in which both the community and the environment was victim to industrial practice. The landscape is made surreal by the mining operation: villages have disappeared; so too have the fields, woods and the roads, until all that is left is a barren landscape, whose topography is metamorphosed by the excavations to comprise dead, uniform hills and lifeless ponds – the mounds of excavated material and craters filled with water. The soundtrack emphasizes the strangeness of the scenery, seen mostly from the air; the sound of dogs howling are heard throughout, connoting madness, desperation. The landscape is one that Volker Braun, who once worked in the industry and who had, like other writers, initially eulogized the transformative potential of such industry, later came to interpret it rather differently:

> *Ausgelöffelt die weichen Lager, zerhackt, verschüttet,*
> *zersiebt, das Unterste gekehrt nach oben und durch-*
> *gewalkt und entseelt und zerklüftet alles*[1]
>
> *[Scooped out from the soft deposits, hacked, spilled,*
> *sieved, the underneath turned upwards and stretched*
> *out and all of it lifeless and cratered]*

Where images of machinery in DEFA's documentary films once connoted progress, the GDR's self-sufficiency or proud industrial character, in Rocha's film they are indiscriminate, ominous, dwarfing the people who operate them; the impersonal tools of industry excavating the land, stripping it bare.[2] And what of the former inhabitants? Rocha's film shows the resident of a traditional, ramshackle farm, an elderly woman in a shawl and smock who, when she watches the television reports, assumes (correctly?) that 'I can't keep up with history'. Others have been rehoused in the prefabricated housing of the *Plattenbau* estates, which seem no less barren than their now former *Heimat*, and here the harmony and integrated community suggested by the GDR's self-description as a 'workers' and peasants' State' ('Arbeiter-und-Bauernstaat') seems inaccurate – the newly arrived folk look depressed and out of place: three figures stare at the camera, saying nothing; another is seen from behind, silent, motionless, looking out of the *Plattenbau* window and staring into the void.

The subjects rarely speak in Rocha's film. When they do, the tone is invariably agitated or resigned. A naked worker highlights the poor conditions in the factory and the camera captures water dripping down from the ceiling, the cracked and dirty walls, the greasy floors. Similar observations are made by a similarly semi-naked worker of a brick factory in Volker Koepp's *Märkische Ziegel* [*Brandenburg Bricks*, 1989], who indignantly points to leaking pipes and general disrepair. The GDR towards the end of its days: all is crumbling, disintegrating. The subtext is clear: the 'workers' state' failed to provide conditions fit for its workers. What remains are ruins, layered histories. In Rocha's film the open cast mines have obliterated the villages but some remnants remain: the shells of buildings, houses barely standing, debris and ruins everywhere. *Schmerzen der Lausitz* is largely a film comprised of images without words, a visual account of the exploitation of nature and the destruction of communities. The eco-documentary is today a well-established genre and the focus on environmental devastation in the drive for profit, often framed in terms of the discourse of globalization and with a particular interest in the human suffering as well as the ecological impact, are among the generic topoi. Environmental concerns in the GDR had far fewer platforms and the damage done to the East German environment (and beyond) as a result of outdated industrial practices, inadequate policies and the near complete absence of any green politics, was a much discussed issue in the early year of unification – so much so that one writer would accuse the Western states of an attitude that bespoke 'green imperialism'.[3]

Representing environmental damage was problematic in the GDR because to do so was to challenge the state on a conceptual/ideological level and to counter its self-understanding as a state that cared for the citizens, that had the East German community's best interests at heart. Such commitment to 'the beautiful homeland' (*Heimat*) was part of the official rhetoric, habitually intoned by young East Germans whenever they sang Herbert Keller's song, 'Unsere Heimat'. Criticism of economic policy and the damage done did exist: 'In lyric poetry', Jacqui Hope explains, 'the ethical imperative of reshaping the landscape was replaced by an emphatic identification with the beleaguered natural world'.[4] This was more difficult to achieve in film but not impossible. Kurt Tetzlaff's *Erinnerung an eine Landschaft – Für Manuela* [*Memories of a Landscape – To Manuela*, 1983] is an early example of a DEFA documentary seeking to capture the damaging impact that open cast mining has on a region in Saxony, whose inhabitants were forced to abandon their villages (and also relocated to a huge *Plattenbau* estate) in order to make way for the diggers that flattened their homes in preparation for lignite mining. Their relocation is a question of rehousing rather than rehoming and the ersatz *Heimat* is no more than that: a simulacrum with a few authentic touches in the shape of rescued artefacts, the vestiges of the disappeared village. Tetzlaff's film, which was screened at the film festival in Leipzig in 1981, made a strong impression on audiences and on those critics prepared to speak their mind, but won the director few favours at the DEFA Studio for Documentary Films.[5] The film was much commended for its authenticity, for revealing the problems faced by a community. Such praise needs to be considered as much for what it does *not* say as for what it does. In praising the film for its true depiction of the subjects we can infer from Hans-Dieter Tok's review, for example, the suggestion that other DEFA films were less concerned with truthful representations than they were with providing confirmation of the state's preferred self-image.[6] *Erinnerung an eine Landschaft – Für Manuela* is by turns melancholic, elegiac, angry; images describe the physical destruction of villages while the narration and spoken dialogue recount the villagers' disappointment, frustration and anguish. It may be unusual in its honest depiction of the suffering that comes as a result of state policy, but the aforementioned adjectives well describe the mood of many East German films and especially those made towards the end of the state's existence; and it is the melancholic turn and the recourse to ruin, both physical and metaphorical, in the films made in the last couple of years of the GDR, in what retrospectively we may term its 'last gasp', that form the principle focus of this chapter.

DEFA's Melancholic Turn

How might one understand the melancholy that informs and is reverberated through different media representations of the GDR? In the case of the DEFA films under discussion the melancholic disposition is more than 'the poetic mood of brooding introspection' described by Mary Cosgrove, more than wistful Romantic rumination, even if we might include it as a further example of a sensibility that is manifest across centuries of German artistic expression.[7] In a piece on German writers and a national tendency towards melancholy and pessimism, Kate Connolly remarks that 'Germans hardly seem to be able to enjoy their lives without sensing its impending demise'.[8] This propensity and the creative energies often attributed to it is taken up by fellow journalist Stefan Klein, who ponders the apparent disjuncture between statistical evidence that reveals the Germans to be more contented than are some of their neighbours and melancholy as an abiding feature of the cultural script.[9] Indeed surveys conducted since unification have routinely revealed the East Germans to be unhappy, or frustrated with important aspects of their lives. Among these are the failure to attain the kind of material comfort to which they had aspired, the uncertainties of life in the free market (financial insecurity and anxieties about pensions and welfare provision) and regional deprivation. These are valid and, in some cases, pressing concerns, and commentators such as Jana Hensel have engaged with East Germans' discontent in order to reflect critically on economic and other disparities in contemporary Germany, and to challenge perceived master narratives about the state and its subsequent collapse.[10]

For Freud, the melancholic remains unconscious of the object of loss, unlike the mourner whose suffering is a painful recognition of the thing(s) that is/are lost.[11] Such a distinction, influential though it has been, is not without its problems, something that Freud himself recognized, and certainly the melancholic mood that pervades many of these films is a consequence of both emotional responses – actual grief that accompanies bereavement (the passing of friends and family; the destruction of homes and demise of communities) as well as a conscious feeling of loss for that which never was or, rather, that which failed to be (the GDR's failure to live up to its utopian aspirations). Some of the films on which I focus seem to be temporally dislocated, appearing to report not at a point in time but a point between times, where not just the future but the past and present seem to be in question. Scholars more commonly associate the transition period (between the demonstrations in 1989 and unification in 1990) as the period of political uncertainty during which unease and trepidation, as well as an overdue reckoning with the state, emerged as themes in the films made by those long absent or indeed by those termed the 'lost generation'.[12] But foreboding and feelings of loss are evident in earlier films, those made before the end was in sight, too. Those films made when the GDR was still a state that claimed a future, reveal a preoccupation with certain themes and emotions – among them frustrated desires, relinquishment of principles and loss – that are constitutive of a melancholic mood.

Unhappy Endings

It is no exaggeration to say that the most discussed of the DEFA films made in the final twenty years of the GDR tend to be narratives of loss, of despair and disappointment. Relationships break down, dreams fail, protagonists die. This is true of many films about contemporary, everyday life released in the 1970s and 1980s and, in contradistinction to prevailing trends, it is also true of many films that were box office successes and/or comedies (see for example Heiner Carow's 1973 film *Die Legende von Paul und Paula* [*The Legend of Paul and Paula*] Frank Beyer's *Das Versteck* [*The Hiding Place*, 1978] or Konrad Wolf's *Solo Sunny*, 1981). We might speculate as to their appeal, that, in addition to simply being well-made films, these narratives thematize something that had often been absent from DEFA films, for these are films that prioritize subjectivity and individualism, films whose characters make (but seldom succeed) in finding their own ways. The films thus provide confirmation of feelings that were widespread in the GDR, rather than affirmation of rhetoric. While many East German films essentially trod the same path, with socialist ideology either foregrounded or underpinning narratives across a range of genres, films that eschewed ideology in favour of following individual stories appeared to have the greatest resonance. How audiences might have originally responded to films, some of which were only rescued from obliged anonymity after unification, remains a matter of past perfect speculation: the films that were banned in the wake of the Eleventh Plenum of 1965 offer a tantalizing glimpse of a new wave cinema that might have been – films that could have changed the way East Germans (and others) saw themselves on screen had they been released to a wider public. It is hard not think along these lines when watching films such as Jürgen Böttcher's *Jahrgang 45* [*Born in '45*, 1966/1990] or his *Barfuß und ohne Hut* [*Barefoot and without a Hat*, 1964] or even earlier films that fell victim to fluctuations to official debates on aesthetics (Falk Harnack's *Das Beil von Wandsbek* [*The Axe of Wandsbek*, 1951], for example). There is a discernible melancholy then, too, in certain reflections of the East German's cinematic past – as is evident in the title of Barton Byg's article 'What Might Have Been: DEFA Films of the Past and the Future of German Cinema' and Dieter Wolf's book *Gruppe Babelsberg – Unsere nichtgedrehten Filme* [*The Babelsberg Group – The Films We Did Not Make*].[13]

That so many of the DEFA films made in the last few years of the state's existence are films that end unhappily, is significant. It is a truism that so-called 'quality films' prefer conclusions that are inconclusive, favour unresolved endings to those that provide answers and solutions. A brief survey of, say, film festival winners will likely confirm such endings to be the norm rather than exception, whereas the reverse is generally true of mainstream films. In the case of DEFA's films, the unhappy ending, or perhaps more accurately endings that avoid triumph or positive affirmation, is a feature common to many films across different genres. It is true, for example, of films such as *Die Besteigung des Chimborazo* [*The Ascent of Chimborazo*, 1989], Rainer Simon's account of Alexander von Humboldt's ascent of the Ecuadorean peak, a film that is reminiscent of Werner Herzog's South American epics in terms of the characterization and plot (obsessional protagonists, tests of endurance, overwhelming challenges) as well as the geographical and production contexts. Simon explained that his film was supposed to demonstrate to young people the importance of having and trying to realize dreams and not allowing these to be taken from them, but the protagonist's failure to reach the summit with which the film ends, following a long wordless sequence documenting the climb, does not celebrate the heroic effort nor does it suggest the struggle to have been a worthwhile cause.[14] Synthesizers and flutes combine to provide a strange and unsettling soundtrack; the final image simply shows the party's weather-beaten faces and anguished expressions. Even crime thrillers such as Horst E. Brandt's *Die Beteiligten* [*The Parties Involved*, 1989] a film set in the 1960s, which begins with a suspected suicide that turns out to be a murder and whose investigation finally reveals a network of corrupt and venal civil servants, barely acknowledges the success of its detectives. The corruption depicted instead represents a belated engagement with the duplicity within the ranks of the ruling Socialist Unity Party (SED) and with individual careerism, topics seldom investigated in East German film and which, notoriously, were issues that had resulted in the censorship of several films in 1965/66, notably Kurt Maetzig's *Das Kaninchen bin ich* [*The Rabbit is Me*, 1965] and indeed the original screenplay for *Die Beteiligten*.

A similar lack of triumph is evident, too, in Rainer Ackermann's melancholic *Über die Grenzen* [*Over the Borders*, 1990], which follows a fictional documentary team as they follow a celebrated East German cyclist on his last outing, the Peace Race ('Friedensfahrt') spanning Poland, Czechoslovakia and the GDR. Instead of being a celebration of success or adhering to the conventions of sports films (triumph over adversity, comradeship, the cost of success and so on), the film reflects as much on the metaphysical as on the physical. Ernst Bloch is indirectly referenced when the director reflects on his youth, his memory of first seeing the race and of the impossibility of returning to childhood. The cameraman is less pessimistic and asks, 'What should we take from our childhood if not a dream?', but the film details their futility, their eventual impoverishment, as is evident in the camera team's shift in interest away from the likely success of their compatriot to the English rider, struggling for most of the film in last place. 'Who's interested in losers in today's world?' asks one of the journalists. It is an ironic question, of course, since loss and losers were precisely the subjects in which many East German filmmakers were interested. Loss, losing and failure are central to Ackermann's narrative. The film details broken relationships and ruptured friendships; even the (fictional) director's decision to make the loser the film's subject ultimately fails. I have suggested elsewhere that East German documentaries, a field in which the director had spent most of his career, were increasingly characterized by a politics of silence, by a notable absence of dialogue, a refusal to offer commentary or guidance, to let the images speak for themselves.[15] Something similar happens here, too: the manager of a local cinema mistakes the director's request to show the film and rushes for an offer of a preview screening, not realizing that the film team only has images without sound; thus the few reels shot are shown in silence, with the result that the race's triumphs are made less triumphant, less dramatic.

The documentary team assumes their compatriot's success in his hometown to be guaranteed, a weary recognition of inveterate corruption through which the state gets the results it wants. The (actual and fictional) director's decision to explore a (meta-) narrative of failure is thus a more subversive choice than it might first seem. Corruption of ideals and the non-realization of dreams are themes to which filmmakers would return time and again after the Wende, only sporadically appeared as topics in DEFA film – for obvious reasons. In the final years, however, it emerges as a concern across a range of films. Herrmann Zschoche's *Das Mädchen aus dem Fahrstuhl* [*The Girl in the Lift*, 1991], for example, demonstrates the ways in which idealism was compromised in the GDR through a twin strategy of intimidation and privilege. When an upstanding teenager, prompted initially by a romantic interest in a new classmate, demands more discussion about assessment and performance at school, he is expelled from the Free German Youth movement (FDJ). Such an action should spell the end of opportunities available to him; in Zschoche's film, however, the parents' connections enable him to move to a privileged apprenticeship. The outcome may be a positive resolution for the young man, but it does not constitute a traditional happy ending. What chance is there for change if freethinking youth can be so easily corrupted? Can principles be so easily compromised? Hans-Werner Honert offers an alternative take on this question in his film, *Ein brauchbarer Mann* [*A Useable Man*, 1989]. A young businessman tasked with retrieving from a disgruntled erstwhile colleague the documents and designs his company needs if it is to match its contractual obligations, begins to sympathize with the man (now a gravedigger on the island of Rügen) whom he has initially befriended in order to get access to the plans. Recognizing that the engineer has been mistreated by the company and that he too has been exploited as collector, he refuses to pass the documents on, only to discover that the other's principled refusal to be bought is less steadfast than he assumed. Betrayal is to be found everywhere in Honert's film: between colleagues, between husband and wife and between friends; and the film's bleak ending offers a particularly depressing image in East German cinema and a somewhat crude metaphor for the erosion of hope:

no longer able to tolerate his life, he takes on the role of the now vacant gravedigger and is finally seen deep in the ground unable to climb out of the hole he has dug. It is hard not to see the crater begun by the older man, and which finally confines the young man, as a metaphor, too, for the older generation's failure to provide for the state's young people (Fig. 13.1).

Where *Ein brauchbarer Mann* ends in a cemetery, with its young protagonist stranded in the grave, Rainer Behrend's *Der Magdalenenbaum* [*The Magdalena Tree*, 1989] and Rolf Losansky's *Abschiedsdisco* [*Farewell Disco*, 1990] both begin in one. A new grave is the starting point for a film about frustrated desires, regrets and tense relationships in the former, while the latter begins with Henning (Holger Kubisch), its teenage protagonist, attending the funeral of a girlfriend killed in a traffic accident. Bereft, the teenager is given to remembering his friend, memories which are played out in hazy flashback sequences, and to imagining her in the present, a spectral figure who appears in hallucinatory visions. Such recollections and imaginings would become a feature of

Figure 13.1: Symbolic excavation: the older generation preparing a grave for the younger generation in *Ein brauchbarer Mann* (1989) © DEFA-Stiftung/Heinz Pufahl.

post-unification narratives (Andreas Kleinert's film *Verlorene Landschaft* [*Lost Landscapes*], for example, Andreas Höntsch's *Der Strass* [*Rhinestones*] and Jens Becker's *Grönland* [*Greenland*] all released in the early 1990s), where the oneiric, dreamlike states serve to connect past and present, to emphasize the transition from one world to another and to underline the world made strange, where madness and the grotesque feature, and characters oscillate between indistinct memories, fantasies and deliria. The remembered scenes and spectral presences in *Abschiedsdisco* are a reference to the protagonist's experience of bereavement but also accentuate his uncertainty as he tries to make sense of the world around him – specifically a region undergoing transformation as (here, too) the area in which his grandfather lives is cleared in preparation for strip mining (Fig. 13.2). Rolf Losansky's screenplay had been rejected in 1983 and again in 1986 and underwent various changes before permission for filming was granted in 1989. As with many other East German films targeted at adolescent audiences, the ostensible focus on issues related to young people yields interesting and often critical commentary on society in general.

Figure 13.2: Henning (Holger Kubisch) helpless against the region's redevelopment in *Abschiedsdisco* (1990) © DEFA-Stiftung/Rigo Dommel.

In *Abschiedsdisco*, the protagonist's desire to seek 'more meaning from life' does not end with any such self-realization. The disorientation and incomprehension Henning experiences as he searches among the houses for his grandfather are not resolved; no answers are provided, no reasons for hope offered. Forced to hide from the police patrolling the area to prevent looters, he takes refuge in the tunnels of the brick factory, where he loses his way. This self-imprisonment (again a feature of later post-unification narratives) clearly represents the loss of hope in the final years of the GDR, its isolation, and perhaps, too, the reliance on the past. Henning's memory of happier times serves to distract him from his entombment, a retreat into the tunnels and under the earth that connects the film with other films surveying the earth and the changing terrain and which anticipates similar explorations undertaken in Volker Braun's 'earthwork'.[16] As in Rocha's and Tetzlaff's and others' films, the ruins bespeak the vanishing of seemingly permanent landmarks, the disappearance of people and transformation of place. Not even the dead can rest: Henning, whose perambulations amid the ruins, and encounters with intruders and other odd figures, has made him increasingly drowsy, is woken from his brief repose by the noise of excavation as the cemetery in which he has inadvertently slept is encroached on, the graves moved and tombstones piled ready to be relocated. The cemetery scene is fitting for a film preoccupied with ghosts of the past (of the dearly departed) and ghosts of the future (the ghost-town to be, the older residents whose connection to place is a connection to a future emptiness). Henning is not the only one haunted by the past. The farewell disco to which the film's title alludes is a subterranean bar, a private repository of memories presided over by a young woman who retreats to the cellar where she plays records whose beats represent the final pulse of village life. It offers only a temporary refuge for Henning and for the girl, a hope that cannot be fulfilled, namely the return of a boy she once met there. Dreams and desires are articulated but only to emphasize their impossibility: Henning's girlfriend can live on only as a memory or phantom; the friend who desires him knows she cannot have him; the few eccentric older residents know their time is up but seek to cling to a place that is disappearing around them. There is but one brief moment of hope, but it is an act of futility and serves to demonstrate the fading of optimism in the GDR or even the hope that films such as Losanky's, released as the state on which they comment fades altogether, might have any sort of impact: together with his friend, Henning plants some apple tree cuttings. It is a gesture of defiance in the face of inevitability but suggests a moment of hope and faith in the future;

in this it is reminiscent of a proverb long attributed to Martin Luther: 'Even if I knew that tomorrow the world would go to pieces, I would still plant an apple tree today'. Were that the final scene, one might think Losansky's film hopeful for the future; the actual ending is much more pessimistic and in keeping with the mood of many of his contemporaries: an image of a bleak, open-cast mine.

    Other films are less austere but no more hopeful and private despair and the threat to the environment emerges as a common theme. Desire figures as a complicated, seldom realized emotion which connects several of the final films. It is a sensation that rarely allows for a positive ending, yielding instead to disappointment, acrimony and anguish. In Rainer Behrend's 1989 *Magdalenenbaum*, a village nurse, Magda (Christine Schorn), is permitted only a fleeting happiness in a romance with a solitary artist who has shunned official commissions in order to concentrate on his own vision (but who finally returns to the city). An adaptation of Jurij Koch's 1984 novella *Der Kirschbaum* [*The Cherry Tree*], Jürgen Brauer's film, *Sehnsucht* [*Longing*, 1990], is aptly named for it concerns a love triangle, again a suggestive device used in several films in the final years – Michael Gwisdek's *Treffen in Travers* [*Rendezvous in Travers*, 1989], Erwin Stranka's *Liane* (1987) and Dietmar Hochmuth's *In einem Atem* [*In One Breath*, 1988] – in which allegiances, devotion and loyalties shift between a young couple (set once again in the Lausitz) and an interloper (Ulrich Mühe).[17] A rare example of an East German film that makes use of *Heimatfilm* motifs – the disruption caused by the arrival of an urbane and urban stranger in a small, seemingly hermetic rural community – *Sehnsucht* is a film that, like others previously mentioned, is concerned with the destruction of *Heimat*. Sieghart (Mühe), an engineer surveying the area, intrudes and disturbs the relationship between Matthias and Ena (Ulrike Krumbiegel), finally marrying the latter and moving with her to Paris. Sieghart's presence in the area is a threat not just to the young couple (the jealous Matthias will die when he crashes the wedding cart carrying the bride and groom he has recklessly driven into a lake, from which he does not emerge) but to their environment – Ena notices the markers engineers have left and which we infer to spell the flooding of the valley and the disappearance of her *Heimat*. The escape to Paris, where Sieghart has been sent, offers no salvation; the West's allure proves short lived. Disorientated and alienated by the city, Ena's homesickness is acute, a feeling compounded by visions of her dead partner. She returns to her village, no longer bathed in a golden glow but rendered uncanny – bare trees, and a mist shrouding the scene of the drowning. Like other films in these final years, the mood in Brauer's film is ominous. The environment made strange connects it visually and thematically with *Magdalenenbaum* in which the tree of the title is seen backlit and similarly surrounded by fog (Fig. 13.3). The composition is portentous; we expect the worst. These images, which recall the still otherworldliness of Caspar David Friedrich, are a prompt for melancholic reflection on lives lost and uncertain futures, the significance of which extends far beyond the rural locations.

Ruin (n. & v.)

Caspar David Friedrich is not only cited, albeit obliquely, in the eerie images in the films mentioned above; he also serves as an absent reference in other films that share a similar fascination with ruins. What do the ruins frequently seen in these films connote? A nostalgic memory of what one was – mnemonic disrupture, ghostly landmarks? Ruins in cultural memory are often a cause for sorrow,

Figure 13.3: The GDR province as ethereal environment in *Der Magdalenenbaum* (1989) © DEFA-Stiftung/Waltraut Pathenheimer.

for melancholic, metaphysical reflection and sensitive contemplation caused by material disintegration, prompts to consider 'the destruction of the spiritual form by the effect of natural forces, that reversal of the typical order' as Simmel saw it.[18] While nature's reclamation comes into play in some of the images seen (a manor house slowly disappearing amid the leaves in *Abschiedsdisco*, overgrown cemeteries and so on), the films' images emphasize human agency – either as conscious destruction (in the form of what planners today euphemistically term 'clearance' and in the deracination and excavation) or wilful neglect (abandonment as the will/prelude to decay). Ruin is a constant theme and visual motif in several films. Were the fascination only on material, manmade decay, on disintegrating buildings, empty properties or abandoned objects, one might consider the films to fetishize decay. But the films do not indulge ruin-gazing, are not simply interested in the sublime beauty of nature's ascendancy, though the images are usually at the halfway point to elimination: the object has not yet fully disappeared beneath the moss or lichen or leaves. This is not the 'pleasure of ruins' as Rose Macaulay termed it, often characterized by a nostalgic and melancholic gaze, a yearning for an imagined or remembered past.[19] As important as the ruined architecture seen is the way in which man, in gaining complete mastery over the environment, is no longer 'the accomplice of nature' but the architect of ruin.[20] In films by Losansky and by Rocha, areas are finally rendered wasteland; nothing will remain. The inhabitants vanish and as the topsoil disappears so, too, do the trees, the grass, the bushes; even colours fade as the environmental palette is reduced to brown and ochre and grey. The regions seen in *Sehnsucht* and *Der Magdalenenbaum* are not yet ruined but we infer them to be on the eve of destruction.

This is not wanton destruction of course but a requirement of progress (and in this respect the films unwittingly foreshadow the post-industrial transformation of the region after 1989); the transfiguration of landscape and the displacement of communities constitute the collateral damage of a mining operation intended to support the wider national community – certainly this was the tenor of official rhetoric, which informs the narration heard in earlier documentary films. At the tail end of the GDR's existence, and in DEFA's later films, such optimistic rationalization seemed more and more far-fetched. Satirizing party rhetoric was not impossible in the GDR but nor was it without risk. In DEFA's final films, those made by a studio that briefly survived its state, we frequently hear socialist newspeak with its reliance on acronyms and grandiloquence lampooned. In *Der Strass*, a photojournalist attempts to explain why a dancer is worthy of an article by utilizing the official idiom; as he talks, the words are lost to a stirring soundtrack and the background transforms from the editor's office to a giant GDR flag, against which the speaker is seen making his speech. Similar satirical moments are to be found in Jörg Foth's *Letztes aus der DaDaeR* [*Latest from the Da-Da-eR*, 1990] and *Grönland*, though such satirical play will become deictic, increasingly difficult to decode for those unfamiliar with the original lexis. In *Abschiedsdisco* Henning's father also parrots official lines, albeit unenthusiastically and apparently sceptical of his own rhetoric, when his son, in what amounts to a further example of the theme of betrayal, discovers that he is involved in evacuating the area. As with the relocated villagers in Tetzlaff's film, all he can do is take with him the village sign as a final remnant, a symbol whose displaced presence represents a double absence – of the sign to a village that no longer exists and here one may see the film as anticipating themes and actions that foreshadow certain 'ostalgic' impulses.

Anticipation was an abiding feature of life in the GDR. The singer Wolf Biermann had provocatively taken up the theme in his song 'Warte nicht auf beßre Zeiten' ['Do not wait for better times'] in 1973, at a time when a call for action, not words, still seemed appropriate. Charity Scribner has commented on anticipation in relation to Heiner Müller's notion of a pervasive 'waiting-room mentality', an outlook conditioned by stasis (as opposed to the west's forward momentum) that allowed for greater phenomenological awareness.[21] The anticipation in these films means something quite different; it is the anticipation of obsolescence, an obsolescence that, later confirmed, would preoccupy many (mainly East German) filmmakers in the years after unification. Holding on to remnants in order to sustain, or facilitate, some connection to the past prefigures the reification of everyday GDR-era objects following unification and the new desirability of quotidian artefacts. Ruin, to be understood as object and action (the architectural remnants as well as that which is ruined, i.e. the landscape, the ideology), represents not simply the past but a present becoming past, as well as a lost future – certainly this is the tone that informs the melancholic mood in films by Koepp, Ackermann, Brandt, Honert and others. It was not always thus. Ruins had long been a feature of the GDR. Where the postwar rubble and the remains of the past had in the early days of the GDR constituted a challenge, were an exhortation to be cleared or rescued and rebuilt for a state fixated on progress (and the early DEFA films abound with sites of destruction), the ruins and extirpation frequently seen in the final films now figure as the wreckage of a state, the atrophy of its ideals.

Just as Müller saw some potential in the state's inertia, some commentators see some emancipatory potential in the past. Žižek for example, argues that the past 'contains hidden, non-realized potentials, and the authentic future is the repetition/retrieval of this past, not of the past as it was, but of those elements in the past which the past itself, in its reality, betrayed, stifled, failed to realize'.[22] In *Ruins of Modernity*, editors Julia Hell and Andreas Schönle argue: 'The reality of ruins at least calls forth a constructive, "manly" rhetoric of looking into the abyss, learning from our mistakes, confronting our enemies, and thus retroactively conferring some modicum of meaning to the senseless destruction'.[23] This well describes the significance of ruins in the SED's historical reflections. Ruins were invoked in the opening line of the GDR's national anthem – 'Auferstanden aus Ruinen' ('Risen from the ruins') – and underlined the past's relevance to the future in the second – 'Und der Zukunft zugewandt' ('And facing the future). Ruins served as a warning but also as cue for ongoing renewal, though the continued presence of ruins in the urban landscape decades after the war came to signify the GDR's material neglect and economic failure. Ruins dating back to the World War II in the GDR could thus also serve as reminders of the state's nonrenewal, while after 1989, ruins of the GDR-era variously represented failed potential, the failure of a system, or, increasingly, symbolized objects of poetic destruction and melancholic decay, as in Allora's and Calzadilla's film, *How To Appear Invisible* (2009).

The focus on ruins and ruination in films such as *Schmerzen der Lausitz*, *Abschiedsdisco* and others is, however, much less a prompt for reflecting on what can be learned or simply an aesthetic fascination with past things, and much more a melancholic contemplation on the state's failure and the elimination of hope. When, in *Märkische Ziegel*, Volker Koepp juxtaposes footage of the same brick factory from the 1950s with the images he has shot, he is presenting visual evidence of the GDR's original aspirations and eventual failure. Here, too, ruins are a theme. The opening narration references the ruin/renewal motif, noting that the bricks produced at the small town of Zehdenick were sent up to Berlin after the war to help rebuild the city; the current working conditions and the employees' deflated mood provide a counter-narrative to the older film's exuberant voiceover and the site's historical significance. Koepp captures a choral group standing in the street singing Heine's 'Lorelei'. In the lyrics Heine's narrator claims not to know the origin of his sadness: 'Ich weiß nicht, was soll es bedeuten, / Daß ich so traurig bin' ('I do not know why it should be | That I am so sad'). The ballad's 'sense of longing for an irretrievable past' assumes a significance that transcends sentimental nostalgia and is well suited to the mood of the film's subjects as it invokes a melancholy that here has a clearly understood, if never articulated, object.[24] The camera shifts from the singers on the town hall steps to the near empty streets adjacent. Koepp reinforces the gulf between past and present: in contrast to the earlier documentary and the focus on people, purpose and activity, these images are characterized by absence and inertia.

Conclusion

The quotidian fears of recrimination and punishment were naturally more acute in a state so tightly regulated as was the GDR, but the films under discussion here are less a testament to those fears than they are representative of a pervasive melancholia, one that comprises complex, even contradictory emotions in response to the region's finitude, personal loss, and physical and psychological exhaustion. Protagonists in the post-unification films and since are prone to geographical and cultural disorientation – themes that, surprisingly perhaps, connect comedies and dramas (from early treatments in the 1990s such as Peter Timm's comedy hit *Go Trabi Go* (1991), or Andreas Kleinert's *Wege in die Nacht* [*Paths in the Night*, 1999] to Christian Schwochow's 2013 film *Westen* [*West*]). The sites through which characters in many of the films pass are ghost sites: abandoned border watchtowers, empty factories, deserted buildings. Scarred landscapes, derelict industries and premises are the markers of a state that has crumbled, its leaders and custodians dispersed, imprisoned or redeployed, the symbols of a past rendered a foreign country. Ruins and debris confirm the end imagined and outlined in the earlier films. In the films discussed above, though, death has either not yet taken place, or is happening. The melancholy that characterizes many of the narratives is partly a response to what appears to be inevitable, death, *pace* Brecht, as the only thing certain in life. Such melancholy anticipates the mood identified in much post-unification discourse, whether the 'melancholic paralysis' of scholars who, as Julia Hell suggests, indulge 'in memories of a lost country in which their dreams had been so heavily invested' or the melancholic tone of post-GDR literature.[25] Melancholy is the undercurrent, too, of the much discussed and too easily dismissed phenomenon of 'ostalgia' (*Ostalgie*), which, as Peter Thompson has argued, represents more than mere nostalgia and 'is actually a longing for a future that went missing in the past rather than for a past that never had a socialist or communist future'.[26]

Ruins in the DEFA films made while the GDR still existed thus connote 'the slow cancellation of the future', the end of (GDR) time and place, though unification would accelerate its termination.[27] In films such as Rocha's and Losanky's the end of place is the result of progressive policy. Space is reconceived as the sites are reordered; in some cases places and times overlap and the past is palimpsest (as with the GDR-era graffiti on a Wilhelmine-era building in Rocha's film made as one state dissolves into another). In others, there are no physical signs of the past as places are obliterated (as in the physical destruction that accompanies mining) to exist only as ghostly imaginings or in fragments, dislocated and relocated (as in the remnants of the villages adorning *Plattenbau* rooms). The films, for as long as they exist, may serve as the final record, but they are objects of melancholy not just in the terms Susan Sontag suggests in her discussion of photography as a means of preserving the past, freezing time and place, but also of capturing its dissolution.[28]

It is hard to resist a teleological reading of films made towards the end of the GDR, hard not to see in them the sense of an ending, some foresight that the state is edging towards extinction. Reflecting on interpretations of the GDR, Christoph Dieckmann has noted that '1989 is always the punchline, as though right from the start history had inevitably been heading towards this conclusion'.[29] We would do well to remember, however, that the GDR's disintegration was unexpected; it was not an event waiting to happen, tempting though it is to try to identify the hairline systemic cracks that would result in structural collapse. Surveys in the West (naturally there were no such files in the East) confirm that few anticipated seeing unification in their lifetime. That the wall was breached was as much about crucial non-intervention (thanks to Gorbachev) as it was about comical misunderstanding (thanks to Schabowski). Rather than seeing in these pre-1989 films some anticipation of the state's collapse, we should perhaps consider them as an index of a particular mood – of a weariness and pessimism discernible across much East German art, particularly in the second half of the state's life (though some might argue has its roots in the German condition). It is worth noting that most of the filmmakers discussed here were born before the state was founded. For many these were among the last films made; whether intended or not, the end of the GDR signified the end of several careers (and that includes film personnel and actors). In contrast to the younger generation, the so-called *Nachwuchs*, many of whom would struggle to make films at all, most of the directors could look back on an ample portfolio. Most of the films being made or released in the GDR's final months were superseded by events; the political ruptures rendered them obsolete and diminished any impact they might otherwise have had – a fate that would also befall the lost generation's final DEFA films. The director Dietmar Hochmuth was ruefully aware of this when he commented, 'Who is going to pay D-Marks after July [i.e. after currency reform] to see a DEFA film?'[30] His misgivings would prove well founded. But twenty-five years later, the earlier films discussed here have acquired a new significance, providing us with the final reflections of a state at the end of its days.

Nick Hodgin is a lecturer in German and Film studies at the University of Sheffield. He has published widely on German film, including *Screening the East. Heimat, Memory and Nostalgia in German film since 1989* (2011), and the co-edited *The GDR Remembered. Representations of the East German State since 1989* (2011). He is currently co-editing books on the filmmaker Andreas Dresen (Lang, 2016) and on international trauma cinema (Palgrave, 2016).

Notes

1. Volker Braun, 'Durchgearbeitete Landschaft', in Volker Braun, *Gegen die symmetrische Welt. Gedichte*, Frankfurt am Main: Suhrkamp, 1974, p. 34. My translations here and throughout.
2. One interviewee, who is operating the excavator (better known as the singer-songwriter Gerhard Gundermann) offers some interesting commentary, using the opportunity to talk less about local issues than about wider issues to do with the West, a subject about which he became even more critical after unification. He would keep his work even when his musical career could have sustained him, a strenuous dual career that may have contributed to his early death aged forty-two in 1998. See [no author] 'Sänger ohne Schutzengel', *Der Spiegel*, 29 June 1998, p. 179.
3. Cited in Nick Hodgin, *Screening the East. Heimat, Memory and Nostalgia in German film since 1989*, Oxford: Berghahn, 2011, p. 66.
4. Jacqui Hope, 'Environmentalism and its Cultural Transformation in the German Democratic Republic: Poetry and Fictional Prose', in Axel Goodbody (ed), *The Culture of German Environmentalism*, New York and Oxford: Berghahn, 2002, pp. 153–71, p. 157.
5. Kurt Tetzlaff, 'Wir waren besessen von der Arbeit', in Ingrid Poss, Anne Richter and Christiane Mückenberger (eds), *Das Prinzip Neugier. DEFA-Dokumentarfilmer erzählen*, Berlin: Neues Leben, 2012, pp. 157–93 (p. 176).
6. For more on Tetzlaff's film see Nick Hodgin, 'Alternative Realities and Authenticity in DEFA's Documentary Films', in Marc Silberman and Henning Wrage (eds), *DEFA at the Crossroads of East German and International Film Culture. A Companion*, Berlin, Boston: de Gruyter, 2014, pp. 281–304.
7. Mary Cosgrove, 'Introduction: Sadness and Melancholy in German-Language Literature from the Seventeenth Century to the Present. An Overview', in Mary Cosgrove and Anne Richards (eds),

Sadness and Melancholy in German-Language Literature from the Seventeenth Century to the Present [= Edinburgh German Yearbook, 6], Rochester NY: Camden House, 2012, pp.1-19 (p.1).
8. Kate Connolly, 'Melancholie und Pessimismus', *Der Freitag*, 30 September 2012 [= https://www.freitag.de/autoren/kraut-sourcing/melancholie-und-pessimismus], accessed 14 March 2016.
9. Stefan Klein, 'Mythos schöpferische Melancholie', *Süddeutsche Zeitung*, 25 October 2012 [= http://www.sueddeutsche.de/gesundheit/kreativitaet-und-niedergeschlagenheit-schoepferische-melancholie-ist-ein-mythos-1.1505245], accessed 14 March 2016.
10. Jana Hensel, 'Der Fremde Blick', *Der Spiegel*, 9 November 2009, pp. 134-35.
11. Sigmund Freud, 'Mourning and Melancholia', in James Strachey (ed and trans.), *The Standard Edition of the Complete Psychological Works of Sigmund Freud*, 24 vols., London: Hogarth Press, 1953, vol. 14, pp. 243-58.
12. See Nick Hodgin, 'Cannibals, Carnival and Clowns. The Grotesque in German Unification Films', *Studies in Eastern European Cinema* 5.2 (2014), 124-38. For more on the DEFA films made after the state had dissolved see Reinhild Steingröver, *Last Features. East German Cinema's Lost Generation*, Rochester NY: Camden House, 2014.
13. Barton Byg, 'What Might Have Been. DEFA Films of the Past and the Future of German Cinema', *Cineaste* 17. 4 (1990), 9-15. Dieter Wolf, *Gruppe Babelsberg – Unsere nichtgedrehten Filme*, Berlin: Das Neue Berlin, 2000.
14. See in Elke Schieber, 'Anfang vom Ende oder Kontinuitat des Argwohns 1980 bis 1989', in Ralf Schenk (ed), *Das zweite Leben der Filmstadt Babelsberg. DEFA-Spielfilme 1946-92*, Berlin: Henschel, 1994, pp. 265-326, p. 316.
15. See Nick Hodgin, '"Only one noble topic remained: the workers". Sympathy and subversion in Jürgen Böttcher's *Arbeiterfilme*', *Studies in Eastern European Cinema* 6.1 (2015), 49-63.
16. See Karen Leeder, '"After the Massacre of Illusions". Specters of the GDR in the work of Volker Braun', in Anne Fuchs and Kathleen James Chakraborty (eds), *Transformations of German Cultural Identity 1989-2009*, [Special edition of] *New German Critique* 116 (2012), 103-18.
17. Jurij Koch, *Der Kirschbaum*, Halle: Mitteldeutscher Verlag, 1984.
18. Georg Simmel, 'Two Essays. The Handle, and The Ruin', *Hudson Review* 11.3 (1958), 371-85 (382).
19. Rose Macaulay, *Pleasure of Ruins*, London: Thames and Hudson, 1953.
20. Simmel, 380.
21. Charity Scribner, *Requiem for Communism*, Cambridge: MIT, 2003, p. 127.
22. Slavoj Žižek, *In Defense of Lost Causes*, London: Verso, 2008, p. 141.
23. Julia Hell and Andreas Schönle, 'Introduction', in Julia Hell and Andreas Schönle (eds), *Ruins of Modernity*, Durham, NC: Duke University Press, 2010, pp.1-14 (p. 5).
24. Kari Lokke, 'The Romantic Fairy Tale', in Michael Ferber (ed), *A Companion to European Romanticism*, Malden, MA: Blackwell, 2005, pp.138-57 (p. 150).
25. Julia Hell, *Post-fascist Fantasies. Psychoanalysis, History, and the Literature of East Germany*, Durham and London: Duke University Press, 1997, p.1. See Anna O'Driscoll, 'Melancholy and Historical Loss. Post-unification Portrayals of GDR Writers and Artists', in Nick Hodgin and Caroline Pearce (eds), *The GDR Remembered. Representations of the East German State Since 1989*, Rochester NY: Camden House, 2011, pp. 37-54; and Franziska Meyer, 'The Past Is Another Country and the Country Is Another Past. Sadness in East German Texts by Jakob Hein and Julia Schoch', in Mary Cosgrove and Anne Richards (eds), *Sadness and Melancholy in German-Language Literature from the Seventeenth Century to the Present*. [= Edinburgh German Yearbook, 6], Rochester, NY: Camden House, 2012, pp. 173-92.

26. Peter Thompson, 'Worin noch niemand war: The GDR as Retrospectively Imagined Community', in Nick Hodgin and Caroline Pearce (eds), *The GDR Remembered. Representations of the East German State since 1989*, Rochester NY: Camden House, 2011, pp. 250–66, p. 252. See also Scribner.
27. Franco Berardi, *After the Future*, edited by Gary Genosko and Nicholas Thoburn, trans. Arianna Bove et al., Oakland: AK Press, 2011, p. 13. Beradi's focus is on capitalism but he does argue that 'all the different families of modern political theory share a common certainty: notwithstanding the darkness of the present, the future will be bright'.
28. Susan Sontag, *On Photography*, London: Farrar, Straus & Giroux, 1973.
29. Christoph Dieckmann, 'Kurt Maetzigs Mail', *Die Zeit*, no. 34, 16 August 2012, p. 12.
30. Hans-Dieter Tok, 'Bissig und bösartig, komisch und ironisch', *Leipziger Volkszeitung*, 16 July 1990.

CHAPTER 14

DEFA's Antifascist Myth Revisited

KLK an PTX – Die Rote Kapelle
[*KLK calling PTX – The Red Orchestra,* 1971]

Sebastian Heiduschke

On 25 March 1971, the premiere of Horst E. Brandt's cinematic extravaganza *KLK an PTX – Die Rote Kapelle* [*KLK Calling PTX – The Red Orchestra*] took place in what, with 1001 seats, was the GDR's largest cinema, the Kosmos, on East Berlin's Karl-Marx-Allee. Even before shooting had begun, Brandt's epic film about underground opposition to the Hitler regime was conceived as an antifascist blockbuster. The conditions – both technical and financial – under which the film was made confirm that DEFA intended *KLK an PTX* to be a special contribution to the history of East German cinema. It was one of only nine films released by DEFA to be made using the expensive 70mm format (rather than the regular 35mm), and was captured on the best ORWO film stock available to the studio at the time.[1] In addition, it featured a star-studded cast with hundreds of extras, had a running time of over 170 minutes, and cost more than six million marks (at a time when one million marks was the norm for most films).[2] Its production was extensively documented in the East German popular press, and its release was positively reviewed across all media outlets in the GDR.

The impact of *KLK an PTX* was remarkable. On its release, the East German press staged an extensive campaign to boost the film's reception, while West German print media and television countered with their own (very different) interpretation of the Red Orchestra's role in Germany's history. Even since reunification, *KLK an PTX* continues to prompt a range of responses (both written and visual) proving that it remains a pivotal work and one that still provokes strong reactions on the part of contemporary viewers.[3]

KLK an PTX, as a review in the Cologne weekly newspaper *Rheinischer Merkur* observed, was intended 'first, as part of an ongoing process of painting communist agents and spies in a positive light; second, as part of an increasingly frenetic communist propaganda campaign designed to inspire hatred of the allegedly "imperialist" Federal Republic of Germany; and third, it was supposed to inspire not only the "struggle against imperialism", but also communist "solidarity" in the drive towards a united popular front led by the communists'.[4] An East German journalist reviewing the film in the television guide *FF dabei* in 1972 described the film's subject matter as an issue of national significance: 'The Red Orchestra – it was originally intended as a term of abuse. But it became a term of distinction that referred to what was one of the largest and most forceful and influential antifascist resistance organizations fighting for a better Germany'.[5] This yearning for a better Germany, as this and other reviews in the East German press claimed, was eventually realized in the formation of the GDR.

The production history of *KLK an PTX* provides a number of insights into the way the film was deployed in the cultural and political context of the late 1960s and early 1970s to re-establish the foundational myth of the GDR as the antifascist Germany (in clear opposition to the Federal Republic), and to do this precisely at a moment in history when détente and a growing rapprochement between the GDR and the Federal Republic seemed to have blurred the political fault lines established by the Cold War. Initially, *KLK an PTX* appeared to be almost an anachronism within DEFA's feature film output of the late 1960s and early 1970s, as it reinstated the thematic cluster of a mutually beneficial relationship between Germans and Soviets as an integral component of the antifascist film genre. *KLK an PTX* fetishized the members of the Red Orchestra as antifascist resistance fighters and communist spies who relayed critical information about troop movements to the Soviet Union via radio transmitters (called 'music boxes' in Soviet intelligence jargon, with the radio operators called 'musicians'). The release of a film with a clear ideological message together with the depiction of a strong and united communist resistance movement against Hitler was designed to reaffirm not only the GDR's commitment to socialism and antifascism, but also to codify its loyalty to the Soviet Union at a critical time of identity crisis for the state.

The portrayal of the Red Orchestra in *KLK an PTX* transformed the resistance movement into something that, in reality, it was not – a centrally-organized communist spy ring – and sent a message that resonated both internationally and domestically. The myth of the Red Orchestra as an essentially communist-led organization was accepted in both the Federal Republic and the GDR (the West branding its members as German traitors and the East celebrating them as heroes) which made it possible for DEFA to exploit the film as an uncontroversial means of cementing the friendship with the Soviet Union while at the same time avoiding any real risk of jeopardizing the progress of détente. Ernst Thälmann, the communist leader sent to a concentration camp for his political beliefs (and the subject of two major DEFA biopics in 1954 and 1955),[6] had become the key figure around which the GDR's foundational myth had been constructed; yet, as a committed communist, he remained unacceptable as an antifascist figurehead in the West. By the same token, West German myths of military resistance (such as that surrounding Claus von Stauffenberg and others in the German military who participated in the 20 July 1944 assassination attempt on Hitler), and bourgeois resistance (by the *Weiße Rose/White Rose* group who resisted Hitler on religious grounds), were clearly at odds with the GDR's (Marxist-Leninist) concept of antifascism.

The Red Orchestra, however, was regarded on both sides of the Iron Curtain as a resistance movement led by communists. East Germans and West Germans alike believed that it had been a single spy organization consisting of hundreds of members operating all across Europe who relayed military secrets via radio to the Soviet Union. Reports by the Gestapo and extremely dubious statements by high-ranking German officers interrogated after the war were simply accepted as true; because of the way these documents were exploited during the Cold War, the Red Orchestra itself was subjected to a process of mythologization that made it impossible to distinguish between fact and fiction. Consisting of, at best, a number of loosely connected groups, the Red Orchestra never existed in the form of a centrally organized movement. *KLK an PTX*, however, makes no effort to point out to the viewer that its focus is exclusively on the activities of what had become known as the Schulze-Boysen/Harnack Group (named after the three founding members, the couple Harro and Libertas Schulze-Boysen and Arvid Harnack, who lived in Berlin). Harro and Arvid were active in the Nazi state apparatus; they had joined the Nazi party, but worked against the system from within. Harro was a member of Hermann Göring's staff, who had been recruited by the intelligence department in the Reich Aviation Ministry in 1934 because of his linguistic skills. Arvid worked in the Reich Economic Ministry as a senior executive officer. Neither knew each other until the couple Greta and Adam Kuckhoff introduced them and brought their respective circles of friends together. United by their common desire to stop the Nazis, the two groups started organized activities in 1939.

Although the Schulze-Boysen/Harnack Group was primarily involved in subversive acts of civil disobedience, such as distributing anti-Nazi leaflets or sticking notices on advertising pillars, some of the information obtained at their workplaces was delivered to contacts who, in turn, passed on the information to the Soviet Union and the United States of America. For example, 'information on German currency and economy, investments abroad, and foreign debt and trade agreements'[7] was given to the US intelligence officer Donald Heath.[8] The group received the nickname 'Red Orchestra' as a result of delivering some information to Soviet spies who then transmitted the information provided by the Schulze-Boysen/Harnack Group to Moscow via two-way radio. The German Reich's Main Security Office (the RHSA) had assigned the operative name 'Rote Kapelle' (Red Orchestra) to a pro-Soviet Union radio espionage network that was operating in western and central Europe. 'The orchestra's radio operators were "pianists", their transmitters "pianos", and their supervisors "conductors"'.[9] When the RHSA intercepted a radio message, they also obtained the names of Schulze-Boysen and Harnack. The Gestapo arrested them and other members of the Schulze-Boysen/Harnack group as members of the Red Orchestra, accusing them of espionage for the Soviet Union. The leaders of the group were executed on 22 December 1942, while a number of others were imprisoned but subsequently released due to lack of evidence.

Confusion surrounding the RHSA's name for the group bolstered the myth of the Red Orchestra, the name used thereafter to refer to the Schulze-Boysen/Harnack group (even though the Gestapo had arrested members from other resistance groups as well). Now known as the Red Orchestra, the Schulze-Boysen/Harnack group also came to be seen by the Nazis primarily as a communist resistance group (which of course was far from the truth). Moreover, in a bizarre postwar development, a number of German detainees continued to lend credence to the idea that the Red Orchestra had been a communist organization. When questioned by US forces, the former NS judge Manfred Roeder, the lawyer Alexander Kraell, and the Rear Admiral Karl-Jesko von Puttkamer all talked at length about acts of espionage alleged to have been carried out by members of the Red Orchestra; in the process, the detainees often invented spurious details, such as knowledge of the Russian and French language, or the occurrence of orgies where activists supposedly gained access to classified material. Fuelled by such testimony, the former resistance organization came to be regarded as a 'Bolshevist Organization for Treason and High Treason' in 1968. With the onset of the Cold

War, the myth of a communist spy organization was exactly what both the Soviet/East German and the US/West German political agendas needed.

In the GDR, the myth of the Red Orchestra was developed into a memorial to an antifascist struggle that, proceeding in sync with the efforts of its 'big brother', the Soviet Union, had succeeded in liberating Germany; in short, the activities of the group were not acts of treason, but heroic deeds worthy of being remembered at a time of postwar political crisis. Accordingly, at this moment of rapprochement between the Federal Republic and the GDR, the film *KLK an PTX* gave the press an opportunity to divert public attention away from the contemporary politics of cooperation with its Western neighbour and refocus it on the GDR's foundational narrative as the 'better' Germany. The political shift of 1969 in the Federal Republic (after twenty-five years in power, the conservative CDU had been replaced in government by the more liberal/left-leaning SPD) and the changing political dynamic triggered by a process of rapprochement between the two German nations was, for the GDR at least, a double-edged sword. On the one hand, the new doctrine of *Ostpolitik* allowed it to enter into diplomatic and economic relations with nations that, up until then, had only had ties with the Federal Republic;[10] on the other hand, rapprochement with the Federal Republic only a few months after the Soviet invasion of Czechoslovakia had brought political reforms there to a halt, was at best problematic and risked souring existing relations with the Soviet Union itself.

All of these concerns are addressed in *KLK an PTX* which announces its commitment to antifascism quite unambiguously in its opening sequence. The film opens in the then contemporary East Berlin of October 1969 with the ceremonial reopening of the Neue Wache on Unter den Linden and the changing of the guard – an event attended by large crowds of (presumably) East German onlookers (Fig. 14.1). Whereas in the prewar era the Neue Wache had been used to honour the dead of World War I, following its remodelling in 1969, it had been fitted out with a glass prism and an eternal flame to commemorate 'the victims of fascism and militarism'; this re-editing of the narrative of history had the effect of defining this public site of memory as something that was, above all, East German – a claim that was further emphasized by scheduling the re-dedication of the space to coincide with the twentieth anniversary of the founding of the GDR. Including such documentary footage as an establishing shot in *KLK an PTX* serves a number of purposes. First, it references the foundational myth of antifascism as the film's overarching thematic strand while affirming the GDR's ongoing commitment to this ideal. Second, it invites the viewer to draw a distinction between the process of memorialization embodied in the Neue Wache in East Berlin, and the annual commemoration of German soldiers who lost their lives in the two World Wars that was centred around existing war memorials in the Federal Republic. In the context of 1971, the year of the film's release, the sequence showing the rededication of the Neue Wache underlines the fundamental ideological difference between the GDR and its neighbour. Finally, inclusion of contemporary documentary footage links the activities of the Red Orchestra to the history of the GDR and implies that there is a correlation between their wartime work as Soviet spies and the existence of the present-day GDR as a sovereign, free and antifascist nation. As the screenwriters of *KLK an PTX,* Wera and Claus Küchenmeister, note in an early treatment for the film: 'It is crucially important that the audience can follow the feelings of our comrades along with the correct political insights, which have been borne out by the existence of our Republic, along with the dramatic action and the adventurous spirit of many of our heroes'.[11]

Instead of producing a counter-narrative to the widely accepted notion in the West that the Red Orchestra was a communist spy ring, the GDR embraced this narrative and developed it further by transforming the members of the group into socialist heroes (thereby embedding the organization into that system of antifascist myths from which the GDR emerged as the state that had done most to come to terms with the legacy of Hitler). Wera and Claus Küchenmeister created a script for director Horst E. Brandt that was designed to play up the (allegedly) major role of communists in the organization. Some seventeen members of the Red Orchestra

Figure 14.1:   Changing of the guard at the Neue Wache, Berlin, in *KLK an PTX* (1971). DVD screen capture.

are introduced during the first hour of the film; and by the end some of them have yet to meet all the other protagonists participating in its activities.[12] Through character sketches that are often juxtaposed (though not always interwoven), the audience is introduced to air force officer Harro Schulze-Boysen, economist Arvid Harnack, dramaturge Adam Kuckhoff, artist Kurt Schumacher, author Walter Küchenmeister and John Sieg, the editor of the communist newspaper *Rote Fahne*, to name but some. The short subplots provide glimpses of the protagonists in their everyday environments. They cover roughly a decade of resistance activities against the Nazis, and include printing leaflets with details about concentration camps, putting up anti-Nazi flyers on walls, stealing military secrets and transmitting information to the Soviet Union using the call sign 'KLK to PTX'. The story begins in the year 1932, just months before the National Socialists became the strongest party in Germany, and ends ten years later with the arrest of many members of the Red Orchestra (leaving out, in the process, many details regarding their trial and execution). Key moments are often exaggerated for dramatic effect, such as the sequence in which Schulze-Boysen searches his superior's office to find classified documents.[13] Historical accuracy, however, was not uppermost in the minds of the two scriptwriters; and, as a note to the studio management reveals, the Küchenmeisters often took considerable liberties with actual events, and invented large portions of the plot in order to foreground particular political aspects: 'A film about the Red Orchestra is not a historical film. It should radiate the revolutionary spirit of our comrades that still impacts upon the present'.[14] For the Küchenmeisters, the story of the Red Orchestra was one that needed to be manipulated if it was to function within the traditions of GDR antifascist cinema and extend these traditions in a way acceptable within the changing political environment of the 1970s.

On the other side of the Iron Curtain, the story of the Red Orchestra had surfaced much earlier as the subject of a number of monographs published in the late 1940s and 1950s.[15] Articles in popular news magazines such as *Stern* and *Der Spiegel* soon followed, in which the Red Orchestra was referred to as a communist spy organization. The author of a 1951 essay in *Stern*, for instance, claimed to have uncovered the supposed 'secrets' of the Red Orchestra: 'It is impossible to offer an overview of the Soviet espionage network in Europe without considering the case of the "Red Orchestra". Under this name, the most influential group of Kremlin agents in Germany was crushed and judged'.[16] *Der Spiegel* published a slightly more balanced account in a nine-week special series authored by Heinz Höhne and

Gilles Perrault, using excerpts of Perrault's book about the Red Orchestra.[17] Yet, even this series of articles was based on the Gestapo papers and interviews with former Nazi party members and did not yield any new discoveries[18] – much like the 1972 seven-part television co-production involving partners from Germany (ARD), Italy (RAI) and France (ORTF). 'The History of a Spy Ring', as the series of articles in *Der Spiegel* was entitled, merely rehearsed conventional Cold War positions and contributed to a still lingering distrust of East German politics (much as *KLK an PTX* had done the year before).

There was little need to present an alternative ('socialist') view of the Red Orchestra in the GDR. With their emphasis on the Red Orchestra's communist roots, West German productions and publications had played into the hands of the GDR and fostered its preferred interpretation of the organization's 'history'. The situation changed in 1967, when the BBC approached Greta Kuckhoff (a former member of the group and the widow of Adam Kuckhoff) with a request for an interview about the Red Orchestra and its role in the resistance.[19] Fearing that Kuckhoff might reveal the true nature of the Red Orchestra in such an interview, the GDR Ministry for State Security intervened. Kuckhoff, according to the official reply to the BBC, was unable to participate in an interview due to illness. Further attempts by the BBC to contact Greta Kuckhoff were similarly thwarted by the Ministry for State Security, who were anxious to protect the myth of the Red Orchestra. Shortly after these attempts, DEFA announced plans for a feature film based on a screenplay co-authored by Wera and Claus Küchenmeister. The BBC's interest may not have been directly responsible for the decision to make *KLK an PTX*; but it seems likely that it was influential in prompting the Ministry for State Security to prioritize the production of a film about the Red Orchestra.

The involvement of the Ministry in this DEFA project is evident in the choice of director and screenwriters. Even though the film's budget at some six million marks was about six times the normal budget allocated to a movie, DEFA did not select a veteran director such as Kurt Maetzig to oversee the production. Instead, the film was given to Horst E. Brandt, who up until that point had worked as cinematographer for the series of satirical short films known as *Stacheltier*. Brandt seemed to be the ideal director: someone who would be sufficiently flattered by being entrusted with such a big project that he could be manipulated, or at least influenced, to accept political guidance in adhering closely to the ideologically prepared script with which he was provided. Written by Wera and Claus Küchenmeister, two committed socialists with ample experience in the production of newsreels, documentaries and politically slanted feature films, the screenplay had already been in the planning stages for some time. The screenwriters readily agreed to collaborate when approached by the Ministry of State Security.[20] This may have been for personal reasons, as Claus's younger brother Rainer had been arrested (as a sixteen-year-old) as one of the youngest members of the Red Orchestra, and his father Walter had been executed by the Gestapo;[21] or it may simply have been for professional reasons and the belief that working on this film would ensure future commissions.

Preparations started with a press campaign spanning several years – one involving DEFA and the press in both the GDR and the Soviet Union – to commemorate the real members of the Red Orchestra, were followed by a tour of the screenwriters to publicize their screenplay, and concluded with media coverage of the film before its official release date. Nearly two years before the film's release on 25 March 1971, GDR audiences were being groomed for the film. In a first step, the *Berliner Zeitung* published an article by Karl-Heinz Biernat entitled 'Sie kämpften für Deutschland' ('They fought for Germany'), in which the author sketches a picture of the members of the Red Orchestra as national heroes.[22] The article does not yet mention any significant anniversary in connection with the Red Orchestra; but it was published in the context of discussions relating to preparations for the twentieth anniversary of the GDR on 7 October 1969. By foregrounding the members of the Red Orchestra, Biernat carefully places them in the context of communist resistance organizations, stressing that the 'core [of such organizations] consisted of communists'.[23] In the weeks to follow, the GDR press followed up with a series of articles in quick succession. On 28 October, *Neues Deutschland* retold the story, this time highlighting the Orchestra's 'patriotic fight for the home of socialism ... and its striving for the unity of the working class' and reiterating to readers that the group's 'legacy was in excellent hands'.[24] Just a couple of weeks later, in November 1969, a further article in the *Berliner Zeitung* ensured that the story and the members of the group remained in people's minds.[25] At the end of that same year, the report of an event in which members of the Red Orchestra were awarded a number of Soviet medals for their engagement as 'antifascist resistance fighters' appeared in *Neues Deutschland*.[26] It is unclear if the award of these medals was an orchestrated move and/or was bound with the increasing press coverage in GDR; however, at the very least, the front page billing together with two pages of photos and biographies of the twenty-nine members of the Red Orchestra suggests that the intention was to anchor the names and faces of the group firmly in the public imagination with a view to reviving the myth of a close collaboration between the group's members and the Soviet Union. By showcasing the medals (for the most part awarded posthumously), the GDR not only turned those members of the Red Orchestra who had lost their lives into martyrs for a greater cause, but also made them emblematic of a (future) GDR–Soviet friendship already anticipated during the latter stages of National Socialist rule. At the end of 1969, the Red Orchestra had become a staple in the GDR press, and the story of its members had been established as one of personal sacrifice in the service of antifascism and the drive towards a new model of socialist society under the leadership of the Soviet Union.

Almost simultaneously with press coverage of the 'historical' Red Orchestra, the GDR public learned about DEFA's plans for a film about the organization when, on 7 December 1969, *Neues Deutschland* included a report about Wera and Claus Küchenmeister's visit to a car manufacturing plant in Eisenach where they discussed parts of their screenplay for *KLK an PTX* with workers.[27] Interaction of this kind between workers and film artists was not uncommon in the GDR, and was seen as an aspect of a classless society in which the arts reflected the desires and realities of the working class. It is unlikely that the discussion forum involving the screenwriters and the mechanics in December 1969 would have triggered alterations to the screenplay or storyline; nevertheless, the relationship between the blue- and white-collar strata of East German society were in urgent need of a thorough reconceptualization at a time when 'the aesthetic principles underpinning socialist realism ... had lost their original meaning and degenerated into a set of empty, conventional forms'.[28]

Just as the staging of the screenwriting process was intended to give an impression of the active participation on the part of the working classes in the commemoration of antifascist heroes in the arts, so too were the shooting of the film and its official premiere both meticulously documented in a variety of GDR publications. A steady series of anecdotes targeted at film fans of all ages helped to create interest in a production that promised to become a GDR blockbuster. Readers of daily newspapers such as *Neue Zeit* learned about the 'genesis of a significant film about the struggle of the resistance',[29] while the FDJ paper *Junge Welt* informed young readers of the work of actress Barbara Adolph in Prague and Dresden by providing numerous stills from two scenes.[30] The SED newspaper *Neues Deutschland* stepped up the campaign shortly before the film's opening night by reminding its readers of the film's 'star-studded cast'.[31] Just days before the premiere, the GDR film magazine *Filmspiegel* ran an extensive feature on *KLK an PTX* as part of a final drive to remind readers of the imminent premiere.[32]

The film was a success in the eyes of critics and audiences – at least if we accept that reports about the public reception in the country's daily papers and magazines actually mirrored the true sentiments of the GDR population.[33] Immediately after the premiere, the well-known film critic Horst Knietzsch emphasized the political importance of the film in *Neues Deutschland*, suggesting that viewing this film was not simply a matter of entertainment but a political necessity for any GDR citizen.[34] Brief notes, detailed reports and letters written to the editors extolled its virtues. A letter published in *Neues Deutschland* on 28 March from Marina Jacobitz, an eleventh-grade student at the Berlin Oberschule Köpenick, claimed *KLK an PTX* was a film for a new generation of young East Germans who had benefited from the sacrifices of the Red Orchestra, and articulated the desire of all her classmates that her school be renamed after one of the heroes, Arvid Harnack.[35] Other letters, for instance those from Irene and Karl Harloff, 'members of the communist party since 1918', and from the office clerk Frank Drechsler, emphasized its universal appeal and far reaching impact on East German society.

KLK an PTX had been conceived as a mythologizing antifascist blockbuster that would fetishize the members of the Red Orchestra as Marxists, from the earliest stages of its planning through to the coverage of critical and public reception in the post-production press. Yet, in terms of the development of East German cinema as a whole, we can discern a shift in the way in which antifascist heroism is celebrated; for *KLK an PTX* abandons the monumentalist style and glorification of individual resistance in DEFA's Thälmann films of the 1950s, in favour of a new aesthetic of collective resistance and collaboration with the Soviet Union. However, this type of approach remained the exception, for with films such as Frank Beyer's *Jakob der Lügner* [*Jacob the Liar*, 1974] and Ulrich Weiß's *Dein unbekannter Bruder* [*Your Unknown Brother*, 1982], DEFA soon returned to the notion of the individual as victim and/or insurgent, and 'telling the stories of people who had risked their lives against an inhumane system'.[36]

The myth of the Red Orchestra as a communist resistance organization lasted well after German reunification. However, in 2003 the documentary *Die rote Kapelle* [*The Red Orchestra*], directed by the German-American artist and filmmaker Stefan Roloff, set out to retell the story of the Red Orchestra and to challenge the myths that had grown up around it. Based on archival research and interviews with survivors active in the Red Orchestra and family members of those who had been executed, *Die rote Kapelle* aims to correct history by showing that the Red Orchestra was not made up of a group of communist activists, but rather was a resistance movement consisting of friends united by a simple common goal, namely bringing about the end of National Socialism in Germany.

Die rote Kapelle stems from the desire to document a portion of the Roloff family history. Stefan Roloff, a German-American painter and film artist, stumbled upon the topic by accident when asking his ageing father, the former professional pianist Helmut Roloff, about his experiences during the Third Reich. Stefan filmed numerous conversations between 1997 and 2001, and in these interviews his father gradually revealed the story of how a group of friends decided to resist the National Socialist regime with acts of civil disobedience. Stefan Roloff then used these interviews as the basis for *Die rote Kapelle*, adding interviews with relatives of other members of the Schulze-Boysen/Harnack Group, with the French journalist Gilles Perrault (who in 1967 became the first person to publish his research on the group),[37] and with the director of the German Resistance Memorial Centre (Gedenkstätte Deutscher Widerstand), Johannes Tuchel. The result of these numerous conversations was the book and subsequent documentary, *Die rote Kapelle*, both of which were created not with a view to discrediting the DEFA film or clearing his father's name, but rather to 'prevent the resistance of the Red Orchestra against the National Socialist regime from being forgotten'.[38]

Even though it was not filmed in direct response to *KLK an PTX*, Roloff's documentary still offers a useful point of reference for a closer analysis of the cinematographic strategies deployed in DEFA's film. *Die rote Kapelle* is, in many ways, the cinematic antithesis of *KLK an PTX*. Whereas the storyline of Horst E. Brandt's film takes liberties with the actual events and writes an alternative history to fit the requirements of GDR historiography, *Die rote Kapelle* is based on archival research and expert testimony, and uses the genres of oral history and survivor testimony to propose a modified understanding of the Red Orchestra as a loose group of friends united by their common repugnance to National Socialism. In contrast to the fast-paced structure of *KLK an PTX,* which was, as one reviewer remarked in 1971 in the weekly magazine *Weltbühne*, not always quite in line with the truth, since 'the film's intention is simply that of re-creating historical events in outline',[39] *Die rote Kapelle* uses Helmut Roloff's narration and the comments of his friends' relatives to foreground the individual stories of the survivor and his executed friends. Together with archival footage in the form of stills and clips that substantiate the oral testimonies, the scholar Johannes Tuchel places the visual evidence in its historical context. The lack of a voiceover allows audiences to take in the information unfiltered, in an attempt to present a less biased presentation of the events. All of the above attest to the key point of the documentary, namely that a number of resistance movements operated both simultaneously and independently from each other. In *KLK an PTX*, by contrast, the narrative string of the radio operation has the function of binding all the protagonists together into a single (mythical) collective. In *Die rote Kapelle* the espionage activities of the organization are confined to the activities of just a handful of members of the Red Orchestra.

In *KLK an PTX* size matters as far as the politicization of the Red Orchestra is concerned. The viewer is introduced to a confusingly large number of protagonists during the first hour of the film. Brief sequences of about five minutes serve as mini biographies of those members of the Red Orchestra who would eventually be arrested and executed by the Gestapo. What is important in these introductory moments, however, is not an in-depth understanding of the individual characters per se, but the fact that they are, or will become, part of the conspiracy to overthrow fascism in Germany. The central message of the film soon becomes clear: a united working class forms the core of this movement, an inference suggested in such slogans as 'Those who used to work with their mind now work with their fist', or in the frequent references to 'class consciousness' that formulate an understanding of the political character of the Red Orchestra early on. The determination to organize and to spread the political message is equally pronounced in utterances like, 'We have to look for contact to other groups', and the decision to organize communist literature for political indoctrination. However, if we believe the interviews in *Die rote Kapelle*, there were no pan-European espionage activities taking place, because the Red Orchestra did not exist as an organization at all. For that reason the documentary focuses on just one circle of friends and their activities. According to the testimonies in the film, their work against the National Socialists consisted of pasting flyers with anti-Nazi slogans or sending anonymous letters exhorting the public to unite against the regime. Accordingly, the scope of such resistance and its overall impact differ markedly between the two films, and are in accordance with their intended messages of, on the one hand, coordinated mass resistance motivated by a common political communist agenda and, on the other, the idea of having the individual courage and humanitarian conviction to stand up for one's beliefs.

In the case of *KLK an PTX* the complexity of the script that had been developed by Wera and Claus Küchenmeister to illuminate the broad impact of antifascist resistance by the purported communist group was also reflected in the film's length. Conceptualized as a two-part opus with a total running time of 178 minutes, the film's expansive narrative eventually unites multiple storylines when the paths of the protagonists cross. In addition, *KLK an PTX* contains extended sequences showcasing both the cinematic expertise and technology deployed throughout the film. Extravagant set designs and a sophisticated *mise en scène* abound, making the film a lavish endeavour. It also required an abundance of extras in authentic costume as evidenced, for instance, by the variety of Nazi uniforms on display when Greta and Adam Kuckhoff meet at the train station and make their way through brown shirts, black uniforms and the green garb of the regular police troops. Filming in many cities inside and outside the GDR required establishing shots of landmarks to help viewers orient themselves during the frequent location changes. Vehicles such as cars, trucks and trams rarely appear in more than one sequence, creating a well-rounded impression of life in the 1930s and 1940s. If the plot takes liberties in depicting the story of the Red Orchestra, then the set design and *mise en scène* create a perfect illusion of 'authenticity' and one designed to reinforce the 'truthfulness' of the story in the minds of viewers (Fig. 14.2).

Roloff's *Die rote Kapelle*, by contrast, is a much shorter film. At only eighty-seven minutes, the audience's attention is shifted away from the wider implications for Germany's future and instead towards the more abstract, prototypical nature of the actions. The images on screen function only as an aid to help the viewer visualize the words of those interviewed. There are multiple instances where Roloff restages events to help audiences imagine them. He ensures a narrative distance by introducing these events with the help of an animated technique

Figure 14.2: 'Authentic' *mise en scène* in *KLK an PTX* (1971). DVD screen capture.

especially developed for the film: 'These scenes are shown in a new black-and-white animation technique that allows an undistorted depiction of events. Scenes filmed to accompany certain interview passages were turned into black-and-white pictures that resemble drawings'.[40] The restagings do not attempt to create an illusion of authenticity; the scenes were obviously filmed in contemporary Berlin. In one example, the interviewee talks about two Gestapo officers coming to arrest a member of the Red Orchestra. In the restaged scene, an older model Volkswagen car stops and two men get out before driving back to the police headquarters. However, what initially appears to be an authentic re-creation of events is exposed as an illusion almost immediately, when we see contemporary cars parked to the left and right of the street and finally notice that the car bears a modern-day German licence plate in the European style (Fig. 14.3). What the viewer originally imagined to be Gestapo uniforms turn out to be simple trench coats. The illusion is meant to be broken; by way of these deliberate (quasi-Brechtian) alienation devices, Roloff maintains the integrity of the interviews.

The restaged animated scenes also avoid the identification of faces and facial expression, keeping the actors anonymous while demanding that the viewer rely

Figure 14.3: Broken illusion: restaging the arrest by the Gestapo in modern-day Berlin in Stefan Roloff's *Die rote Kapelle* (2003) © Stefan Roloff.

on the real faces presented in the form of mug shots taken by the Gestapo. In black and white, like the animated portions of the film, these mug shots morph into each other during the final credits of the film. Using this unique cinematic, computer-animated tool seems to mock the notion of the Red Orchestra members as one united movement. The faceless actors in the restaged scenes and the real faces on the mug shots stand in stark opposition to the star-studded cast of the DEFA film. In *KLK an PTX*, the well-known television actors Horst Drinda and Barbara Adolph together with the movie stars Eberhard Esche and Günther Simon were cast as a further means of promoting the film to the general public at a time of crisis for GDR cinema, which saw declining attendances due to competition from television and film imports from the West.

KLK an PTX was not only an attempt to revitalize the antifascist film or to (re) claim the Red Orchestra as a communist resistance movement; it was also a showcase for technology and a playground for cinematographers. In order to ensure it was developed as a prestige production for the big screen to combat both domestic and international competition, DEFA shot the film in the expensive 70mm format to allow for a higher resolution and more detail; and the use of high quality Orwo film stock made it possible to emphasize vivid colours. Brandt hired two experienced cinematographers to work on the film, Werner Heydn and Günter Haubold. Both used their respective expertise to select interesting camera positions and angles, such as the positioning of a mobile camera on a sailing boat.

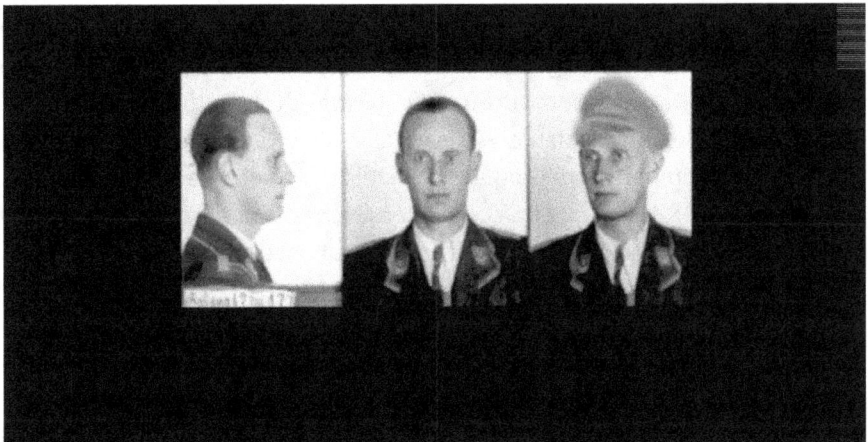

Figure 14.4: Morphing faces using Gestapo mug shots of members of the Red Orchestra in Stefan Roloff's *Die rote Kapelle* (2003) © Stefan Roloff.

Finally, the inclusion of an extensive soundtrack by Helmut Nier (performed by the DEFA symphonic orchestra) and the use of an editing style in keeping with that of a high-paced thriller contributed to the perception of *KLK an PTX* as a popular entertainment film with an emphasis on action. Such a reading becomes even clearer when seen in contrast with *Die rote Kapelle*. The latter production was done on a much smaller scale. Shot in Digibeta with only one camera (mostly in a static position), a small cast and no crew, the documentary relies above all on the power of the narrative and the still images from the archive, and is enhanced only by the animated sequences and an evocative soundtrack by Martin Rev (which sampled nondiegetic synthesizer music and effects within a unique soundscape to accompany the film).

The contrast between the films is striking, as each approaches the topic of the Red Orchestra with a different purpose and from a different angle. For Brandt and DEFA, *KLK an PTX* is essentially a political tool, produced, promoted and marketed with the intention of relaunching the antifascist cinema genre after a hiatus. This attempt at modernizing antifascist cinema opted for technological sophistication over historical accuracy and merged the distinctive qualities of the genre with those of the biopic – only this time with the goal of creating a myth of collective resistance. The fact that the myth of these political role models had been originally created by the Gestapo and continued to be propagated in the Federal Republic did not matter. In DEFA's eyes, the Red Orchestra was little more than 'collateral damage' in the Cold War, and was ruthlessly exploited in the pursuit of a political goal regardless of the consequences for the individual members of the group. This becomes even more evident when we take a closer look at the story of the Red Orchestra as told by the survivors in *Die Rote Kapelle*. Roloff's documentary is, in virtually all respects, the corollary of the imaginary version of history produced by DEFA. It references – and at points reveals – the GDR's appropriation of the Red Orchestra as a means of exploiting an established myth in order to convey a sense of political stability at what was a precarious moment in postwar history.

Sebastian Heiduschke is Associate Professor in the School of Language, Culture and Society, and Affiliate Faculty in the School of Writing, Literature and Film, at Oregon State University. He has published the monograph *DEFA. East German Cinema and Film History* (2013) and essays on the marketing, distribution, and fan cultures of DEFA film.

Notes

1. http://www.instereouk.com/DEFA_List.html, accessed 15 March 2016. DEFA used a camera engineered in its own workshop, the DEFA 70 Reflex, to shoot its features in this format. See also http://www.filmmuseum-potsdam.de/Kameras.html, accessed 29 January 2015.
2. Ralf Schenk, 'DEFA (1946-1992)', in Michael Wedel, Chris Wahl and Ralf Schenk (eds), *100 Years Studio Babelsberg. The Art of Filmmaking*, Berlin: teNeues, 2012, pp. 114-19.
3. See for example Shareen Blair Brysac, *Resisting Hitler. Mildred Harnack and the Red Orchestra*, New York: Oxford University Press, 2000; Stefan Roloff, *Die Rote Kapelle. Die Widerstandsgruppe im Dritten Reich und die Geschichte Helmut Roloffs,* Berlin: Ullstein, 2002; Günter Jordan, 'Der Verrat oder Der Fall Harnack', in Ralf Schenk, Erika Richter and Claus Löser (eds), *apropos: Film 2004* [= Das Jahrbuch der DEFA-Stiftung, 2004], Berlin: Bertz + Fischer, 2004, pp. 148-73; Anne Nelson, *Red Orchestra. The Story of the Berlin Underground and the Circle of Friends Who Resisted Hitler,* New York: Random House, 2009; Mariana Ivanova, *DEFA and East European Cinemas, Co-Productions, Transnational Exchange and Artistic Collaborations,* unpublished PhD Diss., University of Texas at Austin, 2011; Joanne Sayner, *Reframing Antifascism. Memory, Genre, and the Life Writings of Greta Kuckhoff,* New York: Palgrave Macmillan, 2013.
4. 'Dieser Streifen dient erstens der seit Jahren betriebenen "Imagepflege" zugunsten kommunistischer Agenten und Spione; er ist zweitens Bestandteil der immer hektischer werdenden Haß-Propaganda der Kommunisten gegen die "imperialistische" Bundesrepublik Deutschland, und er soll drittens ein Stimulans im "antiimperialistischen Kampf" sowie in der kommunistischen "Bündnis"-Politik auf dem Wege zu der von den Kommunisten geführten Einheits- und Volksfront sein'. Helmut Bärwald, 'Kundschafter des Friedens. Spione im Kampf für den "Sieg des Sozialismus"', *Rheinischer Merkur* (Cologne) 21 May 1971, p. 89.
5. 'Die Rote Kapelle – das war als Schimpfname gedacht. Er wurde zum Ehrennamen für eine der größten, wirkungsvollsten und einflußreichsten antifaschistischen Widerstandsorganisationen, die für ein neues besseres Deutschland kämpften', *FF Dabei* 12/1972 (6). All translations are my own, unless indicated otherwise.
6. See Hunter Bivens, '9 March 1954: *Ernst Thälmann – Sohn seiner Klasse* Marks High Point of Socialist Realism', in Jennifer Kapczynski and Michael Richardson (eds), *A New History of German Cinema*, Rochester, NY: Camden House, 2012, pp. 347-52.
7. Brysac, p. 227.
8. Ibid., pp. 224-27.
9. Richelson, Jeffrey, *A Century of Spies. Intelligence in the Twentieth Century*, New York: Oxford University Press, 1995, p. 126.
10. For more on the Hallstein Doctrine, see for example William Glenn Gray, *Germany's Cold War. The Global Campaign to Isolate East Germany 1949-1969*, Chapel Hill: University of North Carolina Press, 2003.
11. 'Konzeptionelle Gedanken zu einem Spielfilm über die Rote Kapelle' by Wera and Claus Küchenmeister [= BArch N 2506/ 57]. Sayner's translation of a passage found in the undated document.
12. For more on the structure of politically effective filmmaking see Detlef Kannapin, *Dialektik der Bilder. Der Nationalsozialismus im deutschen Film. Ein Ost-West Vergleich*, Berlin: Karl Dietz Verlag, 2006.
13. Sayner, p. 163.

14. 'Ein Film über die Rote Kapelle ist kein historischer Film. Er kann und muß im Sinne der Genossen revolutionären Geist ausstrahlen, der in unseren Tag hineinwirkt'. Wera and Claus Küchenmeister, 'Konzeptionelle Gedanken zu einem Spielfilm über die Rote Kapelle', undated [= BArch N 2506 / 57], pp. 26-35.
15. Wilhelm Flicke, *Die Rote Kapelle*, Hilden: Vier-Brücken, 1949; David Dallin, *Die Sowjetspionage. Prinzipien und Praktiken*, Cologne: Verlag für Politik und Wirtschaft, 1956.
16. 'Wenn man das über ganz Europa gebreitete Netz der sowjetischen Spionage darstellen will, dann kommt man um eine Aufrollung des Falles Rote Kapelle nicht herum. Unter diesem Namen wurde mitten im Kriege die entscheidende Agentengruppe des Kreml in Deutschland ausgehoben und abgeurteilt'. *Der Stern*, No. 18, 6 May 1951 (14).
17. See Heinz Höhne, 'ptx ruft moskau. Die Geschichte des Spionagerings "Rote Kapelle"', *Der Spiegel* issues 21 (20 May 1968) to 30 (22 July 1968).
18. Former members and relatives of the Red Orchestra refused to be interviewed by reporters. See *Der Spiegel*, 21 (20 May 1968), 5.
19. Sayner, p. 149.
20. Johannes Tuchel, *Der vergessene Widerstand. Zur Realgeschichte und Wahrnehmung des Kampfes gegen die NS-Diktatur*, Göttingen: Wallstein, 2005, pp. 232-70 ('Das Ministerium für Staatssicherheit und die Widerstandsgruppe Rote Kapelle in den 1960er Jahren').
21. Wera and Claus Küchenmeister, 'Dieser Film war uns ein Bedürfnis', *Neues Deutschland*, 24 March 1971.
22. Karl-Heinz Biernat, 'Sie kämpften für Deutschland'. *Berliner Zeitung*, 14 September 1969.
23. 'Der politische Kern waren Kommunisten', Biernat, 'Sie kämpften für Deutschland'.
24. Karl-Heinz Biernat, 'Patriotischer Kampf in Liebe und Treue zur Heimat des Sozialismus', *Neues Deutschland*, 28 October 1969.
25. 'Sie kämpften unter den Augen der Faschisten', *Berliner Zeitung*, 4 November 1969.
26. 'Hohe sowjetische Orden für antifaschistische Widerstandskämpfer', *Neues Deutschland*, 23 December 1969.
27. Inge Topf, 'Ein Drehbuch der DEFA im Gespräch', *Neues Deutschland*, 7 December 1969.
28. Seán Allan, 'Representations of Art and the Artist in East German Cinema', in Marc Silberman and Henning Wrage (eds), *DEFA at the Crossroads of East German and International Film Culture*, Berlin, Boston: de Gruyter, 2014, pp. 87-105 (p. 100).
29. Helmut Reinhard, 'Kündend von den Quellen unserer Kraft: Zum Entstehen eines bedeutenden Films über den Widerstandskampf', *Neue Zeit*, 13 September 1970.
30. Peter Lux, 'Berliner Taxi in Prag', *Junge Welt*, 23 July 1970.
31. 'Selbst die kleinsten Rollen wurden mit hervorragenden Schauspielern besetzt. KLK an PTX. Die rote Kapelle', *Neues Deutschland*, 7 February 1971.
32. Bruno Pioch, 'KLK an PTX - Die Rote Kapelle', *Filmspiegel* 6/1971 (17 March), 4-7.
33. Often, party officials or sympathizers wrote these letters in newspapers. While letters may not be a reliable way of gauging the interest of the general public, they still provide important information on the desired reactions of an intended audience.
34. Horst Knietzsch, 'Ein Zeugnis großer Menschlichkeit', *Neues Deutschland*, 27 March 1971.
35. Marina Jacobitz, Letter to the Editor, *Neues Deutschland*, 28 March 1971.
36. Christiane Mückenberger, 'The Anti-Fascist Past in DEFA Films', in Seán Allan and John Sandford (eds), *DEFA. East German Cinema, 1946-1992*, New York, Oxford: Berghahn, 1999, pp. 58-76 (p. 74).
37. Gilles Perrault, *L'Orchestre Rouge*, Paris: Fayard, 1967.

38. Roloff, p. 15.
39. 'Der Film kann und will das historische Geschehen nur in Ausschnitten nachbilden': Lothar Kusche, 'Das Menetekel an der Wand', *Die Weltbühne*, 6 April 1971.
40. http://when6is9.de/red_orchestra/filmkonzept.html, accessed 20 June 2016.

CHAPTER 15

DEFA's Afterimages
Looking back at the East from the West in *Das Leben der Anderen* [*The Lives of Others*, 2006] and *Barbara* (2012)

Daniela Berghahn

Twenty-five years after the fall of the Berlin Wall, the familiar images of East and West Germans celebrating at Berlin's Brandenburg Gate are beginning to fade. Instead of documentary footage of this momentous historical event, fictionalized accounts of life on the other side of the Wall circulate prominently in the media. Mention the German Democratic Republic to anyone who has not actually lived there and what springs to mind are film scenes, publicity stills and DVD covers such as the polarized portrait of Alex Kerner (Daniel Brühl) and his mother Christiane (Katrin Sass) in shades of red and beige. The image is overlaid with the film title of Wolfgang Becker's *Good Bye, Lenin!* (2003) in large black and red capital letters, with the five-pointed communist star replacing the full stop underneath the exclamation mark. Arguably more evocative is the close-up of a man's face from *Das Leben der Anderen*, his eyes large and alert as he listens attentively through his oversized headphones. Whereas in the former image communist red conveys a cheerful mood as befits a comedy, in the latter, sombre shades of grey predominate: the man's bald head and furrowed face are ashen, his anorak an inconspicuous grey and the background black. This monochrome image of Stasi Captain Wiesler (Ulrich Mühe) in *Das Leben der Anderen* has come to encapsulate the all-pervasive surveillance of the *Staatssicherheitsdienst* (State Security), which infiltrated every aspect of East German society – even intimate relationships. A third image, albeit one circulated less widely, shows a blond woman (Nina Hoss), her hair pinned up, riding an old-fashioned bicycle. Her rather elegant attire (a woollen jacket, colour-coordinated knee-length skirt and high heels) look somewhat incongruous amidst the natural setting of boulders and bushes, as if the cyclist had been transplanted from the city to the countryside. Even more intriguing is the fact that, instead of keeping her eyes fixed on the uneven terrain she has to negotiate, she is looking backwards over her shoulder as if to check whether someone is following her. Although the furtive backward glance indicates suspicion and anxiety, it is a gesture too subtle and ambiguous to convey that the film is actually set in the GDR. That is why the UK and US DVD covers of Christian Petzold's film *Barbara* carry the tagline, 'Anyone who loved *The Lives of Others* should see this', thereby trying to capitalize on the spectacular success of Florian Henckel von Donnersmarck's film about the Stasi.

All three films won numerous prestigious prizes on the international film festival circuit and were Germany's contenders for the Oscars – though only *Das Leben der Anderen* actually won one; all three depict life in the GDR but were made by filmmakers who grew up in the West. While this in itself is not remarkable, it nevertheless begs the question why films made by filmmakers who were trained in the GDR have not gained similar visibility as these three, be it in terms of box office success, critical acclaim or media coverage. Have West German filmmakers colonized our subconscious – to adapt Wim Wenders's famous remark about the impact of American popular culture upon postwar West Germany – by projecting perversely seductive images of the GDR onto the silver screen?

Compared with DEFA films that were released around the time of the Wende, productions made by filmmakers from the West enjoyed a huge competitive advantage. Randall Halle, who outlines the very uneven conditions of production and distribution East and West German directors faced after the Wende, suggests that the majority of DEFA directors 'appeared tainted to their West German counterparts' and cites Volker Schlöndorff, who was appointed artistic director at the Studio Babelsberg after DEFA was privatized, as having publicly announced, 'The word DEFA will hopefully disappear; I find that it does not smell good'.[1]

It is thus hardly surprising that the difficulties East German filmmakers encountered, when trying to adjust from state-based methods of funding and distribution to the more market-orientated film industry of the Berlin Republic, ultimately led to their marginalization.[2] Although I acknowledge that access to funding sources, publicity budgets and skilfully orchestrated marketing campaigns significantly contributed to the critical and/or commercial success of films like *Das Leben der Anderen* and *Barbara*, these industrial factors will remain outside the concerns addressed in this chapter. Moreover, and in contrast to much of the scholarly and media debates surrounding *Das Leben der Anderen* and *Barbara*, I am less interested in the contested issue of the films' historical authenticity than in the question of how they construct a fictionalized memory of the former GDR. In particular, I want to explore how they engage with the extensive archive of cinematic representations of East Germany in DEFA films, notably Roland Gräf's *Die Flucht* [*The Flight*, 1977] and Frank Beyer's *Der Verdacht* [*The Suspicion*, 1991], two films about similar themes: attempted *Republikflucht* (illegal escape from the GDR) and the corrosive atmosphere of fear and mistrust associated with surveillance by the Stasi. And finally, I seek to explore what narrative and visual strategies identify von Donnersmarck and Petzold's films as *Nachbilder* or 'afterimages' of 'Stasiland' that look back at the East from a recognizably Western vantage point.[3] In the context of memory studies, the term 'afterimages' denotes multi-layered narrative and/or visual constructs that draw on and conflate living memory, postmemory (typically family memories that have passed down from one generation to the next) and prosthetic memory that is mediated through film, television and other mass media.[4] In the introduction to *Nachbilder des Holocaust*, Inge Stephan and Alexandra Tacke offer the following evocative definition:

> *Afterimages are brief, fleeting memories that, created by rays of light, remain on the retina. If we close our eyes the afterimage remains for a short moment before fading away slowly, losing its sharpness, and finally – as soon as we open our eyes again – becoming overlaid and replaced with other images. In this figurative sense, images of the Holocaust have been burned into our cultural memory and have left their mark. Although, with the passing of the first generation of witnesses, there is a danger of such images becoming blurred and fading away, or being replaced by other images, they continue to make an impression even today.*[5]

Afterimages, Stephan and Tacke argue, are always in dialogue with 'Vor-Bilder' (preceding images), which they refract, cite, affirm or disavow.[6] Hence, the concept underscores that what is at stake is not so much the mimetic relationship between image and reality (around which authenticity debates revolve) but the relationship between images and preceding images. Offering fictionalized accounts of the past, afterimages not only construct alternative historical imaginaries that compete with eyewitness accounts in documentaries but, more significantly, they do not necessarily purport to be historically true.[7] For the first generation, who actually experienced or witnessed the Holocaust, any form of fictionalization is anathema. The second and subsequent generations, by contrast, have no qualms about using a history that is not their own as rich source material for fictions that propose radically new perspectives and thereby challenge the master narratives of previous generations.

What prompts me to invoke the critical framework of afterimages, which has been developed in the context of cultural memory of the Holocaust, to films about the memory of the GDR's totalitarian regime, are two influential frameworks of memory studies:[8] Michael Rothberg's 'multidirectional memory' and Alison Landsberg's 'prosthetic memory'. Like afterimages, these concepts are based on the premise that the fading of living memory due to generational shift results in a significant transformation of collective and cultural memory. Furthermore, Landsberg and Rothberg challenge the essentialist logic that posits an exclusive link between a particular group identity and their collective memory. In the age of transnational media flows, mass-mediated images of traumatic pasts, notably the Holocaust, slavery and the violent struggles of decolonization, have become so widely accessible that collective memory is no longer the sole property of one particular community. Whereas in the past, memory was predominantly passed down the generations through oral history, family photos and other memorabilia, nowadays the mass media have gained an increasingly important role in the transmission of memory. The global circulation of mass-mediated images of the Holocaust and of other traumatic pasts has led, in Rothberg's words, to 'a confluence of disparate historical imaginaries'.[9] He proposes that through 'the dynamic transfers between diverse places and times during the act of remembrance' a multidirectional memory arises 'which is partially disengaged from exclusive versions of cultural identity and acknowledges how remembrance both cuts across and binds together diverse spatial, temporal and cultural sites'.[10] Whereas Rothberg's concept of multidirectional memory foregrounds the idea that the boundaries between memory and identity are fluid, negotiable and overlapping, Landsberg's concept of prosthetic memory underscores that these memories 'mark trauma' and are artificial insofar as they are 'derived from engagement with mediated representation (seeing a film, visiting a museum, watching a television mini-series)'.[11]

I would like to propose that *Das Leben der Anderen* and *Barbara* are such afterimages and that their genesis is based on processes of prosthetic and – in the case of von Donnersmarck's film – multidirectional memory. The directors' relationships to the collective memory of the GDR are not only determined by the distance that separates the living memory of the experiential generation from that of successive generations but, additionally, by the fact that both grew up in the Federal Republic, not the GDR. Petzold explained that for him the GDR was merely a 'Projektionsraum' (projected space), but neither a 'Lebensraum' (living space) nor an 'Erinnerungsraum' (memory space).[12] This important distinction has determined the aesthetic choices he made in *Barbara*. In the numerous interviews Petzold has given about the making of *Barbara*, the reference points and inspirations he cites are books – notably Hermann Broch's novella *Barbara* (1936) and Werner Bräunig's *Rummelplatz* (1965/2007) – Gerhard Richter's famous painting of his daughter *Betty* (1988, whose pinned-up hairstyle resembles Barbara's chignon) and a fairly eclectic mix of films, including Howard Hawks's *To Have and Have Not* (1944), Roberto Rossellini's *Stromboli* (1950), Alan J. Pakula's *Klute* (1971), William Friedkin's *The French Connection* (1971) and remarkably few DEFA films: Jürgen Böttcher's *Jahrgang 45* [*Born in '45*, 1966/1990] and Joachim Hasler's *Heißer Sommer* [*Hot Summer*, 1968].

Christian Petzold is one of Germany's most critically acclaimed contemporary directors and he is a prominent representative of the Berlin School (a point to which I shall return when analysing his aesthetic approach).[13] He was born in Hilden in 1960 and grew up in Haan, a small town somewhere between Wuppertal and Düsseldorf, as the son of East German refugees who had left before the erection of the Berlin Wall. When the Transit Agreement (1972) between the two German states made it possible to visit family and friends, the Petzolds would regularly spend three weeks in the summer in the GDR. The memories he recounts in interviews are surprisingly positive, which might explain why the atmosphere and the colour palette of *Barbara* contests the dominant media images of a dull, grey and dismal life on the other side of the Wall. During summer holidays in the GDR, he explains:

> *my parents totally changed their behaviour. They had a social surrounding, they were laughing, they could dance. They were a couple in love. And I didn't see that in the West. ... This German Democratic Republic was their home. The other mysterious thing was that after 1989, when the wall tumbled down, they didn't visit the German Democratic Republic anymore. ... I think they weren't just visiting the towns and friends of their youth, they were visiting socialism. And then socialism was gone, so a big part of their lives and their dreams was gone too.*[14]

Although journalists have prompted Petzold time and again to authenticate *Barbara*, he does not dwell too much on his biographical credentials as a refugees' son and even stresses that, when shooting the film, he deliberately avoided those *Erinnerungsorte* (memory spaces) to which his parents returned during their summer visits.[15]

Florian Henckel von Donnersmarck, by contrast, whose actual experience of the GDR is far more limited, has tried to get as much mileage as possible out of his putative East German background. He was born in Cologne in 1973 to aristocratic parents who had been expelled from the Reich's Eastern territories at the end of World War II, i.e. years before the GDR was founded. He enjoyed a privileged upbringing and spent his childhood and youth in New York, Berlin and Frankfurt. After school he studied in St Petersburg and Oxford, before graduating from the Munich Film Academy. *Das Leben der Anderen* is his début film. In interviews, von Donnersmarck recalls his brush with the Stasi surveillance state during visits to relatives in the GDR, when his mother was 'subjected to particularly humiliating checks' even being strip-searched when crossing the German-German border, presumably because she was 'on a special Stasi list' and considered a traitor 'to the communist cause' on account of having moved to the West.[16] Interestingly, in a lecture he gave at Cambridge University in 2008, he admitted: 'I don't really have much experience of the GDR. I just researched this and looked into that, but that's not what journalists want to hear. So I just dug into the very few connections I had to East Germany and talked about those at length. But really, I only visited the GDR a few times as a child when I was eight or nine, when we were pretty much just driving through'.[17] It seems as if von Donnersmarck bowed to media pressure since the film's successful publicity campaign did not miss a single opportunity to sell the fictional account of a Stasi officer who redeems himself by protecting the target of his surveillance as historical truth. Prominent East German artists, including writer Thomas Brussig and the dissident folk-rock performer Wolf Biermann, were called upon to testify that *Das Leben der Anderen* offers a realistic image of 'Stasiland'. Despite highlighting a few factual errors, Biermann concludes his article in *Die Welt* with the astonishing suggestion that 'It's quite possible that the deeper analysis of Germany's second dictatorship is now being carried out more effectively by those without first-hand experience of its misery'.[18]

I consider the whole authenticity discourse as a red herring because it is precisely the *lack* of personal involvement that enabled von Donnersmarck to transform the memory of the East German surveillance state into a melodrama of universal significance, constructing a compelling afterimage of the GDR with enormous popular appeal. In addition to the Oscar for Best Foreign Language Film in 2007, it won some fifty-seven other awards and is, alongside Oliver Hirschbiegel's *Der Untergang* [*Downfall*, 2004] and *Good Bye, Lenin!* one of the top-grossing German films at the international box office. Ironically, as filmmaker Andreas Dresen, who grew up in the East, laments, 'this film has about as much to do with the GDR as Hollywood has to do with Hoyerswerda',[19] whereas more realistic depictions of the GDR, made by filmmakers who worked or were trained at the DEFA studios, have systematically failed to reach large audiences.

When in November 1989 the *Hauptverwaltung Film*, the department in the Ministry of Culture in charge of censorship, ceased to exist, East German filmmakers were, at last, free to address subject matters hitherto regarded as taboo, notably the devastating effect of the Stasi on people's lives, as in Roland Gräf's *Der Tangospieler* [*The Tango Player, 1991*], Frank Beyer's *Der Verdacht*, Michael Gwisdek's *Abschied von Agnes* [*Farewell to Agnes,* 1994] and Sybille Schönemann's documentary *Verriegelte Zeit* [*Locked-Up Time,* 1990]. Unfortunately, the timing was wrong. 'The GDR was finally gone, and with it the social and discursive context that would have made these films politically urgent', Joshua Feinstein observes. 'Criticism that once might have been explosive was now pedantic; broken taboos were now mere clichés'.[20] When Frank Beyer, one of DEFA's most acclaimed directors, was interviewed about his film *Der Verdacht*, he commented upon the dilemma he and his colleagues faced: that there were certain things people did not want to remember because they had a guilty conscience but, also that 'Today films dealing with the former GDR really need to focus on important and exceptional stories if they're to capture the interest of an audience'.[21]

Der Verdacht is precisely not one of those important and exceptional stories, something that distinguishes it from *Das Leben der Anderen*. Set in the 1970s and based on Volker Braun's novella *Unvollendete Geschichte* (1975) and a screenplay by Ulrich Plenzdorf, *Der Verdacht* tells the story of Karin (Christiane Heinrich), the daughter of a council chairman (Michael Gwisdek) in a small town on the German-German border, and her boyfriend Frank (Nikolaus Gröbe), who has a criminal record. Karin's father 'has been informed', as he puts it, that Frank 'is planning something' – but this something is merely a vague suspicion. He asks Karin to end her relationship with Frank because it jeopardizes her future career and might have repercussions for his own. Intimidated by two Stasi officers and pressurised by her family, she leaves her boyfriend. Frank thereupon attempts to commit suicide, is rescued and falls into a coma. Weeks later he awakens but suffers from partial memory loss.[22] Although the allegations of planned *Republikflucht* against Frank are not upheld, his life has been destroyed – as has that of Karin. She is expecting a baby, has forfeited her opportunity to study and will either be sent to work in production (officially advertised as a consciousness-raising experience) or find employment in the hairdressing salon where her sister works. The film's last shot of the young couple walking down a straight, tree-lined avenue recalls the final frames of Konrad Wolf's antifascist film *Lissy* (1957), in which the eponymous heroine has found her place in the antifascist resistance and is walking along a similar tree-lined avenue towards a bright socialist future. The ending of *Der Verdacht*, by contrast, vehemently denies the kind of optimism of the early days of the GDR.

Der Verdacht centres on ordinary people who are morally shallow and who protect themselves and their families through a blend of blind obedience and accommodation with the structures of power. Karin's father, though caring about his daughter's happiness, has internalized 'the totalitarian nature of bureaucratized evil',[23] to such an extent that he has lost touch with his conscience. The oppressive mood, the grey winter landscapes with dirty, slushy snow in the streets, coupled with the film's cynical ending make this DEFA film a far cry from those afterimages that take a much more reconciliatory and empathetic look at what many have dismissed as a bleak dictatorship.

Das Leben der Anderen as a foundational multidirectional memory film

Set in the Orwellian year of 1984, *Das Leben der Anderen* centres on Stasi Captain Gerd Wiesler, who is put in charge of 'Operation Lazlo', an intensive round-the-clock surveillance of the successful playwright Georg Dreyman (Sebastian Koch). During the course of 'Operation Lazlo' the idealistic Stasi officer begins to sympathize with the writer and his actress-girlfriend (Martina Gedeck) and changes sides: instead of finding incriminating evidence against Dreymann, he protects him from persecution. The film's coda fast-forwards to the time of the Wende when Dreymann discovers in his file in the Stasi archives that he had actually been the target of surveillance but that a Stasi officer with the code name HGW XX/7 saved him. Dreymann writes a novel entitled *The Sonata of a Good Man* and dedicates it 'To HGW XX/7 with gratitude'. In the final scene, Wiesler sees the book displayed in a shop window and purchases it (Fig. 15.1 and Fig. 15.2). Through the belated recognition of his essential goodness and humanity, Stasi Captain Wiesler has been redeemed.

Von Donnersmarck uses one of the most compelling narrative formulae of Hollywood cinema, the redemption plot. As Robert McKee has argued, a significant number of Hollywood's most successful films follow this narrative paradigm, which is particularly rich in irony and 'a magnet for Oscars'.[24] It traces the transformation of someone evil, or at least morally ambiguous, into someone good and represents an ironic version of the success story, an even more popular Hollywood

Figure 15.1: Wiesler discovers Dreymann's novel at the Karl Marx bookshop. DVD screen capture.

Figure 15.2: Wiesler's hands holding Dreymann's novel *Sonata for a Good Man* in *Das Leben der Anderen* (2007). DVD screen capture.

plotline. But whereas protagonists of success stories get what they wanted all along, protagonists of redemption plots 'stand to lose, if not their lives, their humanity'.²⁵ A sudden revelation allows them 'to glimpse the ruinous nature of their obsession [... and then] throw away what they once cherished'.²⁶

Captain Wiesler's trajectory is a textbook example of Hollywood's tried and tested narrative formula, in as much as he abandons his unquestioned loyalty to the regime and changes sides. Though his transformation from skilful inquisitor and vigilant spy is gradual, the moment of Wiesler's revelation occurs when he listens to Dreymann playing the 'Sonata for a Good Man' on his piano.²⁷ Lest

Figure 15.3: Dreymann's hands picking up the piano score 'Sonata for a Good Man' in *Das Leben der Anderen* (2007). DVD screen capture.

Figure 15.4: Wiesler is listening to the 'Sonata for a Good Man' with tears in his eyes in *Das Leben der Anderen* (2007). DVD screen capture.

audiences might miss this moment of supreme narrative significance, von Donnersmarck has taken care to amply mark it: the camera lingers for a few seconds on the title of the score (Fig. 15.3) and then cuts to a close-up of Dreymann's hands playing the piano. Wiesler, who hears the music over the surveillance headphones, is affected profoundly. Momentarily, his stern, expressionless features soften and tears well up in his eyes (Fig. 15.4).

Das Leben der Anderen is a memory film, as defined by Lu Seegers. It resonates with historical imaginaries that circulate in the public sphere at a particular moment in time, capturing dominant interpretations of the past while simultaneously constructing new ones.[28] Even though von Donnersmarck rides on the wave of media interest in the GDR that peaked with 'ostalgic' comedies like Leander Haußmann's *Sonnenallee* [*Sun Alley*, 1999] and *Good Bye, Lenin!,* the repertoire of images and narratives he invokes are neither derived from these comedies nor from historically more authentic DEFA films but instead from Hollywood films about the Holocaust. *Das Leben der Anderen* is an apt example of a multidirectional memory text in which heterogeneous emanations of burdened pasts (the Holocaust and the GDR's totalitarian regime) form the layers of a palimpsest.

The film replicates the narrative trajectory of Steven Spielberg's *Schindler's List* (1993) and Roman Polanski's *The Pianist* (2002), two *Greuelmärchen*, or fairy tales of horror. David Bathrick applies the Brechtian term *Greuelmärchen* to the considerable number of films about Holocaust survivors and argues that, although they are often based on personal testimonies of survivors, these films nevertheless convey the misleading impression that the (success) story of survival was the norm, whereas in reality it was a total anomaly.[29] Just as these two Holocaust films single out exceptional good Germans, who saved the lives of those victimized by the Nazi regime, *Das Leben der Anderen* focuses on the exceptional case of a good Stasi officer who spares his target from prosecution. But whereas Oskar Schindler and the German Wehrmacht officer Wilm Hosenfeld (who helped the Jewish pianist Władysław Szpilman survive) actually existed, there is no historical precedent of a Stasi officer who falsified evidence to protect his target. Moreover, Schindler (though a Nazi Party member) and Hosenfeld (though a Party member and Wehrmacht officer) were saviours, not perpetrators, whereas Wiesler is a perpetrator turned saviour.

Das Leben der Anderen echoes two emotionally powerful scenes of these Holocaust films. When Captain Hosenfeld (Thomas Kretschmann) discovers Szpilman (Adrien Brody), almost starved and emaciated, amongst the ruins of

Warsaw and learns that he is a pianist, he asks him to play. Deeply moved by Szpilman's passionate and accomplished performance of Chopin's Sonata in C sharp minor, he spares his life. The idea that high culture, especially music, has a humanizing effect is, of course, also the chief premise of von Donnersmarck's film. A similar correspondence exists between the coda of *Das Leben der Anderen* and that of *Schindler's List*, both of which dramatize the proof of gratitude of those who were saved: Dreymann's dedication 'To HGW XX/7 in gratitude' and the Jews saved by Schindler placing memorial rocks on his grave in Jerusalem.

Das Leben der Anderen can be regarded as the prototype of a multidirectional memory text and, according to Timothy Garton Ash, has played a pioneering role in superimposing the memory of the Stasi on to that of the Nazis:

> *One of Germany's most singular achievements is to have associated itself so intimately in the world's imagination with the darkest evils of the two worst political systems of the most murderous century in human history. The words 'Nazi', 'SS', and 'Auschwitz' are already global synonyms for the deepest inhumanity of fascism. Now the word 'Stasi' is becoming a default global synonym for the secret police terrors of communism. The worldwide success of Florian Henckel von Donnersmarck's deservedly Oscar-winning film* The Lives of Others *will strengthen that second link, building as it does on the preprogramming of our imaginations by the first. Nazi, Stasi: Germany's festering half-rhyme.*[30]

These layers of multidirectional memory work in a way similar to genre conventions, which, according to Leo Baudry, 'lure ... audiences into a seemingly familiar world'.[31] The formulaic narrative process of film genres, their well-rehearsed iconography and conflict resolutions offer a sense of reassurance that 'stabilizes ideological conflicts in society through dramatic closure'.[32] The reference to genre is pertinent here because *Das Leben der Anderen* has captured the imagination of domestic and, even more so, international audiences, not only because it resonated with familiar images of evil Nazis but also because its powerful generic mix pulls all the right emotional chords. Von Donnersmarck himself described it as 'a melodrama with thriller elements' reminiscent of *Casablanca* (Michael Curtiz, 1942 – referenced in the code name 'Operation Lazlo'),[33] while scholars have identified additional genre conventions, notably those of heritage cinema and the Cold War Spy film.[34] Jaimey Fisher's comprehensive analysis of how *Das Leben der Anderen* combines heritage cinema's fetishized representational authenticity with stock scenes and props of the police thriller, while adding the music, pathos and clear moral legibility of melodrama, leaves me little scope to add anything.[35] Except perhaps the observation that the film's melodramatic modality sidelines politics and invites us to take an emotional approach to the politics of memory so that we end up empathizing with a perpetrator. This takes us back to Landsberg's argument that prosthetic memory, a commodified type of memory, mediated through 'mass cultural representation', has the capacity to 'generate empathy' with a past distinct from one's own.[36] It allows a Western filmmaker like von Donnersmarck to see through the eyes of the 'Other' and to engender a sense of forgiveness and reconciliation – an attitude inconceivable for those who actually experienced the totalitarian regime.

Barbara as an afterimage of DEFA's *Alltagsfilme*?

While international distributors and film critics have treated *Barbara* as something of a companion piece to *Das Leben der Anderen,* director Christian Petzold is reluctant to embrace this comparison and describes von Donnersmarck's film as precisely not a GDR-film. 'It's more like Hitchcock. Here the GDR is simply a studio reconstruction – an artificial backdrop for a story that never actually took place there'.[37] In *Barbara* he was less interested in the historical authenticity of the props, costumes and settings, and more in capturing the corrosive atmosphere of suspicion and subterfuge that permeated all human relationships. That is why the Stasi in his film is not some kind of 'moloch', but part of everyday life. That is why *Barbara* does not feature the microphones with which people's flats were bugged but instead people's fear of these microphones.[38] This fear is captured in the way in which the protagonists, Barbara and André (Ronald Zehrfeld), look at each other; one can never be quite sure whether their long and intense glances are motivated by suspicion or by love. In this way, Petzold shows 'how structures of power infiltrate love relationships'.[39] Rather than making the GDR an object of historical or political enquiry, the film's effervescent physicality evokes the emotional and bodily experience of people who lived under such a regime.

This also explains why Petzold's approach to historical authenticity differs markedly from that of von Donnersmarck. He does not aim for the heritage cinema look. There is not a single portrait of Erich Honecker on the wall; Hans Fromm's camera never lingers long on authentic props like the tram, the faded wooden sign at the railway station announcing 'We are looking towards the future with optimism' or the hard-to-come-by *Quelle* mail-order catalogue from 1980. And yet, it seemed important to the director and Kade Gruber, the production designer, to reconstruct the sensuous experience of everyday life in the GDR as evocatively as possible. The initial rehearsals, Petzold recalls, 'were acts of collective remembrance. What did the GDR sound like? What did it smell like?'[40] It is arguably the film's sensory reconstruction of the everyday that creates a particular mood and sensibility akin to DEFA's *Alltagsfilme*, although it could hardly be mistaken for 'the real thing'.

Alltagsfilme (films about everyday life) emerged during the 1970s and represent a departure from DEFA's *Gegenwartsfilme* (films about contemporary life), their earlier counterpart. Both centre on the ordinary lives of East German citizens and feature the workplace as the centre of social interaction. Whereas the *Gegenwartsfilm* is 'based on a progressive vision of history', the *Alltagsfilm* 'emphasizes ahistorical existence, the diurnal'.[41] In *The Triumph of the Ordinary*, Joshua Feinstein identifies *Jahrgang 45*, made in 1966 and one of the films banned in the wake of the Eleventh Plenum, as an important precursor of the *Alltagsfilm*. Its meandering narrative centres on a drifting non-conformist young couple and their marital problems while the workplace plays a subordinate role. The focus is on individuals instead of the socialist collective and the nuanced depiction of everydayness does not 'compete with a narrative driven by ideological logic'.[42] It is one of the few DEFA films which Christian Petzold has cited as a source of inspiration, not in terms of its plotline but in terms of its aesthetics and atmosphere. This slow-paced, contemplative film with long takes of Berlin's Prenzlauer Berg neighbourhood, crisp ambient sound and an eye for the poetry of ordinary life is as close as DEFA ever got to a *nouvelle vague*.

What *Barbara* shares with DEFA's films about everyday life is a quintessential East German sensibility. It positively affirms one of the GDR's central values, labour as the cornerstone of individual and collective identity. As in DEFA films, the place of work is not only the dominant setting but also the site where people meet and fall in love (Fig. 15.5). 'Production is the site where love blossoms' ('Liebe gehört in die Produktion') Petzold declared in an interview,[43] deliberately using an expression that enjoyed wide currency in the GDR. Admittedly, he opted for a fairly 'glamorous' type of work since the protagonists are not exactly manual

Figure 15.5: The workplace is the site where Barbara and André's love blossoms. *Barbara* (2012). DVD screen capture.

labourers in production, but highly qualified doctors in a hospital, a setting that serves as the backdrop for countless popular films and television series.

Set in 1980, *Barbara* tells the story of Barbara Wolff, an attractive paediatrician in her thirties who, following a period of incarceration, has been posted to a small provincial hospital on the Baltic Sea as punishment for having applied for an exit visa to West Germany. Despite having been demoted from the GDR's flagship hospital, the Charité in East Berlin, Barbara is entirely committed to the patients at her new place of work, especially to Stella (Jasna Fritzi Bauer), a teenage girl from the nearby Jugendwerkhof Torgau (a reformatory for deviant teenagers) who has contracted meningitis and who is expecting a baby. During secret trysts, Barbara's West German lover Jörg (Mark Waschke) showers her with presents and supplies her with a bundle of Deutschmarks and a detailed escape plan. His promise, 'Once you've come over, you'll be able to sleep late. I earn enough, you won't need to work' is, however, less enticing than he realizes. After all, Barbara was socialized in the workers and peasants state and work is an integral part of her identity.

Moreover, she appears to be gradually falling in love with her colleague André. On the night of her planned escape, she takes Stella to the appointed place by the sea and puts the teenage girl (and the unborn baby she carries) on the motorized raft that will take her across to Denmark. The film ends with Barbara joining André by the bedside of a critically ill patient in hospital.

The ending lacks the narrative closure and uplifting emotional tenor of *Das Leben der Anderen* and releases the audience with many questions to ponder: Will Barbara and André get together? What consequences will Barbara face for having arranged Stella's escape to the West? The film's open-endedness and narrative ambiguity is comparable to that of *Der Verdacht*. And yet, it *feels* much more optimistic, even if we have not read the screenplay, which mentions the possibility of a kiss (albeit in the conditional) and which concludes with the sentence 'because everything is just fine'.[44] No such firm reassurance is offered in the film's actual ending. Barbara returns to her place of work and sits down quietly on a chair, facing André. A series of shot-counter-shots traces the glances they exchange, not a single word is spoken. Barbara takes a deep breath in and then breathes out. One can hear birds singing outside. The end. Cut to the credits, accompanied by Chic's cover version of the 1980s song 'At Last I Am Free'.

The film's final scene marks Barbara's arrival (*Ankunft*) both literally and figuratively; now she has truly arrived in the sense of having (freely) accepted her life in the GDR, whereas in the film's opening scene she merely arrives at the hospital, eager to leave again as fast as she can. For me at least, the German word *Ankunft* in this context evokes the title of Brigitte Reimann's novella *Ankunft im Alltag* [*Arrival in Daily Life*, 1961], a programmatic literary text that lent its name to the GDR's so-called *Ankunftsliteratur* ('arrival literature'). Like the literary heroes and heroines of the *Ankunftsliteratur* of the 1960s, who have to reconcile their high socialist ideals of a perfectible society with the sobering reality of socialism as it actually exists, Barbara too becomes reconciled with the life she has got, despite its many shortcomings.

Herein lies the film's East German sensibility. It is the way in which it chimes with particular attitudes familiar from East German literature and film that lends *Barbara* an emotional and psychological authenticity very different from *Das Leben der Anderen*. Closely related to this is the portrayal of the Stasi. Whereas von Donnersmarck's film showcases the Stasi's surveillance and interrogation techniques and even makes a Stasi officer the hero, in *Barbara* the local Stasi official (Rainer Bock) is an ordinary man who appears to be very much part of the daily life of the local community. He has his own worries (his wife is terminally ill with cancer), although this does not mean that viewers are invited to empathize with him. In this respect, *Barbara* is closer to DEFA films like Kurt Maetzig's *Das Kaninchen bin ich* [*The Rabbit is Me*, 1965/1990] and Roland Gräf's *Die Flucht*, where Stasi officials make fairly brief (though still threatening) appearances at Maria Morzeck's home and at the hospital where Dr Schmith (Armin Mueller-Stahl in his last DEFA role before leaving for the West) works. The Stasi official in *Die Flucht*, who questions Dr Schmith about a colleague's *Republikflucht*, is portrayed as a polite bureaucrat and certainly far less sinister than the West German trafficker who is organizing the doctor's own escape to the West.

Because of its plotline, *Die Flucht* evinces a number of conspicuous similarities with *Barbara*. Both films centre on paediatricians who are planning to defect to the West: Barbara because she wants to join her boyfriend in Düsseldorf; Dr Schmith because he is disillusioned with the lack of resources for his medical research into neonatal mortality. Both protagonists are portrayed as loners who 'separate' themselves from the socialist collective. Unexpectedly burgeoning romance with fellow doctors adds emotional conflict that complicates their carefully planned escapes. Though popular with East German audiences, Gräf's film – the first attempt to address the taboo topic of *Republikflucht* since Konrad Wolf's *Der geteilte Himmel* [*Divided Heaven*, 1964] – did not fare well with East German critics, despite its cautionary ending (Schmith pays with his life for attempting to flee). In the East German press, it was dismissed as an unsuccessful attempt of marrying an *Alltagsfilm* with the genre of a thriller. 'Instead of a genuine solution rooted in social reality, what we have is a cinematic fantasy-ending – all in all a poorly conceived thriller that fails to address the seriousness of a question that is posed in all sincerity'.[45]

Barbara, too, combines the generic conventions of the thriller (even in the absence of nondiegetic music to heighten suspense) with elements of DEFA's *Alltagsfilm*. However, what identifies this period drama as an afterimage is a distinctive aesthetic approach, indebted to the principles of the Berlin School, rather than the aesthetic doctrine of socialist realism. Petzold's prosthetic memory transfigures the GDR of the 1980s into an aesthetic object in which ordinary life becomes suffused with a sensuous intensity, even beauty, as we hardly ever see it in an *Alltagsfilm* (with *Jahrgang 45* being a rare exception). The film's 'sensuous engagement with the past', to cite Landsberg once more, deliberately eschews the drab colours, the ubiquitous shades of brown and grey, that have come to dominate the visual archive of the GDR (at least in the minds of people in the West).

This may in part be due to the fact that the handful of DEFA films which found an audience in the West were actually black-and-white films, notably the forbidden films that were censored and banned after the Eleventh Plenum of 1965. When they were eventually released in 1990, they elicited a certain voyeuristic frisson on either side of the Wall precisely because they had been forbidden. The 'ostalgic' comedy *Sonnenallee* makes a tongue-in-cheek reference to the visual cliché of a monochrome GDR when colour footage fades to black and white and Nina Hagen sings, 'Du hast den Farbfilm vergessen, Micha, nun glaubt kein Mensch wie schön's hier war' ('You've forgotten to use colour film stock, Micha, now nobody will believe how nice it was here!').

Obviously, DEFA produced films in brilliant colours, although these were predominantly fairy tale or genre films, such as the afore-mentioned *Heißer Sommer*, a hugely popular musical about a teenage holiday camp on the Baltic coast. Indeed, Petzold cites his memories of having watched *Heißer Sommer* as influential for the colour scheme of *Barbara* and as evidence that 'East Germany had to regard itself as colourful, too'.[46] In contrast to von Donnersmarck, whose cinematographer Hagen Boddanski has gone to great lengths to capture the GDR in its (supposedly) true colours by draining out all reds and blues from the film stock, Petzold has taken exactly the opposite approach. His cinematographer Hans Fromm creates a visual counterpoint to the prevailing media image that denounces 'the GDR, and socialism, as lacking in colour and, hence, vitality'.[47] Petzold rejects the clichéd image of the GDR as a grey and cold place as some kind of Western propaganda; in his visual universe, the sunflowers in the former East were just as tall and bright yellow as they were in the West. In order to show the GDR in its richest, warmest and 'most human' colours, *Barbara* was shot on Kodak 35 millimetre from late summer through to October, a time of year when the light is particularly golden and luminous.[48]

The most memorable images are long takes of Barbara riding her bicycle in the wide open landscape on the Baltic Sea, accompanied by the sound of a gusty breeze, rustling trees, bird song or crying seagulls. The astonishing clarity and, indeed, poetry of 'the ambient diegetic sounds ... provokes in us a sense of wonder about the materiality at the heart of the everyday', Marco Abel notes.[49] The fields are golden and the sky is mostly translucently blue. There is nothing claustrophobic about the former East here; in fact, the sheer beauty of the countryside would appear to make Barbara's decision to flee difficult – even though she refers to it as a country in which one can never find happiness. Only her habitual glance over the shoulder (Fig. 15.6), to check whether somebody might be following her, explains why she feels this way.

Equally powerful is the visceral physicality of those scenes which dramatize the invasiveness of the surveillance state: the piercing ring of the doorbell that announces yet another intrusion of the local Stasi officer, Herr Schütz, who has come to search every nook and cranny of Barbara's spartan flat. And, worse still, when the female Stasi officer slips on a pair of surgical rubber gloves and beckons Barbara to the bathroom, we can physically sense on our bodies what living in 'Stasiland' must have felt like.

Petzold relies on the power of images and eschews overt political messages. In fact, his films have been praised for their subtle investigation of the 'politics of the image' and for refusing to 'cater to the well-worn strategies of cinematic representation'.[50] Nevertheless, Berlin School filmmakers like Petzold, Angela Schanelec, Christoph Hochhäusler and Ulrich Köhler, to mention but a few members of the group, intervene in political debates about post-unification Germany and the logic

Figure 15.6: Wherever Barbara goes, she feels that somebody might be watching her. *Barbara* (2012). DVD screen capture.

of contemporary capitalist culture. Although *Barbara* is not a film with a political message as such, through the construction of prosthetic memory it forges collective identifications and allegiances that recuperate those aspects of life under real existing socialism that stand in stark (and positive) contrast to the excesses of contemporary capitalism. 'That's also what the GDR was – a utopian dream'. Petzold explains, 'a dream in which all basic needs were satisfied, an antifascist utopia in which there was genuine equality and in which the greed for profit did not sully everyday life. If the film appears to be so 'colourful' that's because capitalism is in a state of crisis'.[51]

Petzold's implicit critique of neoliberalism and the excesses of capitalism in the Berlin Republic is also a dominant concern in several of his previous films, notably *Yella* (2007), all of which are set in contemporary Germany. Perhaps what I have identified as the East German sensibility of *Barbara*, actually points towards an a-temporal convergence of the leftist political stance that underpins much of the work of the Berlin School as a whole, and the socialist utopia, a dream that kept the GDR going for forty years but that was readily cast aside in the process of German reunification. While *Barbara* disavows the bland 'ostalgic' longing for the GDR's material culture of the kind to be found in *Good Bye, Lenin!* and similar comedies, it nevertheless reflects a nostalgia for certain socialist values that are sorely missing in contemporary Germany's rampantly capitalist culture.

Conclusion

Das Leben der Anderen and *Barbara* project memories that betray the vantage point of distant chroniclers, whose retrospective engagement with the collective memory of the GDR evinces a Western vantage point. Both films illustrate in exemplary fashion the processes of prosthetic memory, insofar as they construct fictionalized accounts of the GDR's last decade that recycle and superimpose commodified memories to form multi-layered palimpsests.

Von Donnersmarck's film superimposes the memory of the Stasi onto that of the Nazis and, thereby, panders to international audiences' gruesome fascination with Germany's burdened pasts. The film's narrative trajectory, which traces the transformation of a Stasi perpetrator to a sensitive and righteous man, is the kind of stuff that Hollywood dreams on celluloid are made of. For DEFA filmmakers, who actually lived in the East German surveillance state, it would have been utterly inconceivable to make a Stasi captain the hero of a film and to manipulate audiences to empathize with him. A West German filmmaker like von Donnersmarck, by contrast, is at liberty to recast and fictionalize the GDR's traumatic past and make it subservient to the demands of the global entertainment industry.

For all its affinities with DEFA's *Alltagsfilme*, *Barbara* is also markedly different and has all the hallmarks of an afterimage. What it shares with the *Alltagsfilm* is its firm focus on work and the everyday, in which even the Stasi official is very much part and parcel of the fabric of ordinary life. What distinguishes *Barbara*, however, from DEFA's films about the everyday is the dichotomy between the cerebral and the sensual. DEFA films were cerebral because they were invariably harnessed to ideological intent. In *Barbara*, Petzold challenges the ossified visual clichés of an austere GDR that have colonized the media and our imagination. By applying the aesthetic principles of the Berlin School to a period film about the GDR, Petzold constructs an afterimage that reveals the rich sensory texture of ordinary life, in which glimpses of breath-taking beauty and moments of breathtaking fear exist side by side. Just as von Donnersmarck boldly rewrites the master narrative of the surveillance state, Petzold infuses the visual memory of the GDR with colour, light, even a haunting beauty that compels us to look – and to look again.

Daniela Berghahn is Professor of Film Studies at Royal Holloway, University of London. She has widely published on DEFA's antifascist and forbidden films as well as on the legacy of DEFA in post-unification German cinema, and is the author of *Hollywood behind the Wall: The Cinema of East Germany* (2005). More recent publications include *European Cinema in Motion: Migrant and Diasporic Film in Contemporary Europe* (with Claudia Sternberg (2010)), *Far-Flung Families in Film: The Diasporic Family in Contemporary European Cinema* (2013) and *Head-On* (2015).

Notes

1. Randall Halle, '*The Lives of Others*, the New Matrix of Production and the Profitable Past', in Paul Cooke (ed), '*The Lives of Others' and Contemporary German Film. A Companion*, Berlin, Boston: de Gruyter, 2013, pp. 59–78, p. 62.
2. For a detailed account, see Daniela Berghahn, *Hollywood Behind the Wall. The Cinema of East Germany*, Manchester: Manchester University Press, 2005, pp. 212–29.
3. 'Stasiland' is a term coined by Anna Funder in her book, *Stasiland. Stories From Behind the Wall*, London: Granta, 2003.

4. Marianne Hirsch, *Family Frames. Photography, Narrative and Postmemory*, Cambridge, MA and London: Harvard University Press, 1997; and Alison Landsberg, *Prosthetic Memory. The Transformation of American Remembrance in the Age of Mass Culture*, New York: Columbia University Press, 2004.
5. Inge Stephan and Alexandra Tacke, 'Einleitung', in Inge Stephan and Alexandra Tacke (eds), *Nachbilder des Holocaust*, Cologne: Böhlau, 2007, pp. 7–17 (p. 7). Unless stated otherwise, all translations from German into English in this chapter are the author's.
6. Ibid.
7. Ibid., pp. 8–9 and p.11.
8. Inge Stephan and Alexandra Tacke apply the same critical framework to the cultural memory of the GDR in the edited collection *Nachbilder der Wende*, Cologne: Böhlau, 2008.
9. Michael Rothberg, *Multidirectional Memory. Remembering the Holocaust in the Age of Decolonization*, Stanford: Stanford University Press, 2009, p. 271.
10. Rothberg, p. 11.
11. Landsberg, p. 20.
12. Interview with Christian Petzold, 'The Making of 1', included in the extras of the German DVD release of *Barbara*; Cristina Nord and Christian Petzold, 'Ich wollte, dass die DDR Farben hat', *Taz.de*, 11 February 2012.
13. The term 'Berlin School' refers to a group of directors, including Petzold, Thomas Arslan and Angela Schanelec, who graduated from the Deutsche Film- und Fernsehakademie (DFFB) in Berlin in the early 1990s. Subsequently, the label has also been applied to Ulrich Köhler, Christoph Hochhäusler, Benjamin Heisenberg, Maren Ade and Valeska Grisebach, who honed their skills at other film schools. See Marco Abel, *The Counter Cinema of the Berlin School*, Rochester, NY: Camden House, 2013.
14. R. Kurt Osenlund and Christian Petzold, 'Christian Petzold on *Barbara*', *Filmmaker Magazine*, 21 December 2012.
15. Nord and Petzold.
16. Florian Henckel von Donnersmarck, 'Thirteen Questions with Florian Henckel von Donnersmarck', [= www.sonyclassics.com/thelivesofothers/externalLoads/TheLivesofOthers.pdfwww.sonyclassics.com/thelivesofothers/externalLoads/TheLivesofOthers.pdf], accessed 20 June 2016.
17. Florian Henckel von Donnersmarck, 'Seeing a Film Before You Make It. Introduced by Christopher Young', in Cooke, pp.19–36 (p. 23).
18. Wolf Biermann, 'Die Gespenster treten aus dem Schatten', *Die Welt*, 22 March 2006.
19. Andreas Dresen, 'Die Bilder der Anderen', *Film-Dienst*, 22 (2009), 32–34 (33).
20. Joshua Feinstein, *The Triumph of the Ordinary. Depictions of Daily Life in the East German Cinema 1949-1989*, Chapel Hill and London: University of North Carolina Press, 2002, p. 240.
21. Cited in Frank Junghänel, 'Zwei Liebende unter staatlicher "Obhut": Frank Beyer verfilmte Volker Brauns "Unvollendete Geschichte" von 1975', *Leipziger Volkszeitung*, 15 November 1991.
22. Petzold's *Barbara* also features a teenage boy, Marco, whose attempted suicide results in a coma and who, when he wakes up, discovers he has lost his emotional memory.
23. Anna Funder, 'Eyes Without a Face', *Sight & Sound* 5 (2007), 16–20, (19).
24. Robert McKee, *Story. Substance, Style and the Principles of Screenwriting*, London: Methuen, 1999, p. 126.
25. Ibid.
26. Ibid.

27. Although the German is perhaps better translated as 'Sonata of a Good Man', I am using 'Sonata for a Good Man' in accordance with the English subtitles.
28. Lu Seegers, 'Das Leben der Anderen oder die "richtige" Erinnerung an die DDR', in Astrid Erll and Stephanie Wodianka (eds), *Film und kulturelle Erinnerung. Plurimediale Konstellationen*, Berlin: de Gruyter, 2008, pp. 21–52.
29. David Bathrick, 'Rescreening the "Holocaust". The Children's Stories', *New German Critique* 80 (2000), 41–58.
30. Timothy Garton Ash, 'The Stasi on Our Minds', *The New York Review of Books*, 31 May 2007.
31. Leo Baudry, 'Genre: The Conventions of Connection', in Gerald Mast and Marshall Cohen (eds), *Film Theory and Criticism* (3rd edition), Oxford: Oxford University Press, 1985, pp. 411–33 (p. 416).
32. Thomas Schatz, *Hollywood Genres. Formulas, Filmmaking, and the Studio System*, Boston, MA: McGraw Hill, 1981, p. 31.
33. Cited in Jaimey Fisher, 'German Historical Film as Production Trend: European Heritage Cinema and Melodrama in *The Lives of Others*', in Jaimey Fisher and Brad Prager (eds), *The Collapse of the Conventional. German Film and its Politics at the Turn of the Twenty-First Century*, Detroit: Wayne State University Press, 2010, pp. 186–215 (p. 197).
34. See Fisher, 'German Historical Film'; and David Bathrick, '*Der Tangospieler*. Coming in from the Cold Once and for All. *The Lives of Others* as Cold War Spy Film', in Cooke, pp. 121–38.
35. Fisher, 'German Historical Film'.
36. Landsberg, p. 24.
37. Stefan Schirmer and Martin Machowecz, 'Was es da an Irren gab', *Zeit Online*, 31 January 2013 [= www.zeit.de/2013/06/Christian-Petzold-Filme-DDR-Osten], accessed 20 June 2016.
38. Christian Petzold, Susanne Beyer and Claudia Voigt, 'Nie Mallorca, immer DDR', *Der Spiegel*, 13 (2012), 138.
39. Petzold, 'The Making of 1'.
40. Ibid.
41. Feinstein, pp. 7 and 6.
42. Ibid., p. 195.
43. Petzold cited in W. Husmann, 'Liebe in Zeiten des Misstrauens', *Zeit Online*, 13 February 2012 [= www.zeit.de/kultur/film/2012-02/berlinale-barbara-petzold], accessed 20 June 2016.
44. Christian Petzold, *Barbara*, Berlin: Deutsche Filmakademie, 2012, p. 112.
45. Manfred Haedler, 'Fehltritt eines Arztes', *Der Morgen*, 15 October 1977.
46. Petzold cited in Jaimey Fisher, *Christian Petzold*, Urbana and Chicago: University of Illinois Press, 2013, p. 162.
47. Sabine Hake, 'On the Lives of Objects', in Cooke, pp. 199–219 (p. 205).
48. Nord and Petzold.
49. Abel, *The Counter Cinema of the Berlin School*, p. 16.
50. Marco Abel, 'Imagining Germany. The (Political) Cinema of Christian Petzold', in Fisher and Prager, pp. 258–84 (pp. 273 and 276).
51. Petzold cited in Schirmer and Machowecz.

Select Bibliography

Abel, Marco, *The Counter Cinema of the Berlin School*, Rochester, NY: Camden House, 2013.
Abel, Marco, 'Imagining Germany. The (Political) Cinema of Christian Petzold', in Jaimey Fisher and Brad Prager (eds), *The Collapse of the Conventional. German Film and its Politics at the Turn of the Twenty-First Century*, Detroit: Wayne State University Press, 2010, pp. 258-84.
Abusch, Alexander, 'Reale Perspektiven unserer sozialistischen Filmproduktion', *Deutsche Filmkunst* 7/1957, 193-94.
Ackermann, Anton, 'Zur Parteilichkeit in der Filmkunst', *Einheit. Zeitschrift für Theorie und Praxis des wissenschaftlichen Sozialismus* 13.4 (1958), 527-38.
Adorno, Theodor W., *Introduction to the Sociology of Music*, trans. E.B. Ashton, New York: Continuum, 1988.
Agde, Günter (ed), *Kurt Maetzig. Filmarbeit. Gespräche. Reden. Schriften*, Berlin: Henschel, 1987.
Agee, James, *Agee on Film*, New York: Random House, 2000.
Agotai, Doris, *Architekturen in Zelluloid. Der filmische Blick auf den Raum*, Bielefeld: transcript, 2007.
Albrecht, Donald and Ralph Eue, *Architektur im Film. Die Moderne als große Illusion*, Basel, Boston, Berlin: Birkhäuser, 1989.
Allan, Seán and John Sandford (eds), *DEFA. East German Cinema, 1946-1992*, New York, Oxford: Berghahn, 1996.
Allan, Seán, 'Representations of Art and the Artist in East German Cinema', in Marc Silberman and Henning Wrage (eds), *DEFA at the Crossroads of East German and International Film Culture*, Berlin, Boston: de Gruyter, 2014, pp. 87-105.
Alter, Nora M., 'Excessive Pre/Requisites. Vietnam Through the East German Lens', *Cultural Critique* 35.1 (1996-1997), 39-79.
Andrews, James T. and Asif A. Siddiqi (eds), *Into the Cosmos. Space Exploration and Soviet Culture*, Pittsburgh: University of Pittsburgh Press, 2011.
Applegate, Celia and Pamela A. Potter (eds), *Music and German National Identity*, Chicago: University of Chicago Press, 2002.
Augustine, Dolores, 'The Power Question in the GDR', *German Studies Review* 34.3 (2011), 633-48.
Axen, Hermann, 'Über die Fragen der fortschrittlichen Filmkunst', in *Für den Aufschwung der fortschrittlichen deutschen Filmkunst*, Berlin: Dietz, 1953, pp. 15-46.
Baer, Willi and Karl-Heinz Dellwo (eds), *Diktatur und Widerstand in Chile* [= Bibliothek des Widerstands, vol. 29], Hamburg: Laika, 2013.
Baier, Christof, André Bischoff and Marion Hilliges (eds), *Ordnung und Mannigfaltigkeit. Beiträge zur Architektur- und Stadtbaugeschichte für Ulrich Reinisch*, Weimar: Vdg, 2011.

Baptist, Edward, *The Half Has Never Been Told. Slavery and the Making of American Capitalism*, New York: Basic Books, 2014.
Barnett, Thomas P.M., *Romanian and East German Policies in the Third World. Comparing the Strategies of Ceaușescu and Honecker*, Westport, CT: Praeger, 1992.
Bataille, Gretchen M. (ed), *Native American Representations*, Lincoln, NE: University of Nebraska Press, 2001.
Bathrick, David, 'From UFA to DEFA. Past as Present in Early GDR Films', in Jost Hermand and Marc Silberman (eds), *Contentious Memories. Looking Back at the GDR*, New York, Washington: Lang, 1998, pp. 169-88.
Bathrick, David, 'Rescreening the "Holocaust". The Children's Stories', *New German Critique* 80 (2000), 41-58.
Bathrick, David, '*Der Tangospieler*. Coming in from the Cold Once and for All. *The Lives of Others* as Cold War Spy Film', in Paul Cooke (ed), '*The Lives of Others' and Contemporary German Film. A Companion*, Berlin, Boston: de Gruyter, 2013, pp. 121-38.
Baudry, Leo, 'Genre: The Conventions of Connection', in Gerald Mast and Marshall Cohen (eds), *Film Theory and Criticism* (3rd edition), Oxford: Oxford University Press, 1985, pp. 411-33.
Becker, Dorothea, *Zwischen Ideologie und Autonomie. Die DDR-Forschung über die deutsche Filmgeschichte*, Münster, Hamburg, London: Lit, 1999.
Berardi, Franco, *After the Future*, edited by Gary Genosko and Nicholas Thoburn, trans. Arianna Bove et al., Oakland: AK Press, 2011.
Berdahl, Daphne, *Where the World Ended. Re-Unification and Identity in the German Borderland*, Berkeley: University of California Press, 1999.
Berg, Michael, Albrecht von Massow and Nina Noeske (eds), *Zwischen Macht und Freiheit: Neue Musik in der DDR*, Cologne: Böhlau, 2004.
Berger, Eberhard and Joachim Giera (eds), *77 Märchenfilme. Ein Filmführer für jung und alt*, Berlin: Henschel, 1990.
Bergfelder, Tim, *International Adventures. German Popular Cinema and European Co-Productions in the 1960s*, New York, Oxford: Berghahn, 2005.
Berghahn, Daniela, *Hollywood Behind the Wall. The Cinema of East Germany*, Manchester: Manchester University Press, 2005.
Betts, Paul, 'The Bauhaus in the German Democratic Republic – between Formalism and Pragmatism', in Jeannine Fiedler and Paul Feierabend (eds), *Bauhaus*, Cologne: Könemann, 2000, pp. 42-49.
Beyer, René, 'Die Etablierung der Merseburger DEFA-Filmtage', in René Beyer and Alfred Georg Frei (eds), *Die Traumfabrik von gestern. Die Merseburger DEFA-Filmtage*, Halle: Cornelius, 2008, pp. 23-52.
Beyer, René and Alfred Georg Frei (eds), *Die Traumfabrik von gestern. Die Merseburger DEFA-Filmtage*, Halle: Cornelius, 2008.
Bien, Fabien, *Oper im Schaufenster. Die Berliner Opernbühnen in den 1950er-Jahren als Orte nationaler kultureller Repräsentation*, Vienna: Böhlau, 2011.

Birgel, Franz, 'The Only Good Indian is a Good DEFA Indian. East German Variations on the Most American of all Genres', in Cynthia J. Miller and A. Bowdoin Van Riper (eds), *International Westerns. Relocating the Frontier*, Lanham, MD: Scarecrow Press, 2014, pp. 37–62.

Bivens, Hunter, '9 March 1954: *'Ernst Thälmann – Sohn seiner Klasse* Marks High Point of Socialist Realism', in Jennifer Kapczynski and Michael Richardson (eds), *A New History of German Cinema*, Rochester, NY: Camden House, 2012, pp. 347–52.

Blackford, James, 'Red Skies. Soviet Science Fiction', *Sight & Sound* 21.7 (2011), 44–48.

Blessing, Benita, *The Antifascist Classroom. Denazification in Soviet-occupied Germany, 1946–1949*, New York: Palgrave Macmillan, 2006.

Blunk, Harry, *Die DDR in ihren Spielfilmen. Reproduktion und Konzeption der DDR-Gesellschaft im neueren DEFA-Gegenwartsspielfilm*, Munich: Profil, 1984.

Blunk, Harry and Dirk Jungnickel (eds), *Filmland DDR. Ein Reader zu Geschichte, Funktion und Wirkung der DEFA*, Cologne: Verlag für Wissenschaft und Politik, 1990.

Bock, Hans-Michael and Michael Töteberg (eds), *Das Ufa-Buch. Kunst und Krisen – Stars und Regisseure – Wirtschaft und Politik. Die internationale Geschichte von Deutschlands größtem Film-Konzern,* Frankfurt am Main: Zweitausendeins, 1992.

Bordwell, David, *Narration in the Fiction Film*, Madison: University of Wisconsin Press, 1985.

Borger, Lenny, 'Ufas Russen. Die Emigranten von Montreuil bis Babelsberg', in Hans-Michael Bock and Michael Töteberg (eds), *Das Ufa-Buch. Kunst und Krisen – Stars und Regisseure – Wirtschaft und Politik. Die internationale Geschichte von Deutschlands größtem Film-Konzern* Frankfurt am Main: Zweitausendeins, 1992, pp. 236–39.

Borries, Friedrich von and Jens-Uwe Fischer, *Sozialistische Cowboys. Der Wilde Westen Ostdeutschlands*, Frankfurt am Main: Suhrkamp, 2008.

Böttcher, Claudia, Judith Kretzschmar and Corinna Schier, *Heynowski & Scheumann. Dokumentarfilmer im Klassenkampf. Eine kommentierte Filmographie*, Leipzig: Leipziger Universitätsverlag, 2002.

Brandes, Ute (ed), *Zwischen gestern und morgen: Schriftstellerinnen der DDR aus amerikanischer Sicht*, Berlin: Lang, 1992.

Braun, Volker, 'Durchgearbeitete Landschaft', in Volker Braun, *Gegen die symmetrische Welt. Gedichte*, Frankfurt am Main: Suhrkamp, 1974.

Braunmüller, Robert, *Oper als Drama. Das 'realistische Musiktheater' Walter Felsensteins*, Tübingen: de Gruyter, 2002.

Briel, Holger, 'Native Americans in the films of the GDR and Czechoslovakia', *European Journal of American Culture* 31.3 (2012), 231–47.

Brockmann, Stephen, *A Critical History of German Film*, Rochester, NY: Camden House, 2010.

Broe, Dennis, 'Have Dialectic, Will Travel', in Terri Ginsberg and Andreas Mensch (eds), *A Companion to German Cinema*, Malden, MA: Blackwell, 2012, pp. 27–54.

Brown, Noel and Bruce Babington (eds), *Family Films in Global Cinema. Beyond Disney*, London: Tauris, 2014.

Brown, Noel, and Bruce Babington, 'Introduction. Children's Films and Family Films' in Brown, Noel and Bruce Babington (eds), *Family Films in Global Cinema. Beyond Disney*, London: Tauris, 2014.

Brysac, Shareen Blair, *Resisting Hitler. Mildred Harnack and the Red Orchestra*, New York: Oxford University Press, 2000.

Buch, Esteban, *Beethoven's Ninth. A Political History*, trans. Richard Miller, Chicago: University of Chicago Press, 2003.

Buhler, James, 'Analytical and Interpretive Approaches to Film Music, II: Interpreting Interactions of Music and Film', in Kevin J. Donnelly (ed), *Film Music. Critical Approaches*, New York: Continuum, 2001, pp. 39-61.

Buhler, James, 'Wagnerian Motives. Narrative Integration and the Development of Silent Film Accompaniment, 1908-1913', in Jeongwon Joe and Sander Gilman (eds), *Wagner and Cinema*, Bloomington: Indiana University Press, 2010, pp. 27-45.

Bulgakowa, Oksana (ed), *Resonanz-Räume. Die Stimme und die Medien*, Berlin: Bertz + Fischer, 2012.

Bulgakowa, Oksana, 'DEFA-Filme im Kontext der "neuen Wellen"', in Michael Wedel, Barton Byg, Andy Räder, Skyler Arndt-Briggs and Evan Torner (eds), *DEFA International. Grenzen und Grenzüberschreitungen. Transnationale Filmbeziehungen der DEFA vor und nach dem Mauerbau*, Wiesbaden: VS Verlag, 2013, pp. 45–60.

Burch, Noel, *Theory of Film Practice*, trans. Helen Lane, New York: Praeger, 1973.

Byg, Barton, 'What Might Have Been: DEFA Films of the Past and the Future of German Cinema', *Cineaste*, 17.4 (1990), 9–15.

Byg, Barton, 'Geschichte, Trauer und weibliche Identität im Film. *Hiroshima mon amour* und *Der geteilte Himmel*', in Ute Brandes (ed), *Zwischen gestern und morgen: Schriftstellerinnen der DDR aus amerikanischer Sicht*, Berlin: Lang, 1992, pp. 95–112.

Byg, Barton 'Introduction. Reassessing DEFA Today', in Barton Byg and Betheny Moore (eds), *Moving Images of East Germany. Past and Future of DEFA Film*, Washington DC: AICGS, 2002, pp. 1–23.

Byg, Barton, 'Spectral Images in the Afterlife of GDR Cinema', in Brigitta B. Wagner (ed), *DEFA after East Germany*, Rochester, NY: Camden House, 2014, pp. 24–50.

Byg, Barton and Betheny Moore (eds), *Moving Images of East Germany. Past and Future of DEFA Film*, Washington DC: AICGS, 2002.

Calico, Joy H., 'The Politics of Opera in the German Democratic Republic, 1945-1961', unpublished PhD Diss., Duke University, 1999.

Calico, Joy H., '"Für eine neue Nationaloper". Opera in the Discourses of Unification and Legitimation in the German Democratic Republic', in Celia Applegate and Pamela A. Potter (eds), *Music and German National Identity*, Chicago: University of Chicago Press, 2002, pp. 190–204.

Calico, Joy H., 'Wagner in East Germany. Joachim Herz's *Der fliegende Holländer*', in Jeongwon Joe and Sander L. Gilman (eds), *Wagner and Cinema*, Bloomington: Indiana University Press, 2010, pp. 294-313.

Calico, Joy H., 'The Legacies of GDR Directors on the Post-Wende Opera Stage', in Elaine Kelly and Amy Wlodarski (eds), *Art Outside the Lines. New Perspectives on GDR Art Culture*, Amsterdam: Rodopi, 2011, pp. 131–54.

Casad, Madeleine, 'Rescreening Memory Beyond the Wall', *The Germanic Review* 88.3 (2013), 320–38.

Castillo, Greg, *Cold War on the Home Front. The Soft Power of Midcentury Design*, Minneapolis: University of Minnesota Press, 2010.

Cho, Joanne Miyang and David M. Crowe (eds), *Germany and China. Transnational Encounters since the Eighteenth Century*, New York: Palgrave Macmillan, 2014.

Chow, Rey, 'When Reflexivity Becomes Porn. Mutations of a Modernist Theoretical Practice', in Jane Elliot and Derek Attridge (eds), *Theory After Theory*, New York: Routledge, 2011, pp. 135–48.

Ciesla, Burghard, 'Droht der Menschheit Vernichtung? *Der schweigende Stern* – *First Spaceship on Venus*. Ein Vergleich', in Ralf Schenk and Erika Richter (eds), *apropos: Film 2002* [= Jahrbuch der DEFA-Stiftung, 2002], Berlin: Bertz + Fischer, 2002, pp. 121–36.

Citron, Marcia, *Opera on Screen*, New Haven, CT: Yale University Press, 2000.

Cooke, Paul (ed), *'The Lives of Others' and Contemporary German Film. A Companion*, Berlin, Boston: de Gruyter, 2013.

Cosgrove, Mary and Anne Richards (eds), *Sadness and Melancholy in German-Language Literature from the Seventeenth Century to the Present* [= Edinburgh German Yearbook, 6], Rochester, NY: Camden House, 2012.

Cosgrove, Mary, 'Introduction: Sadness and Melancholy in German-Language Literature from the Seventeenth Century to the Present. An Overview', in Mary Cosgrove and Anne Richards (eds), *Sadness and Melancholy in German-Language Literature from the Seventeenth Century to the Present* [= Edinburgh German Yearbook, 6], Rochester, NY: Camden House, 2012, pp. 1–19.

Courtade, Francis, 'Die deutsch-französischen Koproduktionen', in Heike Hurst and Heiner Gassen (eds), *Kameradschaft-Querelle. Kino zwischen Deutschland und Frankreich*, Munich: Institut Français de Munich, 1991.

Crowe, David M., 'Sino-German Relations, 1871–1917', in Joanne Miyang Cho and David M. Crowe (eds), *Germany and China. Transnational Encounters since the Eighteenth Century*, New York: Palgrave Macmillan, 2014, pp. 71–96.

Dagron, Alfonso Gumucio, *El cine de los trabajadores*, Managua: Taller de Cine Super 8 de la CST, 1981.

Dahlhaus, Carl, *Musikalischer Realismus*, Munich: Piper, 1982.

Dallin, David, *Die Sowjetspionage. Prinzipien und Praktiken*, Cologne: Verlag für Politik und Wirtschaft, 1956.

Davidson, John E. and Sabine Hake (eds), *Framing the Fifties. Cinema in a Divided Germany*, New York, Oxford: Berghahn, 2007.

Deeken, Annette, 'Die Erfindung des DEFA-Indianers. Eine deutsch-deutsche Mediengeschichte', in Thomas Koebner (ed), *Indianer vor der Kamera*, Munich: edition text+kritik, 2011, pp. 158–80.

Deloria, Philip J., *Playing Indian*, New Haven, CT: Yale University Press, 1998.
Dika, Vera, 'An East German Indianerfilm. The Bear in Sheep's Clothing', *Jumpcut*, 50 (2008) [= http://www.ejumpcut.org/archive/jc50.2008/Dika-indianer/], accessed 16 June 2016.
Donnelly, Kevin J. (ed), *Film Music. Critical Approaches*, New York: Continuum, 2001.
Dorgerloh, Annette, 'Die Räume des Ingenieurs. Zur Szenographie des verbotenen DEFA-Films *Der Frühling braucht Zeit*', in Christof Baier, André Bischoff and Marion Hilliges (eds), *Ordnung und Mannigfaltigkeit. Beiträge zur Architektur- und Stadtbaugeschichte für Ulrich Reinisch*, Weimar: Vdg, 2011, pp. 85-90.
Dorgerloh, Annette, 'Nachkriegsmoderne als Herausforderung. Konsträume zwischen West und Ost in DEFA-Filmen der fünfziger Jahre', *Kunsttexte.de* (January 2014) [= http://edoc.hu-berlin.de/kunsttexte/2014-1/dorgerloh-annette-2/PDF/dorgerloh.pdf], accessed 20 June 2016.
Durovicová, Nataša, and Kathleen Newman (eds) *World Cinemas, Transnational Perspectives*, New York: Routledge, 2010.
Dyer, Richard, *Stars*, London: BFI, 1998.
Eckert, Stefanie, *Das Erbe der DEFA. Die fast unendliche Geschichte einer Stiftungsgründung*, Berlin: DEFA-Stiftung, 2008.
Elliot, Jane and Derek Attridge (eds), *Theory After Theory*, New York: Routledge, 2011.
Engelke, Henning and Simon Kopp, 'Der Western im Osten. Genre, Zeitlichkeit und Authentizität im DEFA- und im Hollywood-Western', *Zeithistorische Forschungen* 1.2 (2004) [= http://www.zeithistorische-forschungen.de/16126041-Engelke-Kopp-2-2004], accessed 16 June 2016.
Erll, Astrid and Stephanie Wodianka (eds), *Film und kulturelle Erinnerung. Plurimediale Konstellationen*, Berlin: de Gruyter, 2008.
Esherick, Joseph W., *The Origins of the Boxer Uprising*, Berkeley, University of California Press, 1987.
Esler, Dominic William, 'Soviet Science Fiction of the 1920s. Explaining a Literary Genre in its Political and Social Context', *Foundation* 109 (2010), 27-52.
Fawkes, Richard, *Opera on Film*, London: Duckworth, 2000.
Feinstein, Joshua, *The Triumph of the Ordinary. Depictions of Daily Life in the East German Cinema, 1949-1989*, Chapel Hill and London: University of North Carolina Press, 2002.
Fellmer, Claudia, 'Stars in East German Cinema', unpublished PhD Diss., University of Southampton, 2002.
Felsmann, Klaus-Dieter and Bernd Sahling, *Deutsche Kinderfilme aus Babelsberg: Werkstattgespräche - Rezeptionsräume*, Berlin: DEFA-Stiftung, 2010.
Ferber, Michael (ed), *A Companion to European Romanticism*, Malden, MA: Blackwell, 2005.
Fiedler, Jeannine and Paul Feierabend (eds), *Bauhaus*, Cologne: Könemann, 2000.
Finke Klaus (ed), *DEFA-Film als nationales Kulturerbe?* [= Beiträge zur Film- und Fernsehwissenschaft, vol. 58] (2001).

Finke, Klaus, 'DEFA-Film als "nationales Kulturerbe"? Thesen zum DEFA-Film und seiner wissenschaftlichen Aufarbeitung', in Klaus Finke (ed), *DEFA-Film als nationales Kulturerbe?* [= Beiträge zur Film- und Fernsehwissenschaft, vol. 58] (2001), pp. 93-108.

Fisher, Jaimey, *Christian Petzold*, Urbana and Chicago: University of Illinois Press, 2013.

Fisher, Jaimey, 'German Historical Film as Production Trend: European Heritage Cinema and Melodrama in *The Lives of Others*', in Jaimey Fisher and Brad Prager (eds), *The Collapse of the Conventional. German Film and its Politics at the Turn of the Twenty-First Century*, Detroit: Wayne State University Press, 2010, pp. 186-215.

Fisher, Jaimey, 'A Late Genre Fade. Utopianism and its Twilight in DEFA's Science Fiction, Literary and Western Films', in Marc Silberman and Henning Wrage (eds), *DEFA at the Crossroads of East German and International Film Culture*, Berlin, Boston: de Gruyter, 2014, pp. 177-196.

Fisher, Jaimey and Brad Prager (eds), *The Collapse of the Conventional. German Film and its Politics at the Turn of the Twenty-First Century*, Detroit: Wayne State University Press, 2010.

Fleury, Antoine and Lubor Jilek (eds), *Une Europe malgré tout, 1945-1990, Contacts et réseaux culturels, intellectuels et scientifiques entre Européens dans la guerre froide*, Brussels: Lang, 2009.

Flicke, Wilhelm, *Die rote Kapelle*, Hilden: Vier-Brücken, 1949.

Flierl, Bruno, *Gebaute DDR. Über Stadtplaner, Architekten und die Macht*, Berlin: Verlag für Bauwesen, 1998.

Flinn, Caryl, *The New German Cinema. Music, History and the Matter of Style*, Berkeley: University of California Press, 2004.

Forster, Ralf and Volker Petzold, *Im Schatten der DEFA*, Constance: UVK Medien, 2010.

Frackman, Kyle and Larson Powell (eds), *Classical Music in the GDR*, Rochester, NY: Camden House, 2015.

Friedrichsmeyer, Sara, Sara Lennox and Susanne Zantop (eds), *The Imperialist Imagination. German Colonialism and Its Legacy*, Ann Arbor: University of Michigan Press, 1998.

Fritsche, Karin and Claus Löser (eds), *Gegenbilder. Filmische Subversion in der DDR 1976-1989*, Berlin: Janus, 1996.

Fritzsche, Sonja, *Science Fiction Literature in East Germany* [= DDR Studien/East German Studies Series, 15], Bern, Oxford: Lang, 2006.

Fritzsche, Sonja, 'The Natural and the Artificial. East German Science Fiction Film Responds to Kubrick and Tarkovsky', *Film & History* 40.2 (2010), 80-101 [Special issue: *Visions of Science and Technology in Film*].

Fritzsche, Sonja (ed), *The Liverpool Companion to World Science Fiction Film*, Liverpool: Liverpool University Press, 2014.

Fuchs, Anne and Kathleen James Chakraborty (eds), *Transformations of German Cultural Identity 1989-2009*, [Special edition of] *New German Critique*, 116 (2012).

Fuchs, Peter Paul (ed), *The Music Theater of Walter Felsenstein. Collected Articles, Speeches and Interviews by Walter Felsenstein and Others*, New York: Norton, 1975.

Funder, Anna, *Stasiland. Stories From Behind the Wall*, London: Granta, 2003.

Furlong, Alison M., 'Georg Wildhagen's *Figaros Hochzeit*. How an Italian Opera Based on a French Play Became a German Socialist Film', MA thesis, The Ohio State University, 2010.

Gad, Urban, *Der Film. Seine Mittel – Seine Ziele*, Berlin: Schuster und Loeffler, 1920.

Galt, Rosalind and Karl Schoonover (eds), *Global Art Cinema. New Theories and Histories*, Oxford: Oxford University Press, 2010.

Gemünden, Gerd, 'Between Karl May and Karl Marx. The DEFA *Indianerfilme* (1965–1983)', *Film History* 10.3 (1998), 399–407.

Genette, Gérard, *Narrative Discourse. An Essay in Method*, trans. Jane E. Lewin, Ithaca: Cornell University Press, 1980.

Gestwa, Klaus, 'Der Kolumbus des Kosmos. Der Kult um Jurij Gagarin', *Osteuropa* 59.10 (2009), 121–52.

Giesenfeld, Günter (ed), *Der DEFA-Film. Erbe oder Episode?*, Marburg: Schüren, 1993.

Ginsberg, Terri and Andreas Mensch (eds), *A Companion to German Cinema*, Malden, MA: Blackwell, 2012.

Gledhill, Christine (ed), *Stardom. Industry of Desire*, London, New York: Routledge, 1991.

Gleijeses, Piero, *Conflicting Missions. Havana, Washington, and Africa, 1959–1976*, Chapel Hill: University of North Carolina Press, 2002.

Goldmark, Daniel, Lawrence Kramer and Richard Leppert (eds), *Beyond the Soundtrack. Representing Music in Cinema*, Berkeley: University of California Press, 2007.

Goodbody, Axel (ed), *The Culture of German Environmentalism*, New York and Oxford: Berghahn, 2002.

Gorbman, Claudia, *Unheard Melodies. Narrative Film Music*, London: BFI, Bloomington: University of Indiana Press, 1989.

Goulding, Daniel J. (ed), *Post New Wave Cinema in the Soviet Union and Eastern Europe*, Bloomington and Indianapolis: Indiana University Press, 1989.

Grandin, Greg, *The Empire of Necessity. Slavery, Freedom, and Deception in the New World*, New York: Metropolitan Books, 2014.

Grant, Colin, *Literary Communication from Consensus to Rupture. Practice and Theory in Honecker's GDR*, Amsterdam: Rodopi, 1995.

Gray, William Glenn, *Germany's Cold War. The Global Campaign to Isolate East Germany, 1949–1969*, Chapel Hill: University of North Carolina Press, 2003.

Groys, Boris, *Gesamtkunstwerk Stalin. Die gespaltene Kultur in der Sowjetunion*, Munich: Hanser, 2008.

Guder, Andrea, *Genosse Hauptmann auf Verbrecherjagd. Der Krimi in Film und Fernsehen der DDR*, Bonn: ARCult Media, 2003.

Gumbert, Heather, 'Cold War Theaters. Cosmonaut Titov at the Berlin Wall', in James T. Andrews and Asif A. Siddiqi (eds), *Into the Cosmos. Space Exploration and Soviet Culture*, Pittsburgh: University of Pittsburgh Press, 2011, pp. 240–62.

Gur, Golan, 'Classicism as Anti-Fascist Heritage. Realism and Myth in Ernst Hermann Meyer's *Mansfelder Oratorium* (1950)', in Kyle Frackman and Larson Powell (eds), *Classical Music in the GDR*, Rochester, NY: Camden House, 2015, pp. 34–57.

Haas, Klaus-Detlef and Dieter Wolf (eds), *Sozialistische Filmkunst,* Berlin: Karl Dietz Verlag, 2011.
Habel, F-B. and Volker Wachter (eds), *Das Große Lexikon der DDR-Stars,* Berlin: Schwarzkopf & Schwarzkopf, 2002.
Habel, F-B., *Dean Reed. Die wahre Geschichte,* Berlin: Neues Leben, 2007.
Hake, Sabine, *German National Cinema,* London, New York: Routledge, 2002.
Hake, Sabine, 'On the Lives of Objects', in Paul Cooke (ed), *'The Lives of Others' and Contemporary German Film. A Companion,* Berlin, Boston: de Gruyter, 2013, pp. 199-219.
Hake, Sabine, 'Public Figures, Political Symbols, Famous Stars. Actors in DEFA Cinema and Beyond', in Marc Silberman and Henning Wrage (eds), *DEFA at the Crossroads of East German and International Film Culture,* Berlin, Boston: de Gruyter, 2014, pp. 197-220.
Halle, Randall, 'The Lives of Others, the New Matrix of Production and the Profitable Past', in Paul Cooke (ed), *'The Lives of Others' and Contemporary German Film. A Companion,* Berlin and Boston: de Gruyter, 2013, pp. 59-78.
Halle, Randall and Margaret McCarthy (eds), *Light Motives. German Popular Film in Perspective,* Detroit: Wayne State University Press, 2003.
Hanisch, Michael, *Nachrichten aus einem Land ohne Schurken, oder In Diktaturen hat der Krimi nicht viel zu melden,* in Ralf Schenk and Erika Richter (eds), *apropos: Film 2001* [= Das Jahrbuch der DEFA-Stiftung, 2001], Berlin: Das Neue Berlin, 2001, pp. 194-222.
Häntzsche, Hellmuth, 'Erste Erfahrung aus der Arbeit der Kinder- und Jugendfilmproduktion', *Deutsche Filmkunst. Zeitschrift für Theorie und Praxis des Filmschaffens* 5 (1954), 7-11.
Hardt, Ursula, *From Caligari to California. Erich Pommer's Life in the International Film Wars,* Providence RI, Oxford: Berghahn, 1996.
Haupt, Stefan, *Urheberrecht und DEFA Film,* Berlin: DEFA-Stiftung, 2005.
Heiduschke, Sebastian, *East German Cinema. DEFA and Film History,* New York, London: Palgrave Macmillan, 2013.
Heiduschke, Sebastian, 'Emerging from the Niche. DEFA's Afterlife in United Germany', *Monatshefte* 105.4 (2013), 625-40.
Heiduschke, Sebastian, 'GDR Cinema as Commodity. Marketing DEFA Films Since Unification', *German Studies Review* 36.1 (2013), 61-78.
Heimann, Thomas, *DEFA, Künstler und SED-Kulturpolitik. Zum Verhältnis von Kulturpolitik und Filmproduktion in der SBZ/DDR 1945 bis 1959* [= Beiträge zur Film- und Fernsehwissenschaft, vol. 46], Berlin: Vistas, 1994.
Hell, Julia, *Post-fascist Fantasies. Psychoanalysis, History, and the Literature of East Germany,* Durham and London: Duke University Press, 1997.
Hell, Julia and Andreas Schönle (eds), *The Ruins of Modernity,* Durham, NC: Duke University Press, 2010.
Hell, Julia and Andreas Schönle, 'Introduction', in Julia Hell and Andreas Schönle (eds), *Ruins of Modernity,* Durham, NC: Duke University Press, 2010, pp.1-14.
Hellwig, Joachim and Claus Ritter, *Mach dir ein paar schöne Stunden... Filmkunst contra Wirtschaftswunder,* Berlin: Kongress Verlag, 1961.
Herlinghaus, Hermann, 'Fellinis Roma', *Film und Fernsehen* 3/1993, 43-47.

Hermand, Jost, 'Attempts to Establish a Socialist Music Culture in the Soviet Occupation Zone and the Early GDR, 1945-1965', in Edward Larkey (ed), *A Sound Legacy? Music and Politics in East Germany*, Washington: AICGS, 2000, pp. 4-19.

Hermand, Jost and Marc Silberman (eds), *Contentious Memories. Looking Back at the GDR*, New York, Washington: Lang, 1998.

Higson, Andrew, 'The Concept of National Cinema', *Screen* 30.4 (1989), 2-26.

Higson, Andrew and Richard Maltby (eds), *'Film Europe' and 'Film America'. Cinema, Commerce and Cultural Exchange 1920-1939*, Exeter: University of Exeter Press, 1999.

Hillich, Reinhard, 'Die Brüste der Göttin. Fiktion und Kritik der Fiktion als Gestaltungselemente in Fritz Rudolf Fries' Roman *Das Luft-Schiff*', *Sinn und Form* 33.1 (1981), 141-62.

Hintze, Werner, Clemens Risi and Robert Sollich (eds), *Realistisches Musiktheater. Walter Felsenstein. Geschichte, Erben, Gegenpositionen*, Berlin: Theater der Zeit, 2008.

Hirsch, Marianne, *Family Frames. Photography, Narrative and Postmemory*, Cambridge, MA and London: Harvard University Press, 1997.

Hodgin, Nick, *Screening the East. Heimat, Memory and Nostalgia in German Film since 1989*, Oxford: Berghahn, 2011.

Hodgin, Nick, 'Alternative Realities and Authenticity in DEFA's Documentary Films', in Marc Silberman and Henning Wrage (eds), *DEFA at the Crossroads of East German and International Film Culture*, Berlin, Boston: de Gruyter, 2014, pp. 281-304.

Hodgin, Nick, 'Cannibals, Carnival and Clowns. The Grotesque in German Unification Films', *Studies in Eastern European Cinema* 5.2 (2014), 124-38.

Hodgin, Nick, '"Only One Noble Topic Remained: The Workers". Sympathy and Subversion in Jürgen Böttcher's *Arbeiterfilme*', *Studies in Eastern European Cinema* 6.1 (2015), 49-63.

Hodgin, Nick and Caroline Pearce (eds), *The GDR Remembered. Representations of the East German State since 1989*, Rochester, NY: Camden House, 2011.

Hope, Jacqui, 'Environmentalism and its Cultural Transformation in the German Democratic Republic. Poetry and Fictional Prose', in Axel Goodbody (ed), *The Culture of German Environmentalism*, New York and Oxford: Berghahn, 2002, pp. 153-71.

Hurst, Heike and Heiner Gassen (eds), *Kameradschaft-Querelle. Kino zwischen Deutschland und Frankreich*, Munich: Institut Français de Munich, 1991.

Imre, Anikó (ed), *A Companion to East European Cinemas*, Oxford: Wiley, 2012.

Institut für Kulturforschung beim Ministerium für Kultur (eds), *Kultur in der DDR. Daten 1975-1988*, Berlin: Institut für Kulturforschung, 1989.

Iordanova, Dina, *The Cinema of the Other Europe. The Industry and Artistry of East Central European Film*, London: Wallflower, 2003.

Ivanova, Mariana, 'DEFA and Eastern European Cinemas. Co-Productions, Transnational Exchange and Artistic Collaborations', unpublished PhD Diss., University of Texas at Austin, 2011.

Ivanova, Mariana, 'Die Prestige-Agenda der DEFA. Koproduktionen mit Erich Mehls Filmfirma Pandora (1953-1957)', in Michael Wedel, Barton Byg, Andy Räder, Skyler Arndt-Briggs and Evan Torner (eds), *DEFA International. Grenzüberschreitende Filmbeziehungen vor und nach dem Mauerbau*, Wiesbaden: Springer VS, 2013, pp. 217-33.

Jacobsen, Wolfgang (ed), *Babelsberg. Das Filmstudio,* Berlin: Argon, 1992.
Jäckel, Anne, 'Dual Nationality Film Productions in Europe after 1945', *Historical Journal of Film, Radio and Television* 23.3 (2003), 237-43.
Janik, Elizabeth, *Recomposing German Music. Politics and Musical Tradition in Cold War Berlin,* Leiden: Brill, 2005.
Janssen, Herbert and Reinhold Jacobi (eds), *Filme in der DDR 1945-86,* Bonn: Katholisches Institut für Medienforschung, 1987.
Jansen, Peter and Wolfram Schütte (eds), *Film in der DDR,* Munich: Hanser, 1977.
Joe, Jeongwon and Rose Theresa (eds), *Between Opera and Cinema,* New York: Routledge, 2002.
Joe, Jeongwon and Sander L. Gilman (eds), *Wagner and Cinema,* Bloomington: Indiana University Press, 2010.
Jones, Chuck, 'Music and the Animated Cartoon', *Hollywood Quarterly* 1.4 (1946), 364-370.
Jordan, Günter, 'Der Verrat oder Der Fall Harnack' in Ralf Schenk, Erika Richter and Claus Löser (eds), *apropos: Film 2004* [= Das Jahrbuch der DEFA-Stiftung, 2004], Berlin: Bertz + Fischer, 2004, pp. 148-73.
Juillier, Laurent, 'To Cut or Let Live? The Soundtrack According to Godard', in Graeme Harper (ed), *Sound and Music in Visual Media,* New York: Continuum, 2009, pp. 352-62.
Kalinak, Kathryn, *Settling the Score,* Madison: University of Wisconsin Press, 1992.
Kannapin, Detlef, *Dialektik der Bilder. Der Nationalsozialismus im deutschen Film. Ein Ost-West Vergleich,* Berlin: Karl Dietz Verlag, 2006.
Kannapin, Detlef, 'Gibt es eine spezifische DEFA-Ästhetik? Anmerkungen zum Wandel der künstlerischen Formen im DEFA-Spielfilm', in Ralf Schenk and Erika Richter (eds), *apropos: Film 2000* [= Das Jahrbuch der DEFA-Stiftung, 2000], Berlin: Das Neue Berlin, 2000, pp. 142-64.
Kannapin, Detlef, 'Peace in Space – Die DEFA im Weltraum. Anmerkungen zu Fortschritt und Utopie im Filmschaffen der DDR', in Frank Hörnlein and Herbert Heinecke (eds), *Zukunft im Film* [= Reihe Bildwissenschaften, vol. 6], Magdeburg: Scriptum Verlag, 2000, pp. 55-70.
Kannapin, Detlef, 'Was hat Zarah Leander mit der DEFA zu tun? Die Nachwirkungen des NS-Films im DEFA-Schaffen – Notwendige Anmerkungen für eine Neue Forschungsperspektive', in Ralf Schenk, Erika Richter and Claus Löser (eds), *apropos: Film 2005* [= Jahrbuch der DEFA-Stiftung, 2005], Berlin: Bertz + Fischer, pp.188-209.
Kapczynski, Jennifer and Michael Richardson (eds), *A New History of German Cinema,* Rochester, NY: Camden House, 2012.
Kelly, Elaine and Amy Wlodarski (eds), *Art Outside the Lines. New Perspectives on GDR Art Culture,* Amsterdam: Rodopi, 2011.
Kersten, Heinz, *Das Filmwesen in der sowjetischen Besatzungszone Deutschlands,* Bonn, Berlin: Bundesministerium für Gesamtdeutsche Fragen, 1963.
Knietzsch, Karl, Kino in den Nachkriegsjahren', in *Kinos, Kameras und Filmemacher. Kinokultur in Dresden.* [= Dresdener Hefte, 23/2 (2005)], 34-39.

Kobán, Ilse (ed), *Die Pflicht, die Wahrheit zu finden. Briefe und Schriften eines Theatermannes*, Frankfurt am Main: Suhrkamp, 1997.
Koch, Jurij, *Der Kirschbaum*, Halle: Mitteldeutscher Verlag, 1984.
Koebner, Thomas (ed), *Indianer vor der Kamera*, Munich: edition text+kritik, 2011.
Kohonen, Iina, 'The Heroic and the Ordinary. Photographic Representations of Soviet Cosmonauts in the Early 1960s', in Eva Maurer, Julia Richers, Monica Rüthers and Carmen Scheide (eds), *Soviet Space Culture. Cosmic Enthusiasm in Socialist Societies*, New York, NY: Palgrave Macmillan, 2011, pp. 103-120.
Koepnick, Lutz, *The Dark Mirror. German Cinema between Hitler and Hollywood*, Berkeley: University of California Press, 2002.
Koerber, Thomas (ed), *Sachlexikon des Films*, Stuttgart: Reclam, 2002.
Koerber, Thomas, 'Problemfilm', in Thomas Koerber (ed), *Sachlexikon des Films*. Stuttgart: Reclam 2002, pp. 465-68.
Kolditz, Stefan, 'Gojko Mitic', in Ralf Schenk (ed), *Vor der Kamera. Fünfzig Schauspieler in Babelsberg*, Berlin: Henschel, 1995, pp. 168-71.
König, Ingelore, Dieter Wiedemann and Lothar Wolf (eds), *Zwischen Marx und Muck. DEFA-Filme für Kinder*, Berlin: Henschel, 1996.
Körte, Konrad, *Die Oper im Film. Analysen des Produktionsapparates anhand von Guiseppe Verdis 'Othello' in der Inszenierung von Walter Felsenstein*, Frankfurt am Main: Lang, 1989.
Kracauer, Siegfried, *Theory of Film. The Redemption of Physical Reality*, with an introduction by Miriam B. Hansen, Princeton: Princeton University Press, 1997.
Kramer, Thomas, *Micky, Marx und Manitu. Zeit- und Kulturgeschichte im Spiegel eines DDR-Comics 1955-1990. Mosaik als Fokus von Medienerlebnissen im NS und in der DDR*, Berlin: Weidler Buchverlag, 2002.
Kranz, Dieter, *Gespräche mit Felsenstein. Aus der Werkstatt des Musiktheaters*, Berlin: Henschel, 1977.
Kuan, Yu-Chien and Petra Häring-Kuan, *Die Langnasen. Was die Chinesen über uns Deutsche denken*, Frankfurt am Main: Fischer, 2009.
Laabs, Hans-Joachim, 'Pädagogische Bemerkungen zum Kinderfilm', *Deutsche Filmkunst. Zeitschrift für Theorie und Praxis des Filmschaffens* 5 (1954), 5-7.
Landsberg, Alison, *Prosthetic Memory. The Transformation of American Remembrance in the Age of Mass Culture*, New York: Columbia University Press, 2004.
Larkey, Edward (ed), *A Sound Legacy? Music and Politics in East Germany*, Washington: AICGS, 2000.
Lawrence, Mark Atwood, 'Hot Wars in Cold War Africa', *Reviews in American History* 32.1 (2004), 114-21.
Leeder, Karen, '"After the Massacre of Illusions". Specters of the GDR in the work of Volker Braun', in Anne Fuchs and Kathleen James Chakraborty (eds), *Transformations of German Cultural Identity 1989-2009*, [Special edition of] *New German Critique* 116 (2012), 103-18.
Levin, David (ed), *Opera through Other Eyes*, Stanford: Stanford University Press, 1993.

Li, Weijia, 'Otherness in Solidarity. Collaboration between Chinese and German Left-Wing Activists in the Weimar Republic', in Qinna Shen and Martin Rosenstock (eds), *Beyond Alterity. German Encounters with Modern East Asia*, New York: Berghahn, 2014, pp. 73–93.

Lichtenstein Manfred and Gerd Meier (eds), *Film im Freiheitskampf der Völker – Chile*, Berlin: Staatliches Filmarchiv der DDR, 1983.

Liehm, Mira and Antonín J. Liehm, *The Most Important Art. Eastern European Film after 1945*, Berkeley, Los Angeles, London: University of Berkeley Press, 1977.

Lindemann, Alfred, 'Die Lage des deutschen Films', in *Der deutsche Film. Fragen – Forderungen – Aussichten. Bericht vom Ersten Deutschen Film-Autoren-Kongreß. 6-9. Juni 1947 in Berlin*, Berlin: Henschel, 1947, pp. 9–19.

Lindenberger, Thomas, 'Terriblement démodée. Zum Scheitern blockübergreifender Filmproduktion im Kalten Krieg (DDR-Frankreich, 1956-1960)', in Antoine Fleury, Lubor Jilek (eds), *Une Europe malgré tout, 1945-1990, Contacts et réseaux culturels, intellectuels et scientifiques entre Européens dans la guerre froide*, Brussels: Lang, 2009, pp. 283–96.

Lischke, Ute and David T. McNab, *Walking a Tightrope. Aboriginal People and Their Representations*, Ottawa: Wilfrid-Laurier University Press, 2005.

Lokke, Kari, 'The Romantic Fairy Tale', in Michael Ferber (ed), *A Companion to European Romanticism*, Malden, MA: Blackwell, 2005, pp. 138–57.

Loos, Helmut and Stefan Keym (eds), *Nationale Musik im 20. Jahrhundert. Kompositorische und soziokulturelle Aspekte der Musikgeschichte zwischen Ost- und Westeuropa*, Leipzig: Gudrun Schröder, 2004.

Ludz, Peter Christian and Johannes Kuppe (eds), *DDR Handbuch*, Cologne: Wissenschaft und Politik, 1979.

Lüthi, Lorenz M., *The Sino-Soviet Split. Cold War in the Communist World*, Princeton: Princeton University Press, 2008.

Lütteken, Laurenz, *Das Monologische als Denkform in der Musik zwischen 1760 und 1785*, Tübingen: Niemeyer, 1998.

Macaulay, Rose, *Pleasure of Ruins*, London: Thames and Hudson, 1953.

Mak Dit Mack, Joël, 'La conquête spatiale à travers le cinéma de science-fiction de la guerre froide (1950-1990)', *Gavroche, revue d'histoire populaire* 155 (2008), 4–11.

Major, Patrick, 'Communist Science Fiction in the Cold War', in Rana Mitter and Patrick Major (eds), *Across the Blocs. Cold War Cultural and Social History*, London, Portland, OR: Frank Cass, 2004, pp. 56–74.

Marchetti, Gina, 'From Fu Manchu to M. Butterfly and Irma Vep. Cinematic Incarnations of Chinese Villainy', in Murray Pomerance (ed), *Bad. Infamy, Darkness, Evil, and Slime on Screen*, Albany, NY: State University of New York Press, 2004, pp. 187–200.

Maurer, Eva, Julia Richers, Monica Rüthers and Carmen Scheide (eds), *Soviet Space Culture. Cosmic Enthusiasm in Socialist Societies*, New York, NY: Palgrave Macmillan, 2011.

McKee, Robert, *Story. Substance, Style and the Principles of Screenwriting*, London: Methuen, 1999.

McLuhan, Marshall, *Understanding Media*, New York: McGraw-Hill, 1964.
Meißner, Werner (ed), *Die DDR und China 1949 bis 1990: Politik – Wirtschaft – Kultur. Eine Quellensammlung*, bearbeitet von Anja Feege, Berlin: Akademie Verlag, 1995.
Meurer, Hans Joachim, *Cinema and National Identity in Divided Germany,1979-1989. The Split Screen*, Lewiston, Queenston and Lampeter: Edwin Mellen, 2002.
Meyen, Michael, *Denver Clan und Neues Deutschland. Mediennutzung in der DDR*, Berlin: Christoph Links, 2003.
Meyer, Franziska, 'The Past Is Another Country and the Country Is Another Past. Sadness in East German Texts by Jakob Hein and Julia Schoch', in Mary Cosgrove and Anne Richards (eds), *Sadness and Melancholy in German-Language Literature from the Seventeenth Century to the Present*. [= Edinburgh German Yearbook, 6], Rochester, NY: Camden House, 2012, pp. 173–92.
Michaels, Jennifer, 'Appropriating the "Other" for the Cold War Struggle. DEFA's Depiction of Native Americans in its Indianerfilme', *Frames Cinema Journal* 4 (2013) [= http://framescinemajournal.com/article/appropriating-the-other-for-the-cold-war-struggle-defas-depiction-of-native-americans-in-its-indianerfilme/], accessed 16 June 2016.
Michel, Robert, 'Geschichte schreiben, Geschichte machen', in Manfred Lichtenstein and Gerd Meier (eds), *Film im Freiheitskampf der Völker – Chile*, Berlin: Staatliches Filmarchiv der DDR, 1983, pp. 103–9.
Michel, Robert (ed), *Politischer Film und politische Aktion. Chile-Zyklus des Studio H&S im internationalen Wirkungsraum*, Berlin: Solidaritätskomitee der DDR Chile-Zentrum, 1976.
Miller, Cynthia J. and A. Bowdoin Van Riper (eds), *International Westerns. Relocating the Frontier*, Lanham, MD: Scarecrow Press, 2014
Mitic, Gojko, *Erinnerungen*, aufgezeichnet von Alex Wolf, Frankfurt am Main: Ullstein, 1996.
Mitter, Rana and Patrick Major (eds), *Across the Blocs. Cold War Cultural and Social History*, London, Portland, OR: Frank Cass, 2004.
Möbus, Karlheinz, 'Die Beziehungen DDR–Chile' in Willi Baer and Karl-Heinz Dellwo (eds), *Diktatur und Widerstand in Chile* [= Bibliothek des Widerstands, vol. 29], Hamburg: Laika, 2013, pp. 209–21.
Moeller, Robert G., 'The Politics of the Past in the 1950s. Rhetorics of Victimisation in East and West Germany', in Bill Niven (ed), *Germans as Victims. Remembering the Past in Contemporary Germany*, New York: Palgrave Macmillan, 2006, pp. 26–42.
Moine, Caroline, *Cinema et guerre froide. Histoire du festival de films documentaires de Leipzig (1955-1990)*, Paris: Publications de la Sorbonne, 2014.
Möller, Harald, *DDR und Dritte Welt. Die Beziehungen der DDR mit Entwicklungsländern, ein neues theoretisches Konzept, dargestellt anhand der Beispiele China und Äthiopien, sowie Irak/Iran*, Berlin: Köster, 2003.
Morsbach, Helmut, 'Vorwort zur Festschrift', in Ralf Schenk, *Eine kleine Geschichte der DEFA*, Berlin: DEFA-Stiftung, 2006, pp. 8–9.

Mückenberger, Christiane, 'The Anti-Fascist Past in DEFA Films', in Seán Allan and John Sandford (eds), *DEFA. East German Cinema, 1946–1992*, New York, Oxford: Berghahn, 1999, pp. 58–76.

Mückenberger, Christiane and Günter Jordan (eds), *'Sie sehen selbst, Sie hören selbst...'. Eine Geschichte der DEFA von ihren Anfängen bis 1949*, Marburg: Hitzeroth, 1999.

Naughton, Leonie, *That Was the Wild East. Film Culture, Unification, and the 'New Germany'*, Michigan: University of Michigan Press, 2002.

Nelson, Anne, *Red Orchestra. The Story of the Berlin Underground and the Circle of Friends Who Resisted Hitler*, New York: Random House, 2009.

Neumann, Dietrich, *Filmarchitektur. Von Metropolis bis Blade Runner*, Munich, New York: Prestel, 2002.

Neumeyer, David, 'Melodrama as a Compositional Resource in Early Hollywood Sound Cinema', *Current Musicology* 57 (1995), 16–38.

Neumeyer, David and James Buhler, 'Analytical and Interpretive Approaches to Film Music, I. Analyzing the Music', in Kevin J. Donnelly (ed), *Film Music. Critical Approaches*, New York: Continuum, 2001, pp. 16–38.

Niven, Bill (ed), *Germans as Victims. Remembering the Past in Contemporary Germany*, New York: Palgrave Macmillan, 2006.

Novotny, Ehrentraud, *Gojko Mitic*, Berlin: Henschel, 1976.

Odenwald, Ulrike, 'Aufbruch zur Kontinuität', in Ralf Schenk and Erika Richter (eds), *apropos: Film 2001* [= Jahrbuch der DEFA-Stiftung, 2001], Berlin: Das Neue Berlin, 2001, pp. 296–327.

O'Driscoll, Anna, 'Melancholy and Historical Loss. Postunification Portrayals of GDR Writers and Artists', in Nick Hodgin and Caroline Pearce (eds), *The GDR Remembered. Representations of the East German State Since 1989*, Rochester, NY: Camden House, 2011, pp. 37–54.

Ostrowska, Dorota, 'An Alternative Model of Film Production. Film Units in Poland after World War Two', in Anikó Imre (ed), *A Companion to East European Cinemas*, Oxford: Wiley, 2012, pp. 453–65.

Owens, Louis, 'As if an Indian Were Really an Indian. Native American Voices and Postcolonial Theory', in Gretchen M. Bataille (ed), *Native American Representations*, Lincoln, NE: University of Nebraska Press, 2001, pp. 11–25.

Pence, Katherine and Paul Betts (eds), *Socialist Modern. East German Everyday Culture and Politics*, Ann Arbor: University of Michigan Press, 2008.

Penny, H. Glenn, 'Elusive Authenticity. The Quest for the Authentic Indian in German Public Culture', *Society for Comparative Studies in Society and History* 48.4 (2006), 798–819.

Perrault, Gilles, *L'Orchestre Rouge*, Paris: Fayard, 1967.

Piel, Victoria, 'Dissonante Repräsentationen. Tendenzen der DEFA-Spielfilmmusik der 70er Jahre', in Matthias Tischer (ed), *Musik in der DDR*, Berlin: Kuhn, 2005, pp. 166–84.

Pinkert, Anke, *Film and Memory in East Germany*, Bloomington and Indianapolis. Indiana University Press, 2008.

Pisani, Michael, 'Music for the Theatre. Style and Function in Incidental Music', in Kerry Powell (ed), *The Cambridge Companion to Victorian and Edwardian Theatre*, Cambridge: Cambridge University Press, 2004, pp. 70-92.
Pomerance, Murray (ed), *Bad. Infamy, Darkness, Evil, and Slime on Screen*, Albany, NY: State University of New York Press, 2004.
Port, Andrew, *Conflict and Stability in the German Democratic Republic*, Cambridge, New York: Cambridge University Press, 2007.
Poss, Ingrid and Peter Warnecke (eds), *Spur der Filme. Zeitzeugen der DEFA*, Berlin: Christoph Links, 2006.
Poss, Ingrid, Anne Richter and Christiane Mückenberger (eds), *Das Prinzip Neugier. DEFA-Dokumentarfilmer erzählen*, Berlin: Neues Leben, 2012.
Powell, Kerry (ed), *The Cambridge Companion to Victorian and Edwardian Theatre*. Cambridge: Cambridge University Press, 2004.
Powell, Larson, 'Une socialiste est une socialiste. Der geteilte Himmel zwischen Bild und Stimme', in Oksana Bulgakowa (ed), *Resonanz-Räume. Die Stimme und die Medien*, Berlin: Bertz + Fischer, 2012, pp. 130-37.
Powell, Larson, '"Wind from the East". DEFA and Eastern European Cinema', in Marc Silberman and Henning Wrage (eds), *DEFA at the Crossroads of East German and International Film Culture. A Companion*, Berlin, Boston: de Gruyter, 2014, pp. 223-42.
Price, Brian, 'Art/Cinema and Cosmopolitanism Today', in Rosalind Galt and Karl Schoonover (eds), *Global Art Cinema. New Theories and Histories*, Oxford: Oxford University Press, 2010, pp. 109-24.
Prinzler, Hans Helmut, 'Fern von jeder Realität. Über die Schauspielerin Gertrud Kückelmann', *FilmGeschichte* 11/12 (1998), 54-57.
Prommer, Elizabeth, *Kinobesuch im Lebenslauf*, Constance: UVK, 1999.
Prommer, Elizabeth and Andy Räder, 'Kinogrenzgänger im geteilten Deutschland (1949-61). Filmgeschmack, Nutzung und Motive des Kinobesuchs', in Michael Wedel, Barton Byg, Andy Räder, Skyler Arndt-Briggs and Evan Torner (eds), *DEFA International. Grenzen und Grenzüberschreitungen. Transnationale Filmbeziehungen der DEFA vor und nach dem Mauerbau*, Wiesbaden: VS Verlag, 2013, pp. 131-48.
Räder, Andy, 'Der Kinderfilm in der Weimarer Republik', in Horst Schäfer and Claudia Wegener (eds), *Kindheit und Film. Geschichte, Themen und Perspektiven des Kinderfilms in Deutschland*, Constance: UVK, 2009, pp. 21-38.
Reed, Dean, *Aus meinem Leben*. Aufgeschrieben von Hans-Dieter Bräuer, 2. aktualisierte und erweiterte Auflage, Leipzig, Dresden: Edition Peters, 1984.
Richelson, Jeffrey, *A Century of Spies. Intelligence in the Twentieth Century*, New York: Oxford University Press, 1995.
Rigg, Robert B., *Red China's Fighting Hordes*, Westport, CT: Greenwood, 1951.
Roloff, Stefan, *Die Rote Kapelle. Die Widerstandsgruppe im Dritten Reich und die Geschichte Helmut Roloffs*, Munich: Ullstein, 2002.
Rothberg, Michael, *Multidirectional Memory. Remembering the Holocaust in the Age of Decolonization*, Stanford: Stanford University Press, 2009.

Rother, Rainer and Julia Pattis (eds), *Die Lust am Genre. Verbrechergeschichten aus Deutschland*, Berlin: Bertz + Fischer, 2011.

Roulé, Antoine and Violette Anger, *Les Nibelungen de Fritz Lang. Musique de Gottfried Huppertz*, Paris: L'Harmattan, 2012.

Ruffinelli, Jorge, *Patricio Guzmán*, Madrid: Ediciones Catedra, 2001.

Rüss, Gisela (ed), *Dokumente der Kunst-, Literatur- und Kulturpolitik der SED 1971-1974*, 3 vols., Stuttgart: H. Seewald, 1976.

Said, Edward W., *Orientalism*, New York: Pantheon Books, 1978.

Saunders, Thomas, *Hollywood in Berlin. American Cinema and Weimar Germany*, Berkeley, Los Angeles, London: University of California Press, 1994.

Sayner, Joanne, *Reframing Antifascism. Memory, Genre, and the Life Writings of Greta Kuckhoff*, New York: Palgrave Macmillan, 2013.

Schäfer, Horst, 'Höhen und Tiefen – Der Kinderfilm in der Bundesrepublik Deutschland in den 1950er-, 1960er- und 1970er-Jahren', in Horst Schäfer and Claudia Wegener (eds), *Kindheit und Film. Geschichte, Themen und Perspektiven des Kinderfilms in Deutschland*, Constance: UVK, 2009, pp. 73-109.

Schäfer, Horst and Claudia Wegener (eds), *Kindheit und Film. Geschichte, Themen und Perspektiven des Kinderfilms in Deutschland*, Constance: UVK, 2009.

Schatz, Thomas, *Hollywood Genres. Formulas, Filmmaking, and the Studio System*, Boston, MA: McGraw Hill, 1981.

Schenk, Ralf, *Eine kleine Geschichte der DEFA*, Berlin: DEFA-Stiftung, 2006.

Schenk, Ralf, 'DEFA (1946–1992)', in Michael Wedel, Chris Wahl and Ralf Schenk (eds), *100 Years Studio Babelsberg. The Art of Filmmaking*, Kempen: teNeues, 2012, pp. 114–168.

Schenk, Ralf (ed), *Das zweite Leben der Filmstadt Babelsberg. DEFA-Spielfilme 19467-1992*, Berlin: Henschel, 1994.

Schenk, Ralf and Erika Richter (eds), *apropos: Film 2000* [= Das Jahrbuch der DEFA-Stiftung, 2000], Berlin: Das Neue Berlin, 2000.

Schenk, Ralf and Erika Richter (eds), *apropos: Film 2001* [= Das Jahrbuch der DEFA-Stiftung, 2001], Berlin: Das Neue Berlin, 2001.

Schenk, Ralf and Erika Richter (eds), *apropos: Film 2002* [= Jahrbuch der DEFA-Stiftung, 2002], Berlin: Bertz + Fischer, 2002.

Schenk, Ralf, Erika Richter and Claus Löser (eds), *apropos: Film 2004* [= Das Jahrbuch der DEFA-Stiftung, 2004], Berlin: Bertz + Fischer, 2004.

Schenk, Ralf, Erika Richter and Claus Löser (eds), *apropos: Film 2005* [= Jahrbuch der DEFA-Stiftung, 2005], Berlin: Bertz + Fischer, 2005.

Schicker, Juliane, 'Beyond the *Gewandhaus*. Mahler and the GDR', in Kyle Frackman and Larson Powell (eds), *Classical Music in the GDR*, Rochester, NY: Camden House, 2015, pp. 135-56.

Schieber, Elke, 'Anfang vom Ende oder Kontinuitat des Argwohns 1980 bis 1989', in Ralf Schenk (ed), *Das zweite Leben der Filmstadt Babelsberg. DEFA-Spielfilme 1946-92*. Berlin: Henschel, 1994, pp. 265-326.

Schöning, Jörg and Johannes Roschlau (eds), *Film im Herzen Europas. Deutsch-tschechische Filmbeziehungen im 20. Jahrhundert*, Berlin: absolut Medien, 2007.

Scribner, Charity, *Requiem for Communism*, Cambridge: MIT, 2003.

Seegers, Lu, 'Das Leben der Anderen oder die "richtige" Erinnerung an die DDR', in Astrid Erll and Stephanie Wodianka (eds), *Film und kulturelle Erinnerung. Plurimediale Konstellationen*, Berlin: de Gruyter, 2008, pp. 21–52.

Shen, Qinna, *The Politics of Magic. DEFA Fairy-Tale Films*, Detroit, MI: Wayne State University Press, 2015.

Shen, Qinna and Martin Rosenstock (eds), *Beyond Alterity. German Encounters with Modern East Asia*, New York: Berghahn, 2014.

Siefert, Marsha, 'East European Cold War Culture(s). Alterities, Commonalities, and Film Industries', in Annette Vowinckel, Marcus M. Payk and Thomas Lindenberger (eds), *Cold War Cultures. Perspectives on Eastern and Western European Societies*, New York, Oxford: Berghahn, 2012, pp. 23–54.

Sieg, Katrin, 'Ethnic Drag and National Identity. Multicultural Crisis, Crossings and Interventions', in Sara Friedrichsmeyer, Sara Lennox and Susanne Zantop (eds), *The Imperialist Imagination. German Colonialism and Its Legacy*, Ann Arbor: University of Michigan Press, 1998, pp. 295–319.

Silberman, Marc, *German Cinema. Texts in Context*, Detroit: Wayne State University Press, 1995.

Silberman, Marc, 'What is German in German Cinema', *Film History* 8 (1996), 297–315.

Silberman, Marc, 'Learning from the Enemy. DEFA-French Co-Productions of the 1950s', *Film History* 18.1 (2006), 21–45.

Silberman, Marc and Henning Wrage (eds), *DEFA at the Crossroads of East German and International Film Culture*, Berlin, Boston: de Gruyter, 2014.

Simmel, Georg, 'Two Essays. The Handle, and The Ruin', *Hudson Review* 11.3 (1958), 371–85.

Simon, Erik and Olaf Spittel, *Die Science-fiction der DDR. Autoren und Werke*, Berlin: Das Neue Berlin, 1988.

Smolkin-Rothrock, Victoria, 'Cosmic Enlightenment', in James T. Andrews and Asif A. Siddiqi (eds), *Into the Cosmos. Space Exploration and Soviet Culture*, Pittsburgh: University of Pittsburgh Press, 2011, pp. 159–94.

Soldovieri, Stefan, 'Finding Navigable Waters. Inter-German Film Relations and Modernization in Two DEFA Barge Films of the 1950s', *Film History* 18.1 (2006), 59–72.

Soldovieri, Stefan, 'Managing Stars. Manfred Krug and the Politics of Entertainment in GDR Cinema', in Barton Byg and Betheny Moore (eds), *Moving Images of East Germany. Past and Future of DEFA*, Washington: AICGS, 2002, pp 56–71.

Soldovieri, Stefan, 'Socialists in Outer Space. East German Film's Venusian Adventure', *Film History* 10.3 (1998), 382-398.

Soldovieri, Stefan, 'The Politics of the Popular. *Trace of Stones* (1966/89) and the Discourse of Stardom in the GDR Cinema', in Randall Halle and Margaret McCarthy (eds), *Light Motives. German Popular Film in Perspective*, Detroit: Wayne State University Press, 2003, pp. 220–36.

Sontag, Susan, *On Photography*, London: Farrar, Straus & Giroux, 1973.
Stanitzek, Georg, *Blödigkeit. Beschreibungen des Individuums im 18. Jahrhundert*, Tübingen: Niemeyer, 1989.
Steingröver, Reinhild, *Last Features. East German Cinema's Lost Generation*, Rochester, NY: Camden House, 2014.
Steinmetz, Rüdiger, 'Heynowski & Scheumann. The GDR's Leading Documentary News Team', *Historical Journal of Film, Radio and Television* 24.3 (2004), 365-79.
Steinmetz, Rüdiger and Tilo Prase, *Dokumentarfilm zwischen Beweis und Pamphlet. Heynowski & Scheumann und Gruppe Katins*, Leipzig: Leipziger Universitätsverlag, 2002.
Stenzl, Jürg, *Jean-Luc Godard – Musicien. Die Musik in den Filmen von Jean-Luc Godard*, Munich: edition text + kritik, 2010.
Stephan, Inge and Alexandra Tacke, 'Einleitung', in Inge Stephan and Alexandra Tacke (eds), *Nachbilder des Holocaust*, Cologne: Böhlau, 2007, pp. 7-17.
Stephan, Inge and Alexandra Tacke (eds), *Nachbilder des Holocaust*, Cologne: Böhlau, 2007.
Stöck, Katrin, 'Die Nationaloperndebatte in der DDR der 1950er und 1960er Jahre als Instrument zur Ausbildung einer sozialistischen deutschen Nationalkultur', in Helmut Loos und Stefan Keym (eds), *Nationale Musik im 20. Jahrhundert. Kompositorische und soziokulturelle Aspekte der Musikgeschichte zwischen Ost- und Westeuropa*, Leipzig: Gudrun Schröder, 2004, pp. 521-39.
Stöck, Katrin, *Musiktheater in der DDR. Szenische Kammermusik und Kammeroper der 1970er und 1980er Jahre*, Cologne: Böhlau, 2013.
Stott, Rosemary, 'Continuity and Change in GDR Cinema Programming Policy 1979-1989. The Case of the American Science Fiction Import', *German Life and Letters* 55.1 (2002), 91-99.
Stott, Rosemary, *Crossing the Wall. The Western Feature Film Import in East Germany*, Oxford: Lang, 2012.
Studio H&S, *Die Toten schweigen nicht (Los muertos no callan): Ein Film von Heynowski & Scheumann, Peter Hellmich*, Berlin: Studio H&S, 1978.
Sturm, Sybille, M. and Arthur Wohlgemuth (eds), *Hallo? Berlin? Ici Paris! Deutsch-französische Filmbeziehungen 1918-1939*, Munich: edition text + kritik, 1996.
Tambling, Jeremy, *Opera, Ideology and Film*, Manchester: Manchester University Press, 1987.
Tetzlaff, Kurt, '"Wir waren besessen von der Arbeit"', in Ingrid Poss, Anne Richter and Christiane Mückenberger (eds), *Das Prinzip Neugier. DEFA Dokumentarfilmer erzählen*, Berlin: Neues Leben, 2012, pp.157-93.
Thiel, Wolfgang, 'Opernverfilmungen der DEFA', *Oper heute* 9 (1986), 276-90.
Thomas, Andrew, *Kul'tura kosmosa. The Russian Popular Culture of Space Exploration*, Boca Raton: Dissertation.com, 2010.
Thompson, Peter, 'Worin noch niemand war. The GDR as Retrospectively Imagined Community', in Nick Hodgin and Caroline Pearce (eds), *The GDR Remembered. Representations of the East German State since 1989*, Rochester, NY: Camden House, 2011, pp. 250-66.

Tiedemann, Rolf (ed), *Adorno. Gesammelte Schriften in 20 Bänden*, Frankfurt am Main: Suhrkamp, 1997.
Tischer, Matthias (ed), *Musik in der DDR. Beiträge zu den Musikverhältnissen eines verschwundenen Staates*, Berlin: Kuhn, 2005.
Tompkins, David, *Composing the Party Line*, Lafayette; Purdue University Press, 2013.
Torner, Evan, 'Casting for a Socialist Earth. Multicultural Whiteness in the East German/Polish Science Fiction Film *Silent Star*', in Sonja Fritzsche (ed), *The Liverpool Companion to World Science Fiction Film*, Liverpool: Liverpool University Press, 2014, pp. 130-49.
Torner, Evan, 'The DEFA Indianerfilm as Artifact of Resistance', *Frames Cinema Journal* 4 (2013) [= http://framescinemajournal.com/article/the-defa-indianerfilm-as-artifact-of-resistance/], accessed 16 June 2016.
Torner, Evan, 'The Race-Time Continuum. Race Projection in DEFA Genre Cinema', unpublished PhD Diss., University of Massachusetts Amherst, 2013.
Torner, Evan, 'The Red and the Black. Race in the DEFA Film *Osceola*', *New German Review* 25.1 (2011), 61-81.
Trumpener, Katie, 'DEFA. Moving Germany into Eastern Europe', in Barton Byg and Betheny Moore (eds), *Moving Images of East Germany. Past and Future of DEFA Film*, Washington DC: AICGS, 2002, pp. 85-104.
Tuchel, Johannes, *Der vergessene Widerstand. Zur Realgeschichte und Wahrnehmung des Kampfes gegen die NS-Diktatur*, Göttingen: Wallstein, 2005.
Tucker, Robert, C. (ed), *The Marx-Engels Reader*, New York: Norton, 1978.
Vérroneau, Pierre, 'The Children of Vertov in the Land of Brecht', in Thomas Waugh (ed), *'Show us Life'. Toward a History and Aesthetic of the Committed Documentary*, Metuchen, NJ: Scarecrow Press, 1989, pp. 417-30.
Vertov, Dziga, *Kino-Eye. The Writings of Dziga Vertov*, Berkeley: University of California Press, 1984.
Villarroel, Mónica and Isabel Madrones, *Señales contra el olvido. Cine chileno recobrado*, Santiago: Editorial Cuarto Propio, 2012.
Vogt, Guntram, *Stadt im Kino. Deutsche Spielfilme 1900-2000*, Marburg: Schüren, 2001.
Vowinckel, Annette, Marcus M. Payk, and Thomas Lindenberger (eds), *Cold War Cultures. Perspectives on Eastern and Western European Societies*, New York; Oxford: Berghahn, 2012.
Wagner, Brigitta (ed), *DEFA after East Germany*, Rochester, NY: Camden House, 2014.
Wagner, Brigitta, 'Introduction. Making History ReVisible', in Brigitta Wagner (ed), *DEFA after East Germany*, Rochester, NY: Camden House, 2014, pp. 1-7.
Warnke, Stephanie, *Stein gegen Stein. Architektur und Medien im geteilten Berlin 1950-1970*, Frankfurt am Main, New York: Campus, 2009.
Waugh, Thomas (ed), *'Show us Life'. Toward a History and Aesthetic of the Committed Documentary*, Metuchen, NJ: Scarecrow Press, 1989.
Waugh, Thomas, 'Introduction' to Pierre Vérroneau, 'The Children of Vertov in the Land of Brecht', in Thomas Waugh (ed), *'Show us Life'. Toward a History and Aesthetic of the Committed Documentary*, Metuchen, NJ: Scarecrow Press, 1989, pp. 417-30.

Wedel, Michael, 'Schuld und Schaulust. Formen und Funktionen des deutschen Kriminalfilms bis 1960,' in Rainer Rother and Julia Pattis (eds), *Die Lust am Genre. Verbrechergeschichten aus Deutschland*, Berlin: Bertz + Fischer, 2011, pp. 25–40.
Wedel, Michael, Barton Byg, Andy Räder, Skyler Arndt-Briggs and Evan Torner (eds), *DEFA International. Grenzen und Grenzüberschreitungen. Transnationale Filmbeziehungen der DEFA vor und nach dem Mauerbau*, Wiesbaden: VS Verlag, 2013.
Wedel, Michael, Chris Wahl and Ralf Schenk (eds), *100 Years Studio Babelsberg. The Art of Filmmaking*, Kempen: teNeues, 2012.
Wehrstedt, Norbert, 'Indianerwestern Made in GDR', in Ingelore König, Dieter Wiedemann and Lothar Wolf (eds), *Zwischen Marx und Muck. DEFA-Filme für Kinder*, Berlin: Henschel, 1996, pp. 55–69.
Weihsmann, Helmut, *Gebaute Illusionen*, Wien: Promedia, 1988.
Wendling, Amy E., *Karl Marx on Technology and Alienation*, New York: Palgrave Macmillan, 2009.
Wiedemann, Dieter, 'Der DEFA-Kinderfilm. Zwischen Resteverwertung und Politikdiskursen. Überlegungen zum Umgang mit einem Kulturerbe', in Horst Schäfer and Claudia Wegener (eds), *Kindheit und Film. Geschichte, Themen und Perspektiven des Kinderfilms in Deutschland*, Constance: UVK, 2009, pp. 111–24.
Willemen, Paul, 'Fantasy in Action', in Nataša Durovicová and Kathleen Newman (eds) *World Cinemas, Transnational Perspectives*, New York: Routledge, 2010, pp. 247–86.
Wischnewski, Klaus, '*Sheriff Teddy*', in: Lissi Zilinski, Götz Barndt, Alfred Krautz, Rolf Liebmann and Gustav Salffner (eds), *Spielfilme der DEFA im Urteil der Kritik*, Berlin: Henschel, 1970, pp. 162–66.
Wischnewski, Klaus, 'Träumer und gewöhnliche Leute. 1966 bis 1979', in Ralf Schenk (ed), *Das zweite Leben der Filmstadt Babelsberg. DEFA-Spielfilme 1946–92*, Berlin: Henschel, 1994, pp. 212–63.
Wojchik-Andrews, Ian, *Children's Films. History, Pedagogy, Ideology, Theory*, New York: Garland, 2000.
Wolf, Dieter, *Gruppe Babelsberg. Unsere nichtgedrehten Filme*, Berlin: Das Neue Berlin, 2000.
Zahlmann, Stefan (ed), *Wie im Westen, nur anders. Medien in der DDR*, Berlin: Panama, 2010.
Zilinski, Lissi, Götz Barndt, Alfred Krautz, Rolf Liebmann and Gustav Salffner (eds), *Spielfilme der DEFA im Urteil der Kritik*, Berlin: Henschel, 1970.
Žižek, Slavoj, *In Defense of Lost Causes*, London: Verso, 2008.
Zur Weihen, Daniel, *Komponieren in der DDR. Institutionen, Organisationen und die erste Komponistengeneration bis 1961*, Cologne: Böhlau, 1999.

Index

A

2001. A Space Odyssey, 8, 224n1
400cm³, 129
Abenteuer mit Blasius [Adventures with Blasius], 224 n10
Abschied von Agnes [Farewell to Agnes], 318
Abschiedsdisco [Farewell Disco], 259, 279–81, 284–86
Abusch, Alexander, 70, 82n19, 123–24
Ackermann, Anton, 70, 82n17, 112, 117, 125n4, 125n11, 125n20, 126n23,
Ackermann, Rainer, 277, 285
Ade, Maren, 333n13
Adolph, Barbara, 301, 307
Adorno, Theodor, W., 47, 49, 51, 58n23, 58n28, 59n35, 60n48, 193, 207n2, 207n4
Aelita [Aelita. Queen of Mars], 215, 221
Agde, Günter, 130, 143, 145n37, 226n34,
Aisner, Henri, 100
Albrecht, Erich, 30, 31, 39n37, 39n42, 39n44–46, 39n48, 39n50, 39n52
Allende, Salvadore, 127, 131–133, 135, 137, 141, 144, 170
All the President's Men, 37
Allora, Jennifer, 286
Alraune [Unnatural], 218
Ankunft im Alltag [Arrival in Daily Life], 327
Apachen [Apaches], 35, 58n25,
Arafat, Yasser, 181
Arslan, Thomas, 333n13
Asriel, Andre, 42
Astronauci [The Astronauts], 213
Atze, 216
Auf dem Weg zu fernen Welten. Ein Buch von der Weltraumfahrt [On the way to Distant Worlds. A Book on Space Travel], 220
Aus dem Leben eines Taugenichts [From the Life of a Good-for-Nothing], 170–75, 179, 186n12–13, 186n17, 187n23, 187n28

B

Badham, John, 263
Ballmann, Herbert, 100, 249, 252–56
Barbara, 11, 312–344
Barfuß und ohne Hut [Barefoot and without a Hat], 276
Bartel, Kurt, 46
Bauer, Horst, 76
Bauer, Jasna Fritzi, 326
Becher, Johannes R., 108
Beck, Werner, 36, 39n34
Becker, Wolfgang, 312
Bedrohte Menschheit [Endangered Mankind], 166n1
Beethoven, Ludwig van, 41, 54–55, 59n29, 59n41, 193, 195, 199
Behrend, Rainer, 279, 282
Belyayev, Alexander, 218
Belz, Uwe, 159–160
Bergman, Ingmar, 55, 59n42, 59n47, 192
Berger, Erna, 202
Besuch aus der Zone [Visitors from the Soviet Zone], 71–72
Beyer, Frank, 31, 52, 275, 302, 314, 318
Biermann, Wolf, 42, 176, 285, 317, 333n18
Biernat, Karl-Heinz, 300, 310n22–24
Blauvogel [Blue Bird], 228
Bleiweiß, Celino, 170–172, 174, 186n12, 187n24
Blier, Bernard, 95
Bloch, Ernst, 214, 277
Blonder Tango [Blond Tango], 26
Blume, Renate, 5, 181, 184
Blutsbrüder [Blood Brothers], 169, 175–77, 182–83, 187n36–37
Bock, Rainer, 327
Böhm, Karlheinz, 218
Böhm, Rainer, 42
Böhm, Rudolf, 100, 116, 126n29
Bonnet, Horst, 201–02
Böttcher, Jürgen, 276, 290n15, 316

Böttcher, Martin, 115
Brandt, Horst E., 277, 285, 292–311
Bratpfanne und Orchester [Concerto for Frying Pan and Orchestra], 257
Braun, Harald, 114
Braun, Volker, 272, 281, 289n1, 290n16, 318
Braun, Wernher von, 212, 218, 219, 221–23, 226n35
Brauer, Jürgen, 33, 272, 282
Bräuer, Hans-Dieter, 180, 186n9
Bräunig, Werner, 316
Brecht, Bertolt, 44–5, 47–8, 54, 73, 95, 144n1, 145n36, 195–6, 208n13, 232, 287, 306, 322
Bredemeyer, Reiner, 42, 56
Brezhnev, Leonid, 175
Broch, Hermann, 316
Brody, Adrian, 322
Brühl, Daniel, 312
Brussig, Thomas, 317
Burning Life, 239
Burton, Tim, 263, 267n30

C

Calzadilla, Guillermo, 286
Čapek, Karel, 214
Carow, Heiner, 24, 29–31, 34–36, 43, 62, 67–8, 72, 249, 257–59, 266n27, 275
Casablanca, 323
Castro, Fidel, 143, 235
Cesta do pravěku [The Journey to the Primeval Age], 224n5
Chamoun, Camille, 181
Chic, 327
China – Land zwischen gestern und morgen [China – A Country between Yesterday and Tomorrow], 148, 153–4, 156, 167
Chingachgook, die große Schlange [Chingachgook, the Great Snake], 43, 230–32, 244
Chowaretz, Rudolph, 181, 187n43
Cody, Iron Eyes, 239
Curtiz, Michael, 323

D

Dammbeck, Lutz, 52
Daquin, Louis, 99, 101–2, 105n41–43

Das Beil von Wandsbek [The Axe of Wandsbek], 276
Das Eismeer ruft [The Arctic Sea Calls], 249, 259–64, 267n32
Das Fräulein von Scuder [Mademoiselle de Scudéry], 112
Das geheimnisvolle Wrack [The Mysterious Wreck], 253
Das hölzerne Kälbchen [The Wooden Calf], 58n25
Das Kaninchen bin ich [The Rabbit is Me], 277, 328
Das kalte Herz [The Cold Heart], 253
Das Leben beginnt [Life starts now], 62, 66–68, 71–2, 74–5, 82n22
Das Leben der Anderen [The Lives of Others], 312–34
Das Luftschiff [The Airship], 43, 51–52, 55–6
Das Mädchen aus dem Fahrstuhl [The Girl in the Lift], 278
Das Prinzip Hoffnung [The Principle of Hope], 214
Das schlaue Füchslein [The Cunning Little Vixen], 194
Das Versteck [The Hiding Place], 275
Davis, Angela, 170, 177, 186n11
Dean Reed erzählt aus seinem Leben [Dean Reed Talks About His Life], 180
Denk bloss nicht, ich heule [Just Don't Think I'll Cry], 58n25, 171
Dein unbekannter Bruder [Your Unknown Brother], 302
Der Augenzeuge [The Eyewitness], 151–2, 196
Der Berg ruft [The Mountain Calls], 7
Der Bettelstudent [The Beggar Student], 201
Der fliegende Holländer [The Flying Dutchman], 201, 208n6
Der Freischütz [The Marksman], 203
Der Frühling braucht Zeit [Spring Takes Time], 62, 65, 78–80, 81n9
Der geteilte Himmel [Divided Heaven], 5, 42–3, 47–8, 51–55, 62, 65, 76–7, 80, 328
Der Kinnhaken [The Punch to the Jaw], 4–5
Der Kirschbaum [The Cherry Tree], 282
Der lachende Mann [The Laughing Man], 129, 143
Der lange Ritt zur Schule [The Long Ride to School], 239

Der Magdalenenbaum [The Magdalena Tree], 279, 282–4
Der Nackte und der Satan [The Head], 218
Der Ochse von Kulm [The Ox of Kulm], 115
Der Rosenkavalier [The Knight of the Rose], 209n22
Der schweigende Stern [The Silent Star], 77, 210–26
Der Scout [The Scout], 227, 239
Der Strass [Rhinestones], 280, 284–85
Der Tangospieler [The Tango Player], 318, 334n32
Der Teufel vom Mühlenberg [Devil from Mill Mountain], 100, 249, 252–55
Der Untergang [Downfall], 318
Der Verdacht [The Suspicion], 314, 318–19, 327
Der weiße Putsch [El Golpe Blanco/ The White Coup], 135, 141
Destination Moon, 210–11
Dessau, Paul, 42, 47, 53, 56–7n6, 195
Die 1000 Augen des Dr Mabuse [The Thousand Eyes of Dr Mabuse], 218
Die Abenteuer des Till Ulenspiegel [The Bold Adventure], 95, 99
Die amerikanischen Schandtaten in Korea – ein Tatsachenbericht [American Crimes in Korea – A Factual Report], 150–51
Die Besteigung des Chimborazo [The Ascent of Chimborazo], 276
Die Beteiligten [The Parties Involved], 277
Die Beunruhigung [Apprehension], 25, 29
Die blauen Schwerter [Blue Swords], 114
Die Drei von der Tankstelle [The Three from the Filling Station], 209n22
Die Elenden [Les Misérables], 99–101, 105n43
Die Erforschung des Mars [The Exploration of Mars], 219
Die Eroberung des Mondes [Conquest of the Moon], 219
Die Familie Benthin [Family Benthin], 57n16
Die Flucht [The Flight], 314, 328
Die Frau und der Fremde [The Woman and the Stranger], 56
Die gefrorenen Blitze [Frozen Lightning], 221–2, 226n41
Die Geschichte vom kleinen Muck [The Story of Little Mook], 253

Die goldene Jurte [The Golden Yurt], 147, 149, 161–65
Die Hexen von Salem [The Crucible], 99, 105n44
Die Hochzeit des Figaro [The Marriage of Figaro], 194, 201, 204–5, 209n23
Die Legende von Paul und Paula [The Legend of Paul und Paula], 29–40, 43, 174–5, 275
Die Leiden des jungen Werthers [The Sorrows of Young Werther], 56
Die lustigen Weiber von Windsor [The Merry Wives of Windsor], 201, 202
Die Mörder sind unter uns [The Murderers Are Among Us), 57n16, 89
Die Reise nach Kosmatom [The Trip to Cosmaton], 224n10
Die rote Kapelle [The Red Orchestra], 302–11
Die schöne Helena [The Beautiful Helena], 33
Die schöne Lurette [Belle Lurette], 201,
Die sieben Affären der Doña Juanita [The 7 Affairs of Doña Juanita], 31
Die Söhne der großen Bärin [Sons of Great Bear], 43, 227–28, 236–37, 241, 247n49
Die Toten schweigen nicht [The Dead Are Not Silent], 137, 145n24
Die verkaufte Braut [The Bartered Bride], 209n22
Die Windrose [The Compass Rose], 154, 176n14
Dieterle, William, 89
Doerk, Chris, 209n22
Domröse, Angelica, 31–33, 36
Don Giovanni, 194, 204–5
Donnersmarck, Henckel von, 312–34
Dordschpalam, Rabschaa, 147, 165
Dorndeck, Wiebke, 170, 178–79, 181
Doroga k zvezdam [Road to the Stars], 211, 219
Dr. Strangelove, 221
Drei Haselnüsse für Aschenbrödel [Three Wishes for Cinderella], 16n38
Dresen, Andreas, 11, 38n11, 318
Drinda, Horst, 307
Du und mancher Kamerad [You and Many a Comrade], 56–7n6
Dudow, Slatan, 21, 44, 61–2, 66, 68, 100, 123–24
Dymschitz, Alexander, 3
Dziadyk-Dymna, Anna, 171
Dziuba, Helmut, 260

E

Efremov, Ivan, 214
Egel, Karl-Georg, 109–10
Ehe im Schatten [*Marriage in the Shadows*], 7, 45
Eichendorff, Joseph von, 170–73
Ein brauchbarer Mann [*A Useable Man*], 278–79
Ein Windstoß [*A Gust of Wind*], 198–99
Eine Minute Dunkel macht uns nicht blind [*One Minute of Darkness Does Not Blind Us*], 135–36, 140–41
Eine sonderbare Liebe [*A Strange Love*], 25
Eisler, Hanns, 41–42, 44–45, 47, 53, 101, 195, 199
El Cantor, 182
Elsner, Hannelore, 171, 186n16
Engel, Erich, 235
Eolomea, 223–24n1, 224n10
Erdmann, Otto, 62, 66
Erinnerung an eine Landschaft – Für Manuela [*Memories of a Landscape – To Manuela*], 273–74
Ernst Thälmann – Führer seiner Klasse, 4, 42–48, 51–53, 55, 219, 294, 302
Ernst Thälmann – Sohn seiner Klasse, 4, 42–48, 51–53, 55, 57n12, 219, 294, 302, 309n6
Esche, Eberhard, 307
ET, 263
Ewald, Charlotte, 255–56, 266n15

F

Felsenstein, Walter, 13, 191–209
Fidelio, 193–94, 197, 198–201, 203, 205
Figaro, 203, 205
Figaros Hochzeit [*Figaro's Marriage*], 201, 209n23
First Spaceship on Venus, 213
Fischer, Adolf, 21
Fischer, Günther, 43
Flash Gordon, 218
Forbidden Planet, 211
Forest, Jean Kurt 195, 208n10
Foth, Jörg, 34, 249, 259, 261, 264, 266n9, 285
Frankenweenie, 263, 267n30
Frau im Mond [*Woman in the Moon*], 216
Frauenschicksale [*Destinies of Women*], 61–62, 66, 68
Freaky Friday, 256

French Connection, The, 316
Freud, Sigmund, 275
Friedkin, William, 316
Friedrich, Caspar David, 283
Friedrich, Götz, 192, 208n8
Fritsch, Gunther von, 218
Fromm, Hans, 324, 329
Funder, Anna, 332n3

G

Gabin, Jean, 100–101
Gagarin, Yuri, 50–51, 54, 216, 217, 219
Gass, Karl, 56n6
Gedeck, Martina, 319
Gejagt bis zum Morgen [*Persecuted Until Morning*], 115
Geldsorgen [*Money Troubles*], 134–35, 141
Gemayel, Amine, 181
Genosse Sziau erzählt [*Comrade Xiao Narrates*], 154, 156
Geschwader Fledermaus [*Bat Squadron*], 235, 237
Geschonneck, Erwin, 169, 185
Glatzeder, Winfried, 30, 31, 36
Go Trabi Go!, 287
Göring, Hermann, 294
Golde, Gert, 30
Goldmann, Friedrich, 43, 52–54, 59n46
Good Bye, Lenin!, 312, 318, 322, 331
Gotthardt, Peter, 36
Gojira [*Godzilla*], 211
Goya, 28
Gorbachev, Mikhail, 288
Gräf, Roland, 314, 318, 328
Great Spy Mission, The, 221
Griffith, D.W., 229
Grisebach, Valeska, 333n13
Gröbe, Nikolaus, 318
Gromnica, Erica, 174
Groschopp, Richard, 43
Groth, Hanns, 68
Gruber, Kade, 325
Gundermann, Gerhard, 289n2
Günther, Egon, 56, 60n50
Gussmann, Manfred, 224n10
Guzmán, Patricio, 127, 141
Gwisdek, Michael, 282, 318

H

Habel, Frank-Burkhard, 185, 186n8
Hacks, Peter, 33
Hagen, Nina, 329
Hannemann, Rudi, 21
Häntzsche, Hellmuth, 250–51
Harfouch, Corinna, 11
Harnack, Avid, 294–95, 298, 302–03
Harnack, Falk, 276
Hasler, Joachim, 43, 115, 117–18, 316
Haubold, Günter, 307
Haußmann, Leander, 322
Hawks, Howard, 316
Heath, Donald, 295
Heine, Heinrich, 286
Heinrich, Christiane, 318
Heinrich, Hans, 107
Heisenberg, Benjamin, 333 n13
Heißer Sommer [*Hot Summer*], 43, 181, 316, 329
Hellmich, Peter, 130, 134, 139, 144n10
Helwig, Gerhard, 62, 120
Hendriks, Jan, 115
Herz, Joachim, 201
Herzog, Werner, 276
Heydn, Werner, 307
Heynowski, Walter, 8, 127–45,
Hirschbiegel, Oliver, 318
Hirschmeier, Alfred, 62, 76–77
Hitler, Adolf, 164, 237, 292–94, 297
Hochmuth, Dietmar, 282, 289
Hochhäusler, Christoph, 330, 333n13
Hochwaldmärchen [*High Forest Fairy Tale*], 271
Hofmann, Heinz, 173
Hoffmanns Erzählungen [*Tales of Hoffmann*], 194, 203
Höhne, Heinz, 298
Holm, Richard, 198
Honecker, Erich, 42, 160, 182, 202, 324
Honert, Hans-Werner, 278–79, 285
Honold, Rolf, 235
Höntsch, Andreas, 280
Hoppe, Rolf, 175
Hosalla, Hans-Dieter, 48–51, 54–55, 58n25
Hosenfeld, Wilhelm (Wilm), 322
Hoss, Nina, 312
How to Appear Invisible, 286

Huisken, Joop, 148, 156
Humboldt, Alexander von, 276

I

Ich war, ich bin, ich werde sein [*I Was, I Am, I Shall Be*], 133–36, 141
Ikarie XB-1 [*Voyage to the End of the Universe*], 211, 220, 223, 224n5
Ikarus [*Icarus*], 249, 257–58
Im Feuer bestanden: die letzten Stunden in der Moneda [*Steadfast in the Fire, the Last Hours in the Moneda*], 135, 137–38
Im Staub der Sterne [*In the Dust of the Stars*], 224n10
In einem Atem [*In One Breath*], 282
Irgendwo in Berlin [*Somewhere in Berlin*], 249–50, 252
Isabel auf der Treppe [*Isabel on the Stairs*], 260
Ivens, Joris, 95, 154

J

Jadup und Boel [*Jadup and Boel*], 56
Jaeuthe, Günter, 172
Jakob der Lügner [*Jacob the Liar*], 52, 302
Jähn, Sigmund, 217
Jahrgang 45 [*Born in '45*], 156, 276, 316, 325, 328
Janáček, Leoš, 194
Jentsch, Gerhard, 154, 156
Johann Faustus, 199
Jürgen, Anna, 228

K

Kaiser, Josef, 76
Kamei, Fumio, 166n1
Karl, Günter, 237
Karzhukov, Mikhail, 211
Katzer, Georg, 42
Keller, Herbert, 273
Kiepura, Jan, 209n22
Kit & Co., 175–76, 183
Kleberg, Bruno, 149
Klein, Günter, 31, 170
Kleinau, Willi, 114
Kleinert, Andreas, 280, 287
Klushantsev, Pavel, 211
Klute, 316

KLK an PTX – Die rote Kapelle [KLK calling PTX – The Red Orchestra], 292–311
Knef, Hildegard, 218
Knietzsch, Horst, 173, 302
Koberidze, Otar, 211
Koch, Jurij, 282
Koch, Sebastian, 319
Koepp, Volker, 272, 285–87
Köhler, Ulrich, 330, 333n13
Kohlhaase, Wolfgang, 218
Kolditz, Gottfried, 28, 58n25, 147, 165, 201, 224n10, 233
Körner, Dietrich, 222
Kosmicheskiy reys [Cosmic Voyage], 215
Kracauer, Siegfried, 193
Krael, Alexander, 295
Krakatit, 224n3
Kranz, Georg, 62, 78
Kraus, Peter, 209 n22
Krenz, Egon, 177, 182, 187n39
Kretschmann, Thomas, 322
Krieg der Mumien [War of the Mummies], 127, 132–33, 135, 138, 141
Krug, Manfred, 5, 169, 175–76, 185, 242
Krumbiegel, Ulrike, 282
Khrushchev, Nikita, 42, 158, 164, 215–16
Kubisch, Holger, 279–80
Kubrick, Stanley, 8, 221
Küchenmeister, Claus, 172–73, 297–301, 304
Küchenmeister, Rainer, 300
Küchenmeister, Walter, 300
Küchenmeister, Wera, 172–73, 186n18, 297–301, 304
Kückelmann, Gertrud, 114
Kuckhoff, Adam, 294, 298–99
Kuckhoff, Greta, 294, 299
Kühn, Siegfried, 24
Kühne, Erich, 31
Kupfer, Harry, 208n8

L

La batalla de Chile [The Battle of Chile], 127–28, 139, 141
Laabs, Hans-Joachim, 250
Lamprecht, Gerhard, 249–50
Lang, Fritz, 44, 57n14, 65, 86, 89, 216, 218

László, Magda, 198
Le Chanois, Jean-Paul, 99–100
Le Nozze di Figaro, 201, 209n23
Leben am Fließ [Life Along the Rivulet], 271
Lem, Stanislaw, 211, 213–14, 217, 219
Lenin, Vladimir Ilich, 164, 183, 215, 220
Letztes aus der DaDaeR [Latest from the Da-Da-eR], 285
Leuchtfeuer [Signal Fire], 112
Leupold, Harry, 33
Liane, 282
Liebermann, Rolf, 203
Lied der Ströme [Song of the Rivers], 154
Lindemann, Alfred, 3, 88
Linke, Marlis, 177
Lissy, 43, 319
Loren, Sophia, 221
Lortzing, Albert, 195, 201
Löscher, Alexander, 21
Losey, Joseph, 192
Losansky, Rolf, 259, 279–80, 282, 284
Lotz Karl Heinz, 259
Lüdecke, Gruskin, 218
Lüdecke, Wenzel, 218
Lukács, György, 195
Luther, Martin, 282

M

Mach, Josef, 43
Mäde, Hans Dieter, 181
Mader, Julius, 221
Mahlich, Hans, 236–37
Maetzig, Kurt, 4, 7, 13, 21, 42, 44–45, 77, 185, 210–26, 235, 277, 299, 328
Magellanic Cloud, The, 211
Mainz, Friedrich A. 218
Man in Space, 219
Märkische Ziegel [Brandenburg Bricks], 272, 286–87
Marten, Walter, 147
May, Karl, 8, 227, 229, 236–37
Mayakovsky, Vladimir, 215
Mazurka der Liebe [Mazurka of Love], 201
Mechte navstrechu [A Dream Come True], 211, 220
Mehl, Erich, 81n15, 112–16, 119, 121, 123, 125

Meine Frau macht Musik [*My Wife Sings*], 107
Menegoz, Robert, 148, 156,
Messter, Oskar, 209n22
Metropolis, 216
Metternich, Josef, 202
Meyer, Ernst Herrmann, 47
Michel, Robert, 130, 138
Millöcker, Carl, 201
Mins, Leonard, 89
Mitbürger! [*Fellow Citizens!*], 132–33, 138, 141
Mitic, Gojko, 169, 176–77, 224n10, 227–47
Mödl, Martha, 202
Mongolia, 161, 163–65
Montand, Yves, 101
Morgenstern, Victor, 211
Mosaik, 216, 220
Mozart, Wolfgang Amadeus, 192, 194–95, 201, 204–06, 209
Mügge, Vera, 115
Mühe, Ulrich, 282, 312
Müller, Alfred, 222
Müller, Hans, 201
Müller, Heiner, 31, 285–86
Mueller-Stahl, Armin, 5, 175, 169, 242
Mutter Courage [*Mother Courage*], 95

N
Na lune [*On the Moon*], 220
Natschinski, Gerd, 43
Nebo zovyot [*The Heavens Call*], 211, 215, 220, 224n4
Neckář, Václav, 183
Neef, Wilhelm, 43–47, 53, 55, 57n16, 230
Ni hao – heißt Guten Tag [*Ni Hao – Means Hello*], 160
Nicht schummeln, Liebling [*No Cheating, Darling*], 35
Nicolai, Otto, 201
Nier, Helmut, 308
Nesvadba, Josef, 214

O
Offenbach, Jacques, 194–95, 201, 203–05
One Flew over the Cuckoo's Nest, 37
Operation Crossbow, 221
Ophüls, Max, 86, 98, 100, 209n22

Oppenheimer, Robert, J., 219
Orpheus in der Unterwelt [*Orpheus in the Underworld*], 201–03
Othello, 194
Osceoloa, 237, 239

P
Pappe, Feodor, 150–51
Pakula, Alan J., 316
Parkplatz zur großen Sehnsucht [*A Car Park Named Desire*], 70, 106, 122
Parsifal, 192
Pasetti, Peter, 69, 113–14, 117
Peletz, Wolfgang von, 130
Peppard, George, 221
Perrault, Gilles, 299, 303
Petzold, Christian, 11, 312–34
Petzold, Konrad, 175–76
Perrault, Gilles, 299, 303
Philipe, Gérard, 95, 99, 100
Philipp der Kleine [*Philipp the Small*], 257
Pianist, The, 322
Piloten im Pyjama [*Pilots in Pajamas*], 129
Planet des Todes [*Planet of Death*], 217
Planeta Bur [*Planet of Storms*], 211, 220
Plenzdorf, Ulrich, 29, 34, 36, 209n27, 318
Pohl, Artur, 7, 12, 62, 68, 71, 106–26
Polák, Jindřich, 211, 224n5
Polanski, Roman, 322
Preludio 11, 235
Professor Mamlock, 58n25
Protozanov, Yakov, 215
Puttkamer, Karl-Jesko von, 295

Q
Quinn, Anthony, 239

R
Rabenalt, Arthur Maria, 7
Radzinowicz, Anatol, 77
Ranke, Leopold von, 242
Rat der Götter [*Council of the Gods*], 115
Rauschende Melodien [*Resounding Melodies*], 201
Reagan, Ronald, 184
Reed, Dean, 12, 168–88
Red Man's View, The, 229
Reeves, Steve, 238

Rehan, Rosemarie, 183
Reimann, Brigitte, 327
Reisch, Günter, 33
Rehfuss, Heinz, 198
Reinl, Harald, 218
Remmert, Mathias, 130
Reschke, Ingrid, 29
Reusse, Peter, 171
Rev, Martin, 308
Richter, Erika, 25–26
Richter, Gerhard, 316
Ritter Blaubart [*Bluebeard*], 194, 198, 203–04
Rocha, Peter, 271–72, 281, 284, 288
Rodenberg, Hans, 168
Roeder, Manfred, 295
Roloff, Helmut, 303
Roloff, Stefan, 302–11
Roman, José, 170
Rosenfeld, Gerhard, 42
Rossellini, Roberto, 316
Roter, Erwin, 57n16
Rouleau, Raymond, 99
Rouch, Jean, 244
Rücker, Günther, 218
Rückwärts laufen kann ich auch [*I Can Run Backwards as Well*], 259
Rummelplatz [*Fairground*], 316

S

Sabine Kleist 7 Jahre [*Sabine Kleist, 7 Years Old*], 260
Santis, Omar Saavedra, 26
Sartre, Jean-Paul, 99, 100
Sass, Katrin, 11, 312
Sasse, Karl-Ernst, 42
Schabowski, Günter, 288
Schanelec, Angela, 330, 333n13
Schauer, Hermann, 218
Schaut auf diese Stadt [*Look at this City*], 56 n6,
Schemmel, Rudolf, 149
Scheumann, Gerhard, 8, 127–45
Schiller, Willy, 62, 73, 75
Schindler, Oskar, 322–23
Schlegel, Egon, 224n10
Schleif, Wolfgang, 7
Schlöndorff, Volker, 203, 313

Schmerzen der Lausitz [*The Pain of Lusatia*], 271, 273, 286
Schmidt, Eberhard, 46
Schöbel, Frank, 181, 209n22
Schönemann, Sybille, 318
Schorn, Christine, 282
Schroeter, Werner, 203
Schubert, Helga, 25
Schulze-Boysen, Harro, 294–95, 298, 303
Schulze-Boysen, Libertas, 294–95, 303
Schwaen, Kurt, 42
Schwochow, Christian, 287
Seemann, Horst, 224n10
Sehnsucht [*Longing*], 282, 284
Sellars, Peter, 192
Selpin, Herbert, 7
Severino, 227
Shepherd, Alan, 219
Signale – Ein Weltraumabenteuer [*Signals – A Space Adventure*], 28, 224n1, 224n10, 239
Signoret, Simone, 95, 101
Simmel, Georg, 284
Simon, Günther, 219, 307
Simon, Rainer, 24, 43, 51–52, 56, 59n41, 59n42, 276–77
Singler, Werner, 7
Sing, Cowboy, sing, 174, 182–84
Smetana, Bedřich, 209n22
Solaris, 224n1
Solo Sunny, 43, 275
Sontag, Susan, 288
Sonnenallee [*Sun Alley*], 322, 329
Spielbank-Affäre [*Casino Affair*], 12, 62, 68, 70, 106–26
Spielberg, Steven, 263, 322
Spira, Camilla, 202
Spitzweg, Carl, 172
Spur der Steine [*Trace of Stones*], 28
Spur des Falken [*Falcon's Trail*], 227
Stacheltier, 299
Stahnke, Günter, 62, 78
Stalin, Joseph, 34, 107, 154, 184, 215, 216, 237
Stanislavsky, Konstantin, 196–97
Star, Janusz, 224n10
Starke Freunde im fernen Osten [*Strong Friends in the Far East*], 149, 153–55, 159

Stärker als die Nacht [*Stronger than the Night*], 100
Stasiland, 332n3
Staudte, Wolfgang, 89, 95, 253
Stauffenberg, Claus von, 294
Sterne [*Stars*], 104n29
Stranka, Erwin, 282
Strauß, Franz Josef, 164
Strauss, Johann, 201
Strauss, Richard, 192, 209n22
Streich, Rita, 202, 203
Stroheim, Erich von, 218
Stromabwärts nach Shanghai [*Downstream to Shanghai*], 159, 160
Stromboli, 316
Strugatsky, Arkady, 214
Strugatsky, Boris, 214
Sword of Lancelot, 236
Syberberg, Hans-Jürgen, 192
Szpilman, Władysław, 322–23

T
Tauber, Richard, 209 n22
Tecumseh, 227
Teichmann, Regina, 30
Tele-Atlas: Japan, 166n1
Tereshkova, Valentina, 217
Tetzlaff, Kurt, 273–74, 285
Thälmann, Ernst, 44, 294
Thiel, Heinz, 4, 174
Thieme, Bernhard, 58n25
Thomas Müntzer, 115
Thompson, J. Lee, 221
Thürk, Harry, 221
Till Eulenspiegel, 52
Timm, Peter, 287
Titanic, 7
Titov, Gherman, 217
To Have and Have Not, 316
Tödlicher Irrtum [*Fatal Error*], 239
Treffen in Travers [*Rendezvous in Travers*], 282
Trenker, Luis, 7
Trivas, Victor, 218
Trübe Wasser [*Muddy Waters*], 99, 101
Tsiolkovsky, Konstantin, 215, 219–20, 226n38
Tuch, Walter, 199

Tuchel, Johannes, 303
Tulpanov, Sergei, 3

U
Und deine Liebe auch [*And Your Love Too*], 4
Uncle Tom's Cabin, 236
Unter Geiern [*Frontier Hellcat*], 236
Unterberg, Hannelore, 257, 260
Unvollendete Geschichte [*Unfinished Story*], 318

V
Valente, Catarina, 209n22
Vávra, Otakar, 224n3
Veiczi, János, 221
Verdi, Giuseppe, 194
Verhoeven, Paul, 253
Verlorene Landschaft [*Lost Landscapes*], 280
Verriegelte Zeit [*Locked-Up Time*], 318
Vne Zemli [*Beyond the Planet Earth*], 220
Vorlíček, Václav, 16n38
Vogel, Frank, 4
Vom Amnok-kang zum Kymgansan [*From Amnok River to Mt Kumgang*], 147, 150, 152–53
Von Wismar nach Shanghai [*From Wismar to Shanghai*], 149, 153, 155

W
Wagenstein, Angel, 104 n29
Wägerle, Karl, 71
Wagner, Richard, 44–46, 53, 192, 201, 202, 207–08n6
Wallace, Mike, 184
Wallstein, Hans-Joachim, 237
War of the Worlds, 211
War Games, 263
Warneke, Lothar, 24, 25–26, 29
Waschke, Mark, 326
Weber, Carl Maria von, 195, 203
Wege in die Nacht [*Paths in the Night*], 287
Weiße Wölfe [*White Wolves*], 227, 240–41,
Welskopf-Henrich, Liselotte, 228, 241
Weltall – Erde – Mensch [*Space – Earth – Human*], 217, 225n26
Welz, Peter, 239
Wenders, Wim, 313
Wendt, Erich, 218

Wenzel, Heidemarie, 30
Wernher von Braun – Ich greife nach den Sternen [I Aim at the Stars], 212, 218, 221, 222, 223, 226n34
Werzlau, Joachim, 43, 253
Westen [West], 287
Wiene, Robert, 209n22
Wilde, Cornel, 236
Wildhagen, Georg, 201, 205
Wilkening, Albert, 31, 32, 100, 113, 123, 218
Willy Wonka and the Chocolate Factory, 256
Winnetou, 218
Wir berichten aus Pan Yü [We Report from Pan Yü], 154, 156–58
Wir sangen und tanzten in China [We Sang and Danced in China], 154, 156–58
Wischnewski, Klaus, 26, 35
Wischnewski, Traute, 130
Wolf, Dieter, 25, 221–22, 276
Wolf, Friedrich, 89
Wolf, Konrad, 5, 6, 21, 24, 42, 43, 48, 50–51, 58n25, 62, 76, 80, 104n29, 183, 275, 319, 328
Wolffhardt, Rainer, 71

Y

Ya byl sputnikom solntsa [I Was a Sputnik of the Sun], 211, 215

Z

Zaveshchaniye professora Douelya [Professor Dowell's Head], 218
Zschoche, Herrmann, 224n10, 257, 278
Zeller, Wolfgang, 45
Zar und Zimmermann [Tsar and Carpenter], 201, 202, 203
Zeffirelli, Franco, 192
Zehrfeld, Ronald, 324
Zeman, Karel, 224n5, 226n38
Zhuravlyov, Vasili, 215
Ziemann, Sonja, 202
Ziethen, Anni von, 21
Žižek, Slavoj, 286
Zwei Tage im August: Rekonstruktion eines Verbrechens [Two Days in August. Reconstruction of a Crime], 166n1
Zwischen Großer Mauer und Perlfluss – Begegnungen in der Volksrepublik China [Between the Great Wall and the Pearl River – Encounters with the People's Republic of China], 160

www.ingramcontent.com/pod-product-compliance
Lightning Source LLC
Chambersburg PA
CBHW072142100526
44589CB00015B/2048